NEW ART

AN INTERNATIONAL SURVEY

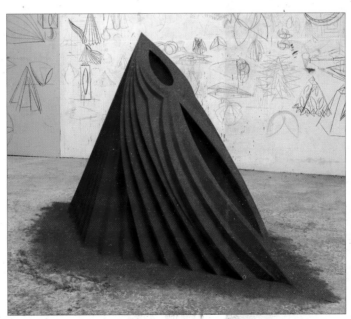

Anish Kapoor, *Mother as a Mountain*, 1985, wood, gesso and pigment, 140x275x105cm

Daniel Buren, *Coïncidence ou: La Place des Colonnes*, installation detail, Moderna Museet, Stockholm, 1984

NEW ART

AN INTERNATIONAL SURVEY

Edited by
Andreas Papadakis
Clare Farrow & Nicola Hodges

Jeff Koons, *Jeff and Ilona (Made in Heaven)*, Venice Biennale, installation detail, 1990, painted wood, 127x271.8x137.2cm

ACADEMY EDITIONS • LONDON

Above: Mario Merz, drawing from *Lo Spazio è curvo o diritto,* 1990, Hopeful Monster Editore, Florence; *Front Cover*: Gerhard Richter, *Abstract Picture*, (detail), 1984, oil, 190x500cm, Marian Goodman and Sperone-Westwater Galleries, New York; *Front Flap*: Luciano Fabro, *Two nudes descending a staircase dancing the boogie-woogie*, 1989, marble, steel, oil, dimensions variable, Ydessa Hendeles Foundation, Toronto, photo SteinGladstone Gallery, New York

Published in Great Britain in 1991 by
ACADEMY EDITIONS
an imprint of the Academy Group Ltd, 7 Holland Street, London W8 4NA

ISBN 1-85490-024-2 (HB)
ISBN 1-85490-046-3 (PB)

Printed and bound in Singapore

CONTENTS

Anselm Kiefer, *The High Priestess/Zweistromland*, (details), 1985-89

INTRODUCTION

New Art – An International Survey is a collection of critical writings, interviews and artists' statements, inspired by five years of editing *Art & Design*. A combination of the most significant articles published in the magazine, together with a number of new commissions, the book provides a platform for the colourful and often conflicting voices of the international art scene, and is based on the principle of critical selection rather than straightforward documentation. While a reading of the texts provides a dramatic picture of the endlessly shifting emphases that have dominated the art world in recent years, there is also an attempt to analyse, define and contextualise new art, to step aside from the accelerated pace of the commercial art scene and to assess the implications of new media in the light of other disciplines and in the wider context of the 20th century.

The background section focuses primarily on the now legendary figures of Joseph Beuys and Andy Warhol who, in questioning the distinction between art and everyday existence, opened up a common ground of communication, embracing new media such as performance, actions, film and mass-media technology, and signifying a continuation of the revolutionary thinking of Marcel Duchamp. Focusing on time, space and energy as fields of action, Beuys' work gave material form to the European orientation towards memory and spirituality; while Warhol, constructing a visual encyclopedia of serial images appropriated from newspapers, consumer products, advertising and the art market, embodied the American experience, defined by Baudrillard as 'hyperreality'. The interaction between language, context and form, together with an experimentation in new technologically-based media, frequently extending beyond the limits of the conventional art space, has characterised much of new art since the 70s, including the work of artists such as Lawrence Weiner, Joseph Kosuth, John Baldessari and Bruce Nauman who have set the scene for the conceptually-based art of today. Utilising the media of language, photography, video and performance, industrial materials and scientific technology, artists such as Jenny Holzer, Barbara Kruger, Cindy Sherman and Hans Haacke have confronted political, economic and social issues, often bringing their messages into a public space.

Against the background of a rapidly expanding art world, many artists have sought to represent themselves in increasingly sophisticated ways, often adopting the roles of critic and businessman, while museums and alternative spaces have attempted not only to document but to define current trends, to come to terms with the spatial demands of new media and advanced technology. The emphasis now is on experimentation, on the interaction of disciplines and the construction of new exhibition spaces, responding to the changes that have occurred over the past decade.

Robert Rauschenberg, *BED*, 1955, combine painting, 191x80x16.5cm

I

BACKGROUND TO NEW ART

Fat Chair, 1964, wooden chair, fat, wax and metal wire, 94.5x41.6x47.5cm

DEMOSTHENES DAVVETAS
JOSEPH BEUYS – MAN IS SCULPTURE

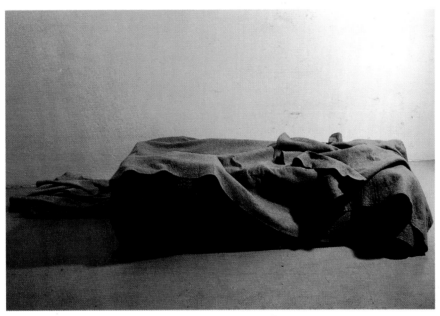

Camp-Bed, 1982, camp-bed, felt, copper, iron and wood installation, 59x242x121cm

Joseph Beuys was born on May 12th, 1922 in Cleves from 'a wound drawn together with plaster'; a phrase he himself uses in his autobiographical notes. Who could imagine that this child was destined in the world of contemporary art, to become the exemplary artist incarnate in whose work the idea of the 'wound' (or Wunde *in German, a word close to* Wunder, *miracle) would play a principal role?*

During the Second World War, Joseph Beuys (again by his own account), whose ambition it was to become a doctor, found himself in the Luftwaffe at the age of 18 as a bombardier. He had such traumatic memories – his plane crash, the death of many of his own friends and imprisonment by the Allies – that he gave up the idea of studying medicine. His life from then on was haunted by nightmares and plagued by feelings of guilt and anguished questions about the future of Man and mankind.

Just as Joë Bousquet, who had himself been physically injured in the previous war, had tried to come to terms with his injury by turning towards writing and poetry, so Beuys turned towards art. In 1944, he enrolled in the class of Ewald Mataré, a teacher at the Academy of Fine Art in Düsseldorf.

Beuys shares with Bousquet the sense that an injury is above all a *moral* trauma. The theme of injury would remain 'radioactive' in Beuys' work until his death, becoming a fundamental component of his artistic language. This theme does not weigh down on the past, but, as with Bousquet, is at the origin of a penetrating analysis by the great German artist on the life and destiny of Man in general: Man is therefore at the centre of the work; *he is the sculpture*; a sculpture gifted with thought, sensitivity and will.

To thought would devolve *the inquiry on traumatism*: What is it? Where is it? What are its consequences? In short, it becomes

an investigative task. To sensitivity would return therapeutic activity: how to heal or dare to heal and see the process of healing. As for will, its task would be to inscribe this endeavour into an historical perspective. Beuys' drawings, his sculptures, his performances, his writing, his political action – everything in his work demands the presence of an anthropological constituent, a constant which conceals creative strength, energy, knowing nature and the will to change it on the condition that Man understands that he is the master of his material and of the possibilities opened up by science.

Thus, with the key that is formed by this anthropocentrism, it becomes easier, as we make our way through a series of works, to interpret compositions such as *Fat Corners* and *Fat Chair*, *How to Explain Pictures to a Dead Hare*, *And in us . . . under us . . . landunder*, *Celtic*, *Coyote* and *Tram Stop*.

A Decisive Stage: *Fluxus*

The determining phase in Beuys' work occurred around 1960, when the controversy around *Fluxus* began. The title is derived from the famous concept of the 'panta reï': 'Into the same river we both step and do not step. We both are and are not.' (Heraclitus, *Fragments*). *Fluxus* represents a sort of continuation of the ironic uprisings and methods in art matter begun by Yves Klein and Manzoni – the extension of an American style

Tram Stop, 1976, iron rail, four iron cylinders, barrel with mouth and head, installation at Venice Biennale

Happening. However, *Fluxus* differs on a fundamental point: during a Happening what occurs is reinforced and amplified by the participation of the audience, whereas in *Fluxus* we can see that there is a tendency to establish, without its formal exclusion, a disciplined relationship with the audience which prevents the 'ceremonial' progression from turning into chaos.

Fluxus aimed to bring together musicians, dancers, painters, poets, sculptors and all other types of artists into an anti-egocentric, anti-nationalist and anonymous platform as a melting-pot of different nationalities and viewpoints. Like the demonstrations of its predecessor, Dada, *Fluxus* aimed at releasing the individual from any type of physical or intellectual and, in particular, political repression.

The fact that *Fluxus* neither set up any discrimination between artistic disciplines nor burdened the multiple space of art with artificial barriers was natural; having both a revolutionary and anti-authoritarian character, *Fluxus* refused to separate art and life. It assumed John Cage's viewpoint that everyday life can be seen as theatre wherein everything can coexist. The obsolete idea of artistic specialisation gives way to the common ground of communication where, inevitably, everything is oriented towards the power of the image, the action, the performance – towards a *superior output of mediatory possibilities.*

In trying to go beyond the strict limits of painting or sculpture and of the national and geographical frontiers of art, *Fluxus* gives value to the mobility of materials and is akin to the old dream of *Total Art.* Any material, no matter what sort and even the most humble, can contribute to the combined, entire idea – the *global concept.* Anyone can be associated with these actions since, being an open, outward movement, it does not allow for ideological enclosure. Rivalling Marcel Duchamp, Beuys is more inclined towards energy and artistic effect, rather than the final product, the work of art.

Fat – Felt

Next came the moment when materials such as fat and felt made their appearance. Both the technical and speculative aspects of Beuys' views on sculpture coexisted within these materials. The moment took place in 1964, on the occasion of a reading given by Allan Kaprow at the Zwirner Gallery in Cologne.

The works of this period such as *Fat Corners* and *Fat Chair* display his 'theory of sculpture' – from the indefinite to the defined, from heat (the 'chaotic') to cold (the 'crystallised'), from the *spontaneous* (the 'formless') to the *intellectualised* (the 'formed'). The transition was not made just in one stage but was the result of a progression, which Beuys has described himself:

My initial intention in using fat was to stimulate discussion. The flexibility of the material appealed to me particularly in its reactions to temperature changes. This flexibility is psychologically effective – people instinctively feel it relates to inner processes and feelings. The discussion I wanted was about the potential of sculpture and culture, what they mean, what language is about, what human production and creativity are about. So I took an extreme position in sculpture, and a material that was very basic to life and not associated with art. At this time, although I had not exhibited, the students and artists who saw this piece did have some curious reactions which confirmed my feelings about the effect of placing fat in a corner. People started to laugh, get angry, or try to destroy it.

The fat on the *Fat Chair* is not geometric, as in the *Fat Corners*, but keeps something of its chaotic character. The ends of the wedges read like a cross-section cut through the nature of fat. I placed it on a chair to emphasise this, since here the chair represents a kind of human anatomy, the area of digestive and excretive warmth processes, sexual organs

and interesting chemical change, relating psychologically to will power. In German the joke is compounded as a pun since *Stuhl* (chair) is also the polite way of saying shit (stool), and that too is a used and mineralised material with chaotic character, reflected in the texture of the cross section of fat.

The importance and consequences of *Fat Chair* and *Fat Corners* were recognised by Beuys:

Now, 15 years later, I can say that without *Fat Chair* and the *Fat Corners* as vehicles none of my activities would have had such an effect. It started an almost chemical process among people that would have been impossible if I had only spoken theoretically.

Interrogations Concerning the Role of the Audience

From now on Beuys' beginnings took a more insistent turn: everything indicated that his temperament would draw his course towards its most extreme limits and that it would not remain fixed. For him the world was not fragmented but whole. Equally, his art created conflicting forces that both created and destroyed in the same instant. Beuys was certain that such a route would, in a chain of events, pass through situations which were not always pleasant. It is precisely there that the artist's strength is revealed: in the deep-seated resourcefulness which allows him to turn every experience to the advantage of his creative development, and Beuys showed that he possessed that strength many times. One of the most typical examples was at the *Festival of New Art*, held at Aix-la-Chapelle in 1964, where, with other artists, he took part in various actions entitled 'Kukei', 'Akopee No!', 'Brown Cross', and 'Fat Corners'. However, at the time of the third stage of the programme planned for the Festival which dealt with word, image and sound, the performance had to be stopped because of the booing from the audience and one of the students punching Beuys in the face. Beuys remained unperturbed and did not renounce his standpoint despite the riot.

These events, as well as his participation a month earlier at *Documenta III* (where he presented drawings and sculptures from the period 1951-56 including *Queen Bee I-III*), played an essential role in what was to follow. Firstly, because his thinking began to be 'infiltrated' by the political factor, and moreover, in an imperative way. Secondly, because he began to consider the creator/community relationship of his actions from a different angle and preferred to put himself in a less vulnerable position in relation to the public.

It should be stressed that the first ideas, which had been the initial theoretical substratum of *Fluxus*, on the 'collective mind', 'anonymity' and the role of the audience in general, paved the way for a new critical phase marked by a change in speculative foundations. Beuys didn't find himself particularly in favour of the tumult and agitation, or the spectators' propensity for destroying certain performances. Nor did he feel the need to continue being left to the exclusive domination of chance during an action. To the contrary, he was looking for a concentration of a different nature to that which presides over the ordinary control of Time: *meditation,* the control of material and space, dialogue with the audience. This kind of attitude, however, should not be analysed as an absolute inclination to control everything with no account of invisible parameters, surprise, the unforeseen, which can all interfere with the more or less lasting development of the action. Rather, it must simply be seen from the point of view of a *ritual.* An open ritual which can then provoke a series of questions, the equivalent of a method which once again would include in its project the awakening of the forces of the mind.

This is why Beuys from now on would place the creator further in the background in the course of his subsequent performances, rendering him more obscure in his relationship

13

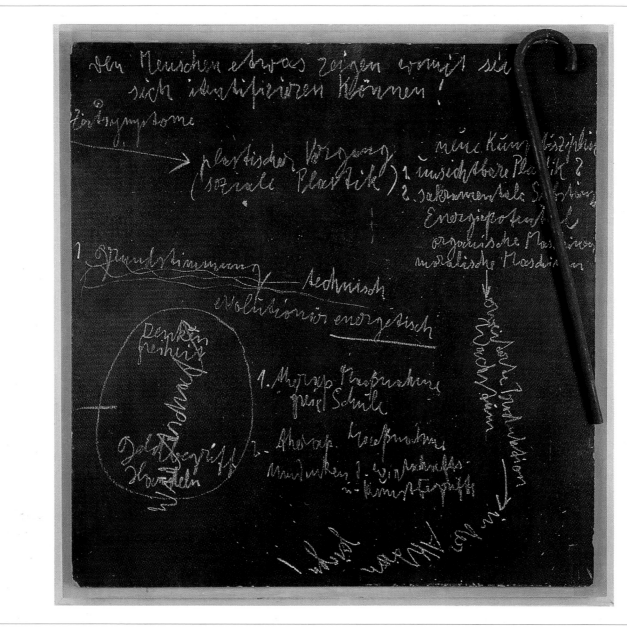

Blackboard, (Action Third Way) II, 1977-78, chalk on board, 130x130cm

with the audience, yet without meaning that communication with the community would be cut off. It was merely another form of dialogue which he would set up in the ritual of the following works.

Parallel Creation

The effect of *Fluxus,* even in the most grandiose and decisive moments of its progress and display, is characterised by a certain determining antithesis which has marked the whole of Beuys' language. On the one hand, there exists an unreserved investiture of oneself, in the 'spirit' of a revolutionary use of new materials for artistic expression and, as a consequence, a radical refusal of the image of the artist as an antisocial and marginal *genius* locked in his studio. On the other hand, however, can be seen the persistent, unwavering determination never to become integrated with groups, organisations or movements.

While confident in the journey he had begun, a journey similar to that of an explorer who investigates every region of human expression hitherto unknown, forbidden or impenetrable to art, Beuys had only explored a part of himself in *Fluxus*. The other part was reserved for the freedom of a continuing personal creation. Besides, he was still an outsider, an observer and a protagonist. He was someone who knew how to delve deep into the spirit of the time, not so as to show it in the heart of a form of reality, but, above all, to transform it into a further element of his thought, which, in having a *total* expression, propelled his artistic language to the furthest depths of humanity's memory.

Time – Space

Beuys has always used Time as well as Space in a particular way. In Beuys' own language, Time and Space as weapons against the materialism of everyday life, its bad organisation and stereotyped production, or as a way of remembering the existence of human dignity, take on different dimensions from their usual ones: they become the field of action of his proposition: supreme Man, the administrator of his production capacities.

We can see an example of this way of perceiving things in *And in us . . . beneath us . . . landunder*, an action which took place in June 1965 at the Parnass Gallery in Wuppertal. During this happening which lasted 24 hours – from midnight to midnight – Beuys, who was curled up in a chair, from time to time would shake his feet and head over a tub full of margarine or would, occasionally, with his ear against a carton, listen to the fat with which the carton was filled. Then he tried to touch the objects which were out of his reach without sliding off his box. Before curling up again, he started a cassette recorder and with a concentrated expression let his head go back to the carton of fat to carry on listening once again. On occasion, he would take hold of one of the two builders' shovels which were left standing against a blackboard and grip it close to his chest.

In this action, it is not the materials which represent the centre of gravity (moreover, some of them, such as the margarine, tape recorder and fat had previously been used) but the anthropocentric factor which, explained in this rather absurd, irritating way, leads to the idea that Time and Space are not exteriorised or far away from Man, but *within* him in all his possibilities. It suffices to have the will power to attempt an approach to things which seem to be beyond likely limits, so we reach a stage of continual dispute with ourselves and thus of strengthened conscience.

Spiritual Dimension
It is natural that this proposition which dominated Beuys' intellectual problematic necessitated new sources of energy. It was vigorously taken up in different forms inherent in the cyclical process of his 'alphabet' since the scheme of traditional thought seemed to him to be exhausted.

Indeed, the law of one permanent 'rational' system was not enough for him: he needed something else, something capable of provoking an awakening of the mind in the form of spiritual relaxation which would reinvigorate the intellect with new strength. It is through the perspective of the necessary resources of Man's spiritual energies that we must consider his next action in 1965 at the Schmela Gallery in Düsseldorf: *How to Explain Pictures to a Dead Hare*.

It went thus: the exhibition hall remained closed to the public who could only see what was happening inside, either through the gallery window or on a screen. Inside, Beuys had put together the following objects, some of which are familiar to us: a stool with one foot wrapped in a sheath of felt, and two bones placed just beside him in which were hidden microphones.

Beuys, his head smeared with honey and gold leaf, held a dead hare in his arms which he carried from one picture to another. The shoes he was wearing had two different soles: one of iron (concealing a microphone) and the other of felt. He sat on the stool and began to murmur in an almost incomprehensible way, explaining painting to the hare and deliberately refusing to address the audience.

Here we find ourselves once again confronted with a metaphor of the artist who invents a ritual through visual representation of his own code. The hare isn't there to suggest the death of art – a point which many have misinterpreted; on the contrary, linked to the ancient goddess Mother Earth, the hare is a symbol of regeneration and underground incarnation; it becomes the power whose aim it is to arouse the dormant *ratio* – reason. *Felt* (whose qualities as a preserving and protective agent are already familiar); *gold* – leaf or powder – (which has its cultural value); *iron* (a metal linked to energy); the *microphones* (transmitting the voice, which is not only for Beuys the vehicle of the *message*, but also, by its very existence, a sculptural material with an energising value); *honey* (by origin, the rise of the vegetable towards the animal and an energising substance which connotes a perfectly structured community); so many elements are used here by Beuys not as an attempt to propose an aesthetic motion but as the wheels of the mechanism of his thought that is guided by a desire: that of drawing out 'dead' intellect from its lethargy (the reason for which Beuys 'honeyed' his head) and – organically uniting thought, action (praxis), matter and form – achieving Creation.

In hexagonal and crystalline wax sculptures, honey – that energising and moving substance – is cast by the bee community. Similarly, Beuys intends to introduce into the structures of reason, movement, plasticity and warmth – essential materials in his theory of sculpture which flow into social and political concepts:

The nature of warmth is latent in honey, wax, and even in pollen and nectar taken from plants. In mythology, honey was considered a spiritual substance and bees were divine. The cult of the bee is fundamentally a cult to Venus . . . It had spread widely and was influenced by all the process of the production of honey, a link between the earthly and the divine. The flow of a substance stemming from all the environment – plants, minerals and the sun – was the essence of the bee cult. The allusion refers to socialism, as it was practised in the large clock and watchmaking cooperatives of the Republic of Bes at La Chaux-de-Fonds (Switzerland). We can still see sculpted bees, the symbols of socialism, on the walls and stone foundations. This doesn't imply State socialism that functions like a machine but a socialist organisation all the parts of which function like a living body. In physiological terms, this organisation is not hierarchical – the queen bee links the head and heart, and the drones become cells which must constantly be renewed. The whole makes a unit whose function is perfect, but in an atmosphere of human warmth founded on the principles of co-operation and fraternity.

The bee is one of the themes that can be found again in Beuys' drawings and in a series of important sculptures: *Queen Bees* (*Bieren Röigen*), the first of which is dated 1947 and the last 1952. All are made in beeswax or wood: two incorporate small feminine figures.

Iphigeniea/Titus Andronicus
This action took place in Frankfurt in May 1969, organised by the German Academy of Dramatic Art, and proceeded as follows: on a stage in a circle of rope, a horse was eating hay while a microphone placed on the stage allowed the noise of his hooves to be heard. Nearby, by various gesticulations and movements Beuys interpreted classic texts: Goethe's *Iphigeniea in Tauride* and Shakespeare's *Titus Andronicus*, which could be heard emitted from a tape recorder in a montage with C Peykmann's and W Wiens' voices. The materials Beuys used from beginning to end were, a microphone, margarine, sugar, a piece of iron, cymbals and a fur coat.

The procedure unfolded like a ceremony that places the artist in an enclosed position as regards the public and provoked different questions. Let us proceed stage by stage. To begin with, we have Goethe and Shakespeare's classic texts: Iphigeniea, a symbol of sacrifice and Titus Andronicus, a symbol of extreme violence. They are two poles (Germanic 'idealism' and Anglo-Saxon 'realism') which, in keeping with his 'Theory of Sculpture' come together in a *glyptic* movement. Then we have the horse who is innocence, beauty, freedom; the a-logos (the animal deprived of *logos*). Finally, we have the artist himself with his gesticulations, his movements, his voice and materials that are carriers of energy.

At first sight, there doesn't seem to be a direct relationship between all these elements. And yet everything can take on different dimensions – if Beuys is seen as the man who moves between conscience, history, and the 'prospective' search between the intellectual and the organic, between chaos and order, then, as the critic Caroline Tisdall describes, we have the unexpected arrival of Man, 'producer of time and space', the 'coordinator', the 'impeller', a man of heightened spirituality, initiated into 'gnosis' and gifted with 'intuition', who knows

Above: Joseph Beuys performing in *Iphigeniea/Titus Andronicus*, Frankfurt 1969; *Below*: *Coyote*, performance at Galerie René Block, New York 1974

how to respect individuality but at the same time, how to play a social role – an image-metaphor that Beuys gives us 'for' Man and the artist. Such an image corresponds to his *anthropocentric language* which, among other things, offers something more in that it theoretically proposes the bringing together of both the individual and the community, and thus the experience of isolation and sociability.

Individual – Collectivity – Theatre (The Nordic Element)
Two actions displayed the similar intention of knowing how to live alone while at the same moment having communal space. This time however they had a Celtic theme. The first floor piece in Edinburgh in 1970 with Hennig Christiansen was entitled *Celtic* (*Kinloch Rannoch*), *Scottish Symphony* (*Schottische Symphonie*) and the second, in Basel, in 1971, *Celtic + ~.*

This was not the first time that Beuys alluded to Nordic mythology – ever since he had read and been influenced by James Joyce's *Ulysses* (in which he had discovered the spiritual values of the North) his tendency to draw from sources of 'a Nordic element' had never left him.

The Celtic performance at Edinburgh had been inspired by the Arthurian legend. As Beuys said: 'On the way to Edinburgh' he had 'absolutely no idea what was the right thing to do'. All he knew was that he would be going to give 'a concert'. But, as usual, he had been cautious enough to order all kinds of materials that constituted the organic part of ideas and obsessions which accompanied him from his childhood years and, as time went by, had transformed into fundamental elements of his language: 'Films, a piano and a whole load of other things'. On the way he 'noticed an old stick' which he considered worthy enough to add to the list. He then spotted an axe in a shop which he 'bought'. . . Later on, he had a look at the hall where he would be giving the performance and, as is his usual way, started fiddling about with everything there. In this way he gradually reached an obsessive relationship with space, a vehement and conflicting dance with all the material surrounding him. The intervention of his partner Hennig Christiansen serves to heighten the rhythmical tension to such a degree that it didn't take him long to find the solution which could enable the performance to spring into life. He asked the question 'What is Scotland?' . . . and suddenly all his impressions, obsessions and ideas buried within him began to burst forth. 'Scotland, King Arthur's Round Table, the legend of the holy grail . . . ' and became elements on which he would base the performance that he carried out.

This theme, as well as the ideas that gravitated around it would not end in the Edinburgh performance but would be resuscitated in the 1971 performance in Basel, which hardly differs in its material from the first performance with the exception that it brought out the relationship between the actor (Man and a strengthened conscience) and the community – the social space – in full relief. And this time, he gathers together the following material:

Three Philips tape recorders, an axe, a grand piano, a microphone, an aluminium ladder, a watering can, an enamelled washbowl with a piece of soap, a basin filled with water the handles of which were decorated with two torches, attached to them by elastic, painted in black, and bound in insulating Scotch tape; there were also white cloths and a blackboard, two film projectors and a screen.

Everything began when Beuys, in the presence of only photographers and cameramen, set about washing seven peoples' feet. Then about 500 spectators could come closer to watch him, lying on the floor pushing back a blackboard three times on which was chalked a drawing. Between each scene he would rub out the drawing and draw another. When it reached the piano, he got up onto his feet and with the blackboard beside him and a shep-

herd's crook in his hand – pointed towards the drawing on the blackboard – began to meditate in a concentrated manner. At that moment three films were played one after another in the same auditorium: *Eurasianstaff*, the performance entitled *Vacuum . . . Mass* and *The Transiberian*.

After that Beuys spattered the walls with gelatine and immediately after, using a ladder and an iron box, picked everything off the wall, bit by bit. Then, standing in the middle of the hall, holding the full box straight over his head with his arms outstretched, he poured the gelatine over himself. He picked up the blackboard on which was drawn a chalice and brandished it (in the same way) above his head like a shield, spluttering inarticulate sounds into the microphone. He let the board fall to his feet, leaving it upright, and sat astride it while he held the crook in his hand like a spear. He remained in this motionless position for more than half an hour and to finish the performance he went straight to a large bucket full of water, attached two torches to his thigh, filled a watering can with water and stepped into the bucket where Christiansen began to drench him with the watering can.

It appears here that the performance's development is cyclical – beginning with an act of offering to the others and finishing with a baptism. Again, this time, the characteristic elements of the artist's world are all reunited: life and death, creation, conscience, the individual, collectivity. The washing of feet – a symbolic image with Christian connotations – raises a socio-political meaning – that the individual is at the service of others (and it is here that the concepts of reciprocity and exchange should be located). However, going beyond individual egoism in no way expresses the individual's negation. To the contrary, during this performance, the individual manages *his* time and *his* space. The idea of the celebrant is especially present:
1) When Beuys keeps away from the audience and does not allow it to approach until after the time of isolation and concentration that he needs to take part fully in the ritual, which, like the cycle of life, comes to a close by beginning again.
2) When Beuys pushes back the board three times with his crook.
3) When he collects the gelatine and holds it above his head.
4) When he brandishes the blackboard with the drawing of the grail above his head.
5) During the films.

This individual (the man-artist) is distinguished by one fundamental trait: creativity. It intervenes through the widening of conscience (the board pushed back each time), going beyond polarities to one solid unit (the theme of the films), and total unity of the individual and surrounding fragments (the collect, lifting the gelatine above his head and pouring it over himself: reproduced on the immaterial level when the board and the drawing of the Grail are lifted: these two movements – the overflowing of the visible and invisible, the contents of the chalice – being synthesised in the final baptism).

This 'concert' of creativity, of conscience, of the individual's relationship to society is maintained as a cycle which constantly opens and closes, and is tirelessly reiterated in a sort of alphabet, a persistent 'work in progress'. Contrary to many others, this takes culture into its field of action which, Beuys thinks, is the way which allows Man to rediscover his integrity and dignity in a social perspective.

Coyote. I like America and America likes me
This particular action, at New York's René Block Gallery in 1974 took place in the following way. An ambulance took Beuys – who was wrapped in felt – from John F Kennedy aeroport where he had just arrived from Düsseldorf to the gallery and left him there with a recently captured Texan coyote. In the space of a few days both the artist – still muffled in felt from head to foot,

17

Joseph Beuys
Plight

Plight, 1985, felt, piano, blackboard and thermometer installation at Anthony d'Offay Gallery, London

'I was interested to point at the necessity to determine the idea of art to us all. To the senses existing in human beings and even to develop new senses . . .'

'One association of my room in *Plight* is isolation. The other is the warmth of the material. Surely this shut off from society is an anti-communicative element; it has a negative, even hopeless feeling as in some Samuel Beckett pieces. The other quality of the felt is to protect people from bad outside influences. So it is also a positive insulator. You can make a suit or tent out of it, like the Mongol tribes. It protects them against cold, storms and the outside world because it contains a lot of warmth. It is organic. This positive side – protecting people from danger – is the other extreme meaning of the piece. So the idea of a concert hall without sound looks completely negative at first, but it is meant to stress a threshold where everything moves to a critical point. Everything beyond that is transformed, transubstantiated, and surely the general meaning of art is the complete, radical change of human beings, beginning with their knowledge of themselves . . . Visual art touches the senses. Balance, hearing, temperature (I find temperature the most important element of sculpture) . . . Those things are interesting because they are translatable into the human psyche. Instead of something you are confronted with outside, all the senses combine to make the human being and the sculptural work one thing. Otherwise "understanding" means only a logical explanation which would be better written down. If the meaning of art is that there is anything to understand immediately; there would be no reason to work with felt or bones or clay or whatever to make forms . . . Thinking is a structured thing, with intelligence on the lowest level, and on the highest level intuition, inspiration and imagination. So a lot of possibilities exist for the development of man's thought and thinking power.'

Joseph Beuys, from interviews with William Furlong and Stuart Morgan, 1985

apart from a stick held pointing outwards from his wrapped form – and the coyote managed not only to coexist but gradually and slowly succeeded in living together. Beuys talked to the animal, walking up and down playing a triangle that he had hung on his neck while noises, emitted from a tape recorder, filled the room. In that space of time, the animal had urinated all over 50 issues of the *Wall Street Journal*, the chronicle of American economic power. It had begun to get on so well with his 'master', becoming calmer and quieter as each day went by, that by the end of the performance he seemed sad and uneasy at no longer having company.

Beuys' fondness for animals was not a new thing. From the beginning of his artistic career, hares, sheep, swans, bees, horses, etc, occupied an essential place in his drawing, sculptures and actions. Indeed, animals embody the elementary forces of life, as opposed to stones and plants which can serve to transmit other higher forces. He recognised the meaning of collective consciousness with them; something distinctly more unreliable in Man, with his thought and freedom and capacity for both good and evil. He also finds many other qualities such as instinct and sense of direction which could be valuable to Man who, as Beuys says, 'needs new sources of energy'.

The coyote in particular, which is gifted with a very powerful instinct, is one of the more symbolical examples of consciousness in the relation between the community and the individual. Being one of the principal animals regarded as divine by American Indians before the arrival of the white explorers, it took on certain symbolic functions of harmonisation between nature and Man. After the arrival of the 'colonialist liberators' the existing harmony was disrupted and from then on appeared the 'wound' – a growing injury which eventually led to the present deadlock of materialism and the inhuman exploitation of technology.

We notice that, remaining faithful to himself, Beuys has anchored the beginning of a work in this 'trauma', a machine for thinking which, leaning towards historical events, aims beyond them. He reaches the depths of one's soul through a revival of an *ante-historic* feeling from signs borrowed from reality.

But let us take a step backward: Man today is generally acknowledged as a wounded being, which is a *de facto* condition of America, but at the same time, is a 'Western' situation. For precisely this reason, Beuys' performance began in an ambulance.

Joseph Beuys
Talking about One's Own Country: Germany

'When I speak about my own country, I cannot base what I say on anything more recent and primal than our language. My path, strange as it is, took me by way of the language rather than my so-called visual ability being the starting-point. As many people know, I started to study the natural sciences, and then came to the conclusion that my possibility perhaps lay in a sphere demanding something completely different from the ability to become a good specialist in some scientific occupation, and that my talent lay in exerting an all-embracing impact on the task facing the nation. The concept of a people is elementally coupled with its language. Mind you, a people is not a race. The fact that this was also the only way of overcoming all the surviving racist machinations, terrible sins, and indescribable darkness without losing sight of them for even a moment led me to decide in favour of art, albeit of an art that took me to a concept of sculpture which starts with speaking and thinking, thereby learning to construct concepts which can and will bring feeling and willing into form if I do not slacken and keep rigorously going, so that forward-looking images will present themselves and ideas take shape. The precondition for a successful sculpture was thus that an inner form first came into being in thought and understanding which could then be expressed in the shaping of the material used in the work.

'. . . The work of art is the greatest riddle of all, but man is the solution. Here is the threshhold which I want to call the end of modernity, the end of all traditions. Together we will develop the social concept of art as a new-born child of the old disciplines. We view the traditional disciplines as entailing architecture, sculpture, painting, music, and poetry, the group of muses which here too appear from behind an iron curtain so that a child may be born: social sculpture, which sets itself the task of apprehending more than just physical material. We also need the spiritual soil of social art, where every single person experiences and recognises himself as a creative, world-determining being, for building, sculpture in bronze or stone, theatrical presentations, and our speech. The slogan "Everyone is an artist", which generated a great deal of excitement and is still misunderstood, refers to re-shaping of the social body in which every single person both can and even must participate so that we bring about that transformation as quickly as possible . . .

'. . . I am not saying that people must believe me but merely that everyone should look inwards, should in fact give words within themselves to whatever their feeling and thinking bring, allowing thinking to influence the will, and the will language, so that there develops an ever-rising spiral process where an acute ego-consciousness, a will to self-assertion, must arise in every human being. We are, after all, highly developed, we all have a rich history behind us, and we even grew up at a time when humanity was capable of acts of genius. So when I assert that everyone is an artist, that is the outcome of my work rather than a fact I assume everyone must believe . . .

'. . . Art is the only still unconsumed function that derives from a profoundly historical past but returns as the future, as the totality of self-aware-man. This is nothing else but art. I say art since art can display various aspects. It can present its past and no longer effective aspect of grand signals, but it can also present its human face, its evolutionary meaning. Here lies the threshhold between the traditional concept of art, with social art as the precondition for an ability. There is, however, a great falsification, fabricated time and again, that maliciously and deliberately maintains that when I say everyone is an artist I mean everyone is a good painter. That was certainly not what I meant though. What was meant was the talent in every job . . . demanding recognition as being part of an artistic task . . .'

Joseph Beuys, from a speech given at the Münchner Kammerspiele, 1985

What is the vehicle's destination? It has to be the place where 'the wounded' exist: America and the Western world and their antagonism between Nature and Technology, Nature and Culture, Art and Science, and the 'Money-God' (evoked by copies of the *Wall Street Journal*). What is the aim of this operation? Nothing but the fundamental will to materialise a desire: that the wound closes and heals and that after that, physiologically, the two incompatible forces (the coyote on the one hand and the isolated individual enveloped in felt on the other) start to coexist in a harmonious symbiosis.

It is not easy to bring such an attempt to a satisfactory conclusion, for let's not forget that between these forces there exists a wide temporal abyss. We thus discover each opponent with his trumpcard. The animal has its instinct and its litter. The 'wounded', who resembles a caretaker or a shepherd (we can picture images from childhood games), has his crook, the triangle, the felt (the insulator of America but transmissive of warmth for the coyote), and above all, his essential 'anthropological materials': will, compassion, thought and knowledge as well as faith in Man.

The 'struggle' was intense. Each one made use of his own domain, his field of action. The man rejects the felt wrapping (that isolated him) and risks coexisting with the animal who proves to be peaceful and content. In Beuys' alphabetic code, to be able to overcome the consequences of a crisis of positivist and materialistic thinking, Western Man needs new energies, and needs to recast conflicts and discussions in one solid unit which can only reside in a better attained development of consciousness.

The central idea of the *Coyote* suggests *transformation*. It entails a metamorphosis of ideology into the idea of ferocity; a metamorphosis of language into an energetic practice; a metamorphosis of the monologue of will into a dialogue between those concerned and a metamorphosis of distrust into communal and creative coexistence.

An interesting example of this performance's effect is the case of Jimmy Boyle, a Scot imprisoned for murder. After seeing some photographs of *Coyote*, he identified himself with the animal and not only did he begin a friendship with the artist, but he also turned his activities to writing and became an author.

Tram Stop
This environment presented at the Venice Biennale in 1976 is

founded on the idea of the monument. The word 'monument' signifies a link with celebration, with memory, and with the past. Traditionally the monument is erected on a central site with roads surrounding it so that it becomes the point of departure, the roads leading away from the centre.

Tram Stop is planned so as to exploit the principles of this spatial arrangement in two ways. Firstly, the notion of the monument is the centre from which every reference here takes its origin and, secondly, its structure follows the physical principles of a traditional monument.

Tram Stop is made up of the following three elements:
1) The monument with a field canon in the centre and four primitive 17th-century mortar bombs clustered around it.
2) A tramline which runs all the way past the monument.
3) An iron tube full of water, embedded in a lagoon in which is fixed an iron bar bent at the surface.

Apart from these principal elements, there is a heap of rubble that comes from where the hole for the tube was sunk; through earth and water. It indicates the exact place Beuys used to get off the tram. Also, the metal bar coming off the water-filled tube is a schematic echo to the linear directions found in the three elements described above, moving vertically and horizontally. The metal bar plays a unifying role among the three constituents.

All the elements are, as is the case in all his work, the fruit of the combination of his life and history. To explain this further:
1) As a five-year-old in Cleves, Beuys would get on and off the tram at the 'monument stop', a monument erected by Moritz von Nassau in 1652. There he would sit on the mortar bombs, surrounded by the three natural elements: air, earth and water.

This intuitive moment from childhood has been interpreted into the work *Tram Stop*, not in order to relive the 'good old days', but primarily in view of a selection of material that can undergo a transposition of universal range. The work itself has kept similar linear directions:
a) The monument is erected vertically with the canon pointing upwards, referring to the air towards which it is pointing.
b) The tramline, the earth, emerges from and is set within it, thus the line is in contact with the earth, running along it horizontally.
c) The tube filled with water relates to the water into which it plunges and is contained by pointing vertically towards the bottom.
2) The first three elements of *Tram Stop* are all made of iron. One is rusted, rough and plain (the canon); the second is smooth, gleaming and rapid (the tramline); the third is submerged and full of water (the tube). These elements are united beyond their different functions, through a common material: iron – a solid and resistant metal.
3) *Tram Stop* also refers to the place where he was born and its physical characteristics. The link between earth and water is particularly accentuated in a region where there exist canals and lagoons; where earth and water constantly intermingle, each one skirting the other.
4) Moritz von Nassau believed that his monument should embody the struggle between love and war. Beuys' monument refers to the struggle of ideas, the inner struggle of the thinking man. This is manifested in the sad expression on the face of the man Beuys sculpted at the top of the canon. He appears to be emerging from the canon in 'the active pain of doing' and 'the passive pain of suffering' (C Tisdall). Between the *passive element* (memory) and the *present* (the embodiment of this memory) a connection between the thesis and antithesis can be expressed. Their synthesis is the duty of the thinking man; he is the centre. He is the monument. Everything radiates from and towards him. He is the future, having the possibilities and capacities to change and redefine tradition.

Voglio vedere le mie montagne

The title of this environment is taken from Segantini. *Voglio vedere le mie montagne* was first shown in August 1971 at the Stedelijk van AbbeMuseum, Eindhoven. The objects used were an old wardrobe with an oval mirror and a drawer, a box and a yellow stool, and above these, a mirror, a packing case and the frame of a bed in the middle of which was a small felt rug.

All these objects which had been assembled together on a sheet of copper (in the centre of the room was a bulb burning over a felt insulating circle while in the four corners were sealed jars of gelatine) were closely related to the artist's memory, for it was the furniture of the room he had as a child. However, its arrangement was not a simple biographical representation; as we know, Beuys sought to bestow another dimension to the things he approached, to give them a poetic place in space and to connect them to sources of energy by imparting to his works a shamanistic course characteristic of creation. This time at the exhibition in Holland a notice advised the public: 'The title of this work is not a direct reflection of what we see. The question arises of what is to be seen there.'

The notice gave another interpretation to the exhibited objects that was not only immediately realistic but, linked to a perspective which displaced them into the imaginary, bestowed upon them a symbolic prolongation. This is confirmed by the fact that, above the exhibited objects can be seen some words written in chalk. On the bed there is the word *Walun* meaning 'alley'. On the wardrobe can be seen the word *adrec(t)* – a Celtic word for glacier. On the packing case, the word *Felsen* – 'cliff', and *sciora* (a mountain range in Switzerland) written on the box. And behind the stool's mirror we find the word 'summit'.

All these matching elements construct a mountain landscape but not through a realistic representation. Here, the 'real' is used as a metaphor: an allusion to nature, its relationship with Man and with his personal memory.

There were also certain other objects such as a photograph on the wall, not showing the wardrobe in the same way as in the work itself; a second photograph on the bed, showing Beuys lying across the bed; and, above all, a rifle on the wall over which is written the word *denken* – 'to think'.

Thus we are able to see the Beuys *lebensraum* and see his transformation through Time. He appears as a 'partisan' who is fighting the confusion of thought. The rifle hanging there, airing, is an allegory of thought. The 'partisan' fights on the side of sensitivity, concentration of thought and the transformation of something into creation in society. Here, we have the artist's regular motif: unity of art and life through a binary relation – individual (personal experience) and social (going beyond the individual to a communal perspective) which depends on flux, evolution, movement and change.

7000 Oaks

In 1982, as a contributor to the *Documenta 7*, Joseph Beuys took advantage of the urban situation in Kassel to launch his project *7000 Oaks*, as part of his views on *social sculpture*. He stated himself that it wasn't purely

> an achievement of urgent necessity to the biosphere and to the pure matter of ecological coherence, but demonstrates during the procedure a much wider understanding of the ecological idea. An understanding which should increase more and more as years go by, because it is our intention to proceed with this activity continuously.

This action is situated between the limits of modern art and what Beuys calls 'anthropological art'. It is the *praxis* of a Shaman; a gesture that requires 'signalling'. Thus he placed a column made of basalt of about 1.20m next to each oak tree:

> This kind of basalt column can be found in ancient volcano

flutes. Cooled down inside the chimneys in a specified and particular manner, it finally brings about its characteristic facets and crystalline shape. With respect to the particular cool-down system which activates an artificial crystallisation-like process, the stone produces these regular 5. 6. 7. 8. cornered shapes. They have been found in the districts of Eifel, showing beautiful and organpipe-like clearness, and can still be found there today, but partly under preservation of the National Trust. However, I haven't been too keen on these fine and special organpipes. It has been of much more importance to me to have a material at my disposal, that I can find in the Kassel region and which shows the characteristics of basalt. Thus I made out the kind of basalt exhibiting a half crystalline and angular shape as well as having a certain amorphous tendency.

Founded on a well-defined plan, the plantation would stretch across many years so that for each tree a stone would be set aside in a storehouse and taken to the planted tree. We can now begin to understand the development of the whole venture: the fewer stones remaining in the storehouse, the more trees planted; and the process will continue until the final stone is taken. While the volume and height of the stone remain constant, the oak tree will slowly grow with the passage of time.

7000 Oaks depends on the movement, change and transformation of life and the social body. Moreover it is a metaphor that incorporates future behaviour into its perspective. Beuys stresses:

As far as the first 7000 trees are concerned it has been of great importance to me to obtain the monumental character though the fact that each living monument is composed of two parties – the living being, the oak tree, steadily altering due to the season of the year; and the other, the crystalline part, preserving its shape, quantity, height and weight. The one and only possible incident able to evoke a change to the stone could be, for instance, taking away a piece from it or, if something splinters off, but never by means of coming up, like the tree does. Hence the two things are united, a continually changing proportionateness happens between the two parties of the monument. For the present we should keep in mind that the above mentioned trees have an eye of six or seven years now, so the stone dominates at first. However, as years go by, the balance between the stone and the tree will be achieved and after a course of time of about 20 or 30 years to come, perhaps we may notice and become aware of it; and the stone gradually and step by step becomes an accessory to the evergreen oak or any other kind of tree.

7000 Oaks is a symbolic action attempting to show that a change in society can be achieved through everyday activity, and that now, more than ever, the search for a 'third course' is needed, passing beyond the bipolar problematic of Marxism and capitalism. Every tree represents a human existence and is a radical outline of the *possible* transformation of the social body to tomorrow's community: a community that will perceive the needs of Man and nature in a different way. As Beuys said himself during the discussion *Difesta della natura* that took place in 1984 in Bologna:

These trees have a life that stretches far beyond any human being and this immediately introduces us to the contemplation of the element of time.

This is perhaps what becomes apparent after certain moments in the life of this German artist, whose work has played such a fundamental role in post-war Germany and still continues to radiate in the history of human ideas.

Object from *Eurasia, 32nd Movement of the Siberian Symphony 1963*, 1966, blackboard, chalk, poles, oil, dead hare, cord, felt and fat installation, 183x230x51cm

ROBERT ROSENBLUM
WARHOL AS ART HISTORY

Despite his maxim, Andy Warhol's own fame has far outlasted the 15 minutes he allotted to everyone else. During the last quarter century of his life, from 1962 to 1987, he had already been elevated to the timeless and spaceless realm of a modern mythology that he himself both created and mirrored. Now that he is gone, the victim of a preposterously unnecessary mishap, the fictions of his persona and the facts of his art still loom large in some remote, but ever-present, pantheon of 20th-century deities. His lofty role in our modern Olympus is recognised not only by the world at large, but by his own artist-contemporaries, young and old, at home and abroad.

Moreover, Warhol's universality in the art world united the conventional factions of Modernist and avant-garde versus conservative or hopelessly square. Just as he exhibited with LeRoy Neiman and with Jamie Wyeth (who painted Warhol's portrait, as Warhol painted his, in 1975),[1] so, too, could he join forces in 1984 on the same canvas as Jean-Michel Basquiat, thereby covering all bases and toppling all hierarchies of élite and populist image-making. Similarly, although museums of conventionally 'modern' art throughout the world have collected and exhibited his work, Warhol was equally at home with the more neo-conservative or, put more positively, Post-Modernist establishment. After all, the New York Academy of Art, which opened in 1980 to promote the revival of traditional instruction in drawing from life models and plaster casts, can claim Warhol as one of its founding board members.

As for Warhol's own images, from the beginning they have nourished not only the vast public domain of everything from advertising to gingerbread cookies (as baked in New York by Pattie Paige in the form of Brillo Boxes or Campbell's Soup Cans), but – the sincerest form of flattery – the work of other artists. Small wonder, that the word *Warholism*, originally coined in 1965 to deride the artist's seeming indifference to traditional values,[2] may have become indispensable in defining the ever expanding mythological mixture of art and public notoriety with which he created, after 1962, a new empire that, in retrospect, may make the last quarter-century be known as the 'Age of Warhol'.

By now, in fact, the phenomenon of Warholism has covered so many different territories – from the populist to the élite, from old-fashioned drawing on paper to films, performance art, and globally recognised logos – that no single view of Warhol ever seems adequate. Indeed, Warhol may end up rivalling Picasso in providing to all comers the most daunting breadth of approaches.

For one thing, the subject matter of his work, now that we're beginning to see it in full retrospect, covers so encyclopaedic a scope of 20th-century history and imagery that, in this alone, it demands unusual attention. To be sure, in the early 60s, his work could be sheltered under the Pop umbrella shared by Roy Lichtenstein, James Rosenquist, Tom Wesselmann, and others, joining these contemporaries in what can now be seen more clearly as an effort to re-Americanise American art[3] after a period of Abstract-Expressionist universals that renounced the space-time co-ordinates of the contemporary world in favour of some mythic, primordial realm. Within this domain, Warhol quickly emerged as a leader, choosing the grittiest, tackiest, and most commonplace facts of visual pollution in America that would make the aesthetes and myth-makers of the 50s cringe in their ivory towers.

This alone, if only in terms of inventory, would have been enough to make him the king of Pop art. But what is less obvious is how Warhol's initial inventory of ugly, counter-aesthetic America expanded to unexpected dimensions. Looking back at his entire output, the sheer range of his subjects becomes not only international (indeed universal in its concern with death) but mind-boggling in its journalistic sweep. What other modern artist's work comes so close to providing a virtual history of the world in the last quarter-century? In terms of the role of the artist as chronicler of his times, Edouard Manet, a full century before Warhol, might be something of a contender. Picasso, too, cut a wide swath, commenting directly or indirectly on every war he lived through, and leaving us a portrait gallery of 20th-century pioneers, from Gertrude Stein and Igor Stravinsky all the way to Stalin. But Warhol's art is itself like a *March of Time* newsreel, an abbreviated visual anthology of the most conspicuous headlines, personalities, mythic creatures, edibles, tragedies, artworks, even ecological problems of recent decades. If nothing were to remain of the years from 1962 to 1987 but a Warhol retrospective, future historians and archaeologists would have a fuller time-capsule to work with than that offered by any other artist of the period. With infinitely more speed and wallop than a complete run of the *New York Times* on microfilm, or even 25 leather-bound years of *Time* magazine (for which, in fact, he did several covers),[4] Warhol's work provides an instantly intelligible chronicle of what mattered most to most people, from the suicide of Marilyn Monroe to the ascendancy of Red China, as well as endless grist for the mills of cultural speculation about issues ranging from post-Hiroshima attitudes toward death and disaster to the accelerating threat of mechanised, multiple-image reproduction to our still-clinging, old-fashioned faith (both commercial and aesthetic) in hand-made, unique originals.

The diversity of Warhol's subject matter is staggering. As for people alone, almost everybody is there: a generic *American Man – Watson Powell* and the *Thirteen Most Wanted Men*; artists like Robert Rauschenberg, Frank Stella, Joseph Beuys, and David Hockney; stars like Elizabeth Taylor and Mick Jagger; statesmen like Chairman Mao and President Nixon; sports champions like Muhammad Ali; and literary celebrities like Truman Capote. But this encyclopaedic *Who's Who* is only one facet, if a major one, of Warhol's vast image-bank of our age. There is a documentary history of modern catastrophes, both man-made and natural, like the jet crash reported on June 4, 1962, which took 129 lives, or the Neapolitan earthquake of November 23, 1980, which may have taken some 10,000 lives. There are inventories of modern ways of death, whether by such lethal commonplaces as knives and revolvers, car crashes, leaps from high-rise buildings, and canned-food poisoning, or by such specialised technological horrors as the atom bomb and the electric chair. There are anthologies of endangered species, both human (the American Indian) and animal (the giant panda and the Siberian tiger), that right-thinking people concerned with our planet's natural, social, and economic history worry about; and there is a pantheon of mythic beings, from Santa Claus and Dracula to Uncle Sam and Mickey Mouse, that both right- and wrong-thinking people the world over simply know about, much as they would recognise Warhol's international symbols culled from art, money, and politics: *The Last Supper*, the dollar sign, the hammer and sickle. And if one includes the hundreds of even-handed, seemingly effortless drawings that Warhol quietly and continuously produced from the 50s to the 80s, the range of his imagery is infinitely amplified, taking in Christ and Buddha, gay sex and breast-feeding.

Even when looked at in terms of more venerable hierarchies of subject matter, Warhol covers all bases. Although, by earlier standards, he might be classified primarily as a history painter and portraitist, he ventured into other traditional territories as well, translating them into his own language, which as often as not means the language of our times.

This remarkable breadth might in itself be enough to make Warhol a singular artist of our century, a strange hybrid of major journalist, chronicling the broadest spectrum of public experience, and media master, who can be at once painter, photographer, draftsman, decorator, sculptor, filmmaker, and illustrator. But it also turns out, looking ahead and back across the decades, that Warhol, essential to any account of Pop culture, commands fully as much attention within the more élite world of high art.

From the 60s to the very last months of his life, Warhol's art, in fact, constantly intersected the major concerns of other artists – seniors, contemporaries, and juniors – casting its glance not only backward to the now remote world of Ad Reinhardt and Mark Rothko but forward to the most youthful activities of the 80s, from the making of art based on reproductions of reproductions, as in the work of Sherrie Levine or Mike Bidlo, to the bald use, in both two and three dimensions, of the most ordinary imagery and commodities from the world of commerce and advertising, as in the work of Jeff Koons or Haim Steinbach. To be sure, in the 60s, when the initial impact of Pop art appeared to threaten the fortified towers of abstract art with a bombardment of visual and cultural pollution, Warhol, like Lichtenstein, was seen on the other side of an unbridgeable gulf that separated a faith in aesthetic purity from the vulgar reality of the life outside the studio door. But in retrospect, this black-and-white antagonism, like the Classic-Romantic, Ingres-Delacroix polarity of the 1820s, has greyed and become a larger whole, making it possible to see how Warhol, for instance, fully participated in the structural changes conventionally associated with the march of formalist innovation from the late 50s onward.

Already in the 60s, in fact, critics began to notice how Warhol, despite the seeming heresies of Pop imagery, could be located on both sides of the high-art/low-art tracks.[5] In 1968, for instance, John Coplans traced in an exhibition and more expansive catalogue the important genealogical table of serial imagery in Modern art from Monet and Mondrian through Reinhardt and Stella, and concluded with Warhol, whose Campbell's Soup Cans and Marilyns may at first have looked like illegitimate heirs in this noble Modernist ancestry, but gradually settled firmly into historical place.[6] Typically, Warhol himself, with his customary no-nonsense succinctness (often worthy of Gertrude Stein), later declared his allegiance to this exalted and primarily abstract tradition by claiming, 'I like Reinhardt when he began painting those black paintings and they were all the same black paintings.'[7] Within this context, we might note, too, how not only Reinhardt's repetitive, rectilinear blackness could provide foundations for Warhol's own version of serial monotony, but how even Rothko's procedures might also be invoked as a precedent from the 50s. For just as Rothko would prune his pictorial world down to the most elemental, head-on format of a

few hovering planes, released from the laws of gravity, and then complicate this image with infinitely nuanced chromatic combinations, so, too, would Warhol take his disembodied soup cans, floating frontally on an abstract ground, and embellish their initial fidelity to the crude factory colours of the original product with a series of lurid variations upon a new Day-Glo spectrum of artificial hues, from torrid orange to sultry purple.

In the 70s, another of Warhol's characteristic devices, the grid, generally used by him to evoke impersonal, belt-line replication, began to be recognised and included in rigorous discussions of this format in primarily abstract art, first by John Elderfield[8] and then by Rosalind Krauss,[9] both of whom located Warhol within the more cerebral company of artists like Agnes Martin, Kenneth Noland, and Sol LeWitt. And even more broadly, seeing the aesthetic skeleton as well as the cultural flesh of Warhol's art, Richard Morphet, in 1971, caught Warhol in a wide net of American abstract artists, quickly suggesting many analogies between the variety of structures characteristically employed by Warhol and those explored by artists ranging from Reinhardt and Kelly, Stella and Andre, Judd and Morris, all the way to LeWitt and his wall drawings.[10]

Now, almost two decades later, when the first battles between Pop and abstract art may seem as remote as our century's earlier theoretical conflicts between the partisans of Cubism and the supporters of pure abstraction, such affinities between Warhol's work of the 60s and that of his contemporaries have become far more apparent, to the point where he now looms large as one of the major formal innovators of the period. For instance, he shares with Johns, Lichtenstein, and Stella an attraction to what might be called a bifocal composition, that is, one that obliges the spectator to look side by side, or above and below, at two identical or equally compelling images, whether of the *Mona Lisa,* a car crash, or Marlon Brando. This vision, often transformed literally into a diptych structure, undermines the absolute authority of those unique images so precious to artists of a pre-Warhol era, setting up instead an either/or situation, or else creating a world of multiple replication, where even the artist's self-portrait is doubled as a means of diffusing any one-to-one focus on what might once have been a singular revelation of face and feeling at a particular time and place. In any anthology of this art of the double, so abundant in the late 50s and early 60s (as in Rauschenberg's *Factum I* and *Factum II,* 1957; Johns' *Ale Cans,* 1960; Lichtenstein's *Step-On Can,* 1961; and Stella's *Jasper's Dilemma,* 1962-63), Warhol must play a central role, exploring every aspect of the structure of duplication, from a shoulder-shrugging indifference toward direct, unique experience to a tonic visual assault on what had become a tedious formula of seemingly spontaneous compositions.

As for the latter, Warhol again occupies centre stage in the history of Minimalism, first as a master of rock-bottom reduction, which, in the case of the single Campbell's Soup Can or the *Gold Marilyn Monroe* of 1962, could convey an aura of sanctity; and then as a master of modular repetition, which, in the case of Coca-Cola bottles or air-mail stamps, would evoke the endless monotony of mass production and consumption. It is telling that beyond, or underneath, these rich cultural associations, the structure of Warhol's art bears close affinities to the abstract innovations of such contemporaries as Stella and Andre, much as they look backward to the crossword-puzzle patterns of Johns' Alphabets and Numbers of the mid-50s. And within this context, it should also be noted that like Andre and Morris, Warhol, in the 60s, often polarised his structures into two compositional extremes: an obsessive order and an equally obsessive disorder. As early as 1962, Warhol could arrange eight-by-24 tidy rows of dollar bills in a perfect grid while, at the same time, he could explode this graph-paper regularity with a total disorder of dozens of dollar bills that seem, like a dropped deck of cards, to have landed all over the surface of the canvas.

The sense of the rigorously disciplined versus the wilfully aleatory (to use the buzzword of the period) was apparent as well in Warhol's three-dimensional art. His *Brillo Box (Soap Pads)* of 1964, for example, is the supermarket *Doppelgänger* of Judd's and Morris' ideal cubes, a building-block of almost sacred, elemental clarity. Replicated in more secular quantities, however, and piled up not in neat rows but haphazardly stacked at casual heights and angles, as they were in their first installation at the Stable Gallery in 1964, they subvert their inherent geometries. It is a dialogue of extreme contradiction that was explored by Morris and Andre in the 60s, when both artists switched back and forth between abstract structures of cerebral purity and an elegant chaos of controlled spill and scatter; as if the theoretical principles of reason and its negation had been isolated in a laboratory and illustrated with palpable forms.

On other levels, too, Warhol's new structures joined forces with the most audacious explorations of the 60s and early 70s. His exhibition of helium-filled Silver Clouds at the Castelli gallery in 1966, consisting of airbourne, ballooning 'pillows' –

the 70s offered to those earlier prejudiced about art as a sacrosanct avowal of a personal world of touch and feeling, a world that reached its apogee in Abstract Expressionism. Here it should be said, too, that Warhol's devaluation of works of art made solely by the hand of the artist-genius has ample historical precedent, of which Jacques-Louis David's faith in the primacy of his images over his personal facture is the most apt.

The importance of Warhol's art in the 60s, whether for the innovations of Pop imagery, new formal structures, or new relationships to second-degree image-making (in the employment of silkscreen techniques and in the faith in photography as the most truthful record of reality for the post-50s generations nurtured on television) has seldom been doubted, even by his sworn enemies. But it has often been assumed that after the 60s or, with more rhetorical precision, after his near-death in 1968, his art drifted further and further from centre stage, catering only to the luxury trade or simply repeating, in ever more diluted form, the once fresh ideas of his youth. Warhol's art of the 70s and 80s was little seen in the United States, and usually only in erratic presentations of a single series rather than in any cohesive scope.

Now that this huge oeuvre, with its daunting quantity and

 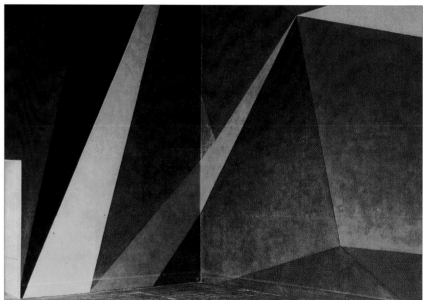

L to R: Ad Reinhardt, *Abstract Painting, Number 33*, 1963, oil, 152.4x152.4cm; Sol LeWitt, *Wall Drawing*, first installation 1987, colour ink washes superimposed

cool but glitzy and festive – once more employed the language of chance and clearly belonged with the kind of imaginative extension of volatile substances as art material that Morris used in his even more ephemeral 'steam piece' of 1968-69. And Warhol's *Cow Wallpaper*, which reached palatial dimensions as the background for the Whitney Museum's installation of his retrospective in 1971, can now be thought of as a counterpart to LeWitt's wall drawings of the early 70s, which similarly disrupted all our deeply ingrained Western assumptions about the proper boundaries of frame and image or the accepted distinctions between primary architectural elements and secondary interior decoration. Moreover, Warhol's accelerating detachment from what to many began to seem an archaic concept of picture-making – a one-to-one, hand-made expression of an individual artist's unique craft and sensibility – prophesied many aspects of Conceptual art, in which the artist conceived images whose material execution could be entrusted to other, anonymous hands (as in the case of LeWitt's wall drawings). Indeed, the metamorphosis of Warhol in the 60s from private artist to the head of a factory of art workers who would manufacture his art products is an integral part of the history of the many challenges

variety is at last being sorted out and as often as not being seen for the first time, it is slowly becoming clear that Warhol's art after the 60s, far from running on a private and ever more peripheral track, not only intersected the development of his contemporaries (Johns, Lichtenstein, and Stella) but was concerned with the same issues as any number of younger artists, from David Salle to Philip Taaffe. In formal terms alone, Warhol's art of the 70s and 80s followed general patterns of evolutions, from the lean austerity of the early 60s – ascetic in colour, sharp in contour, frontal and spaceless in structure – to far more intricate period styles. The passages of bravura brushwork that literally surfaced in the 70s over the silkscreened images below them, shared with Stella and Johns, among others, that growing sense of painterly virtuosity as a kind of homeless, disembodied decoration over a pre-existent structure, creating new kinds of spatial layering and transparencies that infinitely complicated the deadpan, frozen lucidity of, say, Johns' first Flags and Targets or Stella's first 'stripes'. Such visual complexities characterised even more fully Warhol's work of the 80s. For instance, the 1985 paintings of Mount Vesuvius in action[11] were both literally and formally eruptive, centrifugal explosions that would be at home with the most flamboyant Stellas of the same decade. Indeed, Warhol's archetypal forms of the 80s might be the camouflage and Rorschach patterns, ready-made abstractions that provided elaborate surface labyrinths under which a densely concealed imagery could be discerned, the visual opposite of the trumpet-blast clarity of the archetypal soup can of the 80s. In fact, the change from the 60s to the 80s could hardly be seen more clearly than in Warhol's updating of his original Campbell's Soup Cans with a new series of 1985-86 commemorating Campbell's newer product (boxes containing pouches of instant soup) and even some new flavours (Won-Ton).[12] These late images offer infinitely intricate variations on the raw, vintage Warhol of the early 60s with suggestions of spatial illusion and layering in the compression of the cardboard boxes, with occasional croppings that indicate continuities beyond the frame, with conspicuous disparities between colour and enclosing contour, and with hues that deviate totally from the harsh, primary clarity of those now 'ancient' soup cans.

But apart from the elaboration of Warhol's visual language, there is also a mood of both personal and public retrospection here, which not only captures the period flavour of the 80s but

revealing that Warhol's subjects in the 60s were almost all contemporary, culled from the news of the day, the celebrities of the moment, the supermarket shelves around the corner. When he did a series of artists' portraits in 1967, they were not, after all, past heroes like Picasso, Matisse, and Pollock, but rather a selection of his own peers from the Castelli stable – Stella, Bontecou, Rosenquist, Johns, Chamberlain, and Rauschenberg. But by the 80s Warhol, like everybody else it would seem, began to look constantly backward, conforming to the century's twilight mood of excavating memories.

Warhol figures large in the mood of the 80s when the history of art, like the history of everything else, floats about in a disembodied public image-bank where Caravaggio and Schnabel can jostle for equal time in weekly magazines and daily conversations. In this context, Warhol is indispensable to an understanding of the imagery of art about art, or the domain of what is called, more fancily, 'simulation' or 'appropriation'. To be sure, in the 60s, following in the footsteps of Marcel Duchamp (who wanted to desanctify the *Mona Lisa*) and Fernand Léger (who wanted to turn her into a machine-age product), Warhol took on this art icon, transforming her into a hybrid movie star and dime-

L to R: Jasper Johns, *Three Flags*, 1958, encaustic, 78.4x115.6x12.7cm; Roy Lichtenstein, *As I opened fire I . . .* , 1964, oil and magna, 172.7x233.7cm, 2 panels

belongs to a mode practiced by some of his contemporaries. Not only did he repeat, often with ghostly variations (such as photographic negatives or concealing sweeps of paint) the single images that had made him famous in the early 60s, but he even anthologised his early works in single paintings, thereby selecting what amounts to his own mini-retrospectives. This series, of 1979-80, usually executed on canvases of large dimensions, presents surrogate Warhol shows, compiling, for example, self-portraits, soup cans, corn-flakes boxes, flowers, cow's heads, Marilyns, and car crashes. These are often printed backwards and/or in black-and-white reversals, which contributes to a phantom mood of floating memory images confusing both private and public domains. But no less telling is the fact that in the 70s and 80s, Stella, Johns, and Lichtenstein all painted comparable anthologies of their own remembrances of art past.

Such retrospection, to be sure, may be characteristic of many artists as they grow older. Picasso, for one, accumulated in his last decades what seems an infinity of layers of artistic and biographical self-reference. But it should also be noted that Warhol's personal retrospection has a fully public face, typical of the rapidly escalating historicism of the late 20th century. It is

store art reproduction in the manner of Rauschenberg's earlier use of the tackiest postage-stamp prints of museum masterpieces. But by the 80s, his quotations of earlier art belonged to another frame of reference, a Post-Modern vision in which any citation from any historical time could turn up in a contemporary context. And mirroring the constant buckshot barrage of art-history images that bounces off us daily, Warhol could go on switching channels, usually with a shrewd irony that reflects Lichtenstein's own art-about-art choices, which would single out ostensibly the polar opposite of his own style (the painterly nuance and sensibility of Monet's cathedrals, the strident *Angst* of German Expressionism). It would be hard, for instance, to think of anything less compatible with Warhol's mass-produced imagery than precious details from Quattrocento paintings by Botticelli, Uccello, and Leonardo, but that is what Warhol startled us with in 1984, varying these unique, hand-made passages by craftsmen from a remote era of image-making with a shrill rainbow of Day-Glo colours worthy of Stella's comparably extravagant palette of the 80s.

Warhol's canny selections from the data bank of art history also reflected, like Salle's borrowings from Yasuo Kuniyoshi or

Carl Andre, *128 Lead Solid*, 1982, lead 128 unit cube, 40x40x40cm

Reginald Marsh, the revisionist thrust of a Post-Modernist view of 20th-century art that would no longer accept the party lines still held in the 60s. Nothing could demonstrate this more acutely than his appropriation of imagery from Giorgio de Chirico[13] in 1982, exactly the same year that the Museum of Modern Art's retrospective offered the canonic truncated version of the old master's art, which presumably ended in decades of shame with endlessly diluted replications of his early, epoch-making masterpieces. But Warhol translated the De Chirico story into something appropriate to himself and to the reversals of taste of the last decade, which began to value precisely those aspects of layered memory and replication so conspicuous in the artist's paraphrases and self-counterfeits of his own glorious, but remote, historical past.

Warhol could also share the 80s taste for treating abstraction as a kind of *objet trouvé*, a phenomenon familiar to the work of, say, Salle and Taaffe, who can approach the widest vocabulary of abstract imagery – from Jean-Paul Riopelle and Barnett Newman to Ad Reinhardt and Bridget Riley – as if it were simply part of, and interchangeable with, the rest of the visual data around us. And in his last years Warhol arrived at what now

looks like, in terms of religion and art history, the ultimate appropriations, the supreme Christian icons of Western art that fix forever Jesus and the Virgin – Leonardo's *Last Supper* and Raphael's *Sistine Madonna* – quoted in their entirety and in parts, and reaching at times vast pictorial dimensions that, like Schnabel's inflated, scavenged images, echo with a death-rattle irony the mural ambitions and achievements of Renaissance frescoes and altarpieces.

Warhol's connections with art history, are not only those of the 80s quotation-mark eclecticism explored by many of his lively younger contemporaries, but also those of more resonant connections that conjure up a wide range of ancestral charts. In nationalist terms, Warhol, like Lichtenstein, can stir up a proto-history of Pop art in America between the two world wars.

European Cubism and Dada can also disclose a multitude of Warhol lookalikes that provide him with a more cosmopolitan pedigree, albeit one that still has American roots.[14] It was, after all, an American product, a box of Quaker Oats cereal, as imported into France, that Juan Gris carefully reproduced (including the cartoon-like emblem of William Penn on the label) in a Cubist still-life of 1915. And it was the milieu of New York and American mechanical products that excited the Dadaist spirit of Francis Picabia (whose work caught Warhol's eye)[15] to create in 1915 such sexually symbolic machine-age portraits as that of a spark plug representing an American girl in a state of nudity or a flashlight representing a phallic Max Jacob, a prophecy, incidentally, of the more cryptically erotic implications of Johns' flashlight imagery.[16] In both of these heretical images from the pages of the magazine *291*, Picabia not only embraced the kind of ordinary, machine-age object familiar to the Warhol-Lichtenstein repertoire of the early 60s but, as much to the point, depicted these mundane appliances in the language of the commercial illustrator, flattening them, clarifying them, and isolating them like disembodied icons against a totally blank, spaceless ground. Such weightless and homeless relics of our machine age, seen without context and rendered in the visual vocabulary of an anonymous image-maker in a technological civilisation, again strike Warholian chords of recognition.

There are more offbeat areas of 20th-century art as well that have become recognised as proto-Warhol territory, most particularly, as already noted by Richard Morphet,[17] the later portraits and news images of the British artist Walter Sickert, whose work still remains unfamiliar to American audiences. Such a fusion of artist and reporter, however, in terms of voyeuristic sensibility, leads back to Manet, who, like Warhol, maintained the stance of an aesthete-observer in the face of any subject, whether a stalk of asparagus or a murder.

Like Warhol, Manet might have shrugged his shoulders while saying, 'There's a disaster every day',[18] pausing perhaps to record the disaster of the day as Warhol paused to record, on the one hand, a man leaping from a high-rise building and, on the other, a bunch of poppies. The customary accusation that the deadpan coolness of Manet's news-photograph surrogate, *The Execution of Maximilian*, is inadequate as a response to its brutal subject is one that might equally be levelled at Warhol, who also seems to approach the facts of modern death with no apparent shift of emotional tone. His use of electric chairs or car crashes as wallpaper-like repeat patterns or as components in larger wholes similarly underscores and contradicts the terror of modern death, the daily statistic that has become so commonplace that the conventional hierarchy of emotional values begins to look like a naïve and outmoded support system for cushioning grief and outrage. We may all owe a debt to Warhol, as we do to

Manet, for reflecting exactly the state of moral and emotional anaesthesia which, like it or not, probably tells us more truth about the realities of the modern world than do the rhetorical passions of *Guernica*. It is not only a question of murderers at large and electric chairs, but also the apocalyptic vision of the atom bomb and devastating earthquakes. It is not only a question of death on the road or in the air, but of the glaring presence of the skulls and skeletons that haunt all living flesh. Indeed, these constant reminders of our private and public mortality, whether as reportage or through the traditional emblem of the skull, can rival in abundance and impact the persistent theme of death as the overwhelmingly inevitable adversary that casts its dark shadow over the work of Picasso.[19]

No less remarkably, Warhol, presumably the most secular and venal of artists and personalities, has even been able to create disturbing new equivalents for the depiction of the sacred in earlier religious art. His galleries of myths and superstars resemble an anthology of post-Christian saints, just as his renderings of Marilyn's disembodied lips or a single soup can become the icons of a new religion, recalling the fixed isolation of holy relics in an abstract space. Elsewhere, the mute void and mystery of death are evoked, whether through the use of photographic reversals that turn their already impalpable images into ghostly memories or, most startlingly, through the use of a blank canvas, as in the case of *Blue Electric Chair*, 1963, in which a diptych (the form itself recalling an altarpiece) offers, at the left, three times five electric chairs silkscreened in a flat blue plane and, at the right, the same blue ground left numbingly empty. But there is also the supernatural glitter of celestial splendour, as when the single image of Marilyn Monroe is floated against a gold background, usurping the traditional realm of a Byzantine madonna. And even the shimmer of diamond dust, redolent of dimestore dreams and the magic sparkle of Wizard of Oz footwear, can waft us to unimagined heights, providing for Joseph Beuys an impalpable twinkle of sainthood, like a pulverised halo, or transforming a touristic snapshot of the vertical sweep of Cologne Cathedral's Gothic towers into an exalted vision of Christian eternity. Both ingenuous and shrewd, blasphemous and devout, Warhol not only managed to encompass in his art the most awesome panorama of the material world we all live in, but even gave us unexpected glimpses of our new forms of heaven and hell.

Notes

1 See Stuart Morgan, Glenn O'Brien, Remo Guidieri, and Robert Becker, 'Collaboration Andy Warhol', *Parkett* 12, 1987, pp95-96. The exhibitions were *Andy Warhol and Jamie Wyeth: Portraits of Each Other*, Coe Kerr Gallery, N Y, June 1976; and *LeRoy Neiman, Andy Warhol: An Exhibition of Sports Paintings*, Los Angeles Institute of Contemporary Art, 1981.

2 By Max Kozloff. On this, see the doctoral thesis by Patrick S Smith, *Andy Warhol's Art and Films*, UMI Press, Ann Arbor, 1986, ch6.

3 Sidra Stich, *Made in USA: An Americanisation in Modern Art, the 50s and 60s*, University of California, Berkeley 1987.

4 See the issues of January 29, 1965, and February 16, 1970.

5 I myself made some preliminary suggestions in this direction in 'Pop and Non-Pop: An Essay in Distinction', *Art and Literature* 5, Summer 1965, pp80-93.

6 John Coplans, *Serial Imagery*, Pasadena Art Museum, California, 1968. For Warhol, *see* pp130-37.

7 Quoted in *Warhol's Campbell's Soup Boxes*, Michael Kohn Gallery, Los Angeles, 1986, p28.

8 John Elderfield, 'Grids', *Artforum*, May 1972, pp52-59.

9 Rosalind Krauss, *Grids: Format and Image in 20th-Century Art*, Pace, NY, 1979.

10 See Richard Morphet, 'Andy Warhol', in *Warhol*, Tate, London, 1971, pp24ff.

11 See exhib cat *Vesuvius by Warhol*, Fondazione Amelio, Naples. Warhol's detached approach to this awesome sight is, incidentally, prophesied by Edgar Degas, who, in a monotype of *c* 1890-93, coolly recorded Vesuvius erupting. (See Eugenia Parry Janis, *Degas Monotypes*, Mass Fogg Art Museum, Cambridge, 1968, no 310.)

12 On these, see above, note 7, which includes a particularly informative essay by Michael Kohn.

13 See Achille Bonito Oliva, *Warhol verso de Chirico*, Electa, Milan, 1982, reprinted in 1985 for Marisa del Re, NY.

14 I have already suggested this field of inquiry in my essay 'Picasso and the Typography of Cubism', in Roland Penrose and John Golding, eds, *Picasso in Retrospect*, Praeger, NY and Washington, 1973, especially p75; and have amplified it in a lecture, 'High Art vs Low Art: Cubism as Pop', first given at the Hirshhorn Museum and Sculpture Garden, Washington, DC, on May 11, 1975, in which I elaborated the many proto-Pop aspects of Cubism, ranging from the use of cartoon imagery to the replication of commercial logos.

15 Warhol's own collection included Picabia canvases of 1934 and 1946.

16 For varying interpretations of these works by Picabia, see William Camfield, *Francis Picabia: His Art, Life, and Times*, Princeton University Press, NJ, 1979, p83; and Maria Lluïsa Borras, *Picabia*, NY, 1985, pp155-56.

17 First suggested in 'The Modernity of Late Sickert', *Studio International* 190, July-August 1975, pp35-38; and then further elaborated in my essay on Warhol's portraiture. For more on Sickert, see exhib cat *Late Sickert: Paintings 1927 to 1942*, Hayward, London, 1981-82.

18 See above note 7, p28.

19 Warhol's Skulls, in particular, and his death imagery, in general, were the subjects of a lecture by Trevor Fairbrother given at the Warhol Symposium sponsored by the Dia Art Foundation, NY, on April 23, 1988. Proceedings to be published.

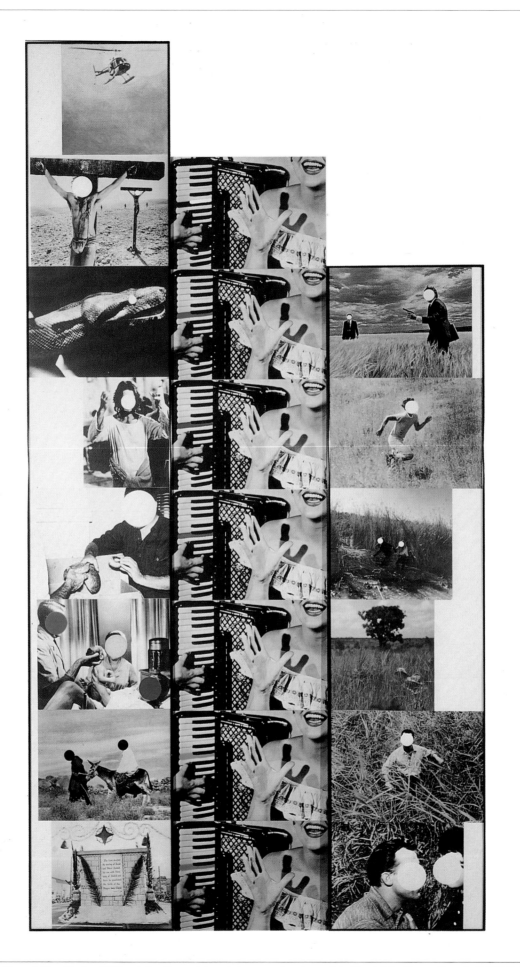

John Baldessari, *Two Stories*, 1987, gelatin silver prints and chromogenic colour prints (C-prints) with acrylic and oil, 243.8x129.5cm

ANNE RORIMER
PHOTOGRAPHY – LANGUAGE – CONTEXT
Prelude to the 1980s

Daniel Buren, *140 Stations du Métro Parisien (Rue de la Pompe)*, 1973, photographic documentation of installation

In a recent essay in which she reflected on the transformations that took place in art during the late 1960s, the art critic Barbara Rose concluded that, after the transitional year of 1967, 'things would never be again as they once were.' Having written about Minimal and Pop art as these movements were developing,[1] Rose contemplated in retrospect the winds of change that were ushering in yet other

approaches to artistic production now broadly labelled Conceptual art. In this regard she succinctly stated:

> If I could sum up the shift that occurred in art and criticism in 1967, it would be the widespread assault on the dogma of Modernism as an exclusively optical, art-for-art's sake, socially detached, formalist phenomenon that inevitably tended toward abstraction . . .[2]

This widely acknowledged shift characterising the art of the 1970s prepared the ground for the art ascribed to the 1980s. A consideration of the specific purposes of a number of artists who first began working over 20 years ago – with no attempt at historical all-inclusiveness – brings the artistic issues of the 1970s (initially defined in the 1960s) into relief in relation to developments in the 1980s (commencing in the late 1970s). It also presents the opportunity to reflect on particular manifestations of, in Rose's words, the 'assault on the dogma of Modernism' or, in less combative terms, the gradual erosion of Modernist doctrine.

'Modernism', in its more recent and limited usage, has been predominantly associated with the views of the eminent art critic Clement Greenberg.[3] Regarded as a father of American art criticism,[4] Greenberg is renowned for his writings since the late 1930s and for his early support in the 1940s and 1950s of Abstract Expressionist artists such as Willem de Kooning, Franz Kline, Barnett Newman, Jackson Pollock, and Mark Rothko, as well as the slightly later Colour-Field painters such as Morris Louis and Kenneth Noland, whose work, he found, fulfilled the Modernist tendency of art to progress towards being a reflection of itself as opposed to a representation of external reality. 'The essence of Modernism lies, as I see it', Greenberg summarised in 1965, 'in the use of the characteristic methods of a discipline to criticise the discipline itself – not in order to subvert it, but to entrench it more firmly in its area of competence.'[5]

For Greenberg, the work of art, as an idealist construct, explores its formal potential within the prescribed limits of painting or sculpture without interference from the economic, social, or political realities that exist outside of its borders. In order to defend the highest cultural values 'against the prevailing standards of society', the artist 'retiring from public altogether', and 'in search of the absolute . . . tries in effect to imitate God by creating something valid solely on its own terms . . . Content is to be dissolved so completely into form that the work of art or literature cannot be reduced in whole or in part to anything not itself.'[6] To accomplish successfully its 'task of self-criticism' – in order to 'find the guarantee of its standards of quality as well as of its independence'[7] – the work of art should not transgress the specifically defined boundaries of its discipline, whether painting or sculpture. That is, quoting Greenberg once again, 'a

Bernd and Hilla Becher, *L to R: Minehead*, Wingles, France, 1967; *Blast Furnace*, Boel, La Louviere, Belgium, 1985

Modernist work of art must try, in principle, to avoid dependence upon any order of experience not given in the most essentially construed nature of its medium.'[8]

A work of art, according to Greenberg, is meant to transcend the chaos of modern life and the contradictions of society.[9] Seeking to attain its own reality within the dictates of its particular medium, it is an autonomous, self-sufficient object that contends with either its two-dimensional or three-dimensional nature as painting or sculpture. Within this scheme, the representation of recognisable subject matter in painting gives way to the 'abstract'[10] so as to ensure to the extent possible the actual two-dimensionality and 'flatness'[11] of the canvas against the slightest allusion to figuration since even 'the fragmentary silhouette of a human figure, or of a teacup'[12] leads to associations with false, illusionistic, three-dimensional space. Insofar as sculpture is concerned, being three-dimensional, it 'exists for and by itself literally as well as conceptually.'[13]

Modernist theory in some respects applies more stringently to the work of Minimal and Pop artists than to that of the Abstract Expressionists, although Greenberg himself did not endorse these ensuing movements.[14] The frequently quoted remark by

Frank Stella about his painting, that there is nothing there 'besides the paint on the canvas' and that 'only what can be seen there *is* there',[15] cogently characterises the paintings and sculptures that, responding to and reacting against Abstract Expressionist works, further clarified the objective nature of their formal content. During the 1960s, for example, Donald Judd, Carl Andre, and Sol LeWitt succeeded in bringing sculpture to its 'purist'[16] state as a non-referential object that essentially is about the fact of being sculpture. With the intent of eradicating all figurative reference and hierarchically arranged compositional elements in order to move 'away from illusionism, allusion and metaphor,'[17] as their contemporary Robert Morris has articulated, these artists have stressed the material presence of sculpture for its own sake.

Paradoxically, the reintroduction of imagery into painting by Jasper Johns in his *Flag* (1954), and thereafter by Roy Lichtenstein with his enlarged depictions of existing comic-book scenes, or by Andy Warhol with his use of existing commercial illustration, confirmed rather than abrogated the flatness of the picture plane so crucial to Greenberg's thinking. Representation of recognisable subject matter, in the form of already flat imagery,

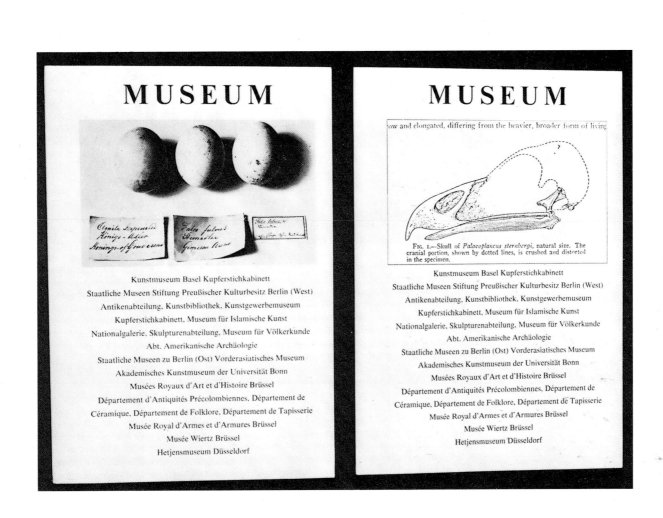

Marcel Broodthaers, covers of the two-volume catalogue, *Der Adler vom Oligozän bis heute*, 1972

re-emerges as a significant factor in painting, but coincides with and indicates its two-dimensionality instead of, as Greenberg feared, obscuring its literal flatness. In this regard, Lichtenstein has claimed that his work 'doesn't look like a painting of something; it looks like the thing itself.'[18] It might further be noted that the insertion of real objects by Robert Rauschenberg into his early paintings – whether the artist's bedding, tipped up and used for *Bed* (1955), or the full-scale stuffed goat standing in *Monogram* (1955-59) – confirmed the pure materiality of paint as paint while also denying illusionism. No longer tied to associative or representational purpose, paint portrays its own reality in Rauschenberg's 'Combine Paintings' at the same time as items from the 'real' world are absorbed into the framework of art without falsifying the two-dimensionality of the canvas surface. Self-referential and non-illusionistic, works of the late 1950s and 1960s may thus be said to have remained within the Modernist idiom.[19] However, having imported materials that do not conform to 'the most essentially construed nature' of the mediums of painting and sculpture as traditionally conceived, they signalled the need for the expansion or reappraisal of Greenberg's criteria.

Attentive to preceding achievements, artists in the late 1960s who followed in the wake of Minimal and Pop art, on the one hand continued the self-reflexive critique of painting and sculpture. On the other hand, however, they reinterpreted what its 'characteristic methods' might encompass. Active experimentation at this time resulted in further re-engagement with pictorial and sculptural representation, as well as in the so-called 'de-materialisation'[20] of the object, and undermined the assumptions of Greenberg's Modernism on two major accounts. Through the exclusive use of photography and/or language, a number of artists called into question the limitation to specific mediums imposed on painting and sculpture, while other artists negated the self-sufficient status of the physical object through the investigation of the contextual conditions of art.

Works of the 1970s break from subordination to an all-encompassing painted framework or sculptural format, while contending with the formal and material issues pertaining to the disciplines of painting and sculpture. Photography and language, employed separately or together, as of the late 1960s provided an avenue for the ongoing exploration of alternatives to previous pictorial and sculptural convention. With major consequence for

Above: Bruce Nauman, *American Violence*, 1981-82, coloured neon, glass tubing, 198x157.5x8.2cm; *Below*: Lawrence Weiner, *MANY COLORED OBJECTS PLACED SIDE BY SIDE TO FORM A ROW OF MANY COLORED OBJECTS*, 1979, spray paint through stencil

the art of the 1980s, artists of the 1970s are responsible for having established the independent use of photography and language as mediums for representation.

Like harbingers of the decade of the 1970s, the early works of Joseph Kosuth, dated 1965, thematically announce the radical break from categorised adherence to traditional concepts of medium. His works of this date consist of three parts: a black-and-white photograph to scale of a utilitarian object – a broom, chair, hammer, lamp, or umbrella, for example; the object itself; and an enlarged photostat of a printed dictionary definition of the object shown. Like ready-mades – functional objects chosen by the artist in the tradition of Marcel Duchamp – Kosuth's objects stand on their own, materially untransformed. Not part of an overall painted or sculptural context, they are bracketed by their mechanically reproduced image and by their linguistic definition. Having been extracted from the 'real' world of use and replaced to function within the work of art, the objects represent themselves. Believing that 'art is the definition of art',[21] and that it is not concerned 'with questions of empirical fact',[22] but 'exists for its own sake',[23] Kosuth has represented the idea of representation *per se* as it may be incurred by photographs or words. As the combination of three equal parts – photography, object, and text – these pieces are statements of fact, not simply about external reality, but about the means to register it.

The work of John Baldessari, and Bernd and Hilla Becher, based on photography, and that of Bruce Nauman and Lawrence Weiner, relying on language, illustrate how these two systems of signification have lent themselves to the artistic purposes advanced in the 1970s. Photography – as an imprint of visible actuality – and language – a series of abstract lexical units that are contiguous with what they mean – affirm the reality of the work in terms of its formal/material self and in terms of its represented content. Because of their inherent representational nature, photography and language exempt the artist from the direct manipulation of materials or the determination of form so that the resulting work might be both what it is and what it is *of* simultaneously.

Early paintings by Baldessari done between 1966 and 1968 betoken his motivation for terminating an involvement with painting on canvas in the interest of photographic representation. By 1965 he 'was weary of doing relational painting and began wondering if straight information would serve.'[24] Desiring to expunge the accepted 'art signals' from painting, he sent standard-size canvases primed by someone else to a sign painter who lettered them as simply as possible across the surface with the statements he provided. These lettered statements, taken from his notebooks, from art books, or from manuals, include such phrases as 'A WORK WITH ONLY ONE PROPERTY' or 'EVERYTHING IS PURGED FROM THIS PAINTING BUT ART'; 'NO IDEAS HAVE ENTERED THIS WORK.' A text covering the entire canvas is, as its title heading states, 'A PAINTING THAT IS ITS OWN DOCUMENTATION'. In a number of these early pieces, furthermore, photographs 'taken to violate then current photographic norms' or 'taken pointing out the window while driving', accompany pronouncements about 'correct' photographic procedures.

Works by Baldessari from this period derive their formal content from their linguistic content and from the application of measures that allowed him to abstain from direct intervention in the act of invention.

With its ability mechanically to reproduce reality, photography has enabled Baldessari to find and arrange existing imagery without having to create it himself. Works such as *Cigar Smoke to Match Clouds that Are Different (By Sight-Side View)* (1972-73) and *Throwing Balls in the Air to Get a Straight Line (Best of 36 Tries)* (1972-73) demonstrate the way in which the camera

positions the artist in relation to his material, not so much as the traditional creator who inspires the work by 'putting himself into it', as one might say, but more as an arbiter of situations set up in advance that seemingly permit the work to transpire of its own accord. In the former piece, Baldessari selected photographs in which his own cigar smoke most closely resembled clouds in the sky. In the latter, photographs document his attempt to make a straight line with four balls tossed into the air. Works such as these are governed by the outcome of events that have been instigated by the artist to preclude his subjective input and to avoid the creation of a subjectively imposed hierarchy of compositional elements and forms.

Like Baldessari, the Bechers have relied on photographic methods to engender pictorial form. Known since the 1960s for their portrayal of industrial architecture, by the late 1950s the Bechers had already found photography to be more suited than painting to their comprehensive study of these structures. For nearly three decades, they have travelled throughout the industrial regions of Europe and the United States documenting industrial buildings: watertowers, cooling towers, winding towers, coal silos, lime kilns, blast furnaces, preparation plants, grain elevators, houses, etc. Individual works by the Bechers may be comprised of separate photographs showing different examples of one particular kind of structure all taken frontally, or may consist of a series of photographs of the same structure from different viewpoints. Images within each work are scaled to identical size and are aligned in equally proportioned rows.

Seeking 'to provide . . . a grammar for people to understand and compare different structures,'[25] the Bechers have maintained for a long time that 'what we would like is to produce a more or less perfect chain of different forms and shapes.'[26] To this end, they render the building in question as objectively as possible, without the 'artistic' effects of figures, trees, cloud formations, or surrounding vistas. Taking advantage of the camera as an instrument of exclusion as well as of inclusion, the Bechers systematically isolate and frame each piece of architecture, either from predetermined and straightforward angles or with regard to particular details. In this way they are able to predicate their work on the permutations of forms that, arising out of functional need, already exist in the industrial landscape and which, with the aid of the camera, they are able to single out, classify, and arrange according to the dictates of their formal enterprise.

Photography has presented artists such as Baldessari and the Bechers with the means of distancing themselves from the traditionally required procedures of constructing a work, while also affording the possibility of producing visual relationships, founded in reality, that would not otherwise be incurred.

In their work, the camera, functioning in accordance with the *a priori* conditions or situations decided in advance by the artist, serves as a tool for focusing on external fact in order to circumvent internally generated fabrication. The photograph is subject to – as well as the subject of – the work as a total construct that comprises the sum of its systemically related, endemic parts, relationally extracted from reality. For these artists, the photograph, resulting from the treatment of the medium as a craft to be mastered, with emphasis on the tonal qualities of the print or in relation to the formal aspect or message of its image, is not a sought-after end.[27] By exempting the artist from subjective decisions regarding compositional content and arrangement, it acts instead to assure the work its own structured reality in direct alliance with forms acquired from reality at large.

As in the case of photographic images, the physical form of words and what they mean are contingent one upon the other. By using language, Bruce Nauman and Lawrence Weiner have made radical use of this relationship within their respective oeuvres. In the work of these artists, language does not encompass a literary aim – although it may possess 'poetic' qualities – but is a vehicle for non-illusionistically fusing form and content.

The continuing search for methods to create meaningful form underlies the diversity of Nauman's work in general and reflects the desire to re-form traditional sculpture. In Nauman's production, words take part in the realisation of three-dimensional objects. Two colour photographs from a set of 11, *Untitled* (1966-67), suggest the nature of Nauman's endeavour. In one, subtitled *Eating My Words*, the artist is shown as he sits at a kitchen table spreading jam on cut-out 'words' made of bread, which he is about to eat. In the other, *Waxing Hot*, one sees the artist's hands in the process of applying wax to individual, standing wooden letters that spell 'hot'. Creating scenarios by acting out 'plays' on words to the letter, so to speak, Nauman has represented words as material, three-dimensional objects, infusing them with physicality. With expressions providing imagery, words take shape.

From 1967 to the present, Nauman has intermittently used neon as a medium to translate verbal form and expression into sculpture. His neon pieces are based on the phonetic, phonemic, figurative, and referential properties of words. Minor changes in the positioning/repositioning, or the addition/subtraction, of single letters in works such as RAW/WAR (1970) or DEATH/EAT (1972) cause major changes in meaning. Illuminating each word in alternating succession, these works in neon often touch on the human and social condition. Sometimes treading the thin line between sense and non-sense, they explore elements that render verbal meaning. Resembling anonymous advertising signs that serve to draw attention,[28] they confer material form on signification and, in this way, alternatively bestow signification on material form.

Whereas language in Nauman's work plays a sculptural role in conjunction with other materials, in Weiner's work, language – because of its representational ability to stand *for* something – stands on its own as sculpture. Weiner came to the conclusion in 1967 that language by itself was sufficient for the production of visual form and meaning. Since then he has created a wide range of works within a broad thematic scope. These works may be either mentally grasped by the viewer or actually physically constructed to yield any number of possible results. In every case, the precise, descriptive interpretation of the work is left open. The piece MANY COLORED OBJECTS PLACED SIDE BY SIDE TO FORM A ROW OF MANY COLORED OBJECTS (1979), for example, does not spell out how many objects might be involved, or of what these objects might consist, or where they should be placed. As the artist maintains in a statement that accompanies all of his work, 'the decision as to condition rests with the receiver upon the occasion of receivership.'

Using language as his material, Weiner deals with the three-dimensional concerns of sculpture by means of pure wording, that is, by what the piece describes. Lettering (or, in some cases, speech) gives the work its necessary presentational form. Usually shown as stenciled, Lettraset, outlined, or hand-drawn words on the walls of exhibition spaces, Weiner's works may also be printed in books or on posters or displayed in countless other ways. By employing language to create specific pieces with unspecified readings and the potential for ubiquitous placement, Weiner frees his work from sole reliance on a particular space or on the spaces designated for art. The shifting contexts in which his works appear alter the frames of reference through which they may be seen so that it is the viewers who, informed by the cultural context in general, ultimately bring their own frame of reference to bear. Weiner treats language neutrally as a means to impart information about the verifiable, external world, and all of his works are grounded in the actuality of observable or possible qualities, processes, conditions, actions, substances, or things. His works vary semantically in the degree of their specificity from a piece like ONE QUART EXTERIOR GREEN INDUSTRIAL ENAMEL THROWN ON A BRICK WALL (1967) to ones such as TAKEN TO A POINT OF TOLERANCE (1973) and MADE QUIETLY (1972).

Referential and self-referential at the same time, works by Weiner are what they describe. A majority deal solely with their own physical nature, as does WITH A TOUCH OF PINK/WITH A BIT OF VIOLET/WITH A HINT OF GREEN (1977), while others may make an intangible occurrence concrete, as in the case of A TRANSLATION FROM ONE LANGUAGE TO ANOTHER (1969), through its materialisation in language and 'translation' into art. By adopting language as his exclusive representational medium and thereby deriving the substance of his work from the import of words, Weiner has succeeded in uniting the subject represented with the object of art. The reality of the former and that of the latter are thus inseparably joined.

Serving to eliminate the signs of execution involving brushwork or manual skill along with the signs of the mental decision-making process, photography and language remove evidence of the artist's participation in the formation of the artwork, so that the form of the work and its content might mutually express one another without subjective comment by the artist. Works of the 1970s employing photography or language further the objective aims of Minimal and Pop artists, who also abolish reference to internally expressive content. As the widely read French philosopher Michel Foucault (quoting Samuel Beckett) has asked, 'What does it matter who is speaking?'[29] Moreover, his contemporary Roland Barthes, in a now well-known text, has asserted that, after all, 'it is language which speaks, not the author.'[30]

Concerned essentially with representation as a tool for social analysis, Victor Burgin and Hans Haacke turned to photography and language at the beginning of the 1970s as a means to bring aspects of the contemporary social situation into their representational purview. Burgin has maintained: 'I wasn't concerned with objects as much as with events in the life of the observer.'[31] In early pieces of 1969-70, he sought to implement language objectively in order to meet 'the demands of a situation'[32] with relation to the viewer rather than to create a material object. His initial involvement with language as a link between viewer and environment instead of with physical objects led him to a consideration of how photographic representation, as a language of images, is manipulated in contemporary Western culture.

A work titled *Britain* (1976), consisting of 11 black-and-white photographs, points in the direction Burgin's work was to follow. The individual photographs, taken by Burgin, include urban and suburban scenes, interiors and exteriors, with or without figures. In all cases Burgin has superimposed a printed text on a portion of the image. Acquired from existing prose found in the media, each text has a specific bearing on the photograph because of its association with it. *Today is the Tomorrow You Were Promised Yesterday* is the subtitle of one of the 11 photographs. Its text, set in the upper left-hand corner of the image, reads partially as follows: 'The early-morning mist dissolves. And the sun shines on the Pacific . . . Wander down a winding path. Onto gentle sands. Ocean crystal clear. Sea anemones. Turquoise waters. Total immersion. Ecstasy.' The message of the text, with its poetic ring, is presumably an inducement to take a costly vacation. The photograph represents a low-income housing complex and off to one side shows a pregnant woman pushing a stroller. The image thus belies the textual injunction for a promised tomorrow in a place where 'pelicans splash lazily in the surf.'

According to the artist, 'the photographic image can carry a large number of different meanings', which generally are 'controlled by its juxtaposition with a verbal text.'[33] His art is motivated by the desire to declare the misrepresentation that 'lies' beneath the surface of photographic representation, particularly in the images of the advertising media with their purely commercial objectives. Conversant from an early date with semiology (the study of signs and signification), most influentially developed by Barthes in the late 1950s and early 1960s, Burgin has articulated the theoretical premises of his work in extensive writings that complement his art. One of his main admonitions is that photographs, whose 'point of view' and 'frame of reference'[34] are not actually admitted within their circumscribed, two-dimensional format, have the ability to cover up 'the actual material condition of the world in the service of specific vested interests'[35] because of the authority of their supposed factual presence. As Barthes affirmed, 'we never encounter (at least in advertising) a literal image in a pure state.'[36] With the intent of investigating the dominant ideology and its attendant social conditions, Burgin believes that the 'job for the artist which no one else does is to dismantle existing communication codes and to recombine some of their elements into structures which can be used to generate new pictures of the world.'[37] For Burgin, decoding photographs leads to a clearer view of the present social system.

Whereas texts and images in Burgin's work contrast with each other, in Hans Haacke's work they connect with each other. Like Burgin, Haacke seeks to penetrate realities of the contemporary social environment as these are disclosed by representation. Approaching his work from an angle slightly different from that of Burgin, he juxtaposes textual and/or photographic information so as to display assembled facts and expose dissembled images in order to reveal the contradictions within the social system.

Haacke approaches his work somewhat like a social scientist gathering empirical data.[38] Since 1969, when he began conducting polls of visitors to exhibitions, he has created works of art that depend on the acquisition of factual material and its presentation in a straightforward, matter-of-fact manner, as in his even earlier weather works that responded to the conditions of their physical environment. Haacke's poll pieces, executed over a period of several years for museum and gallery exhibitions, define an early interest in pinpointing certain kinds of information. During a one-person exhibition in 1969 at the Howard Wise Gallery, New York, he tabulated the birthplaces and current residences of the visitors, having asked them to place red and blue pins, respectively, on maps of Manhattan and the five boroughs of New York.[39] The resulting accumulation of demographic data determined the form of the piece, which foregrounds its viewers' 'backgrounds' within its own framework.

For a slightly later work of 1971, Haacke applied this fact-finding approach to a more elaborate and pointed inquiry into relationships between individuals, geographic location, and housing. *Shapolsky et al Manhattan Real Estate Holdings, a Real-Time Social System, as of May 1, 1971* comprises two enlarged maps (showing the lower East Side and Harlem), in addition to 142 black-and-white photographs of building facades or empty lots, framed above typed data sheets. The accompanying pages give the address of the piece of property concerned, its block and lot number, lot size, and building code as well as the corporation or individual holding title, with addresses and names of officers, its date of acquisition, prior owner, mortgage, and assessed tax value – all found in public records. Also included are six charts of business transactions connected with the ownership of the buildings. The work is an exhaustive, sweeping survey of one family's real estate holdings in lower-income sectors of New York. It brings together the particulars of a situation that, unless systematically compiled, would remain hidden and disregarded. Displayed on the wall and framed as an aggregate of separate but

connected units, the piece opens the door to speculation, not on the value of real estate, but on the 'real' value, in broader terms, of extremely limited private ownership. Facts, made visually concrete by Haacke's method of analysis, contribute to a greater understanding of the factors at work in the economic and social sphere.

The work of Dan Graham, Daniel Buren, Marcel Broodthaers and Michael Asher coincides on the essential question of the object's autonomy. Each of these artists has contributed to dispelling the idea that a painting or sculpture is an isolated object disconnected from its physical, social, economic, or historical context. Within the parameters of their aesthetic production, each addresses the idea that a work of art in contemporary culture, as part of the economic system of buying and selling, is itself a commodity by definition. Although works by these artists may be purchased and owned, they cannot be detached from their supporting conditions to circulate freely, if blindly, through the established channels of commerce. Such works self-referentially analyse how they function as art by questioning their relationship to their surroundings. In so doing, they revolutionise the traditional definition of painting as a flat, separately enframed surface, and sculpture as a freestanding, three-dimensional object.

As early as 1965, Dan Graham perceived the contradictory nature of the artwork's claim to autonomy vis-à-vis its reliance on invisible, but nonetheless real, socio-economic systems of support. From works of this date, which appeared in magazines, to his recent architectural 'Pavilion/Sculptures', Graham has sought to resolve the contradictions inherited by and inherent in the socially isolated object in space. *Figurative* (1965), one of a number of Graham's magazine works, appeared in *Harper's Bazaar* in March 1968 instead of being shown in an art gallery or a museum. A section of an actual cash register receipt, with the amounts paid for numerous, inexpensive items aligned in standard, columnar fashion, endows the work with its 'figurative' content. Bracketed on page 90 of the magazine between two advertisements – one for Tampax and the other for a Warner's bra – *Figurative* functions on several levels. For one, representational material and presentational method become inseparable since the work exists simultaneously *on* the page and *within* the timely – not timeless – context of a magazine. Furthermore, if the format of the magazine gives the work as a whole its form, the figuration on the shopping receipt, at the end of the buying process, contrasts with the two surrounding ads beckoning to the potential consumer.

Graham abandoned the magazine pieces after 1969 in order to realise his ideas through engagement with a range of other media, including performance, film, video, and architecture. His use of video as part of installation works beginning in 1974, without accounting for all of his past and present activity, illustrates some of the ways in which he has explored alternatives to the convention of sculpture as a volumetric object that is not connected with the social environment. As employed by Graham in his installation pieces, video, from the Latin 'to see', serves to convey an image of a reality that is present from one time segment to another or from one place to another.

A piece entitled *Yesterday/Today* (1975), for example, linked the activities of one room of an art gallery such as its office space with its exhibition area. Ongoing routine and daily activities as they occurred in the former were displayed on the monitor placed on view. An audio recording of the sounds and conversations taped in the same room during the same time period, but on the day before, played over the visual imagery. This work, in effect, succeeded in 'documenting what is normally not expressed . . . in front of the artwork,'[40] that is, 'the functional, social and economic realities of the art gallery,'[41] here divided between

35

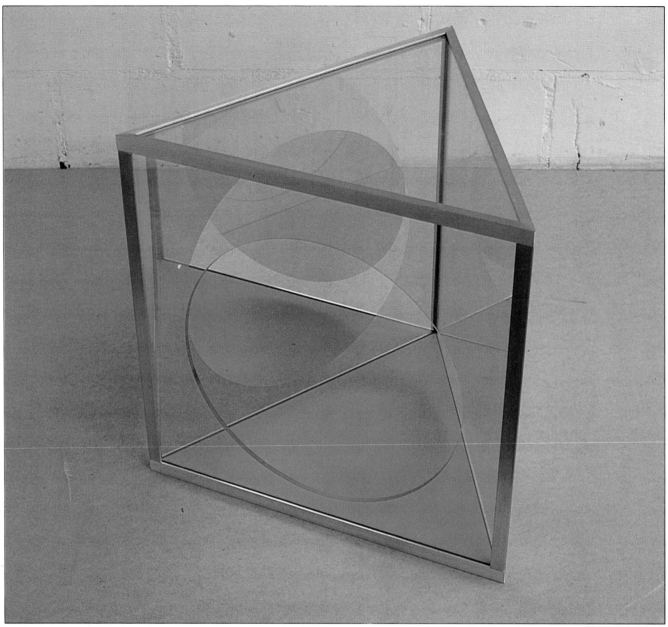

Dan Graham, *Three Linked Cubes*, 1988, two-way mirror and transparent glass

visual and aural modes of representation. These two different modes of delivering information yielded only minor discrepancies in the parallel narratives that unfolded when the work was shown. Other video pieces by Graham, similarly based on video as a conductor of existing information, expose realities behind the facades of office buildings, shopping arcades, urban malls, or suburban homes by making them visible.

For the last ten years, Graham has turned his attention to outdoor 'Pavilion/Sculptures', as he terms these freestanding structures made of transparent, reflective, and mirrored glass. Grafting onto sculpture a reference to specific yet generic architectural forms such as the bus shelter or glass skyscraper, he imparts the potential for their social use. The 'pavilions' are meant to be viewed from within as well as from without. The distinction between interior and exterior points of view is irrelevant insofar as images of spectator and setting, mutually fragmented, merge and are united within the material body of the sculpture. Visually assimilated into their surroundings, Graham's works dispense with the traditional object's outer shell in order to blend with, while reflecting (on), the nature of their physical and social environment.

Whereas Graham's work pertains to sculpture, the work of Daniel Buren has evolved from issues related to painting. For over 20 years, Buren has been working *in situ*, that is, in direct relationship to a given location or situation. Perhaps the first artist to adopt this Latin phrase, now used extensively to describe pieces done on site, Buren associates it with all of his works, whether executed in museums, art galleries, private collections, or outdoor public spaces. Initially desiring to strip painting of any and all illusionistic reference or expressive characteristics so that it might function purely as a sign of itself, Buren arrived at the decision in 1965 to reduce the pictorial content of his work to the repetition of alternating white and coloured vertical bands 8.7cm in width. He realised, moreover, that he did not have to paint them himself, but could purchase canvas used for awnings or outdoor furniture or order mechanically printed material to suit his particular needs.

Commercially obtained, prefabricated material with vertical stripes – intended to be as neutral a (de)sign as possible – serves Buren in an aesthetic practice that frees the work from the framing edge of the canvas and from the allotted exhibition space. Since the end of 1967, Buren has directed his concerns away from the canvas field in order to examine and expose the work of art's affiliation with its external surroundings. The placement of striped material governs the form and meaning of each of Buren's works. Having dispensed with the canvas as an arena for exclusive activity, he explores and visually highlights its contextual frame of reference. 'Right from the start', Buren has asserted, 'I have always tried to show that indeed a thing never exists in itself . . .'[42]

For a group exhibition in Paris in 1970, Buren did not install his work in the provided exhibition space, but instead installed it in the Paris Métro stations. For this work, *140 Stations du Métro Parisien* (installed again in 1973 and open to future installations), Buren glued vertically striped blue-and-white rectangles in the upper right-hand corner of 140 large billboards at each of 140 Métro stations. Typically found at every station platform, the billboards provide a backdrop for passengers entering, exiting, or waiting for the train. The available space at the upper right-hand corner of all of the billboards determined the location and size of the striped, rectangular units, which Buren pasted uniformly throughout the stations.

140 Stations dramatically inverted prior assumptions concerning the definition and province of art. With reference to the signs of expression and style deliberately eliminated from them, the vertically striped rectangles functioned like generic paintings. They took their place among the commercial messages already occupying the billboards where they mediated between the cultural domain of art and the commercial realm of mass-media advertising. Commenting on the shared features of these normally separate systems of display, the blue-and-white striped rectangles pointed to the fact that the Métro billboards – ironically framed like enormous paintings – supplied an alternative and equally viable support for the work. However, although each striped rectangle aligned itself with products of mass-media propaganda, the work as an open-ended whole, encompassing the entire series of Métro station billboards, escaped the consolidated, material form of a commodity. Unlike a solitary, precious object, exhibited in (splendid) isolation, the work had to be seen at multiple spatial and temporal intervals, as a matter of course during daily or routine travel and in conjunction with the surrounding reality.

Works by Buren participate in the given, non-art reality while concurrently commenting on the authority of the museum or gallery whose delegated exhibition spaces they often circumvent. 'Where the empty canvas was once both the authority and the obstacle as a medium for experiment, today the authority of the institution is the only medium available for the artist',[43] according to Buren. *Voile/Toile, Toile/Voile* (Sail/Canvas, Canvas/Sail) (1975-76), a work in two phases, exemplifies how existing reality may give visible shape and form to a work and how the art institution sanctions it. For the first phase of this piece, Buren organised a sailboat race on the Wannsee in Berlin. Nine boats were rigged with sails striped a different colour – white with yellow, blue, red, green, orange, etc. Steered by children, they could be observed from the shore as the wind propelled them through the water. For the second phase some months later, Buren hung the sails like paintings on a wall in the Berlin Akademie der Künste in the sequence of each boat's arrival at the finish line of the race. As the double-entendre of the French title suggests, canvas sails and sails as paintings became one and the same. In this work as in others, Buren fused form and function. He also revealed – and bridged – the gap between an art and non-art context, while connecting the museum with the reality outside its 'hallowed' halls. By thus unveiling the museum's authority in the process of circumventing it, Buren's work dialectically inquires as to whether or not the institution of art can exist separately from society's institutions for it.

During a short but influential career, the late Marcel Broodthaers (1924-1976) produced works of major importance that also were directed toward a consideration of the museum. *Der Adler vom Oligozän bis heute* titles a work that was conceived as a temporary exhibition at the Städtische Kunsthalle Düsseldorf, May 16-July 9, 1972. It belongs to a larger enterprise undertaken by Broodthaers during 1968-72 under the general heading of 'Musée d'Art Moderne, Département des Aigles' (Museum of Modern Art, Department of Eagles). The subheading for the Düsseldorf exhibition is the 'Section des Figures'.[44] Although only a part of his total production, the Düsseldorf 'Section des Figures' indicates the essential nature of Broodthaers' aesthetic investigation.

Hoping 'to provoke critical thought about how art is represented in public',[45] Broodthaers reversed the normal practice of participating in a museum exhibition by actually organising one himself. Rather than simply placing examples of his 'own' work on display in the museum, as is customary, he followed the curatorial procedure of borrowing objects from elsewhere and grouping them to illustrate a particular theme or subject. The subject of his exhibition was the eagle as it has been known or represented from prehistoric times to the present.

For the purpose of presenting what essentially appears to have been an exhaustive survey exhibition, Broodthaers secured the loan of 266 objects from museums and collections in Europe and America. A two-volume catalogue conceived and designed by the artist records the broad range of items bearing the image of the eagle, from its existence as a geological fossil to its rendering as a mythological creature or ideological symbol. Broodthaers included all manner of eagles in the exhibition, from the bird's depiction in the story of Ganymede in a painting by Rubens in the Museo del Prado, Madrid (reproduced in a photograph), to its heraldic function as a coat of arms on a 16th-century tapestry from the Kunsthistorisches Museum, Vienna, to its use as a brand name on a 1910 typewriter from a private collection in Düsseldorf. The exhibited works belonged to all categories of media and included painting, sculpture, drawings, prints, and decorative arts from ancient to modern times, as well as representations of the eagle in non-art contexts – on cigar boxes or wine bottle labels, in the comics, or on national emblems. Ironically, a number, but not all, of these items from contemporary popular or commercial culture belonged to the artist's own 'Sammlung Département des Aigles' (Collection of the Department of Eagles), not to an officially established public or private collection. The image of the eagle unified the vast array of material hung on the walls of the museum or placed in glass vitrines. In treating objects of all kinds as if they had the same aesthetic, historical, or functional importance, Broodthaers did not submit them to any discernible system of hierarchical ordering.[46] He catalogued each one in the standard manner, but organised the checklist alphabetically – from Basel to Zurich – according to the city from which each piece was borrowed.

Most significantly, all exhibited items in Broodthaers' exhibition received an accompanying plastic label with the catalogue number above and a qualifying statement below that alleged in French, German, or English, 'Ceci n'est pas un object d'art' / 'Dies ist kein Kunstwerk' / 'This is not a work of art'. With this unrelenting and ubiquitous statement – based on René Magritte's famous painting *La Trahison des Images* (The Treason of Images) (1929), that represents the image of a pipe and the painted words 'Ceci n'est pas une Pipe' (This is not a Pipe) – he paradoxically opened to question the viewing of the assembled objects as a whole. If objects long acknowledged to be art were not, then what were they doing in a museum, whether in Broodthaers' fictional museum or in those that owned them? One had to wonder if, and deny that, the artist in fact possessed the power to determine whether these were or were not works of art and whether language alone could support such an edict. In 1917 Marcel Duchamp had raised a common, non-art urinal to the status of sculpture by entering it into an art exhibition as an object of his authorial choice. Broodthaers, explicitly indebted to Duchamp[47] but using exactly the opposite tactics, demonstrated by means of his exhibition that what sustained Duchamp's original move was the authority of the museum or exhibition context, not simply the artist's own prerogative.

Der Adler vom Oligozän bis heute, in the form of an exhibition instead of an object in an exhibition, exemplified, while commenting on, the authority of the museum. It demonstrated the way in which the museum is able to accord a deceptive wholeness to works, and actual fragments, from other periods and cultures that perforce have been taken from their original historical and physical settings. By amassing a cross-section of objects unrelated to each other except through the image of the eagle, Broodthaers succeeded in relocating and reclassifying works already relocated and reclassified within the respective museums or collections that owned them. He thus subordinated a broad range of objects to a further process of decontextualisation and reassembly so as to re-view the process itself. Mixing works from art and non-art contexts, moreover, he crossed the line automatically dividing the two, permitting both within the confines of his museum display. Since the myriad examples of eagles, in the end, did not actually yield a single, universal statement about this bird, but only specific manifestations of it in many different contexts, they posited the way in which the museum is able nonetheless to subsume its contents into a seemingly unified ensemble.

By means of his explicitly fictional museum, Broodthaers examined the unspoken fictions surrounding art that empower the museum to sanctify its contents. Just as he subjected the eagle – who 'is even scared of a bicycle'[48] – to scrutiny, bringing him down from his lofty heights and emblematic position of power through a process of levelling, Broodthaers pointed to the mythic proportions that art can assume when divorced from the original conditions of its creation. Representing an amalgamation of objects in the possession of others, the 'Section des Figures' defied its own relocation and commodification since it could not be disassociated from the institutional support it simultaneously acknowledged and subverted.

Broodthaers called the museum into question insofar as such institutions bestow autonomous value on artworks, emphasising qualities such as uniqueness, antiquity, originality, or authenticity, but obscure the socio-economic realities that account for their 'worth' in the contemporary culture. Attentive to the potential of art's fossilisation – like that of the fossil eagle exhibited – and the threat of its 'failing social relevance',[49] Broodthaers pitted the fictions of his museum against the mythical stance of art, as distinct from artefact, in isolation from its social framework. He thereby sought to reinvest art with power in place of unfounded mystique so that it might survive in a social system dominated by commercial goals. But, without illusion as to his success in light of contemporary reality, he

reminded the reader that the eagle, whose wings he has clipped in the work, nonetheless still 'remains unhurt in advertising'.[50]

During the last two decades, Michael Asher has sought to develop methods of redefining the established relationship between an object of art and its context. To this end he has, since 1969, created works that are contingent on existing reality and the conditions of their presentation. A relatively recent work, for the 74th American Exhibition at The Art Institute of Chicago in 1982, expressed the vital function of the museum as an institution for exhibiting art. For this work – initially proposed for the institute's permanent collection – he engaged two groups of viewers to stand at a designated time (one-half hour each day for practical purposes only) in front of two different paintings in the permanent collection galleries: specifically, *Nude in a Bathtub* (1910) by Marcel Duchamp and *Portrait of Kahnweiler* (1910) by Pablo Picasso. Asher selected these two particular paintings because of the disparate degree to which they had been reproduced in books, on posters, or on postcards, etc – the Duchamp hardly at all and the Picasso extensively – and disseminated in the public domain as secondhand images. He explained the rationale behind his choice of works on printed handouts that also referred visitors to the location of each piece. On the verso of the handouts he listed 50 books in which the Picasso has been illustrated and nine in which the Duchamp could be found.

Asher took cognisance of the fact that the same institutions that provide original works of art are also those that make available photographs and reproductions. His 'model' viewers, installed at normal viewing distance in front of two paintings in the same room and paradigmatic of museum visitors, demonstrated the point at which the museum's primary role to present, and the visitors' to perceive, intersect. Seeking to dismantle the barriers to direct perception engendered by reproduction, with its capacity to substitute for, and dull, the experience of the original, Asher's work reproduced as a concrete actuality the process of viewing that takes place in a museum. Rather than being a work, however, that is physically and conceptually independent of its institutional context – yet nonetheless dependent on it for its display – it could not be disengaged from the existing situation it sought to consider critically. Having abandoned the convention of sculpture in the round, the work revolved around the viewing process by materially and thematically embodying it. With coterminous reference to both art and reality, the Chicago piece serves as a quintessential example of the desire to destroy illusion – including that of the work itself – through the removal of obstacles hindering perception.

Referring simultaneously to their own material formation and to physical or social reality as firsthand experience, works by the artists considered in this essay integrate the object of art with external actuality. With the intention of dispelling illusion, these artists have called into question the Modernist interpretation of art as an entity unto itself that timelessly transcends the conditions of its existence. Through their endeavour to eliminate the autonomy of material and form by the use of photography or language or through their investigations into the role of context, they have succeeded in transforming previous concepts of art.

Notes

1 The artists whose work is linked with these movements had begun their careers by the second half of the 1950s or early 1960s.

2 Barbara Rose, 'Remembering 1967', in Janet Kardon, ed, *1967: At the Crossroads*, Institute of Contemporary Art, University of Pennsylvania, 1987, p34.

3 For discussions of Modernism in relation to Post-Modernism, see Brian Wallis, ed, *Art After Modernism: Rethinking Representation*, The New Museum of Contemporary Art, New York, 1984. See also Hal Foster, ed, *The*

Anti-Aesthetic: Essays of Post-Modern Culture, Bay Press, Port Townsend, Washington, 1983.

4 Donald B Kuspit, *Clement Greenberg, Art Critic*, The University of Wisconsin Press, Madison, 1979, p19.

5 Clement Greenberg, 'Modernist Painting', in Gregory Battock, ed, *The New Art: A Critical Anthology*, E P Dutton & Co, New York, 1966, p101.

6 Clement Greenberg, 'Avant-Garde and Kitsch', in *Art and Culture*, Beacon Press, pp5-6.

7 Greenberg, 'Modernist Painting', p102, *ibid* note 5.
8 Greenberg, 'The New Sculpture', in *Art and Culture*, p139, *ibid* note 6.
9 Kuspit, *ibid* note 4, p41.
10 Greenberg, *ibid* note 6, pp5-6.
11 Greenberg, *ibid* note 5, passim.
12 *ibid*, p104.
13 Greenberg, *ibid* note 8, p145.
14 Kuspit, *ibid* note 4, pp114-116.
15 Frank Stella, quoted in Bruce Glaser, 'Questions to Stella and Judd', in Gregory Battcock, ed, *Minimal Art, A Critical Anthology*, E P Dutton & Co, New York, 1968, pp157-58.
16 Greenberg, *ibid* note 8, p139: 'The arts are to achieve concreteness, "purity", by acting solely in terms of their separate and irreducible selves.'
17 Robert Morris, 'Notes on Sculpture, Part IV: Beyond Objects', *Artforum*, April, 1969, p54.
18 Roy Lichtenstein, quoted in G R Swenson, 'What is Pop Art?', in John Coplands, ed, *Roy Lichtenstein*, Praeger Publishers, New York, 1972, p55.
19 For a more specific account of Pop art in relation to Modernism, see Carol Anne Mahsun, *Pop Art and the Critics*, UMI Research Press, Ann Arbor, 1987, pp23-40.
20 For a year by year account, see Lucy Lippard, *Six Years: The Dematerialisation of the art object from 1966 to 1972*, Praeger Publishers, New York, 1973.
21 Joseph Kosuth, 'Art After Philosophy', in Gerd de Vries, ed, *On Art: Artists' Writings on the changed notion of art after 1965*, M Dumont Schaubert, Cologne, p158.
22 *ibid*, p150.
23 *ibid*, p156.
24 John Baldessari, in *John Baldessari*, Municipal van Abbemuseum, Eindhoven and Museum Folkwang, Essen, 1981, p6.
25 Bernd and Hilla Becher, interview with Lynda Morris, in *Bernd & Hilla Becher*, The Arts Council of Great Britain, London, 1974, unpag.
26 Bernd and Hilla Becher, 'Anonyme Skulpturen', *Kunst-Zeitung Nr 2*, Jan 1969, trans Richard Bairstow.
27 For an important consideration of relationships between photography and art, see Abigail Solomon-Godeau, 'Photography After Art Photography', in Wallis (note 3), pp75-85.
28 Brenda Richardson, *Bruce Nauman: Neons* (The Baltimore museum of Art, Baltimore, 1982-83, p20.
29 Michel Foucault, 'What is an Author', in Josué V Harari, ed, *Textual Strategies: Perspectives in Post-Structuralist Criticism*, Cornell University Press, Ithaca, NY, 1979, p141.
30 Roland Barthes, 'The Death of the Author, in *Image-Music-Text*, Hill and Wang, New York, 1977, p143. For a discussion of the relevance of Foucault's and Barthes' definitions of authorship to recent art, see Craig Owens, 'From Work to Frame, or, Is There Life after "Death of the Author"?', in *Implosion: a Post-Modern Perspective*, Moderna Museet, Stockholm, 1988, pp207-213.
31 Victor Burgin, in catalogue entry on *Room* (1970), in *The Tate Gallery 1972-74: Biennial Report and Illustrated Catalogue of Acquisitions*, Tate Gallery, London, 1975, p96. Originally quoted in Victor Burgin, 'Situational Aesthetics', *Studio International,* Oct 1969, pp118-121.
32 Burgin, *The Tate Gallery*, ibid, p94.
33 Victor Burgin, 'Art, Common Sense and Photography', *Camerawork* 3, July 1976, p2.
34 Victor Burgin, *The End of Art Theory*, Humanities Press International, Inc, Atlantic Highlands, NJ, 1986, p16.
35 Burgin, *ibid* note 33, p1.
36 Barthes, *ibid* note 30, p42.
37 Burgin, *Work and Commentary*, Latimer New Dimensions Ltd, London, 1973, unpag.
38 For a specific discussion of this aspect of Haacke's work, see Howard S Becker and John Walton, 'Social Science and the Work of Hans Haacke, *Framing and Being Framed: 7 Works 1970-75*, The Press of the Nova Scotia College of Art and Design, Halifax and New York University Press, NY, 1975, pp145-53.
39 See Brian Wallis, ed, 'Catalogue of Works: 1969-86', in *Hans Haacke: Unfinished Business*, The New Museum of Contemporary Art, NY and MIT Press, Cambridge, Mass, for complete, descriptive information on this and the following works discussed.
40 Dan Graham, 'Present continuous past(s), (1974)', in Benjamin HD Buchloh, ed, *Dan Graham, Video-Architecture-Television Writings on Video and Video Works 1970-78*, The Press of the Nova Scotia College of Art and Design and New York University Press, 1979, p46.
41 *ibid*, p45.
42 Daniel Buren, 'On the Autonomy of the Work of Art', in *Daniel Buren: around "Ponctuations"*, Nouveau Musée, Lyon, 1980, unpag.
43 Buren,'On the Institutions of the Art System', *ibid* note 42.
44 For a more detailed discussion of this work, see Rainer Borgemeister, '*Section des Figures*: The Eagle from the Oligocene to the Present', *October* 42, 1987, pp135-44.
45 Marcel Broodthaers, 'Section des Figures', in *Der Adler vom Oligozän bis heute*, Städtische Kunstalle, 1972, vol 2, p18. Translated from the German for the author by Angela Greiner.
46 Borgemeister, *ibid* note 44, p139.
47 See Broodthaers, 'Methode', in *Der Adler vom Oligozän bis heute*, *ibid* note 45, vol 1, p13. For a discussion of Duchamp's work in relation to institutional and cultural contexts, and as background for Broodthaers, see Benjamin H D Buchloh, 'The Museum Fictions of Marcel Broodthaers', in AA Bronson and Peggy Gale, eds, *Museums by Artists*, Art Metropole, Toronto, 1983, pp45-56.
48 Broodthaers, 'Sections des Figures', in *Der Adler vom Oligozän bis heute, ibid* note 45, p18.
49 *ibid*.
50 *ibid*, p19.

Victor Burgin, *Today is the tomorrow you were promised yesterday*, 1976, gelatin silver print on aluminium

Joseph Kosuth, *Zero & Not* (*New York*), 1986, offset printing on paper

II

TOWARDS A DEFINITION OF NEW ART

Jenny Holzer, *Selections from Truisms*, 1988-89, electronic billboard, Piccadilly Circus, London, sponsored by Artangel Trust

ROBERT ROSENBLUM

TOWARDS A DEFINITION OF NEW ART

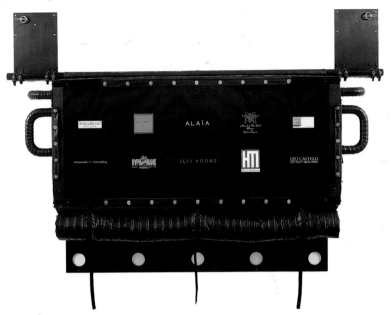

Ashley Bickerton, *Commercial Piece # 1*, 1989, anodised aluminium, wood, leather, acrylic paint, rubber, 117.8x257.1x40.6cm

In the following sequence of Art & Design *interviews, interspersed with critial papers from the Tate Gallery Symposia, organised by Academy Forum, New York critic and art historian Robert Rosenblum consolidates his thoughts on current trends, definitions and phenomena in the international art world of the 80s and 90s, above all asserting the continuing relevance of history to the creation of new art.*

New Art and Popular Culture

– How would you describe the audience for contemporary art?
I can't imagine when there was ever as much popular interest in art as there is now. It used to be the case – and I'm thinking back to the situation in New York in the heyday of Abstract Expressionism – that art, especially contemporary art, was perceived by an audience that you could count on the fingers of both hands. Today there is a huge audience out there just waiting to pounce on the next new artist, not to mention to go again and again to see retrospectives of middle-aged artists, or venerable artists. Just in statistical terms, in New York in particular, the sheer quantity of people out there who are involved with art, who rush around from one gallery to another, and who will go to every museum exhibition on the books, is absolutely staggering.

I think the main effect of it hasn't anything to do with purifying people's lives, saving their souls or anything of that sort. Probably the main effect is to fill in time because there's much more leisure time now for 'cultural activities' which are meant to be good for you and high-minded. The effect is also to make money because the whole international art market scene now is pretty spectacular in terms of a network of finances. The number of people who buy and sell and exchange things all over the world must infinitely surpass anything that's ever existed in the history of art as commerce.

I think it's a good thing. Although it was very nice to say that

Van Gogh or Picasso, Kline or Pollock, were starving to death at a certain point in their lives, I don't see why this is good. I don't see any reason why artists shouldn't make money the way other people do. The whole myth of the artist being pure and poverty-stricken and not having the goods and comfort of ordinary people is ridiculous. There've been a lot of rich artists throughout history who were just as great as the poor ones. If artists realise that art is a commodity and that they can make money out of it, I don't see any reason why this is bad or why it should in some way pollute their art. Artists ideally have patrons, and they always did. It was the 19th and early 20th centuries that tended to upset that balance. Now things have caught up. Artists always used to complain that they were alienated, but they aren't any more. We should all be happy that art is thriving and selling, at least on my side of the Atlantic.
– Would you say it was symptomatic of a trend towards a more predominantly visual culture as opposed to a literary culture?
One of the reasons art is so successful in the late 20th century is, among other things, TV. The fact is that most people have stopped reading, or being involved with any high-minded cultural activity that takes too long a time. People's attention span in the late 20th century is very, very short. Most people can't wait for the commercial to come on because the news itself is too lengthy. Art seems to be perfectly attuned to the minimal attention span

Gilbert & George, *One World*, 1988, mixed media, 227.3x254cm

Barbara Kruger, *Untitled* (The Marriage of Murder and Suicide), 1988, photographic silkscreen/vinyl, 205.7x259.1cm

for culture. If you listen to music or read a book, it takes imposed minutes, or hours, or days, whereas you can look at a work of art at your own tempo. The number of seconds that people devote to each work of art is probably pitiful, but then there's so much art to see. But I think it is an activity that can be reduced to practically nothing more than blinking, and people register things very quickly. It's a kind of instant gratification that suits the unbelievably rapid tempo of information we receive in the late 20th century. Now I think that's really one of the reasons it's been such a huge success.

– *Do you think this has an effect on the kind of art people produce? Are they tending to produce works that will have more of an initial sensory impact that doesn't stand up to continual re-examination and exploration of detail?*

I think that a lot of art is geared to making a big show in a fast way. Most artists have to deal with the attention span of gallery-goers or museum-goers and they have to make them look fast. They have to shout their identity and be recognised. It's certainly clear in Gilbert and George. The identity thing is an important issue. I think that obviously the big bang image reigns today, but

I don't think that it necessarily dominates many artists who are now, in a kind of 'neo' way, going back to old-fashioned oil paint techniques and looking like Tintoretto, El Greco, Rubens, etc.

– *Would you say that the expansion of visual culture and the widening of the audience has produced an inquisitive attitude towards the past?*

Oh yes. The thirst for information and new things to see appears to be unquenchable. The sheer expansion of knowledge about 19th- and 20th-century art, not to mention pre-19th-century art, in the last 10 to 20 years has been mind-boggling. Now there's a whole new repertory of lesser artists, and this has been happening all over. It has to do with museums, and it has to do with dealers who have to sell new things, and it has to do with a kind of sating of a large part of the informed art audience with familiar things, and the need to see unfamiliar things, to dig them up, excavate them, dust them off and start from scratch. Otherwise people would get bored. The sheer quantity of things from the past to look at these days surpasses anything that we've known in the mid or early 20th century and I don't know when it will stop. I mean the data banks are flooded, and it keeps coming.

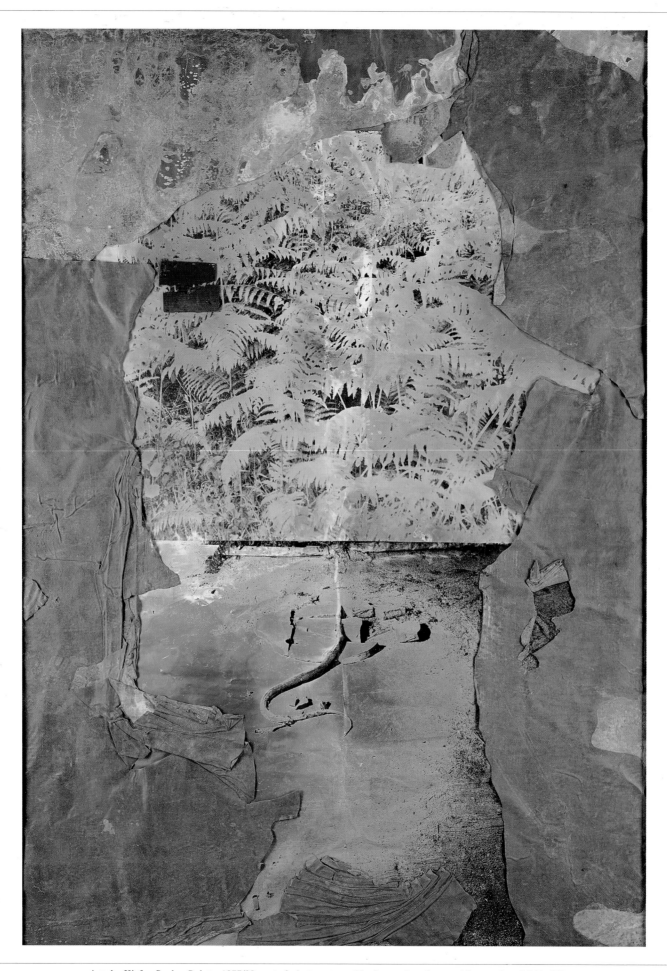

Anselm Kiefer, *Broken Palette*, 1977/88, part of a battery, treated lead over photo in a steel frame, glazed, 240x170cm

Richard Long, *Mountain Lake Powder Snow*, 1985

Romanticism and Retrospection

– Do you think that the tradition you discerned in your book The Northern Romantic Tradition *is important to painting at the moment in any way?*
There is no more impossible word than Romanticism and though I use it as does everybody else, very casually and carelessly, I would be very hard put to define it. It is of course infinitely contractible and expandable. In terms of the general patterns that I try to trace in *The Northern Romantic Tradition*, were I to write a supplementary chapter to it – I stopped with Rothko and Abstract Expressionism – I would probably include earthworks of the late 60s and 70s. Those seem in some way to be the last gasp of that tradition of trying to find some sort of connection with the Great Beyond or the Void. My own sense of what might be called Romantic today, insofar as it resembles in an obvious way historical Romanticism, is really part of the whole constellation of 'neo' movements, so that what one thinks of as Neo-Classicism, whether by Finlay or Mariani, is to be thought of in the same category as works by Christopher Le Brun which look to me like neo-Gustave Moreau or neo-Symbolist painting. The Romanticism of the present is really Romanticism in terms of historical retrospection and reflects the whole condition of neo-ism, revivalism and retrospection that we have in the 1980s. The big historical break in continuity took place in the 1960s and anything younger today is likely to be self-consciously retrospective rather than part of the same tradition.

The revival of Gothic architecture in the 1980s, or even Gothic furniture, could nominally be categorised as Romantic insofar as the Middle Ages is regarded as a token of Romantic revival, but it really is better seen in the same spirit as the revival of Mondrian or even Barnett Newman. It's a question of the incredible environment we have of history and art history in the 1980s.
– Some people have a very fixed idea of what Romanticism is. Do you think it is something existing outside the mainstream of art?
I assume that there are always artists of a provincial or insular kind who, remote from the more sophisticated centres, will go on, for example, doing watercolours of landscapes and injecting into them some kind of traditional sentimentality. I guess these can be considered as vestigial Romantic explorations of a long and great tradition. There are also, on the same wave length, in the States for example, younger painters who are not continuing so much as reviving the Romantic landscape, such as Diane Burko, Joan Nelson and April Gornik who resurrect landscape traditions of sublime mountain heights *à la* Friedrich or Hodler, or even the tradition of painting vast gloomy expanses, foggy skies and infinite horizons. But they again do it quite self-consciously as a revival style just in the way that Mariani or Finlay would revive the look of Neo-Classicism of the late 18th and early 19th centuries. I think that is really the deeper affinity between their works. The Romantic and Classical artists that we

have today are really all manifestations of the same retrospection; for example, Philip Johnson can do a building in a Gothic mode as well as in a Classical mode now. That very eclecticism is again part of the historicism of the early 19th century. It's a kind of double revival, a Chinese Box situation, of a revival of styles now being a revival of the kind of eclecticism that characterised so much Romantic painting and architecture. It seems to me that all these artists of the 1980s are in a way fleeing the present by living in history, but this has been done so many times before that it has to be done now with a lighter touch. Nobody believes that these are going to be therapeutic changes and therefore it's all done, as it were, in quotation marks.

I honestly think that most high-minded ideals about art and morality, art and society, art and Utopia have been almost completely dashed. A stake has been driven through the heart of all optimistic beliefs in art as a goal for purification and change. That's certainly my impression from the younger generations in New York. There may be some last-gasp geniuses like James Turrell who still is, with Caspar David Friedrich's monk by the sea, all alone looking at the universe and the night sky, and he's great. But in general, a younger 1980s generation is living very much here and now in the world of art as commerce, communication and computer systems. I think there are precious few artists of any real interest today who claim for art some kind of spiritual and moral force in the modern world.

The whole Romantic tradition of ruins and having melancholy thoughts about ruins, has had a new lease of life in the 1970s and 80s with people like the Poiriers, or, in the States, Charles Simmonds-type archaeological fantasies. But they again don't have the grand historical wallop that they had when they were originally invented and experienced at the end of the 18th century when they had to deal with the great cycles of civilisation. I mean it really is done more as a kind of quotation or with a kind of chic irony about an earlier way of feeling and seeing. So no matter what you do it seems to be separated by a vast historical gulf. It's art as an imitation of past historical revisions, past imagery, past emotions; it never seems first-hand.

There's been such an enormous dissemination of art history today that everything has become interchangeable. David Salle, for example, can throw in quotes from Watteau, Géricault, Reginald Marsh, Kuniyoshi or Riopelle, it doesn't seem to make any difference. It's just a question of juggling images and devaluing them all. I don't in any way mean to suggest therefore that artists who do this are less good than artists who don't, but rather that this is the condition we all live in, as you can tell by looking at any museum shop anywhere in the world.

An artist I would think of as still working within an older unbroken tradition of Romanticism is Richard Long, who really doesn't have the irony of the 1980s, but he's been doing this for a long time. If I had to have a candidate for somebody who perpetuated the imagery, the feelings, the emotions of someone like Constable or Wordsworth, I'd vote for him. He is somebody who continues those endless magical communions with nature by walking, touching, feeling and accumulating. I find this very direct in terms of his experience and really very moving as a kind of endangered species. It still works with him but I think he is the last of his race.

There's also a German artist, Wolfgang Laib, who spends a lot of time in the woods gathering such things as pollen and forming minimal geometric patterns out of gossamer and natural materials such as honey or pollen of various kinds. It is some kind of ecological last gasp of communion with the pure and beautiful stuff of nature. I guess this attitude is expiring even though it may, as in the case of Richard Long, still produce some marvellous artists.

– *Do you think that landscape or nature is a source for imagery distinct from that of the past?*

As I suggested earlier, Diane Burko, Joan Nelson and April Gornik are in fact in the tradition of sublime landscape painting, but they still seem to produce it in an ironic, knowing way as if they were not continuing this tradition in an intuitive manner but somehow wilfully resurrecting it in the way, say, Philip Johnson might resurrect a Gothic cathedral.

I think that Kiefer might certainly have some claim to being a living survivor of the endangered species of German Romantic painting as he sometimes seems to echo in the direction of Friedrich. But then I also feel too that this is a kind of Post-Modern situation, since he's so filled with historical retrospection, not only in terms of German history but of German painting, especially Friedrich, or German Neo-Classical architecture. He also belongs to the category of historical quotation from the other side of the gulf, and I have to confess that I have been susceptible to his epic sweep. There is a feel in Kiefer that, for want of a better word, I would call Romantic. He's somebody who has the grandeur of Victor Hugo, somebody who has a giant retrospection upon a nation's past, immediate and remote. This is done in a heartfelt, thrilling way. I would think seriously about Kiefer as a candidate for continuing – I'm not quite sure whether it's the real thing or a post-neo-thing – a grand panoramic tradition of German culture and art.

The word Romanticism is so slippery in semantic terms that the meaning of it could be stretched to include a wide range of artistic activity these days which involves a sort of personal introspection rather than historical retrospection. This has usually again been thought of as one of the products of the Romantic movement, the ability of artists to present psycho-biography in their work. Artists like this, especially Jasper Johns in recent years, paint pictures that are practically intimate journal entries. This is relatively new in terms of 20th-century art and it may be some curious permutation of a Romantic progeny. Many of the works of Clemente, in terms of their exploration of his own sexuality, fantasies, dreams and nightmares belong in that way to this tradition and probably not so much in a self-conscious historical quoting way but in terms of an ordinary human need to explore private feelings. One could think about that as a more recent manifestation of Romantic attitudes. But those may just be human constants, the need for personal revelation.

Johns' paintings about the cycle of the four seasons are heartbreakingly intimate and tragic comments on the passing of time, nature and personal biography. As such, they really seem to extend the great traditions of Western art, in particular of Romantic identity with nature. But he's an artist of an earlier generation and probably can still work within that mode. He was doing that kind of personal diary-entry art already in the 1950s. It's just a more complicated version now. They seem to be projections of his own life viewed against the passing seasons and that's a traditional theme, God knows, in Western art. The pictures not only have that universal aspect of going from spring to winter but also all kinds of cryptic as well as decipherable references to his own art, biography, and past. They're very meditative, like the works of some great poet who is contemplating his life, his career and his future against the aspect of eternity. They are directly moving in the grand old tradition rather than being infused with a kind of detachment or cynicism that seems to characterise most younger artists who have emerged in the last ten years or so.

– *It's interesting that in those paintings he uses a lot of imagery and obviously structures the paintings with a traditional theme when he has been celebrated for his desire not to use imagery. Do you think that is part of the spirit of the times, this move towards using imagery and a structural device like the seasons?*

I think he's always liked some kind of system to cling to, some sort of impersonal pattern, whether it be alphabets, or numbers or the structure of the American flag, the Stars and Stripes, or the map of the States. In this particular case he likes the imposed order – it's like a poet deciding to use sonnet or sestina form. He's imposed the pattern of the four seasons upon himself and adapted his personal intimate biography as well as his professional artistic public biography upon that scheme.

– *Do you feel that there's anyone else dealing with those kinds of themes at the moment?*

Not on that level. As I mentioned, artists like Clemente certainly explore issues, like love and death in personal terms but they do it in a far more lightweight, capricious way than Johns. He is a master and the recent work is in some ways a summation of three decades of his art, so it has all kinds of experience and mastery behind it. On the other hand, it's interesting to compare it to the kind of retrospection and work of another artist of Johns' generation, Roy Lichtenstein, who in the 1980s has also done any number of inventories of his past achievements. But he's always doing it in a kind of tongue-in-cheek way. Although one might think about these as a kind of personal and public retrospection, it has – and that's one of the points about Lichtenstein – none of the potent emotions that are so apparent in Johns' work.

– *Blake, both in his paintings and poetry, had a visionary side to his imagination and believed that there is a particular way of seeing things that is uplifting and contrary to the way that life is led. Do you think that particular attitude is something that people don't hold or can't have in art at the moment?*

That seems very ingenuous to me these days. I have the feeling that the last really important artists who felt things like that were the Abstract Expressionists, and then extending that, I would think that some of the people like Robert Smithson, Michael Heizer, Walter de Maria, and above all James Turrell, whom I admire endlessly, belong to this category of lonely visionaries. But in the big cities where most of the art is made and seen and sold it's a pretty rare attitude. William Blake was doing it in London. I don't know if anybody's doing it in London today, but certainly not in New York.

In a way Andy Warhol summed it up when he reported on the earthquake in the south of Italy, near Naples, that killed presumably about 10,000 people. A great Romantic painter would have perhaps painted a huge disaster picture with memories of the eruption of Vesuvius in 79 AD. Andy Warhol just replicated the front page of the Italian newspaper that reported on it and I can't think of a better way to extinguish that Romantic catastrophe tradition. So Andy Warhol as usual marks a profound change between BC and AD in the history of later 20th-century art. He won't take it personally; he sees it always in terms of the mass distribution of what used to be a private response. He was the first artist of major significance to sense the realities of reproduction, of commercialisation of art, of commodity, of distribution of information in the 1960s and 70s. I think he pinpointed the total change in our times and that's an amazing achievement.

It's rather like what Manet did when he painted the execution of Maximilian or when he painted the escape of Henri Rochefort from a penal colony in the South Seas: there's no overt drama, as Goya or Géricault would have done it, it's just a kind of newsflash. That was one way of killing Romantic vestiges in terms of the modern urban situation in Paris and I think Warhol did the same thing in the 60s and 70s.

– *Is that something you admire?*

It's not a question of admiring, it's a question of telling the truth. I think that, one, it's the way things are more and more, and it's the way they've certainly become in the last 30 years; and, two, I happen to think that Warhol is a great artist for, among other reasons, the fact that he took on this cultural phenomenon and

turned it into art. If I think that the human situation involved is lamentable, it is nevertheless a fact and I can't blame Warhol for bringing the news to everybody; he is just reflecting it so it's not about good or bad. Anyway I'm enough of an old-fashioned aesthete to think that we're after all talking about art and not culture. Art has its own hierarchy of good and bad and we don't judge works of art on the basis of what the human messages are, otherwise we'd have a very strange selection. So the bottom line is still in the way it looks.

– *Some people claim that Britain is the home of a sort of intrinsic Romantic tradition associated with landscape and nature. Is that valid?*

It may well be because one of the things that is always fascinating about Britain to an outsider is that it does seem more insular (literally and figuratively) than other countries, and doesn't seem usually to be clocked by the same time machines as the rest of the Western world. It may well be that if there are pockets of continuing Romanticism in the West, Britain's probably the best place to find them. I guess there's been more of a geographical and cultural shedding-off of the 20th century in Britain than there has been in most other industrialised countries. It's just out of sync. If you're clocking it by international Western time, then I guess it is anachronistic, like the monarchy and attitudes towards the House of Windsor. But if you live here and that's the major way of telling time and seeing things, then the rest of the world may seem out of joint.

– *Another aspect of the interest in Romanticism is the revival of interest in Neo-Romanticism in Britain. Do you think that's anything more than an academic or historical interest?*

Perhaps in terms of the dynamics of British art and culture there's some significant trend here, but, looking at it more internationally, there has been such an incredible archaeological unearthing of various suppressed moments of 20th-, not to mention 19th-century art, that it may be nothing more than a symptom of this voracious desire to uncover all of our historical past. In the United States, for example, there have been all kinds of younger art historians working on American artists of the 1940s in particular, those who were passed by because of the stampede of Abstract Expressionism. But the same is true of the 1930s and 20s, you name it. It belongs to this ongoing encyclopaedic eagerness to uncover it all. So my more cynical view would be to suggest that very often these revivals of the past are not so much a response to a particular fascination or affinity with the art but simply a part of the ongoing obsessive historicism to disclose more and more of what the Modern Movement had hidden; the same thing is happening with the 19th century galore.

– *So people aren't looking at those works because they particularly like Romantic art of that description?*

One likes it, but one always should remember that history is part of aesthetics too, that is one very often enjoys looking at works of art because they emanate nostalgia for a particular period. When we look at Art Deco, for example, part of the reason that we enjoy looking at it is that we like the feel of the 1920s and 30s, just as the 1950s and 60s now have terrific charges. So, any work of art that has a period flavour seems to be a time-capsule of magic moments in the past. There's a whole concept of history as aesthetics, of works of art that radiate the flavour of a particular decade or period and produce that association in themselves. The interest in Neo-Romanticism in Britain may in good part be a kind of nostalgia for the 30s and 40s. But one feels nostalgia for everything in the 20th century it seems to me. I can't wait for the 70s revival; the 60s are there already.

– *Are there any younger artists, particularly in Britain, that you would see as drawing on Romanticism in any way?*

In a strange way I find David Mach rather fascinating as an artist who will upset conventions. He's a model demonstration of

Jasper Johns, *The Seasons*, *Above L to R*: *Spring*, 1986; *Summer*, 1985; *Below L to R*: *Fall*, 1986; *Winter*, 1986, all encaustic on canvas, 190.5x127cm

Romantic chaos. One of the things that's so exciting about his work is that he breaks all barriers literally and figuratively and things just come bursting through the walls and the windows. It's the equivalent of being confronted, if you were a Romantic voyager or painter, with the Niagara Falls. A lot of the images do have the overtone of the end of the world, some sort of debris that is left after the apocalypse. On the other hand, very characteristic of the 80s, their success depends upon the fact that they are done with a certain amount of detachment and irony. I love *The Hundred and One Dalmatians*. It's just that introduction of a Walt Disney myth into what could also look like the aftermath of bombing and the confusion of those two things which give it a very contemporary flavour, so that you aren't allowed to take it as seriously as would have been the case had it been a Romantic artist painting the aftermath of the destruction of Pompeii and Herculaeneum. So he is somebody who might be thought of in the crazy category of Romantic disaster images that have been tailored to 1980s cynicism.

– Do you think that Romanticism is a defunct term as it's traditionally understood?

I really think it's an impossible term to use. It's hard enough to apply it to the later 18th and early 19th centuries, the time when it was historically relevant. I talk about it all the time and realise I don't know what I mean, except that I feel I know what I mean, but can't articulate it. But if you expand it into the present you're on even thinner ice, as I guess the fact that we've been talking about every artist from the last 20 years indicates.

– Do you think any of the traditional American myths about the landscape – the country as an ideal – as in the work of Andrew Wyeth, are alive today?

I think it's only there in terms of grass-roots popular imagery or fantasy. Andrew Wyeth is an artist who probably could be thought of as extending all kinds of Romantic, especially American Romantic premises. But the fact of the matter is that he seems, to sophisticated eyes at least, to be more of a commercial product, in the old-fashioned sense – not a commercial product like Haim Steinbach and Jeff Koons – than a high serious artist. Which isn't good or bad, but it's just that he's selling old-fashioned Romantic American myths the way, say, a movie-maker might. They have a kind of soap-opera mentality with predictable formulas and they work for vast audiences. They seem to preach loneliness, closeness to nature, hard work, the prairie, the wilderness and so on. Those are ancient Romantic myths that still have popular currency, but they certainly don't seem to have much genuine currency in the work of younger inventive artists.

– Do you feel things have changed to such an extent that if you use more traditional terms such as Romanticism and Classicism it's not really an effective way of describing what's going on?

I agree that they're not really adequate but I don't have any new words to substitute. I think Romanticism or Neo-Classicism are alive and well today only insofar as they are part of the wide vocabulary of historical styles that have been replicated with variations by younger artists, but I don't think they are living extensions of the original movements any more than the Houses of Parliament are living extensions of Gothic secular architecture.

– Do you think that the sense of the sublime that Rothko and Barnett Newman celebrated no longer inspires people?

I really think that those days are over. I don't think that's for better or for worse; it's an historical fact, just as the way people thought that art could change people's politics. I don't think there are very many people who believe that any more. We're living in a much more cynical, realistic time.

Enzo Cucchi, *We must remove great paintings from the landscape*, 1983, mixed media

Mike Bidlo, *Les Demoiselles d'Avignon*, 1984, oil, 243.8x233.6cm

Post-Modernism

I'm not very good at defining '-isms'. I always remember a student asking me to define Romanticism: that proved impossible, and Neo-Classicism was not so easy either, so I will make no effort to say what Post-Modernism is. But I want to begin with a brief anecdote to indicate that it obviously reverberates and has ordinary colloquial meaning. The last time I was in London my wife and I went to see *Follies*. After the first act, my wife, who does not read Baudrillard or Derrida, said 'this is so Post-Modernist.' Throughout the first act I was thinking that I had to give this lecture today, and was also amazed at how Post-Modernist I thought *Follies* was. It is extraordinary that just through ordinary conversation we had converged with this word which obviously represents something new.

Thinking back over other recent events, I was walking down 5th Avenue and there at Steuben Glass on 56th Street was an exhibition of interiors – little tableaux which utilised Steuben glass. The most extraordinary of them was by Michael Graves, who did a tableau that is clearly, unabashedly, a plagiarism or quotation from a famous Juan Gris Cubist still-life of 1914. This, anybody would say, is Post-Modernist in feeling. Then most of us have seen the Musée d'Orsay, and among other responses to that great building is that it is absolutely the essence of Post-Modernism both as architecture and as conception of the contents. As a building, it has extraordinary layers of nostalgic associations. It looks, amongst other things, like the railway station it originally was; sometimes I feel that I can hear the trains going through it; at other times it looks like one of the destroyed Les Halles pavilions or like a great 19th-century department store. In any case it is a building that is absolutely fraught with historical resonance.

In looking at the collections of the Musée d'Orsay the history of Modernism seems to have collapsed at our feet, and the counter voices, the arrière-garde, are given equal time. All of this suggests, among other things, an extraordinary reshuffling of the view of our historical past in which the monorail of Modernism seems suddenly to be complicated by all kinds of intersecting local trains.

To add to one's recent experience of phenomena that immediately elicit the word Post-Modernism, I also offer you the view of a New York artist's studio. His name is Mike Bidlo and the first time I visited him, his studio looked as if it were a kind of arsenal for the Third World War, where the treasures of 20th-century art would be kept, from Léger and Lichtenstein to Warhol and Matisse. On another occasion I visited him and he was doing his own Picasso Museum in rivalry with what had happened in Paris. This seemed to be an extraordinary statement of what had to be a new point of view, which could even be carried to further astonishing extremes with the photo witness of Mr Bidlo's recreation of *Guernica* – it is meant to look identical. This in turn is a kind of reproduction of the famous photographs of Picasso painting *Guernica* in the late spring of 1937 on the Quai des Grands Augustins. Moreover, just to add fuel to this Post-Modernist fire, there is the New York artist Sherrie Levine who does reproductions after reproductions as in her cluster of works after reproductions by Joan Miró. This seems to say something

about the way in which we have rearranged our experience of the past.

There is also in New York City an artist named Elaine Sturtevant who in the late 1960s did exact replications of works by the then hot young artists who were coming through Leo Castelli's Gallery, like Jasper Johns and Frank Stella. But it isn't only a question of Stella and Johns being replicated, it covers the entire anthology of styles in history. And of the things that fascinate me in particular (and this is said as someone who spends a lot of time loving and reviving the original Neo-Classicism, which in itself was a neo-movement) is the fact that many artists today seem to be doing the same kind of thing, at a second or third degree. There is, for example, Carlo Maria Mariani who is infatuated with, amongst other artists of the late 18th and early 19th centuries, Jacques Louis David, whose *Death of Marat*, was expanded by him with the intrusion of Charlotte Corday, the murderess.

This kind of reconstruction of the past, as in the case of the Romantic movement, can mean all kinds of past. It could be the 1960s or the 1970s, or could take on archaeological turns, as in the case of Carlo Maria Mariani's efforts to reconstruct a famous lost revolutionary painting by David of the revolutionary martyr, Lepelletier de Saint Fargeau. There is some evidence as to what the original picture looked like – a drawing after the lost painting by a student of David – and Signor Mariani fleshed it out a little bit more. As a student of David's work, I always had dreams that one day I would find the lost picture, but Signor Mariani has painted it for me!

The point I am hoping to make here has to do with the fact that the things that we seem to reach for a new word to describe – and the word, for better or worse, is Post-Modernism – have to do with a strange new attitude towards history, towards the past, that is an experience of the 'neo', of revivalism, which paradoxically is the kind of thing the Modernist movement hoped to stamp out. Those of us who are old enough, like myself, remember that the whole point of understanding the history of later 19th- and 20th-century painting or architecture was, in a way, to wipe out the past, and to posit something that was new and forward looking. But now in a strange reversal of history we are looking backwards, and either with irony or with poignant sentiment, we are trying to revive the look of that long lost world. This can be very close to us in terms of historical time: the look even of the 1960s can be the subject of this revivalist attitude. For example, Philip Taaffe sometimes redoes Barnett Newman, as in his re-creation of Newman's *Who's Afraid of Red, Yellow and Blue* of 1967, and it's obvious that Taaffe was as afraid of Newman as Newman was of the primary colours, but wanted to exorcise his power by translating it into a kind of computerese style in which the sublime zips of Newman become a kind of abstract wiring that conjures up the electronic imagery of the later 20th century.

In fact, we don't have to look only at neo-Neo-Classicism, or neo-60s abstraction to see this phenomenon. For example, one of the fascinating phenomena concerns the way in which so many post-war German artists have tried to revive the culture of pre-

World War I Germany in various ironic or grave ways. I remember the first time I saw a painting by Rainer Fetting of 1980, I had a kind of déjà vu experience, my art historical computer bank reached back to works by, for example, Kirchner, including a World War I painting of soldiers showering. In Germany one can also find what has been called, quite correctly in terms of description, Neo-Expressionism, in the works of Georg Baselitz. Even though they seem to hang upside down, they very often look as though they might have been included with the Die Brücke group, along with Nolde and company.

In fact, there are many works around these days by both younger and older artists that speak for this fascination with history. They use it as though it were the subject of art and experience itself. For example, there is a pair of New York artists who are New York's younger generation response to Gilbert and George. Their names are McGough and McDermott, and they work together, are seen together, dress alike and paint pictures that are really historical time trips, in which they try to resurrect, just like archaeologists, the look of various nostalgic moments in the history of relatively recent art. They even date them according to the year they have in mind. There is a picture which has a kind of New York Dadaist look with what would then have been a naughty subject redolent of the red-light district. This they dated 1923. They also made an effort to reconstruct the look of a late-Victorian mosaic which they dated 1894 and is meant to be evangelical in character, though that evangelism is again resurrected at a mock distance which speaks of an ironic predicament I think we all know in the later 20th century.

This attitude, which seems to suggest an abrupt rupture with the past, is of course something that historians like myself are now obliged to trace. When did it first begin? As usual, when we try to find the beginning, we discover that while we think we may have pinpointed it to such and such a year, there are always precedents which suggest that the tradition goes back earlier. But at least in more obvious ways, in terms of the history of the last quarter century, clearly the 1960s represent an overt break with the Modernist tradition. How else could we explain that an artist such as Roy Lichtenstein, who was nurtured in the high traditions of Modernism, could look back to the sacrosanct images of Mondrian or Picasso and translate them with a witty smirk into printer's dots of yellow and blue ink? In fact, the distance here suddenly seems to be that of an unbridgeable gulf. Even the angst, the psychological horror of Picasso's *Head of a Woman* seems to have been filtered out of Lichtenstein's interpretation of it as early as 1963.

Another very clear demonstration of the death of the Modernist tradition can be seen in Lichtenstein's 1974 spoof of one of the canonic images of the forward march of the Modern Movement; namely Theo van Doesburg's aesthetic transformation of an ordinary Dutch cow, which looks as though it might have been painted by Paulus Potter in the 17th century, into a pure abstraction which seems to represent the most unpolluted ivory tower of a forward-looking Modernism. As soon as Roy Lichtenstein had a go at it in 1974 you knew that that tradition was dead and a stake had been driven through its heart. It is fascinating, in terms of the effect on our view of the historical past, the way that attitudes have tended, especially in the last 15 years or so, to reshuffle dramatically our evaluations of some of the most venerable figures in the pantheon of 20th-century art.

When I was growing up in New York it was considered that Pablo Picasso, great as he was, went pretty sour after the 1940s and 1950s – you could date the decline when you wanted – and this was pretty much an *idée reçue* that was even maintained in the great Picasso retrospective in the Museum of Modern Art some seven years ago. But if I'm not mistaken most younger people, and most alert spectators, have newly experienced the late work of Picasso, which seems to carry a new potency, possibly because it shares the same kind of retrospection, sometimes a kind of sad, Proustian retrospection, of things past.

In terms of other curious rearrangements in our assessment of what is good and bad in the early, middle and late work of an artist there is the fascinating, and I think very symptomatic case of Picabia. When I was learning about the history of Modern art, Picabia was terrific as long as he was first a Cubist and then a Dadaist in New York in his teens. But then he went completely to pot. Current opinion has shaken this up and the later Picabia of the 1930s and the 1940s, which used to seem completely outrageous and go against Modernist tradition, suddenly looks fresh and usable to younger artists. It is curious to see that a young Post-Modernist artist, David Salle, is fascinated by late not early Picabia, and has absorbed it into the contemporary experience of art by paraphrasing or paying back his debts to Picabia in works that seem to combine academic drawing with layered double, or sometimes even triple, images.

I couldn't help noticing that the Tate seems to be displaying three late works by Derain. When I went to school Derain was only acceptable insofar as he was in the Modernist line, first as a Fauve, then as an almost-Cubist. His work from the 20s, 30s and 40s was completely ignored. That is obviously not the case today. The most typical example of the strange reversal in direction in what used to be thought of as the bankruptcy of an artist's late work, is the case of Giorgio de Chirico, who we all used to think had gone to seed entirely by the late teens and the early 20s. In fact only recently the Museum of Modern Art in New York had a De Chirico show which put him to rest in the 1920s, though there were just a few feeble indications that he went on to live many decades after that. But all of this has been turned unexpectedly upside down. It was only last summer in London when I saw a late De Chirico show which suddenly looked more alive and well than early De Chirico, which was making us all yawn a little bit after over-exposure. And in some very perverse way a late De Chirico of 1971, which is a kind of Post-Modernist paraphrase of an early work of 1914, seems to have a few more layers of experience that are completely in tune with what appeals to us today.

In 1982 Andy Warhol did a whole series of reproductions of De Chirico in which the Chinese box situation became extraordinarily apparent. Andy's version of who knows which *Hector and Andromache*, early, middle or late, shows he understood about the power of reproduction and could even translate it into a simplified linear image. So we have here a very strange genealogical table which takes us from an artist of a young Post-Modernist generation, Warhol, to a classic artist who, one might say, in his old age became a Post-Modernist. There is a canonic work that is always called Post-Modernist, Charles Moore's Piazza d'Italia, in New Orleans, which is usually as melancholic in terms of the absence of people as the piazzas of De Chirico himself. But it is this kind of cardboard reconstruction of the past, the feeling of loss, of empty spaces with no centre, that seem to be so much a part of our recent experience. This kind of revival of revivals can extend not only from the Neo-Classicism of David to Bridget Riley, but also extends throughout the history of architecture. And it's not surprising to see that, for instance, Richard Meier in the 1970s – I have no idea if he would hate being called a Post-Modernist – can, in his Chambers House, seem to offer us a kind of *déjà vu* experience of one of Le Corbusier's houses of the 1920s such as the Ozenfant studio of 1922.

Topically, it was fascinating to learn as I did recently of the design by Max Gordon for the National Gallery extension. To look at the interior of the Saatchi Museum, I assume that everybody would think it belonged fully to the Modernist tradition and that Mr Gordon was part of that camp. But on the other side of the coin, when he had to design an extension for the National Gallery he very Post-Modernly used an unbuilt project by Inigo Jones for Whitehall, geographically and stylistically appropriate, as his idea for extending the spaces of Wilkins' Neo-Classical building, this being a perfect example of a Post-Modernist view. It is the kind of thing, in fact, that extends from high art to popular art. I was rather pleased in this symposium to hear all the references to Disney World which, it seems to me, since the death of the Modern Movement, has to be incorporated into any sensible history of what has happened in the modern world, modern architecture and modern culture since the 1950s. When I went to Epcot, it was, so it seemed to me, yet another example of this replication or simulation that we have been experiencing in later 20th-century art and architecture. Compared to the real San Marco, for example, Epcot's resurrection of it in the 3-D fantasy collage of Italy is not quite life-size, a diminutive quality that gives it a curious sensation of being a kind of time-capsule we are treasuring in the late 20th century, a precious bit of history to be preserved with the love and fear of a shrine.

Equally astonishing is the fact that it was just last year that the Barcelona Pavilion that we used to know only through black and white photographs was reconstructed on the same site. This veneration, the idea that you can redo or replicate a famous monument, certainly indicates that the tradition behind that monument has to be a moribund if not an absolutely dead one. It's the same kind of thing as the efforts to complete Gaudí's Sagrada Familia in the same city. It used to be thought of as a kind of madcap thing, but it is now part of that dead domain of the Barcelona Pavilion, something from another modern world which we can only gaze upon or reconstruct, rather in the way that 19th-century architects completed Cologne Cathedral based on medieval plans, something the Modern Movement and histo-

rians of architecture who believed in it used to laugh at as one of the characteristic follies of the mid-19th century. With this in mind, our experience even of the history of the architectural past keeps getting reshuffled. For example, Ludwig II's reconstruction of Versailles near Munich used to be thought of as a kind of crazy folly. But these days when we look at Ludwig II's Spiegelgalerie and at the real Galerie des Glaces, they may seem to be a kind of prophetic view of late 20th-century attitudes. The same is true of the Parthenon, as it was reconstructed in Nashville in the 1890s, and then reconstructed again in the 1930s of more durable materials. Suddenly what used to be a joke can become a monument to the history of architecture, just as Ludwig van Klenze's Walhalla on the slopes of the Danube suddenly takes on a new lease of life as a kind of preview of various acts of simulation and historical nostalgia of the 1970s and 80s.

Lastly, though I am asking more questions than answering them, I should try to make some kind of statement about why this is all happening. I hope I'm wrong, but the fact of the matter is that since World War II the future has seemed to be very dim and is becoming dimmer and dimmer. The most optimistic last gasp of the 19th century, the Trylon and Perisphere from the 1939 New York World's Fair, opened with grim historical irony during the first year of World War II. The last death rattle of this thinking is Buckminster Fuller's famous geodesic dome from the US pavilion in Montreal at the International Fair of 1967. But already when this building was erected clouds hung over all of our heads – the clouds of the atom bomb of 1945. And this ghastly spectre, it seems to me, is looming larger and larger as the 21st century looms so close to the horizon. I recently read a marvellous aphorism by Mason Cooley: 'Posterity, the forlorn child of 19th-century optimism, grows ever harder to conceive'. This, it seems to me, would be one way of interpreting the art we see around us.

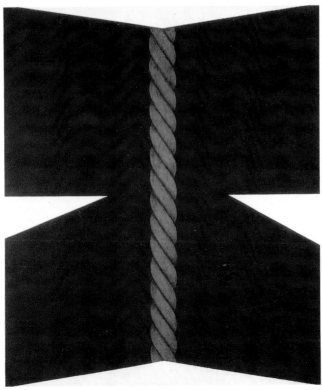

Philip Taaffe, *South Ferry*, 1985-86, linoprint collage, acrylic, 110x95cm

Cindy Sherman, *Untitled*, 1989, colour photograph, 104.1x81.3cm

Peter Schuyff, *The Weld*, 1985, acrylic on linen, 304.8x304.8cm

The Art of Quotation

– In your text written to coincide with the recent MoMA retrospective, you discuss the influence of Warhol on the New York art world, the phenomenon of artist as businessman and media figure, and the concept of art as a commercial product in a mass consumer market. Do you see Warhol as the most significant influence on young artists working today?

Well I have to say that looking backwards I can think of no artist from the past 25 years who seems to have loomed so large as an ancestor figure, as the muse and guiding light of the younger generation, as Warhol; and my own sense is that he is for the last quarter century, what Picasso was to the first half of the 20th century. He seems to be everywhere and the potential of his art never seemed as huge as it suddenly did in the retrospective. So on every possible account he seems to be, for the moment, the great father figure. However, in a strange way he probably had more of an impact in spirit than in visual fact, because one of the odd things about Warhol is that, at least on this side of the Atlantic and especially in New York, the actual work was very seldom exhibited. It's a kind of irony that in spite of his international fame, there has not been a proper Warhol retrospective in New York City since the early 70s. So for an entire younger generation, his art was virtually invisible, except of course in reproduction and in terms of its myth-making capacity.

– Have there been any major revelations about his art for the younger generation of artists?

One of the great revelations had to do with a supplementary show we had at New York University, which was shown at the same time as the major retrospective and which concentrated exclusively on his work of the 50s – a whole decade of Warhol when he was a very successful commercial artist. I compare this – though I'm sure a lot of people would think it blasphemy – to the *Early Cézanne* show insofar as it disclosed a whole premature decade of activity which, once seen, changed forever our perception of what was to come. For example, there's a prevailing myth that Warhol virtually began from scratch around 1960-61 as a grass-roots artist who did very coarse, ugly, 'bottom of the social ladder' imagery – *New York Post* headlines, that sort of thing. In fact, as the exhibition here proved, in that decade he was working, among other things, in high style commercial art – he worked with Tiffany's, for instance – and was completely immersed in the fusion of art, commerce and advertising in a way that suggests that his choice of low-down imagery and in the course of time, of commercial illustration, was a very conscious and sophisticated one.

So it was not a question of someone at the bottom of the social and economic ladder starting at rung one, but rather somebody who had, in a very wilful and elegant way, chosen to descend from the top. I would also say about the Museum of Modern Art retrospective, in addition to showing us acres of work from the 60s and 70s that we had never properly seen in New York or seen at all, that it was, at least for me, something of a revelation in terms of the very late works. My own sense was that the late work was under-exhibited in much the same way as the late work of Picasso was. I think the reason for that was that,

David Salle, *Demonic Roland*, 1987, acrylic and oil, 238x345cm

in order to show it in proper quantity and to give it a fair spread, it simply would have taken up too much room – many of the late paintings are huge. For example, a proper display of the variations of *The Last Supper* and works like those would have taken practically an entire museum. I suppose, given a choice of having a full representation of the serial pictures of the 60s or the work of the last four or five years, they chose the former.

– You talk about Warhol's late works in which he is quoting from art history – from Leonardo, Munch, De Chirico etc – as intersecting the interests of younger artists. Do you think these artists were actually influenced by Warhol?

I don't think so. I think it's more a question of *Zeitgeist*, because my own guess – it's almost more than a guess – is that very few younger artists, at least in New York, were aware of these Warhol works about other works of art. He did for instance have an exhibition of late De Chirico paraphrases, quotations after quotations; but it was amazing to me how little attention it was given – nobody seemed to have gone to see it or to talk about it – and my own hunch is that if you had asked most savvy New York art people five years ago about Andy Warhol and Munch they would never have known that he had done works after Munch. So all of this was almost an underground activity and when it

was exposed, really for the first time, it was a kind of 'eureka' sensation that he clicked into place. I think what we ought to emphasise sufficiently is how invisible Warhol has been in New York over the last ten years or so. He had never been given a fair shake.

– Warhol's statement, 'Being good at business is the most fascinating kind of art', seems to have particular relevance to today's artists.

Yes, I think the spirit of Warhol, which may have started in a kind of mock ironic way in the early 60s, has really replaced in a full-fledged way the earlier mythology of the artist as being totally uninterested in the world of money, of bourgeois values and so on. I would say that this is a myth like the previous one and has just totally turned that one upside down. But as we all know from the late 19th century, right through the 1940s, 50s and 60s, people had the idea, and artists had the idea, that art ought to be a kind of taking of vows; that if you were going to be an artist, it was a fact that you were not interested in material values, you rejected the world of commerce, the world of middle-class pleasures and so on. This was obviously a very fertile myth and many people have lived by it. The Abstract Expressionists in New York were probably the last gasp of faith in that sanctity of art and the feeling that it had nothing to do with the here and now of commerce and materialism in our society. But that myth seemed to have become pretty silly

Peter Halley, *Prevention Mechanism*, 1989, Day-Glo acrylic, acrylic and Roll-A-Tex, 195.6x328.9cm

or moribund by the 1960s with the Pop generation, and Warhol was probably the strongest and earliest voice to deflate it. Now I think the prevailing myth, the prevailing fantasy about art, is that art is business like everything else, it's like fashion or entertainment; there's absolutely no reason why artists should have this 'holier than thou' attitude towards what they do.

– Does this mean that the public in New York now sees art purely in terms of fashion and entertainment, rather than in more serious terms as a form of aesthetic or social critique?

I think it's absolutely true that the atmosphere, especially in New York, of going to openings of art exhibitions, museums, retrospectives, even symposia and discussions, has the flavour of carnival, of fun culture, of high society. It has to do with the sense of esteem that one can have by being associated with the most current trends of the art world; it's very equatable with the world of fashion and high style and all this has permeated the thinking as well as the look of the work of young artists.

– But do you think this has had a negative effect on the quality of art being produced?

No. My own sense is that in terms of the mythologies – the cultural support for works of art – I don't think it makes very much difference

one way or another about good or bad because my own feeling is that throughout history, at any given time there is only a handful of really terrific artists. There have been many periods in the history of Western art in which the prevailing myths and patrons that create art have been absolutely obnoxious, but great art has been produced. What I'm simply saying is that art and the cultural myths that it exploits are not identical and I've seen terrific works of art from the 1980s that may be about art as a commodity but that doesn't mean that the concept of art as a commodity is good or bad; rather it has to do with the quality of the art itself.

– Some critics have seen artists as merely responding to the demands of the New York art market, the pressure from dealers to come up with new gimmicks that may last for only one season, raising the artist to instant commercial success, only to be replaced the following season by yet another, more commercially viable product.

I think that's probably true. I would say that the tempo of change and also the tempo of interest and curiosity about new works of art may be greater now than it has ever been in the past. I always find it a little heartbreaking for example that artists whom I myself have been very enthusiastic about, I've then totally forgotten about because they've been instantly replaced by somebody else who fills the screen. I think

59

this may get sorted out, it may just be the phenomenon of being in the present. Looking back on the 60s for example, the tempo of change also seemed to be very rapid. It may just be that now the present is coming up with such rapidity that things have trouble enduring in our memory.

– Frederic Jameson has used the phrase 'the perpetual present' in relation to the tempo of the art world in New York; and philosophers such as Jean Baudrillard have seen the influence of the media, particularly of television, as having had a significant impact on the work of younger artists and on the visual demands of the market. Do you think this is true?

Well I think it's true, but it should also be said that a 'perpetual present' also involves a 'perpetual past', because one of the characteristics of our perpetual present is to be endlessly curious in terms of resurrecting, re-examining works from decades ago; and the market, it seems to me, and our ability to get sated are such that people are always looking for more and more to see, to re-examine, to buy. And it's not only a question of younger artists but also of older artists; it's rather amazing for example how many revivals there have been of art of the 50s, the 60s, the 70s – the museums are doing it all the time. So it's not just a question of being interested in the new and the young, but of being interested in everything. The excavation of the recent historical past is greater than it's ever been.

– How do you view Neo-Geo art in the context of current New York trends?

I am interested in a lot of these abstract artists, including Peter Halley and Peter Schuyff. One of the things I enjoy about them is the degree of absolute frigidity in their work; they all seem to be hell-bent to make pictures that are so tough, so cold, so unfeeling that you might think a robot or a computer was responsible for them. It seems to me that the new emotional experience is something that has to do with feeling a new range of sub-zero temperature, that is, how cold can you get? How completely impersonal, how chilly and computer-like can you be? It has to do with certain literary counterparts of fictional deadpan description; you sense different ranges of temperature, of wilful lack of feeling and it turns sort of inside out, upside down; it's a coldness that is so cold that it becomes exciting in itself. This is a kind of complaint that used to be levelled against artists like Mondrian who were considered to be absolutely unfeeling, cerebral and without emotions. Nobody says that anymore and I think the same thing is going to happen to these artists. For the moment a lot of people accuse them of looking as if they were robots rather than feeling painters, but I think that their range of emotions will become far more apparent in years to come.

– Would you say that their work evolved primarily as a reaction to the Neo-Expressionist paintings of the early 80s?

Yes, very much so, because there seemed, especially after the 1970s which were so dominated by cerebration, to be this absolute volcano of personal liberation, as if every artist's id had exploded. There was a free-floating world of fantasy images coming from both sides of the Atlantic, sometimes terrific, sometimes boring, as is always the case within any range of artists. I think this cold-hearted calculation is a kind of check, and also in a fascinating way, as in the case of Philip Taaffe, it has to do with permutation once again. His pictures very often take the classics of the 1950s, works say by Barnett Newman and Bridget Riley, and put them into a deep computer freeze. So it's as if some electronic artist had metamorphosed the impersonal look of Bridget Riley onto another level of frigidity. These artists of the 1980s are thus quoting in various degrees of seriousness or irony the art of the 1960s and earlier; and it is now clear that the whole history of Modernism is something that is completely in the past tense and has to be looked at from a completely new angle.

– Do you see then the art of Neo-Expressionism as looking more towards the future in the sense that it was conceived as a definite reaction to Modernism and a return to figurative art?

Everything that is new looks towards the future, even if it is nominally looking at the past; although one of the things I must say about these Neo-Expressionists is that they too have this retrospective character. I'm thinking particularly about German painters such as Georg Baselitz or Rainer Fetting, who quite consciously look back to the Expressionists of the early part of the 20th century, to Emil Nolde, Ernst Kirchner and so on. So that their Expressionism is very much 'neo' in the same way that when Philip Taaffe does Barnett Newman again he's 'neo', but they're just as much a part of this looking backwards to the Modernist past as the abstract painters of the Neo-Geo movement.

– How do you regard the controversial figure of Julian Schnabel, both in terms of Neo-Expressionist painting and in the context of the contemporary art world of New York as a whole?

Schnabel seems to me rather fascinating as an artist who is trying to be, as it were, a neo-mythological hero of modern art. I think he built up a programme and a look for himself that would revive the whole sense of greatness and grandeur of the macho artist in his studio attacking the world. I think he thought of himself as a neo-Picasso and there is something second-degree about this too. It's theatrical and it's almost another example of the role-playing, the retrospective role-playing that we've seen so often in the 80s.

– How does the art of Eric Fischl and David Salle fit into the context of this retrospective painting of the late 80s?

Fischl and Salle are both artists I like immensely for different reasons. Fischl I must say seems very off-beat in terms of artists of the 1980s. One of the reasons is that, at least in his earlier works, he seemed to be so completely unsophisticated, just recording like a photographer the facts of American upper-middle-class life, which was a kind of programme that no other artist I can think of took on. His work has covered a whole range of experience that seemed absolutely impossible for the high-style painting of any other artist – I don't know how he ever dreamed up the possibility of doing it or imagined transcribing it. For me, he put his finger on the pulse of modern America in a way that is miraculous. The only painter I can compare him to is Edward Hopper, who managed to translate into visual terms what must have been the feel of America in the 1920s, 30s and 40s; and it would seem to me that for 21st-century sociologists or historians, if they want to find out the way a good section of American life looked and felt in the 1980s, they could do no better than to turn to Eric Fischl's work.

He seems to be most concerned with recording directly commonplace but intimate experience, which as a rule he takes from the model or, if he works from photographs, he still paints in a first-hand way. On the other hand, one of the odd ironies of this is that even though it seems to be direct pictorial experience, it is the kind of work – I just mentioned Hopper before – that summons up a long genealogical table in terms of the history of American realist art. For one thing it very wilfully evokes images like those of Winslow Homer, an artist who looms large in terms of American parochial history – national history – but who may seem very secondary in terms of International Modernism. But Fischl has in some way looked backwards to this realist tradition which was pretty much ignored by most ambitious artists from the 1950s on. So in this unexpected way he might be said to participate in the retrospective mood of our time. But his subject matter is certainly unique and extraordinarily valuable in that he has managed to produce images that we in America recognise instantly. It's that marvellous feeling we have when a novelist like Nabokov pinpoints an ordinary experience that nobody has troubled to record before.

David Salle is a quite different sort of artist and would certainly be a central figure in any discussion of art of the 1980s, not only from the level of appropriation – quotations from artists from an earlier range of art history – but above all in terms of the collision, the juxtaposition, of completely disparate images. It's become an absolute cliché in the 80s to talk about this mirage of multiple, contradictory images experienced in everyday life, and I guess the archetype of this is our television sets where we just switch channels. But in any case, it may be a platitude, but it's also a fact of the way we live now and David

Salle with his see-through effects and his constant jarring – everything from abstract textural designs, of fabrics and paintings, to academic drawings of nudes, side by side – is very much a part of the facts of visual life today. He has grasped that in a very personal style.

Once again, like everything else, it may seem very new, but in retrospect any number of distinguished ancestral roots come to mind; for instance, it very much recalls the split-screen imagery of James Rosenquist or even Magritte. Likewise the large scale is very American in quality and is one of the things that gives David Salle his special look. It's a billboard scale that was established in the 60s by Rosenquist, and this is very much part of Salle's background. He's just retranslated it into a very fresh and 1980s look that reflects the mood of the television generation.

– *How important is feminist art in New York at the moment?*
I can't speak for the individual artists, but what I can say, and I think it's a heartening thing, is that there is now an amazing number of prominent women artists who demand completely as much attention as men and their programme in art usually has no conscious relationship with feminism. There was a period when such art had to be programmatic to make its point – I'm thinking of the overtly feminist works of Judy Chicago – but now we talk about Barbara Kruger, Jenny Holzer, Judy Pfaff, Jennifer Bartlett, Sherrie Levine, Elizabeth Murray, the list goes on and on, in terms that may have little or nothing to do with their gender. And the fact that we just think about them as artists *per se* seems to be an enormous triumph. They're very well represented in the galleries and they are, it seems to me, completely integrated into the contemporary art world; their numbers are very satisfying. In fact there was a recent exhibition, now circulating in the United States, called *Making their Mark*, which is really about this theme, namely the effect of feminist movements in art during the last 20 years, and the exhibition itself turns out to be first an anthology of terrific artists who happen to be women. And the fact that they are terrific artists and that secondarily they happen to be women seems to indicate that something very good has happened.

Above: Eric Fischl, *Bayonne*, 1985, oil, 259.1x327.7cm; *Below*: Rainer Fetting, *Untitled (Desmond)*, 1989, oil, 139x109cm each

Deconstruction and déjà vu in Art

It seems to me that in a funny way, the traditions of taking apart, of fracturing, fragmenting and reconstructing from the *tabula rasa*, are really part of the heritage of 20th-century art. Many of the examples of Deconstructionist art look very 'neo-' or 'retro-' in the sense that they seem to be nostalgic revisions, or revisitings, of experiences that we have had in the 20th-century historical past.

One of the things that is constantly referred to, in terms of the directions before and after the First World War, has to do with the way in which Cubism, in particular, seemed to offer us a kind of 'de-' or 'dis-' vision of the world – with fragmentation, things coming apart, clashing, a collision of opposites – whereas after the war, especially in that brave new world of Utopian visions, the images tended to turn out elemental forms that looked as though they were the theoretical, abstract ground plan for a new vision of society, with, as its hero, the anonymous worker of the new post-war world. This kind of vision of deconstruction, if I dare use that word, followed by reconstruction is one that can be exemplified in the evolution of, say, Mondrian, whose works that come from the domain of analytic Cubism, with its decomposition of a solid object, precede and oppose the more lucid and stable images of primary colours and basic shapes, that would in some pure empyrean provide the visual sources for a new constructive future.

We all know as well, from the history of early 20th-century art, that the boundaries between painting and sculpture and architecture, in terms of constructive visions, are very fluid. An example is Malevich's architectonic sculpture, abstract blueprints for a new language, not only of painting and sculpture but of architecture and, by implication, all of society.

It is interesting, however, that already in the 1920s, after this basic ground plan was laid, there seemed to be prophecies of a kind of defiance of gravity, of law and order, even within the vocabulary of these early Utopian masters. It's interesting to see the way this rhythm of putting together and coming apart can vacillate so rapidly. It seems to me, looking back from the 1980s, that this is a very familiar pattern that we see repeated often in the 1950s and 60s when, under the banner of Minimalism, which had a very Constructivist thrust, the style of the 1950s was annihilated by elemental shapes that could lead to architecture, to sculpture or to painting. Even this Minimalist trend, however, could be first established and then deconstructed very rapidly. In the early 1960s, firebrick pieces by Carl Andre or installations by Robert Morris looked about as elemental as art can look, but then one suddenly discovered that by the later 1960s, Morris and even Andre could shake all this up, loosen it, make it look, in the fashionable word of the 1960s, 'aleatory'. In other words, there is again this kind of rhythm of getting down to absolute essentials and then destroying them, and once more starting from scratch.

The famous, or infamous, black paintings of Frank Stella of 1959, look like a pictorial blueprint of some new aesthetic world, the exact pictorial equivalent of one of Carl Andre's firebrick pieces, but by the 1960s, 70s and 80s, Stella had turned into a quite different artist who I suspect could offer all kinds of analogies to the whole series of descriptions that begin with 'de-' and 'dis-', having to do with defiance of the law of gravity, having to do with the disjunction of forms, having to do with deception or the combination of fact and fiction, but also having to do, so it seems to me, with earlier historical precedents. I'm

rather surprised that in the discussions of Deconstructionist architecture, more references haven't been made to another period of extraordinary disharmony in architecture, namely the Mannerism of the 16th century, as in one of the touchstones of Mannerist decoration – Giulio Romano's Hall of the Giants in his Palazzo del Te, with the fall of the giants and the collapse of architecture.

It's fascinating to see that in terms of a period style of the 1980s the work of Frank Stella, which seems to turn its back entirely on his works of the late 50s and early 60s, has any number of analogies with the art of other artists of a younger generation, such as Judy Pfaff's installation pieces of the early 1980s in which we have a kind of free-flow funhouse that offers the widest eruption of deconstructive elements. On a more overtly architectonic level, it is worth mentioning how many sculptors – or are they architect/sculptors? – of the 1970s and 80s seem to offer a visual vocabulary that fits into place with much Deconstructionist architecture. For example, works by Alice Aycock (such as *How to Catch a Manufactured Ghost,* an almost literal version of a dream house) and by Alice Adams are fictional experiments in the elements of architecture that are only temporarily, it seems, constructed. They are images that seem to play with the elements of the basic building blocks of architecture but produce a completely irrational result.

One of the most relevant of these artists who defy the category of architecture versus sculpture is, I believe, Siah Armajani who, beginning in the 1970s, composed in three-dimensional terms what he called a dictionary for building, namely, he took the most rudimentary elements we all know from domestic architecture – doors and windows, tables, closets, stairs and so on – and began, as it were, from zero on the drawing board, putting them together in rather disconcerting combinations. It is rather worth noting that his combination of a closed door and an open door, which both seem to lead to nowhere, has a very clear antecedent in Duchamp's famous *Door* of 1927, which can simultaneously be opened and closed, a bit of cerebral as well as utilitarian Deconstructionism which he used to defy the concept of a closed or an open space, if not to defy the concept of a closed or an open door.

It is very hard to look at an abstract hybrid of sculpture/architecture, what have you, like this, without thinking of the work of Frank Gehry. I recall Gehry saying that his predominant concerns are 'cheapness' – well, that used to be the case – but then he goes on, 'destruction, distortion, illusion, layerings and Surrealism'. It's interesting that he uses the word 'Surrealism' because I think one of the important components is exactly this element of the fantastic re-introduced into architecture – fantastic insofar as it seems to defy the laws of gravity, fantastic insofar as it seems it may topple upon you even though it is perfectly secure, fantastic because it seems to be, as it were, the *id* of the super-ego of solid Classical architecture, somehow surfacing and disturbing us in a way that the projects of these sculptor-architects do.

Vito Acconci is one of the most prominent of these artists at the moment in America. His *An Instant House* is both the absolutely secure permanent cubic form and, at the same time, collapsible. To make it more complicated and more collisive, it also has emblems of two major world powers in constant proximity or else tensely separated, depending on whether the house is open or closed.

Even in the domain of furniture, we can see what I've referred to as this constant rhythm of rediscovering the wheel and then destroying it, as in the rock chair by Scott Burton, and a chair by Mr Acconci, of 1987, which in a Surrealist way, seems to have proliferated with other kinds of chairs, so that you have here, just in terms of furniture design, a kind of example of what Gehry had called destruction, distortion, illusion, layering and Surrealism.

On quite a different level, which has to do with a kind of visual or conceptual or Pirandellian deconstruction-reconstruction, there are many examples in, say, the work of Jennifer Bartlett, who loves playing the theatrical game of true or false, fact or fiction – something that again, is as old as the hills in terms of 20th-century art. I'm thinking back to that fact and fiction world of the Cubists in terms of what is real and what is illusion. Bartlett's Volvo commission in Sweden, offers us both real painted furniture and then complicated painted illusions of the same thing, so that you hardly know what is true, what is false, what can be sat on, and what can only be contemplated as in a painting. That can be seen in other examples of her work, such as the dialogue of 'yes' or 'no', true or false, between a real constructed house on the site as opposed to the painted version which is split in two by a screen. This is a perfect example, I would say a kind of semantic Deconstruction in visual language in which things can be looked at in any number of ways, including two-dimensional, three-dimensional, or maybe two-and-a-half-dimensional. One has to scratch one's head and remember whether these are paintings or real objects. They are like theatre sets. On a further level of this kind of semantic multiplication, *Rhapsody,* a very ambitious piece set up in New York in the 1970s takes primary elements like the archetypal, Monopoly-set house, and then deconstructs them into all kinds of modular component parts, offering us an endlessly complex inventory of vocabulary and syntax of the language of primary imagery or the language of primary image-making.

Thinking back again to the early 20th century, particularly in Russia, it's fascinating to see how often this tempo of coming apart and fitting together and then the same pattern repeated seems to turn up in the 1980s. The kind of vision of Malevich's *tabula rasa* that he presented again and again with his Suprematist vocabulary, his new system in art which shows us the purity of a circle and a square (presumably once again the building blocks of a new world of form which could be pictorial or sculptural or architectural or all three at once), has had rather extraordinary consequences in the 1980s in a sequence of events that I'm sure can be put into the grammar of Deconstruction. There is a vintage photograph of what Malevich exhibited in Petrograd in 1915, at what was called *The Last Futurist Show.* Then, in 1980, when at the Los Angeles County Museum there was a big show of Russian avant-garde art, this photograph was reproduced again, blown up on the walls, so that people could have it as historical layering and remember what the Utopian dreams of Russia on the eve of the Revolution looked like visually. Then, in a typically historicising way, the museum tried to reconstruct the actual room in Petrograd where the Malevichs were seen, and they managed to pull together many of the paintings that were shown there, some 65-odd years before. This in itself is some kind of strange nostalgic

reconstruction of the past, but it could also be put to positive use by an artist of the 1980s – David Diao – in New York, who took that now canonic photograph from 1915, and used it as the source for his reconstruction not only of the past but also for his own pictorial vision of the present, which is further complicated by the fact that it also refers to 'Henri Matisse and His Public', an allusion to the cover of Alfred Barr's great monograph on Matisse, so you have here a kind of double historical reference, and you have *Margins of Philosophy,* his own variation of the same photograph with another famous Malevich of this period, desanctified by Warhol-like repetition into a marginal pattern. This sort of phenomenon is, in fact, very common in the art of the last ten years. We are all used to seeing, in the work of such artists as Julian Schnabel or David Salle, the collision courses that are run between completely different sorts of images, some of which actually protrude from the canvas space, compressed, to use Peter Eisenman's phrase, by some kind of anaconda-grip that makes everything seem to be exploding or gasping for breath at the same time. There is a collision of two popular worlds of culture in Julian Schnabel's *The Exile.* Among other allusions is one to the famous Caravaggio *Bacchus,* which is put into this disjunctive mix of images and real things, like the protruding antlers. This kind of equation between canonic images from the past that are reproduced *ad infinitum* in our own time, and abstract paint is a phenomenon familiar to our moment in history. David Salle loves a binary structure that offers a disjunction between the academic style of drawing the nude and the completely counter-style of Abstract Expressionism.

Lastly, I should like to suggest that Deconstruction might have something to do with the Western tradition of the making of ruins, the contemplation of ruins, or the painting of fictional ruins. The image of the apocalypse or of some sort of time cycle, whether it be slow, as in Gibbon's *Decline and Fall,* or rapid as in the 20th century when we think we're all going to die the day after tomorrow, is something that seems to be at the very core of these images of disquiet, of discontinuity, of the defiance of gravity and solidity. The famous 18th-century painter, Hubert Robert took the great monuments of antiquity and deconstructed them, making us feel that time brought on the inevitable upheaval of this civilisation, and this kind of image is really common coinage in the language of the late 18th and early 19th centuries, although perhaps more desolate and without the prospective energy of most of today's Deconstructionist architecture.

Finally, however, I wanted to indicate that, as usual, this kind of vision seems to be capable of working in both ways: they are, shall we say, the two sides of the same coin and I think that the Deconstructionist mode is really the flipside of the classicising Post-Modernist mode. Just as the great Romantic painter Caspar David Friedrich could do all kinds of things both constructive and positive or destructive and melancholy – he could both offer us a kind of Post-Modern vision of a new cathedral, all shiny, new and glorious, that seems to have risen from the ruins, or else he could deconstruct a cathedral into a melancholy vision of the end of the world – I rather suspect that these forms and emotions may lie at the foundations of some of the imagery, the moods, the feelings, that continue to disturb and to inspire us today.

———— * ————

Ashley Bickerton, *Landscape #4 (Fragmented Biosphere)*, 1988, mixed media construction with black leather cover, 244.5x152.4x111.8cm

Barbara Bloom, *The Reign of Narcissism* (detail), 1988-89, mixed media installation, hexagonal room 609.6x609.6x365.8cm

In Search of the New

– By selecting new art as the focal point of this discussion, one must inevitably begin by questioning the concept of the new in the context of contemporary art. New York is considered by many to be the centre for new art. But beyond the market's constant demand for novelty and the emergence of unknown artists onto the international scene, is it possible to define an art that is actually exploring new ground?

I don't know how one can make a clear distinction between new art, meaning something unseen before and fresh, and art that is exploring grander, more serious new territory. That will have to be something that settles into history. What I find phenomenal is the way in which new art seems to have a shorter and shorter lifespan; the very concept of the new seems to be so ephemeral that it's quite useless. For instance, in 1988 Jeff Koons might have seemed like the newest of new artists and suddenly in 1989 he seemed like an old master. Now in the 90s we are no longer thinking about him as a new artist and he has left a void for another new artist to fill. So the concept of newness has been so diminished in terms of timespan that Andy Warhol's prophecy about everybody being famous for 15 minutes seems to have been reduced to 15 seconds!

Part of the concept of the new also has to deal with the concept of what is new in the old, since reputations among mid-20th-century artists from the 40s, 50s and 60s are now being resurrected and turned into something that is hot and new. An interesting phenomenon concerns the whole generation of 1960s Colour-Field painters written

about by Greenberg and his disciples. The younger and newer elements of the 70s and 80s completely ignored them, but now they are being re-exhibited and re-experienced, producing the same effect of novelty and shock as the younger generation. Similarly, countless artists from the 19th century are being excavated, dusted off and given new reputations, so it's not really a phenomenon that is confined to contemporary art. In that sense, the search for novelty, for freshness, for something that is unfamiliar, all helps to keep the art market going. I don't mean this as a negative thing, I'm just describing a phenomenon that is very familiar today.

– You don't agree with critics who might see this as a sign that art has been exhausted, that everything has been invented, and that all that remains is to re-experience and restructure the language of art history?

Things have not really changed, artists have always quoted from the past. Manet spent the early part of his career creating great paintings that were quotations from the past and Sir Joshua Reynolds did appropriations all the time. But this did not mean that the history of art was exhausted, it just meant that they reinvented tradition in their own unexpected ways. So I don't think for an instant that that is the situation today.

– Germano Celant has written that 'What we perceive is not the "new" but the linguistic reflection on the pervasive and communicative ability of things that are already made. Previous knowledge is rear-

ranged, and no "newness" is sought.' Would you agree with this statement?

I don't know if that is true, since it always turns out that the art of the past – and it is as true for Cubism or Abstract Expressionism as it is for art today – when it was first seen appeared to be startlingly new but was subsequently rearranged both linguistically and historically as a perfectly logical continuation of existing art forms.

– Jeff Koons has recently compared the creative process to the rearrangement of existing chemical compounds to form something totally new.

I like that idea and I think about it in particular in terms of his own work. When I first saw the beautiful kitsch sculptures that he exhibited last year I was absolutely bowled over and shocked with both pleasure and horror. I found them really startling and they made me feel as though the ground had shaken and I had to compose myself. Then I discovered that this 'shock of the new' (to use a traditional phrase) was something that I had experienced when I first saw the comic-strip paintings by Roy Lichtenstein over a quarter of a century ago. His paintings had the same combination of something that began as ugly but that turned out to have a new kind of beauty. So Jeff Koons initially seemed to be very, very new but he subsequently came to seem like a

Flavin. When we first saw one of his fluorescent lightbulbs his art seemed totally unprecedented. Then, as the medium became familiar, we became fascinated instead by his combinations of lightbulbs. The same thing has now happened with Jenny Holzer. Initially the medium itself seemed startlingly new but now the electronic signs just look like 'Jenny Holzers' and we are interested, not in the novelty of the medium, but in the various new combinations and permutations of her style. It's just a principle that there is nothing new under the sun; rather there are new variations of existing things. Whatever the discipline, you can't make something totally new out of nothing; it will always have its roots.

– Analysing the constant changes and novelties in his work over the last decade, Jeff Koons seems to communicate a sense of the accelerated history of the commercial art world and the emphasis on the new. Do you see this as a very self-conscious aspect of New York art at the moment?

Yes, I think this is certainly the case with Jeff Koons, and other artists like him. Part of the force of his art has to do with his irony. He is completely aware of the art-as-commodity situation today and, instead of throwing up his hands and bemoaning the fact that art used to be alienated and spiritual, he is embracing the current facts of life. The

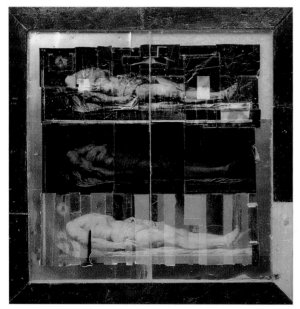 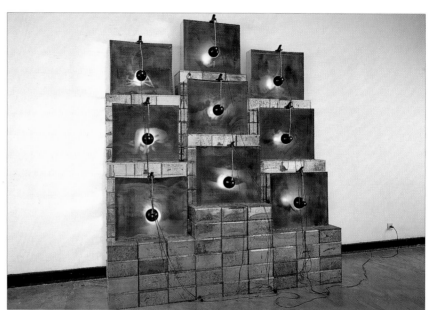

L to R: Doug & Mike Starn, *Triple Christ*, 1986, mixed media, 162.5x162.5cm; Christian Boltanski, *Reliquaire: Meurtres*, 1989/90, mixed media

modern mutation of an experience that I had already had. Then in turn, looking at Lichtenstein I remember having the feeling that, although this seemed totally unprecedented, it was to be construed, at least by me, as a recombination of components that one can find, say, in the work of Seurat, who was so excited by cartoons, caricatures and commercial illustrations, and perhaps even in some aspects of Cubism. However new something seems at first, you quickly get used to it and then in retrospect it seems to be part of a long Darwinian evolution. So I don't really think that Koons' work is earth-shaking, it is just an unfamiliar combination that seems totally new, but when investigated begins to reveal its traditional roots.

– What art have you seen recently that has struck you as being new and unfamiliar?

Two days ago I saw the Ashley Bickerton show and, although I'm familiar with his work, his latest show at first seemed startlingly unfamiliar. I was really rivetted by his images and constructions which looked like something from a different planet. Once again I'm sure we will get used to them and begin to see all sorts of precedents, but at least for the time being they threw me. Even Jenny Holzer's use of electric sign boards, which in itself was startlingly new a few years ago, has become very familiar. Exactly the same thing has happened to Dan

feeling is that if you can't beat it, join it. He is making the most of his art, treating it as fashion and changing the season's model. I don't see why he shouldn't, it is his approach to it and it's a perfect reflection of the business world of art today.

– Can you account for the current resurgence of interest, among international artists, dealers and critics, in Conceptualism, in artists such as John Baldessari, Bruce Nauman and Joseph Kosuth? How does the new Conceptualism compare to that of the 70s and is it a sign that the 80s' tendency towards Expressionism has been exhausted?

I would never say that anything has been exhausted. It seems to me that Nauman, Baldessari and Kosuth were kind of leapfrogging in terms of their art. They represented for a long time the kind of 'hands off' art of the 70s – 'hands off' in the sense that they never looked as though they were using traditional means of making paintings or constructions. They looked pretty irrelevant for a while, but now that so many artists are trying once again to reflect the whole world of commerce, of signs, images, television, billboards, electric sign boards etc, these artists certainly have a new 'ancestor' look and I think that's probably the reason for their sudden relevance. However, the new artists have a much more hip, younger-generation attitude towards commerce and luxury goods than the 70s artists ever did. I'm thinking in particular of

Barbara Bloom. Her grain of narcissism is something that comes ultimately from that 70s' mould but it has a completely new flavour which has to do with high luxury and total vanity, total narcissism, which is a perfect mirror of artists in society today. She is, in terms of influence, taking us back to the art of the 70s and has skipped over figurative painting, but I certainly don't think that's dead. We all know from the history of art that every time something is deemed to be dead it resurfaces a few seasons later, so I never believe in any such statements.

– *Many artists seem to be distancing themselves more and more from the artworks themselves, adopting a certain objectivity towards their art, and embracing other roles such as that of the critic, the philosopher, the spokesman and writer, placing an increasing emphasis on the use of photography and language.*

That is true insofar as there certainly seems to be a whole new wave of young artists getting as far away as they can from the hand-made and that look of the hand-made which was a kind of signature of anti-Conceptual art in the early 80s. So I think that this is probably the kind of generalisation that holds, but that is not to say that there is not a lot of good hand-made painting and sculpture going on now and that it cannot just as quickly replace the synthetic, commercial look of so

signs – this has always been more obvious in America than in Europe and the whole history of 20th-century American art is proof of the fact. On the other hand, I think that it's much too easy to turn this into a black and white situation as French thinkers such as Baudrillard always do.

– *Do you think that new art can be politically effective?*

No, I have never thought that any art, certainly any art of the last 10 or 20 years that has had a political position has been in any way politically effective. Basically the audience is much too narrow. You can't have politically effective art because only the art world sees it. Even if, within that world, it is at first shocking or makes people twinge with embarrassment at their values or lack of them, you soon get immune to that. That's one of the things about Jenny Holzer. Although you may read her messages, and some of them really hit hard, you swiftly forget about the messages and just look at them as a kind of light spectacle. That's certainly what happened in the last show at the Dia Foundation. I think that is true about Hans Haacke or Leon Golub, both ferociously political artists. They make us face, make us confront head on, some of the hardest human and economic issues of our times. But the fact of the matter is that they very quickly look just like a good or a bad 'Hans Haacke', or an early or a late 'Leon Golub'. So I really think that although political ambitions may fire an artist and make him work, in

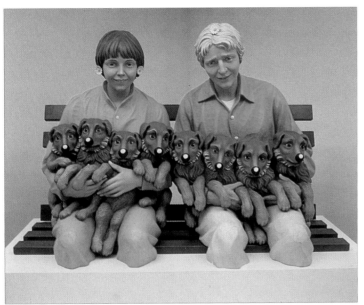

L to R: Jeff Koons, *String of Puppies*, 1988, polychromed wood, 106.7x157.5x94cm; Haim Steinbach, *Untitled (dolls, carriage)*, 1990, 124.5x203.2x55.9 cm

much good art of the late 80s. I think actually they are running concurrently. I don't think of it as first black, then white; I think these tendencies are going along together now.

– *Can we discuss the influence of the media on new art, an issue that has been highlighted in a number of recent exhibitions including* A Forest of Signs *in Los Angeles and* Image World *in New York?*

All we have to do is to look at the attitude of Haim Steinbach, Barbara Kruger, Jenny Holzer or Ashley Bickerton to realise that the whole look of the modern world is being mirrored back to us by them and this seems very, very fresh. However, yet again, the newness of it is in only relative because that immediately reminds me of the way in which James Rosenquist, in the 1960s, was using images from advertising billboards, and Lichtenstein and Warhol suddenly forced us to re-think images from daily newspapers. So it's an old story in the history of art; this is just the latest chapter in it.

– *Baudrillard has described the influence of consumer signs and mass-media images in terms of 'this new hyperreality', a phenomenon that Donald Kuspit sees as distinguishing and defining the American culture. Can you comment on this?*

Well I think certainly the experience of facsimiles, of being bombarded by replicas of everything, the sheer abundance of commercial

the end they have no effect.

– *Do you think this is because the artists you mention are operating from within the commercial market and have become successful and acceptable within that context?*

Well that's certainly part of it. The fact of the matter is that the collectors will instantly buy, and the dealers will immediately show whatever's supposed to be offensive or counter-establishment and the swiftness with which such art is now accepted as art is absolutely dumbfounding. I rather think that if Picasso's *Guernica* was exhibited for the first time today, it would immediately be thought of only as a work of art and not as a political painting. But what's happening in fact has always happened, for even *Guernica* which had such a strong message, very quickly became just another painting by Picasso of 1937. I don't believe that art can save lives or change people's politics and attitudes. But I don't deny artists the right to feel that they can change the world.

– *So you do not believe that artists can really communicate to a mass audience?*

I think that statistically artists have communicated to a mass audience. And certainly if by communication you mean that more and more people know their names and look at their work, there can be no doubt

Leon Golub, *Prisoners I,* 1985, acrylic, 304.8x434.3cm

that the audience today is much larger than it has ever been in the history of art, but I don't know whether this communication is effective.

– Do you see the many interviews, writings and statements by artists as a means of communicating their ideas to a larger audience?

Well to be honest I think it's not so much part of communicating, it's just part of the whole commercial network. The interviews with artists, not to put down the seriousness of what the artists say, are really another form of advertising. The truth of the matter is that very few people read them, in fact few people read most of the art texts which are being published in large quantities today. So I think that statements are just another form of publicity and of course interviews are just like taking out a couple of two or three page ads which you see again and again and that's part of their message.

– Do you think there is a problem in reconciling the many critical and theoretical interpretations surrounding new art with the writings and statements of the artists themselves?

I think this has always been the case; for instance at the time of the Abstract Expressionists there were endless speculations about the parallels with Existentialism.That is just one example. The whole history of the response to Cubism in the early 20th century has been riddled with quasi-philosophical explanations, not to mention Einsteinian physics and so on, and this has generally tended to blow a lot of foggy air around the art. So there are things said about all kinds of art that the artists themselves may not even understand, but the situation itself is not new and it usually evaporates, leaving the art behind.

– In the catalogue text to A Forest of Signs *the curators stated their aim as being to show 'history in the making' , 'history not yet fully written'. Do you think there is a growing tendency among contemporary art museums to play a more active role in defining and promoting new art?*

Yes I think so and I am very grateful for the experience of having seen *A Forest of Signs.* I am New York based and the story here is that it is usually assumed that because we have all the galleries we don't need the museums to make anthologies for us and to tell us what is going on. But if you have a wise curator, as in the case of *A Forest of Signs,* then she can pull things together and make order out of the confusion of the contemporary and perceive patterns of similar artists while the patterns are being established.

– How important are alternative artists' spaces in promoting and defining new art?

My own guess is that they are not very important. Whether we like it or not, the huge glut of art today really means that you only have time to pay attention to what you hear most about, and what you hear most about is effectively what is being publicised. I think the idea of alternative spaces is an idealistic situation but in reality it is one that doesn't work. You have to make your choice from just a handful of galleries and they tend to be the famous and international galleries.

– *Victor Burgin has said that 'the job for the artist is to dismantle existing communication codes and to recombine some of their elements into structures which can be used to generate new pictures of the world'. Do you think that the use of photography combined with written text in Burgin's art, and the work of other artists including Richard Prince and Thomas Lawson, is succeeding in generating 'new pictures of the world'?*

Yes. I think it's a story that begins with Rauschenberg and Warhol in the late 50s and early 60s. They were really the first artists to use photography in high art, in paintings and constructions, and these artists are new variations on that theme. The problem was how to re-introduce images from the real world into the ivory tower of painting. People like Rauschenberg and Warhol realised that the contemporary way to do it was to use the kinds of images that were being used in the media and were being reflected in photographs, so that their mixture of photography and non-photography, painting and sculpture, is really critical in artists like Victor Burgin, Thomas Lawson and Richard Prince. They're really modern variations on Warhol's use of photography. What I do find very bewildering is how to distinguish between photography as photography and non-photography, paintings and sculpture. It's a very strange distinction and one that is becoming less and less clear, but this hybrid form is one that has become more common to our experience. It's typical that the work of Cindy Sherman is not in the domain of modern painting and is equally not in the domain of photography. It is in the domain of, I hesitate to say it, high art – it's such a broad term. It's very funny that we're uncertain in distinguishing between the two territories, it's disconcerting that this has happened. I remember at the *History of Photography* exhibition at the Royal Academy in London, it was to my pleasure and surprise that Andy Warhol and Christian Boltanski were included and I suddenly realised that, although I had never thought about them as being in the history of photography, they were really quite relevant to the history of another kind of art. So the confusion or fusion now is at a maximum.

– *Would you categorise the work of the Starn Twins, who fragment and transform the photographic medium, in terms of art rather than photography?*

It is true that the audience for the Starn Twins seems to be more and more an art audience rather than a photography audience. In fact they have been recently been doing things with photographs of paintings by Picasso so that they are now trespassing on the territory of artists who did art about art. In the same category, Gilbert & George always seem to have that art constituency but in fact they could just as easily be fixed in the history of photography. The boundaries are very ambiguous.

– *David Salle has recently exhibited his new paintings at Waddington Galleries in London. Do you think his art has changed in any way, and where would you place him in the context of new art?*

My impression from his last show in New York is that he hasn't changed in any significant way, although perhaps he has changed in terms of his theatre sets of which I have only seen photographs. But my sense of him now is that he's a kind of old master. That sounds strange with such a short career, but he has had a big show at the Whitney already and he is a perfect example of how the new is no longer new. There is no question that he belongs to an older generation of establishment figures.

– *Would you put Julian Schnabel into the same category?*

Exactly. One looks back to them as one looks back to figurative artists. It's a funny phenomenon although they have been around for quite a while, practically a decade. I sometimes think we consider the tempo of art is so rapid now but one realises, as we just did here in New York with the Cubist Show at the MoMA, that what we're looking at is only seven years of work by Picasso and Braque between 1907 and 1914. By the end of seven years the whole thing looked museum-worthy and everything looked quite different directly afterwards. The tempo change has always been more rapid than you would think. When you experience it of course it seems much faster, but in retrospect things have always been fast. In terms of their careers, Seurat only lived for a decade and the same is true of Van Gogh, but they changed everything. The next decade everything was very different. So I don't think the tempo now is quite as rapid as it seems.

– *Donald Kuspit has contrasted the sensibilities of American and European artists, arguing that in Europe the orientation tends much more towards memory, and that the emphasis is not on the new, it's not on the future, but is much more concerned with coming to terms with the past. Would you agree?*

It's certainly true of many German artists, and I know that Donald Kuspit has been particularly prolific in writing on the contemporary German situation. The history of retrospection, both political and aesthetic, is certainly much stronger in Germany than it is here. On the other hand I also think that the look of many new artists here, from Barbara Kruger and Haim Steinbach to Jeff Koons is also, to a certain extent, a question of looking back because much of this can be thought of as a kind of recycling of the 60s and the whole American tradition of embracing the modern. Every situation has its retrospective character and this does as well. But clearly the situation in Germany is concerned with memory and that's probably true in Italy as well.

– *In Germany, the influence of Beuys on younger artists seems to be as great as that of Warhol in America.*

I think it's amazing, although it may just be a false polarity, but both Warhol and Beuys have been set up as major father-figures. Every young artist in America looks back with some veneration to Warhol, and in Germany the same can be said for Beuys.

– *Do you think it is important for artists to confront international issues? Would you describe Jeff Koons' work for example as being international?*

I think it's international in the sense that the audience for that artist's work is global but that doesn't mean that the character of his work is *esperanto*. I think it's just a phenomenon of the airport vision of art exhibitions that take place all over the world. I think good artists tend to be international in that their work is seen all over the world. But I think that the concept of being an international artist in terms of having no national inflection is unfounded, I can't think of an artist who can be seen in those terms. It is possible that art will eventually become international due to the fact that people can travel so much and that art travels so much and the very clear distinctions between traditions have blurred. Nevertheless it strikes me that Jeff Koons, like Barbara Kruger or Jenny Holzer, is very American. I can't imagine their work being made by anybody outside New York, nor can I imagine Gilbert & George being anywhere other than London; likewise Kiefer couldn't be anything but German. I don't see artists as being internationalised except in terms of commerce.

---
*

Bertrand Lavier, *Mirior No 7*, 1989, acrylic, gold paint and glass, 138.5x77cm

GERMANO CELANT
UNEXPRESSIONISM
Art Beyond the Contemporary

Gretchen Bender, *Untitled*, 1989,Type-C print

Coming to terms with the accelerated history of an artworld obsessed with the new, Celant recognises the difficulty in attempting to articulate or define the present. Perceiving the significance of the negative, the anonymous, and the lack of 'originality' in new art, he evolved the term 'Unexpressionism'. In this extract from his text, he expands his theory, establishing a definition for 32 new artists.

Unexpressionism is not devoted to the contemporary, it does not believe in its ritual simplifications. Rather, it is so profane and sceptical that it sets out on the road of non-being. It prefers interfering with the cold and empty condition of currency, wherever the horizon of 'new' experience and its originality has descended. Conscious that today originality serves as a promotional element yet does nothing but keep reiterating the same aspect;[1] Unexpressionism is not interested in opposing knowledge with inspiration and invention. Instead, it moves through the field of appearance and its application. It draws attention to the fraudulence of languages, including that of art. It does not perform, it strips itself naked. It flaunts its paradoxes between entities of meaning and meaninglessness. It presents itself virtually 'all at once' without legitimising any conclusion. It enunciates the substances of the contemporary, but does not wish to justify or judge them, much less indicate which lines to follow. It is thought of not as a solution, but as a 'symptom' with an absence of traumatising use and debasement of language, and with a serene and almost neutral recourse to what exists.

The Unexpressionist totalities investigate the forms of arguments applied in all fields of seeing and constructing. They work on and with the media, as languages that have no subject because they are applied to all subjects. They reveal their artifices and techniques of persuasion, they verify their universality and autonomy. Hence they work upon the rhetoric of advertising, photography, movies, architecture, and design in order to examine their figures and genres and make their eloquence obvious. However, the assemblages are not functional, not goal-oriented; they are emblems of an elaboration aimed at exposing the workings of systems which adulterate and counterfeit the image.

They draw strength from the failure of quotationalism to create the new, and they lucidly analyse the reasons that have produced the dead centre, where, for the crisis of invention, verisimilitude and verity, copy and original are one and the same. In these terms, they try to establish an anti-rhetorical attitude. Thus, if Neo-Expressionist painting is based on the mannerist excesses of the image, Unexpressionist art studies the cold and geometric arrangement and assembly of things and apparatuses without dissimulating technological artifice; it seeks the meaning of the communication technologies such as advertising and photographic reproduction, which are available for any use whatsoever and utilisable for any goal whatsoever. In this sense, Unexpressionism looks at the Baroque, its cold marble forms, which become alive and palpitating ***Jeff Koons** lucid and rigid masses, in which rhetoric or the art of persuasion makes them passionate and impassioned, elegant and graceful. The intent is to show the 'exercises of ingenuity' contained in the 'neutral' images,[2] whose simulated and theatrical appearance is not accidental, but constructed in terms of mechanisms and technologies.

Devotion to and mannerist deformations of the sacred image of Art and the Contemporary are replaced by a non-subjective presentation and an overall situation that evince the theatrical and cinematic character of the present. **Marco Bagnoli** In other words: by juxtaposing and constructing artificial images, the Unexpressionist artists reconnect the contemporary to theatre and cinema, offering art as a 'stage' practice in order to define it as a hypersensitive instrument of persuasion. Their inventions on paper and film, on canvas and the screen, in the environment and with things, make the artificial speak in the artificial, the image in the image, and the reproduced in the reproduction. Their works are a representation of twofold fiction and construction: they exploit the typically Baroque idea that life and the present are nothing but spectacle and simulation.

We must also point out that if an artwork uses the show-business media and rhetorical effects, resorting to billboards or neon signs that can display the processes of persuasion and invention applied to planning visual communication, this artistic attitude revives discourse and criticism. It speaks about images and its technologies, about its laws of mimesis and artifice; it distinguishes those images, and in this case it seems to go back to the conceptual assumption, although developing it by using the image against the image. Unexpressionism adopts a practical – rather than a discursive or written – demonstration for figures and objects, spaces and contexts. It does not resort to logical models or abstract philosophical arguments. Instead, it makes abundant use of small models and stage-sets, **Juan Muñoz** plans and designs, substituting the practical image for speech, while pursuing a commentary on the means of communication.

For Unexpressionism, being a 'conceptual Baroque' signifies critique and parody, a displacement and a construction/deconstruction of economy and information, consumption and ideology of the languages of the public and the mass media. It assumes a judgement on their functioning and their foundations, squandering them, that is, making excessive and over-abundant use of their materials and technologies. Indeed, the overall Unexpressionist approach is excessiveness. It stages things and figures that are located at the centre of the environment, enunciating a spatial geometry, in which art is no longer a tapestry, but an architecture, a real place, based on the pleasure of building and constructing.

The preparations and elaborations of the Unexpressionists are limitless proliferations; they play non-stop with the object or the lost image – a sensual and artificial game that has no aim other than waste and squandering, visual luxury for the sake of pleasure. Hence, they go back to smooth bodies, covered with industrial glazes and plastic **Jan Vercruysse** laminates, dazzling opaque materials, refined surfaces and textures, meticulous and chiselled craftsmanship, almost as if produced by a goldsmith or designer, engraver or conjuror, in order to 'define' a smooth and sparkling world, polished and marmoreal, like our everyday life.

By means of the play of balance and imbalance, the grafting and multiplying of thingly bodies, whether heavy or light, the Unexpressionist totalities are translated into constellations of clouds and stars, moons and rainbows that rotate at unequal speeds. They rise and fall, **Niek Kemps** they intertwine playful and voluptuous movements, negating their rigid reality.

These cosmologies trace the possible co-ordinates and potential laws that rule the contemporary. They are understood as ensembles of values and representations, of models and behaviour at a given moment of society. They are totalising visions of the present, syntheses in which every aspect is integrated in an articulate and structured system.

Gerhard Merz, *Untitled* (from *Io Son Architetto*), 1988, pigment, linen, 40x14cm

Günther Förg, *Untitled*, 1988, bronze, 270x80x40cm

From this perspective, they hope to trace the censorial and psycho-visual determinations of the relationship between the historical and artificial conditions of existence and the communicational plan. This is an attempt at prefiguring **Matt Mullican** the transmission of signs and emblems, their solidification in the collective subconscious.

We find here iconographic elements belonging both to memories and new icons, products of the most advanced sciences and technologies. In some cases, the choice of 'figures' is an attempt at finding a code and an order that regulates the identity of experience in an osmosis to the social language. They focus on the surfaces, the archetypes of male and female, of the industrial and the political, in which the electronic and mass-media tribal culture is identified. We are absorbed into its vortex and suspended in the aleatoriness and transience of the signs of indefinite existence, in order to discover a more definite existence. Hierophancies and primary events are projected, baring the force of collective persuasion that governs the artificial and simulated dream of repetitions and reproductions. They are made to meet and dance together, **Ange Leccia** they mobilise in order to form a block that, seizing the daily utensils consumed by the wear and tear of habit, restores them as stratifications of beliefs and illusions.

The spell exerted by figurations and metamorphoses based on the analogy or contrast of images serves to introduce, through the pleasure of combinations and associations and sometimes even jokes, the subject of analysis concerning the linguistic process of art. By crisscrossing **Joseph Kosuth** or superimposing kindred or antithetical images, whose acme and element of intensity derive from *a priori* dynamics, such as the play on words or the customary vision, consensus, and unconscious absurdity, artists attack the unambiguousness and pretentiousness of art. A challenge that should remove the creative inhibitions, so that the art of imagination and the art without imagination can co-exist and enter into a dialectical relationship.[3]

The proof that one can create without inventing the new and without a laborious expenditure of energy, suffering, and precious materials, can offer amusement and pleasure, liberating the artistic process from its weighty romantic and idealistic impediments. Art becomes truly lighter, but the adjective 'light' does not mean 'weak' or 'weightless', it means 'airy' and 'mobile', **Rebecca Horn** in the sense of an overflowing into unexpected, unforeseen territories.

However, in order to liberate himself, the artist has to be *inside* the image, not in front of it. He has to travel through its interior and understand its mechanics and mechanisms of transportation and transmission. He must therefore live in the transparency between fullness and reflection, float in the vacuum of light that fixes figures and scenes. Operating in this continuum, which is made up of mediated vectors, such as photography and cinema, one can verify the brief journey of private and public images. One can make evident the service of the human being, male and female, with respect to the impulses of cinematic and TV literature.

Unexpressionism tends to reveal the absolute absurdity of 'existing for' **Barbara Kruger** the image, and it tries to destroy its commodification logic, making the sublime parody of stereotypes. For these artists, living the experience of 'special effects' and verifying their refractions on themselves constitutes a fantastic tour in the retransmitted infinity of images relativised by television and illustrated magazines. This is a tourism without territories, formed by luminosity and immateriality, offering a profusion of unreal and artificial copies. On the transparent and imperceptible threshold of their contexts, we find the play of alternation between fiction and reality as well as between light and dark, public and private. The figures are offered as a

Robert Longo, *CX (Unknown)*, 1989, oil on cast aluminium, 61cm globe

'terminal' factor, on which imperceptible electronic impulses give shape to an ephemeral visual density; at the same time, the artworks are established as insensitive and impersonal transmitters of cinematic subjects and stories. The results are monuments to the immaterial and the invisible, **Jenny Holzer** whose writings and figures of light are intangible apparitions that mould spectral visions, like Las Vegas.

Thus, the Unexpressionistic automatons are offered as machines for transmission, communication, and telecommunication, which produce optical and visual effects having no depth of time or field. The screens and monitors are therefore new vanishing points with no perspective or history: the continuity of cinema and television transmits the images, but does not frame them in time or in the present. The dramas of the contemporary pass by and are forgotten.

The space of the imagination is submerged in a continuum whose tricks and deformations are constructed by technology. They are synthetic images, which the eyes cannot believe; they work towards concealing and they provide a shelter against the inclemencies and tragedies of history.

The process of experiencing 'special effects' and verifying their refractions upon themselves and upon the everyday context is a fantastic voyage through the system of the media. It is a tourism without territory, formed of luminosity and impalpability, and offering a profusion of unreal and artificial copies. It is a place of the phantoms of consumption, which pass **Annette Lemieux** through the screen and the monitor. It takes place in the 'good' parlour, which manages to comprehend such artistic figurations as soap operas, frames, and lamps. It is part of the 'style' of the house. However, it is in the urban anamorphism, whose perimeter is open to all transits of images and things,[4] that the neutral and anonymous behaviour of non-subjective actions, of systems of transmission and communication shows its 'wealth'. We are at the 'full void' of bodies and congealed things, whose reality is outside any definable order. Figures without identity or density, which, in their fullness, occupy the urban spaces and stretches. They are 'creatures' **Robert Longo** whose 'monstrosity' (they are always 'replications') serves to give form to the 'marvellous' and the 'surprising', which depend on the genesis of our civilisation, which, in turn, is based on the speed of retransmitting our appearance, inside and outside ourselves, as subjects and objects.

Reinhard Mucha, *The Underlying Problem with Figures in Baroque Architecture (For you alone only the grave remains)*, 1985, mixed media

The figures constructed by Unexpressionist artists, expressed by elements that travel through one another, recall the energetic and dynamic experience of the Futurist matrix, which lives by way of the urban magma. In these 'places', one experiences the ubiquity of spatial and cultural distances, as well as the removal of the physical dimension. Everything lives on a shattered perception, centred on the formlessness and instability of images, homologous to the flat, empty reflection of their swift whisking, without content, across the TV screen and electronic monitor.

The image is transparent. It leaves no trace or imprint. It travels in an instantaneous time. It is a quantity without space, but with a primitive force. It appears and disappears. But it generates a magic ritual indicating the cultural roots of a society. Consequently, in order to make that society visible, **Gretchen Bender** one has to fetishise it, enclose it in an armature or petrify it in the handwriting memorised by a computer.

The equivalence of formation and information promotes a utilisation of the media as instruments of continuous transit, and their advent on the screen of art makes the implausibility and unreality of its existential and naturalistic stratifications defini-

tive. The media doubles have indeed been confirmed as a diffuse and generalised attempt at assassinating everything that is derived from the 'realist' situation. Operating with shadows, television, photography, and cinema have definitively transformed the projected and ephemeral double into an object. They have created crystallisations of human activities, of logos and nature; they have managed to sell any product. Thus, it comes as no surprise that after Claes Oldenburg, the generation of the 1980s has dedicated itself to objectalising the volatile images of consumption.

Nevertheless, the images are more and more frequently constructed by the transmission of data and figures on screens; and it is thanks to its high technology that the concept and experience of the 'surface' – whether visual or painterly have changed. The surface is turning into an evidence or an iridescent face, which reorganises itself inside the eyes. It has been transformed from a wall or solid and imperceptible plane into a technology for controlling the spectral portraits of the collective – money, death, food – and the individual. The overhaul of the surface as a perceptual continuum in motion magnifies not only the epidermis of the mass-media screens, but also the bark **Günther Förg**

Barbara Kruger, *Untitled* (*God sends the meat . . .*), 1988, photographic silkscreen/vinyl, 282x334cm

of objects and architecture. The wall environments and sculptural constructions, the skyscrapers and residential buildings, the galleries and museums can be taken as 'transmitters', on the surface of luminous spaces and events. They are screens that, like a frame or a film, absorb and consume images with their sensitive membranes. They continuously alter and convey data that can be retaken in colour or black and white. Their surface becomes appearance and a measure of sensitivity, and image-plane and a purely visual object.

Demonstrating that surfaces are luminous and informative 'faces' – a reminder of the Baroque – the Unexpressionists emphasise that the contemporary substance has gone beyond itself; that it has put its physical depth at zero, diminishing and emptying its interior. It is reduced to density by being projected externally, towards the space in front of it. Nevertheless, the awareness that even this surface is staged, has impelled them to act upon it and to control the luminous and chromatic sensations. This control, with a high technological and sensory value, **Ettore Spalletti** has fused points and lines, transforming tones and transparencies, so that the progressive emergence of images attains a sublime quality.

Obviously, they can exercise such a control by using the electronic typesetter, mixer, and scanner. Or else, in the manual field, by resorting to prodigious techniques like plaster and gilding, impasto and fresco – ancient crafts that are tied to representation. Both approaches carry the quality of materials and the capacity for simulation to the point of paroxysm. Colours, strokes, textures, forms are generated by artifice and, without expressing any creative furore, they communicate to the public the softness of steel hair, the colour of plaster flesh, or the brightness of objects in laminated plastic. They transform marble into a veil shaken by the wind or the composition of luminous points into amorously embracing bodies. What counts is the miracle of manual craft or the naturalness of the technological image, as formed by Jannis Kounellis or Nam June Paik.

The alignment of surfaces or points in space produces something exact and perfect. For this, art and the technological methods are once again 'sciences of measurement' and of visual intelligibility. Whether using static vectors, such as paintings, sculptures, or photographs, or dynamic vectors such as monitors and projectors, these are all systems of 'illumination' – to employ a favourite term of Walter Benjamin's. They materialise

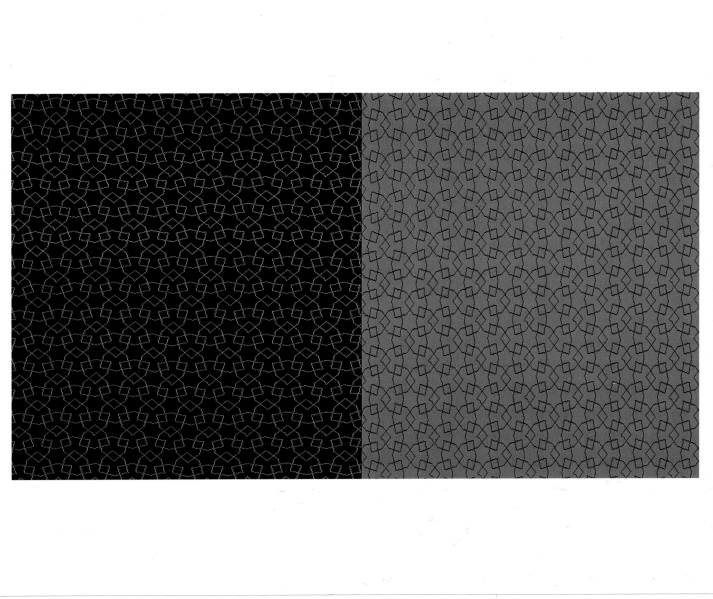

Rosemarie Trockel, *Untitled*, 1988, knitted wool, 160x320cm

a practice that is on non-subjective trial for scientific diagnoses; or at least, it works according to a non-aleatory and personal perspective-based, however, on a measuring process that is ciphered and numerical, synthetic and optometric. The light ray is the maximum reference; for this reason, lending dimension to an object or a figure, a lip or a column, a totem or a robot, means sublimating it with fine light, reducing it to an optical illusion, in which space and time, environment and architecture are confused in a sort of Empyrean of visuality and energy. Confusing near and far, surface and volume, they pass through appearances to their maximum immateriality and transparency. They abolish distances in order to knock consciousness out of whack, to produce an effect of suspension on the present.

The surface 'consistency' of objects and images is thus examined in order to pinpoint other unexpressive and Unexpressionist features. Above all, it is chosen for its compactness and uniformity. It is a sheet of crystal or a film polished and shining like a mirror. Its goal, no doubt, is a continuum, a total space, assuring a support for all reflections, and proving the density of its existence. Basically, it tends to give the impression of being homogeneous, while revealing its warp and warf, its typographi-

cal dots, its artificiality and porosity. It does not present soft, supple sides, it is not flaccid or pasty. Rather, it is a hard fluid made up of glassy and synthetic materials, it is a thick, lucid film. It tends to create the effect of an industrial object, which conquers space and metamorphoses every element with its lava. Beyond the environment, it recovers the human figures, whose sensuality congeals in Unexpressionist works, becoming a mask of ice. It evokes a cadaverous monstrosity of death that is instantaneous or 'in a snapshot'. The splendid skin **Cindy Sherman** of male or female faces passes into the beauty of a corpse, and food loses its delight and freshness, offering itself as a putrid magma. In either case, it is always the eyes that are attacked; the images are chemical processes for transforming eyesight, makeup is food for the eyes.

Between the modalities of appearance, the surfaces of the Unexpressionists summon the reflecting materials, for which illumination makes objects almost mirror-like and radiant. The objects become totalities reflecting at a high density, and they fascinate us with the seductiveness and vivification of bright and painted forms. In the reflecting object, depth is wiped out and only the light message is repeated. It becomes a flat camera,

Annette Lemieux, *Initial Sounds*, 1989, latex, acrylic, 274.3x213.4x3.8cm

capable of a flat reply: a surface of lights and shadows, on which a reflection, rather than being fixed, glides over the cold and compact body.

With its reflection and its radiation of light, the Unexpressionist's object reflects its aura upon the environment and the surrounding architecture. It establishes a journey – we are always dealing with the rapid transit of images – that radiates out, touching the external. The reflection can come with artificial light as well as the light of natural colours, **Remo Salvadori** which wraps up instruments and furnishings, paintings and sculptures, studios and galleries in a translucent sheath. For the Unexpressionists, the process of colouring is developed on fullness. More than suggesting a third dimension, more than being an irregular materiality of lumps and oils, powders and pigments, their colour is generally mechanical, reflecting the vitality of printed colours. This process is neither natural nor organic, it translates a transmission of chromatic information. It is a red, a yellow, an ochre, a black, a green, a false gold – from the printer's book of colour samples. It is the essence of colour, with no history or emotions – so much so that it can give life to things. It connects with figures and objects, **Allan McCollum** forming and composing them. It is a minimal discharge. It claims an autonomous dimension of the language of advertising and television. It implies reproduction, dislocation, and being *en route* without claiming any link to any one image over another. It conveys a notion of 'travelling through'. It superficially dresses things in light and seems to incorporate things by virtue of its crude and dense luminescence. Its visual charge does not separate from a weightiness and a certain gravity that exclude every internal fermentation and levitation; yet it liquefies and anchors things to the ground. Colour is not content to promote a visual modification of objects and surfaces; it turns forms upside down, triggering their maturation as full entities. By ripening them, it swells their smooth epidermis, and this stage indicates a previous stage in the succession of routes.

Thus, the theme of transit and crossing is frequent in the Unexpressionists, and they evoke it with such subjects as the station, the monitor, the subway, the page, the billboard, and the supermarket counter. These are places of acceleration and deceleration in which the everyday continuum is measured as are its changes and interruptions. They configure time and the halting of images, which run at an intense speed.

These are dynamic exhibition galleries, in which the signs glide by at a steady rhythm, devoid of ground supports. Actual jet engines hurl all sorts of things into the void: particles of light and sound, virtual images of synthetic communication. Yet we must remember that the terminal of these systems is the human body. The reader or viewer, that is, the personnel assigned to transmitting and receiving, has eyes filled with data and information. These eyes are a territory covered with communicational reflections, clad in marks and electronic impulses. Thus, the texture covering the body is a further transit space for the distinctive signs of industry, advertising, and television. It is swaddled **Rosemarie Trockel** in colours and logos, acquiring the screen traversed by the evidences and appearances of the contemporary. The era of nudity is over and done with: the surfaces of bodies are semblances and fashion masks, as well as monitors and means of circulation they are covered with stitches or fabrics, but such outer trappings convey figurations and industrial insignia, in the latest fashion. To conclude: Unexpressionism moves simultaneously with the swift propagation of the notions and fissions of the contemporary; it is triggered by an accelerating escalation, in which particles and photons, electrical and electronic impulses occupy the 'non-place' of mass vision. Unexpressionism tries to refer to the hypersensitive field of advertising and telecommunications and it confronts its limits and its degree of velocity. Co-existing with its endless presence, Unexpressionism begins to sense that art now risks losing its central role and becoming an uncertain and decentralised joint and screen displaying images of discarded and recycled things. In order to flee an uncontrolled and overwhelming vertigo, Unexpressionist art introjects the essential ties to these systems of appearance and artifice. It uses them to camouflage itself and it assumes the role of critical and deconstructive interpretation. It declares itself available to mediated behaviour and to the unexpressive mentality in order to seek its autonomy in the planetary system of artefacts and manufactured products. It emancipates itself not in the original, but in the copy of the copy, **Richard Prince** in the reproduction of the reproduction, in the simulacrum of the simulacrum, in order to keep pace with communicational repetitivity. And in order to achieve this result, Unexpressionism adjusts to becoming a sophisticated and precise technology, alert to its mode of artificial production. It calculates its projectivity and its geometric and volumetric routes. It no longer relies on accident and spontaneity; instead, it banks on the sciences and technologies. Having to operate in a space and time 'without dimension', because it is propagated and multiplied by electronic means that fuse and confuse, create and recreate figures and objects at an uncontrollable rhythm, Unexpressionism no longer operates on contemporary time; rather, it seeks to transfer its production 'beyond time' and 'beyond space'. This 'producing beyond' has nothing in common with the communicational present, in which high and low, first and last, past and future, back and front exist. It has more in common with the ultrasonic speed that passes into the ether, confusing temporal chronologies and spatial topologies. It goes beyond the present and the past, beyond the contemporary and the future. This 'beyond' is not metaphysical; it is physical on the microscopic scale of the nuclear and the photonic. We can therefore be at the ultimate vigil and vigilance of art, when the contemporary vanishes into the infinitesimal in order to continue to manage the depth and complexity of images, whose transmission will be momentary, whose representation will be precarious and whose passage will be very brief. Nevertheless, a lost condition will not help to find another one, equivalent to the wave length of contemporary vision beyond the contemporary.

Notes

* The insertion of artists' names into my text is not tied to an interpretation or description of their work, even if it opens up correspondences between ideas and images that strike me as interesting. These insertions are a way of leaving the dialectics between the parts open, interweaving them, interrelating them, without forcing them to illustrate one another. The territories run parallel, but they look at one another and, as in the book, they reflect one another.

1 Marc Jemenez, *Adorno: Art, Idéologie et Théorie de l'Art*, Bourgois, Paris, 1973, p75.

2 Severo Sarduy, *Barocco*, Editions du Seuil, Paris, 1975.

3 Giulio Carlo Argan, *Immagine e Persuasione*, Feltrinelli, Milan, 1985, p108.

4 Paul Virilio, *L'Espace Critique*, Bourgois, Paris, 1984.

Barbara Bloom, *Confession to Godard*, 1987, mixed media installation

LISA PHILLIPS
IMAGE WORLD: ART AND MEDIA CULTURE

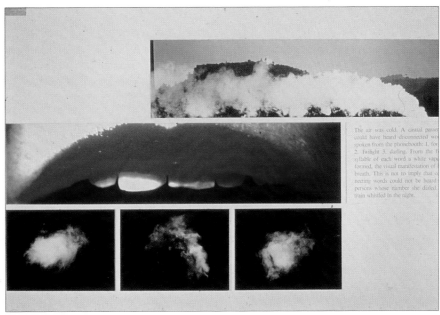

William Beckley, *Deirdre's Lip*, 1979, cibachrome print, 249x406.4cm

'Everything is destined to reappear as simulation. Landscapes as photography, women as the sexual scenario, thoughts as writing, terrorism as fashion and the media, events as television. Things seem only to exist by virtue of this strange destiny. You wonder whether the world itself isn't just here to serve as advertising copy in some other world.' **Jean Baudrillard, America, 1988**

Mass reproduction of the image and its dissemination through the media has changed the nature of contemporary life. In a century that has seen the intrusion of saturation advertising, glossy magazines, movie spectaculars, and TV, our collective sense of reality owes as much to the media as it does to the direct observation of events and natural phenomena. The media has also changed the nature of modern art. As image makers, artists have had to confront the fact that this new visual mass communication system has in some way surpassed art's power to communicate. Over the past 30 years, they have come to terms with the mass media's increasing authority and dominance through a variety of responses – from celebration to critique, analysis to activism, commentary to intervention. The ascendancy of this new visual order has raised a host of critical issues that many artists have felt obliged to confront: Who controls the manufacture of images? Who is being addressed? What are the media's strategies of seduction? Has the media collapsed time and history into a succession of instants? What are the effects of image overload, fragmentation, repetition, standardisation, dislocation? Is the photograph still a carrier of factuality? Where is the site of the real? Is understanding 'reality' a function of representation? All of these questions have directed attention away from aesthetics to the nature of representation itself as the principal problem of our age. Since much of experience is mediated by images, the issue of how meaning is constructed through them has become central. Artists have also had to recognise that as our relationship to the visual world has changed so has the role we assign to art. This awareness has precipitated nothing less than a complete transformation of the function of art and the conventional guideposts used to define it.

In the 1970s, a new generation was coming of age. Many of these young artists were working in the studios of the California Institute of the Arts, founded in 1961 by Walt Disney.[1] This was a TV, rock-and-roll generation, bred on popular culture, and it took images very seriously. They were media literate, both addicted to and aware of the media's agendas of celebrity making, violence-mongering, and sensationalism.

These artists had been trained to question critically their relationship to social institutions. But, unlike their predecessors and more like Pop artists, many became increasingly cynical about the real possibility of maintaining an oppositional position toward these institutions. What made it difficult was art's increasing public acceptance and absorption into the mainstream of American life. Artists who attempted to make anti-object art that would resist commodification found it necessary to seek some kind of institutional support from museums and alternative spaces in order to have an audience (and often their works were reclaimed by the market). No matter how artists tried, it proved almost impossible to resist institutional forces. The avant-garde tradition as it had always been known came to an end. The only way for artists to engage it was as an image, a representation.[2]

The conceptual point of convergence for the emerging generation of artists was the recognition that there can be no reality outside representation, since we can only know about things through the forms that articulate them. According to Douglas Crimp, who introduced some of these artists in the landmark *Pictures* exhibition at Artists Space in 1977: 'To an ever greater extent our experience is governed by pictures, pictures in newspapers and magazines, on television and in the cinema. Next to these pictures firsthand experience begins to retreat, to seem more and more trivial. While it once seemed that pictures had the function of interpreting reality, it now seems that they have usurped it. It therefore becomes imperative to understand the picture itself, not in order to uncover a lost reality but to determine how a picture becomes a signifying structure of its own accord.'[3] Pictures, once signs of the real, had been transformed into real objects by TV, advertising, photography and the cinema.[4]

The premise that representation constructs reality has direct implications for theories of subjectivity. It means that gender roles and identity can be seen as the 'effects' of representation.[5] This became a natural line of inquiry, particularly for artists involved with feminist issues. In a group of early collages, Sherrie Levine extracted images of female models from fashion spreads and advertisements and used them as the 'background' material for silhouette portraits of George Washington and Abraham Lincoln. These mass-media depictions of women are literally inscribed and contained within the broader symbolic realm of mythological heroes and great male leaders. In her *Untitled Film Stills* (1977-80), Cindy Sherman takes active control of her own image as she directs herself acting out a series of canned film stereotypes for the camera. She inverts the logic of commodification by exposing self-expression as a limitless replication of existing models (in this case, models defined by masculine desire). In another serial work from the late 1970s, Sarah Charlesworth photocopied the front pages of the *International Herald Tribune* for one month and then blocked out the texts, so that only the masthead, layout, and photo reproductions remained. The sequence of images as well as their sizes and relationship to each other on the page create a new story. The altered pages at first seem to reveal nonsensical, Surrealistic conjunctions of images. But seen as an aggregate they show how the news is presented, who and what is deemed important, and the astonishing paucity of female representation. Deprived of its textual content, the autonomous system of the newspaper page becomes apparent.

Not only do found materials and their re-framing show how social reality and representation 'subject' us, but the process again raises the issues of uniqueness, authorship, and originality, which had always been the defining characteristics of art and greatness. Like the myth of individual creativity, the original and the unique were now seen to be effects of a social fiction of mastery, control, and empowerment. This fiction is made patently manifest in the rephotography of Richard Prince and Sherrie Levine, for instance, where found reproductions were re-presented with little alteration. Only the image's context was changed – but that was enough to make its social codes and their peculiar unreality apparent.

By the end of the 1970s, it was increasingly clear that the deconstructive method had become dry and pedantic. American artists' direct experience of the media's special effects, their awareness of how the media affects our lives, set them off on a fantastic voyage through the media system – its unreality, artifice, immateriality, and replication. Art entered the spectacu-

lar realm, further exploiting the very strategies that made the media so powerful. The works grew dramatically in scale, the surfaces became glossier and more colourful, the imagery more grandiose, and the compositions more graphically arresting. Aesthetics re-entered the art discourse, but with the revised notion of beauty – alienated and weird – offered by the media's spellbinding seductions. The younger generation, at home with this familiar language, nevertheless approached it with a mixture of love and hatred, respect and fear, dependence and resentment.

Pictures of ambivalent and alienated desires emerged. Robert Longo's *Men in the Cities* series (1979-82) is a good example. In these monumental, larger-than-life drawings, conceived by Longo but executed by a commercial illustrator, men and women strike poses that alternately allude to pleasure or pain. The aesthetic was similarly ambiguous in its relation to the media. Was it distanced and critical in its alienated imagery or was it complicit – simply mimicking the media's techniques?

What made the situation confusing was that some artists seemed to combine the crowd-pleasing strategies of entertainment with the spirit of critical investigation.[6] The new politicised style quickly attracted media attention and was offered as an innovative and stimulating commodity. Artists were enlisted as members of the 'research and development' team of commercial culture.[7] Not only was the 'look' of art adopted by commerce, but in the 80s the concept of the avant-garde itself was used as a marketing strategy, most often by concentrating on the artist as personality. Companies such as Cutty Sark, Rose's Lime Juice, Absolut Vodka, Amaretto, and The Gap have featured endorsements by artists ranging from Philip Glass to Ed Ruscha. Over the past few years, the art and entertainment press have repeatedly featured artists, critics, and curators in fashion and life-style spreads as the latest chic commodity. Some artists, however, were quick to discover a newfound power in this development and began to reclaim public spaces usually occupied by the media for their own political messages. Bus shelters (Dennis Adams), electronic signage (Jenny Holzer), flyposters (Barbara Kruger, the Guerrilla Girls), and advertising placards (Gran Fury) are just some of the sites that artists have invaded, interrupting the expected channels of information with compelling visuals and independent voices.

The fame and success artists have acquired in the last decade have presented a dilemma. After analysing and commenting on signs borrowed from the media, they now must encounter their own media image and consider the role they play in the construction of consent. Suddenly their position is unclear: are artists using media strategies in order to expose them or to expose themselves? Even when theoretical justification is vigorously offered, it is often quickly overshadowed by personal publicity and celebrity attention.

Jeff Koons is the hyperrealisation of the contradictions of our age. After selecting sentimental chatchkes, images, and collectibles from pop culture, Koons has them sumptuously executed by expert craftsmen in stainless steel, porcelain, or polychromed wood and enlarged to near human scale. These images of American juvenilia – from TV, film stills, advertisements, and rock music – are themselves the sculptural embodiment of cinematic spectacle. Added to the effect of the works is Koons' carefully conceived PR campaign for his public persona; he has taken control of his own image in the media, packaging himself through a series of elaborately staged, airbrushed 'advertisements' that feature the artist in a variety of situations. These situations – artist with buxom babes, artist at the head of the class, artist as animal trainer – successfully mock the ultraperfect world of advertising, where images of sex and power are used to dominate and control.

But no matter how sharply focused, such messages are far

from clear. One is left with a sense of unreality and incredulity; aware of how images are deployed by the media, we are still held captive by their force and entranced by their narcotic magic. Even if at times it seems that the artist's involvement with media images has become an institution - a new academy of sorts which, by definition, has played itself out - at other times it seems that this art is just at the beginning of an epic scenario. The seductions and manipulations of the media remain so persuasive and powerful that they must be addressed. And artists will continue to respond in unexpected ways.

Notes

This essay is reprinted from the catalogue for *Image World: Art and Media Culture*, held at the Whitney Museum of American Art from November 8, 1989 to February 18, 1990. This text has been excerpted and edited by Academy Editions.

1 Among the graduates were David Salle, Matt Mullican, Troy Brauntuch, Sherrie Levine, Allan McCollum, Jack Goldstein, Barbara Bloom, and Larry Johnson. John Baldessari, an original faculty member, taught for 18 years and was a guiding force at Cal Arts, along with Conceptualists Douglas Huebler and Michael Asher.
2 See Hal Foster, 'Between Modernism and the Media', in *Recodings: Art, Spectacle, Cultural Politics*, 1985, Bay Press, Port Townsend, Washington, p35.
3 Douglas Crimp, *Pictures*, exhibition catalogue, 1977, Artists Space, New York, p3.
4 This commingling of art and commerce spawned a new type of exhibition in the late 70s and early 80s - exhibitions that incorporated materials from the mass media (food packaging, anonymous photographs, commercial advertisements). *It's a Gender Show*, 1981, by the artists' collaborative Group Material, Barbara Kruger's *Pictures and Promises: A Display of Advertisings, Slogans and Interventions*, 1981, at the Kitchen, and exhibitions organised individually by Marvin Heiferman and Carol Squiers at PS 1 testified to the global penetration of the mass media and naturally drew critical fire from purists. See Carol Squiers, 'The Monopoly of Appearances', *Flash Art*, No 132, February-March 1987, pp98-100.
5 For further discussion, see Kate Linker, 'When a Rose Only Appears to Be a Rose: Feminism and Representation', *Implosion*, pp189-98.
6 See David Robbins, 'Art After Entertainment', *Art Issues*, No 2, February, 1989, pp8-13; No 3, April, 1989, pp17-20.
7 See Richard Bolton, 'Enlightened Self-Interest', *Afterimage*, 16, February, 1989, pp12-18.

Larry Johnson, *Untitled, (Hard to Believe)*, 1987, ektachrome print, 101.6x101.6cm

83

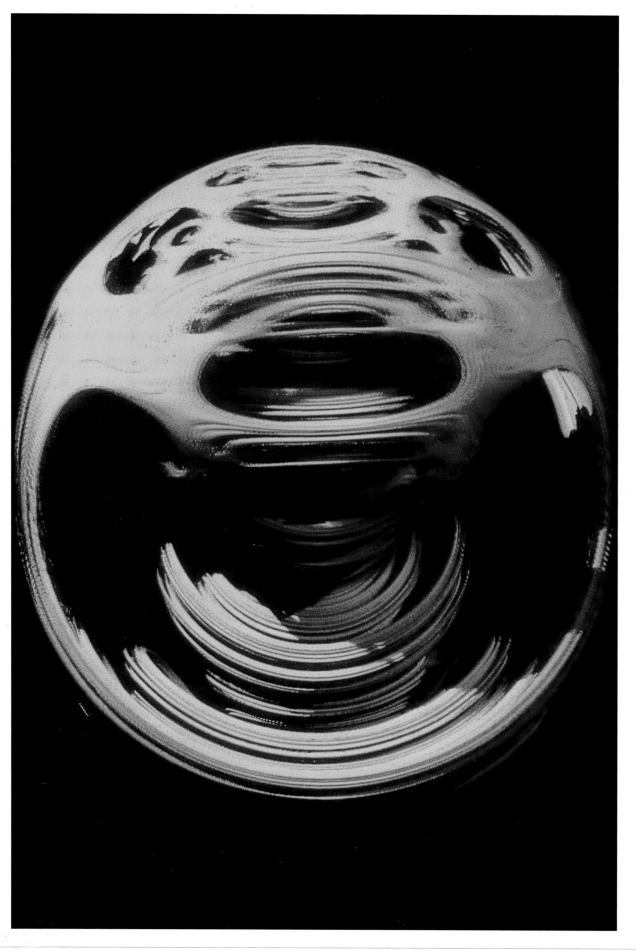

(Art)^n, *Chaos/Information as Ornamentation*, 1989

LAURA TRIPPI

THE STRANGE ATTRACTION OF CHAOS

The ideas embedded in the language and images of chaos science strike a familiar, strangely seductive chord. Like the shapes and figures of its 'fractal' geometry, our daily experience is fragmented, fraught with randomness and arbitrary juxtapositions. Patterns of perception and social practice are assaulted by an onrush of information. 'Reception', Walter Benjamin wrote as early as 1936, is 'in a state of distraction, which is increasingly noticeable in all fields of art and is symptomatic of profound changes in apperception . . . '[1] Under the pressure of new computer and video technologies, we seem to be undergoing a *quantum leap* in the state of distraction identified by Benjamin as a perceptual effect of the rise of film and photography. Leisure time, work, and art, our bodies and so also ourselves – all are absorbed into the breathing and buzzing surreality of simulation culture, global information networks and cybernetic machines.

'Chaos Science' is an umbrella term for two related and flourishing fields: fractal geometry and the study of complex dynamical systems. If its computer-generated video graphics, with their images of a randomised geometry and of systems in chaotic states, strike in us a sympathetic chord, perhaps it is because of our immersion in an atmosphere turbulent with new technologies. The guiding myths and models of modernity have been hopelessly infiltrated and frayed, and even the once invigorating concept of 'crisis' itself seems to have collapsed. This is a journey into space – the 'phase space' of turbulence and 'sensitive dependence'; of 'multi-dimensional degrees of freedom', of the decay, creation, and random fluctuation of information. In the allure of chaos science lies a search for the strangely *fractured* fairy tales of an emerging apperceptual and technological regime.

Border Skirmishes

Benoit Mandelbrot's compendium and guidebook, *The Fractal Geometry of Nature*, was published in 1983. In 1985, Goethe House, New York, sponsored the first exhibition of fractal graphics, produced by scientists and offered in unaltered photo-reproductions as art.[2] By the mid-80s, the shapes and formulas of fractal geometry had begun to appear in the work of practicing artists. But forces other than the discourse of science seem to have prepared the ground for the expropriation of its latest images and ideas.

A new branch of geometry, the study of fractals, breaks with the Euclidean tradition of idealised forms, relying instead on fragmentation and irregularity. With an infinite nesting of pattern within pattern, repeating across scales, fractal images open onto an area devoid of fixed co-ordinates. Because the mathematical operations that produce fractal 'landscapes' depend on the introduction of chance (random number generation), each repetition of a given pattern asserts a fractional difference from all others. The notion of boundary, too, is confounded. On closer look, the line dividing two regions reveals unexpected complexity. Instead of a clear line of demarcation, one finds an endless regress of detail: surfaces that give way on inspection to more surface, boundaries that never resolve.

As Post-Modernism, Post-Structuralism, multi-cultural questionings of the canon, feminism, post-linear historiography, and now even a post-Euclidean geometry, wreak havoc with received habits of thought and practice across a variety of fields, a picture of cultural rupture presents itself, patterned and pockmarked by the 'border skirmishes' of a boundary that refuses to resolve.[3] But forces other than those of discourse *either* in the sciences *or* in the arts would seem to have prepared the ground for such a cultural rift.

Figuring Phase Space

Complexity science is to time in the physical sciences as fractal geometry is to space: in the terms of Thomas Kuhn, a 'revolution', an exchange of operative paradigms.[4] With its concentration on the properties of fluid motion, it joins together fields whose common theme is the study of flows of information – weather patterns, population growth, epidemiology, prices on the international exchange, but also brain waves, the pumping action of the heart, stellar oscillations. All are *open*, *dissipative* systems, meaning that they take in energy from outside which leaves in the form of heat, and that they generate *entropy*, the measure of disorder that accumulates.

Like fractal geometry, complexity science relies on computer technology to produce its simulations of physical systems. *Phase space* plots the successive states (or phases) of a system in an abstract *multi-dimensional* space, with as many dimensions as a given system has *degrees of freedom* (heat, speed, viscosity, for example). A point in phase space represents the total state of the system at a particular point in time. With a dramatic increase in the value of the variable(s) driving the system, its course through phase space can suddenly leave the *limit cycle* (or *periodic orbit*) marked out by the system during a stable state. This phase transition marks the onset of turbulence, where prediction proves impossible. The turbulent system will never visit the same point in phase space twice, but traces an intricate path, careening through a region that gradually, surprisingly, begins to take shape. The system has found what is called its *strange attractor* and entered a chaotic regime.

Concentrating on phase transitions, the study of dynamical systems notes a more or less abrupt change of behaviour as some parameter – degree of freedom – reaches a critical value. Linear temporal flow is translated into a figural dimension. Wrapping infinite difference into a bounded region of phase space, the strange attractor twists and jumps and creases endlessly, not tending toward a final culmination. It could be said that if the system seems to *jolt* or *explode* from a periodic orbit into a chaotic regime, once it has reached the wider region that describes the limit of its strange attractor, it *implodes* as it 'settles onto' its new orbit, exhibiting an oddly compelling property of stable instability, predictable unpredictability, determinate indeterminacy: deterministic chaos.

By an alternate means of computer diagram, complexity science finds that this leap from a stable orbit to a chaotic regime leads through the scenario of *period doubling*: points of stability become unstable as the value of a given variable is raised, and split into two. At a critical juncture, the period-doubling reaches an extreme degree and gives way to the *bifurcation cascade*, the threshold that marks the onset of turbulence. 'Chaos is spontaneously generated, creating randomness from purely deterministic origins.'[5] In phase space, an elegant, filigreed structural stability emerges: the strange attractor. Bifurcation diagrams, however, give a different twist to the story. Once the system has entered a chaotic regime, windows of order arise spontaneously. In the midst of entropy, a self-ordering principle appears. The tendency of dissipative systems toward ever-increasing disorder is off-set by intermittent calls to order, emanating from *within* the very horizons of the chaotic.

Deterministic chaos offers a model of change for which our current vocabulary is conspicuously lacking: development, evolution, advancement, progress, even unfolding (though this seems to approach the idea), all carry with them the sense of a final cause toward which each intervening event tends. Other than these, we have digression, deviation, deflection, departures, swerves, and lapses – terms to which the French intellectual historian Michel Foucault looked for describing what, in the action of history, he called 'the singular randomness of events.'[6]

The Coming of Urgent Indeterminacy

If such ideas, presaged by Henri Poincaré's 1903 study, *The Three Body Problem in Celestial Mechanics*, announced a 'revolution' to science of the 60s, the notion of determinate indeterminacy was already informing compositional practice in the arts by the late 50s.[7] The work of John Cage, in particular, is exemplary in this regard. In his lecture on 'Indeterminacy' of 1958, the horizon of the aesthetic arena was characterised by a bewildering onslaught of demands, of information and new technologies, with a corresponding transformation of regular, measured time into a plastic, even spastic flow.[8] By now, the state of technology has drastically changed. In the place of Cage's almost quaint 'telephony', we have *telecommunications*, an ever-increasing yield of new and newer technologies: the portability and pervasiveness of video – camcorders and global MTV – but also computer networks, cash machines, call waiting, fibre optics, laser discs, world news tonight or at any time of day, memory chips and microelectronics, computerised checkout counters, the promised arrival of High Definition TV and the suddenly ubiquitous Fax, computerised trading on the international exchange. The number of cues and available options, to borrow Cage's only partly metaphoric model, has multiplied at an almost exponential rate. With this, time seems not so much to *flow forward* as to *eddy* and *swirl*, proceeding by jumpcuts and montage; backward into the future and forward into the past.

The highwater mark of process art came and went with the 70s. Traversing a dispersal of the aesthetic (in a move somewhat misleadingly dubbed 'dematerialisation'), artistic practice re-emerged in the 80s in an expanding field of market operations, a realm of investment, speculation, sometimes even *entertainment* pure and simple. What appeared in theory as a clean break with the modernist past, emerges in practice as a tangle of diverse operations, a dizzying array that confounds the sense of boundary, a fray of finely wrought 'transactions'.

No sooner had opposing streams of Neo-Expressionism and Picture Theory art been identified – each with a more-or-less programmatic logic of semantic flows and valences peculiarly its own – than a third tributary came into view.[9] While artists of the first group entrenched themselves in the fixed-point of an individualism already in actuality exhausted, those of the second have circled the grounds of art on a strategic night-watch of appropriation, arrayed against the reifying imperatives of practices of representation. The introduction of this third 'body' of artists, however, running the gamut from Neo-Geo to commodity art, from post-appropriation simulation to a quasi-conceptual (and yet emotionally charged) environmentalism, has worked to destabilise the entire system.

The trajectory of art history, proceeding in the past by way of incremental alternations between classic and baroque, abstraction and representation – a series, in short, of bifurcations – stepped up the tempo of its oscillations to the point where, in the 80s, alternation gave way to a kind of cascade of 'post' and 'neo' stylistic variations. On the shoals of a collapsing capacity for critical distance, the course of art has churned and scattered, passing into an arbitrary flux of formal and conceptual variations, of 'hyper-simulated critical forms' and 'hybrid neutralisations'.[10]

The discourse of Post-Modernism sets up within the aesthetic a situation of extreme urgency and indeterminacy. Now more than ever, as they say on TV, we would seem to feel the force of Cage's call for performers in the aesthetic *cum* cultural arena with 'a mind in one piece', 'alert to the situation, and responsible' (p39). Too sophisticated to invoke outmoded models (other than with the flourish of a high ironic style), profoundly sensitised to the complexities and uncertainties of current conditions in culture, artists, curators, and critics alike find their loyalties torn, divided between the paradigm of a critical practice past and the demands of an art world increasingly dominated by the market, with 'value' itself glorified and jeopardised by the new 'real estate' of art.

Chaotic Regimes

Economics borrows its notions of 'flow' from physics, and with that its mathematics, and from the beginning has been bound up with the development of complexity science. In a figurative aside from the main line of his argument in the article 'Strange Attractors', the mathematical physicist David Ruelle has offered a provocative picture of an economics informed by the science of chaos.[11] Driven by an exponential rise in the value of the *single* variable 'technological development', the economy in Ruelle's model undergoes a phase transition (p47). Periodic cycles grow unstable and split into two. The economy enters a chaotic regime. Wildly unpredictable locally – turbulent, discontinuous, *hysteretic* – it is globally 'stable' at the same time – a change in state that is also, irreversibly, a change in phase space shape.

Ruelle's 'metaphoric but . . . suggestive' model points to the idea that capitalism itself has changed shape, overflowing the boundaries between productive and reproductive or leisured space, overflowing the Euclidean geometries of a fixed system of social relations, subsuming the entirety of time to a logic of maximum circulation – in particular the almost instantaneous circulation of information (p47). 'Turbulent motion', writes Robert Shaw in *Strange Attractors, Chaotic Behaviour, and Information Flow*, is 'governed by information generated continuously out of the flow itself . . . preclud[ing] both predictability and reversibility.'[12] Following the line of argument developed by Eric Alliez and Michel Feher in their essay, 'The Luster of Capital', this transformation of capitalism stems in part from the social revolts of the 60s, and brings with it a renegotiation of the terms – the *narrative* terms – in which capitalism is conceived:

> [A]n economic crisis always appears as an abnormal situation inevitably leading to an after-crisis: either a 'healthy' capitalism or the advent of socialism . . . However, the current articulation of both a new regulatory mode of economic activity and of a new regime of capital accumulation . . . tends to turn this so-called 'crisis' into an ordinary, if not permanent state of affairs.[13]

What gathered and took shape in the guise of a crisis, promising to pass to a resolution, arrives instead as a *liquidation* of the very time-space of capitalist social relations. An apocalyptic model gives way to a new formation, setting the stage for a sea change in the climate of culture. Humans and machines become equivalent, 'assimilat[ed] . . . as cogwheels or relays in a vast machinic network for the productive circulation of information' (p316).

In *Chaos: Making a New Science*, James Gleick wrote of the effect of chaos science: 'One account of nature replaces another. Old problems are seen in a new light and other problems are recognised for the first time. Something takes place that resembles a whole industry retooling for a new production.'[14] Gleick's 'machinic' metaphor is striking, and its implications are at one and the same time exhilarating and frightening. In an essay contributed to the catalogue for the Goethe House exhibition, *Frontiers of Chaos*, Herbert Franke all but argued that the *cultural function* of the new science – of fractal graphics and phase space maps – is tutorial in subtle, cybernetic, and far-reaching ways:

> If we employ language as a means of communication, a linear medium arranged as a time-series, we automatically favour linear organising principles, eg causality or historical process. Visual languages allow us on the other hand to see those very important connections which manifest themselves as loop processes, interactions, communications networks, and so forth. Perhaps our inability to think in terms of networks is due in no small measure in our restriction to the descriptive system of verbal language.[15]

Our collective incapacity for thinking 'in terms of networks' is only equalled by the earnestness of our efforts to do so, as if the patterns traced by technology itself served as a kind of figural key to an emerging mode of social and economic exchange.[16] Witness, for example, our concerted conversion to an ideology of 'networking', with its own analogous operations of 'flows', 'loop processes', human cogs or relays, and vexed or digitised 'interactions'. Or again, consider the luminous but really rudimentary depictions of AT&T's global information network, with its imaginary circuits smoothly humming. We might, though, also consider one last proposition from Alliez and Feher. In this emerging phase, they argue, capitalism 'leads to the dereliction of people and spaces that cannot be "plugged in" to the network' (p316). It is in these 'vacant spaces and bodies . . . only affected by the *flow of wasted time*' that the true chaos of the cultural moment would be seen to reside (p317, emphasis mine).

Losses and chaos of *all kinds* have recently called into question the ground on which aesthetic practice in the past relied. From the collapse of the autonomy of the aesthetic, artistic practice (and even the exhausted, now highly suspect, art *object*) re-emerged both

humbled and exalted in its status as a prototype of 'interest' and 'investment'. In this dispersed aesthetic arena, of speculation and electronically charged transfers, of corporate sponsorship and governmental control, the issue for art seems to grow more urgent and indeterminate by the day.

'Distraction', Walter Benjamin wrote as early as 1936:

> and concentration form polar opposites which may be stated as follows: A man who concentrates before a work of art is absorbed by it . . . In contrast, the distracted mass absorbs the work of art . . . The public is an examiner, but an absent-minded one. (p240)

Benjamin argues that 'the tasks which face the human apparatus at the turning points of history cannot be solved by optical means, that is, by contemplation, alone'. (p240) With a newly-inflected emphasis on the complex processes of circulation and production, art becomes both measure and model of the shifts in apperception wrought by technology. The exponential increase in the value of the cultural variable, technological development, gives to Benjamin's 'absent-mindedness' an unexpected spin:

> Dear Reader:
> When you need information to help you make important decisions in your life, where do you find it? How do you even know what's out there? And, how can you get your hands on it, fast?[17]

If the new science offers a set of tools (specifically, seeing eye tools) for transiting to an unimagined form of collective subjective experience, the question concerning technology becomes one of *who is absorbing whom*, and art becomes a *matter* of *distracting* our collective state of distraction. Artistic practice is issued a strange new challenge, a kind of awful but domestic imperative. While there is no ordinary score, a determinate array of strategies makes itself available as a figure for the digressions and deflections of cultural history begins to take shape. At once elegant and unpredictable – elegiac perhaps, unnerving – art and culture appear here as a 'venture' that does not progress, but instead cycles endlessly on an erratic orbit, shot through with the energy of saturated video graphics, exerting a well-nigh disconcerting and mesmeric appeal.

Notes

1 Walter Benjamin, 'The Work of Art in the Age of Mechanical Reproduction', in Hannah Arendt, ed, *Iluminations: Walter Benjamin*, 1969, Schocken Books, New York, pp217-252, p240.

2 Peitgen and Richter, *Frontiers of Chaos: Computer Graphics Face Complex Dynamics*, exhibition catalogue, 1985, Forschungsgruppe Konplexe Dynamik, Universitat Bremen, pp61-100, pp72, 66.

3 *ibid*, p66.

4 Thomas Kuhn, 'The Structure of Scientific Revolutions', *International Encyclopaedia of Unified Science*, 1962, 1970, Otto Neurath, Ed-in-Chief, vol 2, no 2, The University of Chicago Press.

5 David Campbell et al, 'Experimental Mathematics: The Role of Computation in Nonlinear Science', *Communications of the ACM* 28, no 4, April 1985, pp374-384, p377.

6 Michel Foucault, 'Nietzsche, Genealogy, History', in Paul Rabinow, ed, *Foucault: A Reader*, 1984, Pantheon, New York, pp76-100, p88.

7 Poincare argued, on mathematical grounds, that while Newton's laws of planetary motion held good for systems of just *two* bodies, the introduction of a *third* has the potential of destabilising the system and rendering orbits erratic, unpredictable. See John Briggs and F David Peat, *Turbulent Mirror: An Illustrated Guide to Chaos Theory and the Science of Wholeness*, 1989, Harper & Row, New York, p29.

8 John Cage, 'Indeterminacy', the second of three lectures on 'Composition', in *Silence: Lectures and Writings by John Cage*, 1961, Weslyn University Press, Middletown, pp35-40.

9 On this, see Tricia Collins and Richard Milazzo, *Hyperframes: A Post-*Appropriation Discourse*, 1989, vol 1, Editions Antoine Candau, Paris, pp13-14.

10 Tricia Collins and Richard Milazzo, *Hybrid Neutral: Modes of Abstraction and the Social*, exhibition catalogue, 1988, Independent Curators, Inc, New York, p8.

11 David Ruelle, 'Strange Attractors', in Predrag Cvitanovic, ed, *Universality in Chaos*, 1984, Adam Hilger Ltd, Bristol, pp37-48.

12 Robert Shaw, 'Strange Attractors, Chaotic Behaviour, and Information Flow', 1981, *Zeitschrift fur Naturforsch*, 36a pp80-112, p106.

13 Eric Alliez and Michel Feher, 'The Luster of Capital', *Zone* 1/2 (nd), pp314-22, p315.

14 James Gleick, *Chaos: Making A New Science*, Viking Penguin, New York, p39.

15 Herbert Franke, 'Refractions of Science into Art', in *Frontiers of Chaos*, pp45-52, p47.

16 On this, see Fredric Jameson, 'Post-Modernism or The Cultural Logic of Late Capitalism', *New Left Review*, No 146, July-August 1984, pp 53-92, where aesthetic production is seen to imitate the dominant mode of production at a given historical moment, and technology serves as a shorthand for the information networks of multinational capitalism. See also Hal Foster, 'Signs Taken for Wonders', *Art in America*, Vol 74, No 6, June 1986, pp80-139, especially note #14.

17 'America Needs Information', Promotional mailing for AT&T Information on CallTM, 1989, p2.

Anne and Patrick Poirier, *Exegi Monumentum Aere Perennius*, 1988, cast aluminium, 193x80x80cm

DONALD KUSPIT
EUROPEAN SENSIBILITY TODAY

Anish Kapoor, *Void Field*, 1989, sandstone and pigment, dimensions variable

Is it possible to find a common ground of sensibility for contemporary European art? Isn't it foolhardy to attempt to find unity in what is so obviously disparate? Doesn't it blur important differences between the artists, and isn't it epistemologically naive, even absurd, to suppose that there must be an underlying 'cause' or 'mood' they have in common? Hasn't the very notion of a

hidden universality become suspect – become an empty transcendence, an ignorant assumption of substratum less innocent than it looks, for it does enormous damage to particular existences and fosters incredible misunderstandings of them? Discontinuity, not continuity, is the rule understanding today; the assumption of uncontradictory relationships is the big intellectual lie. A century's epistemological warnings against weaving different existential threads in one intellectual rope should make us wary of any construction of sensibility. Yet lurking within all the differences, stylistic as well as materialistic, generational as well as national, it seems to me there is a situation-bound emotional approach that makes for a certain unconscious communality among European artists, that makes the conscious individuality of each seem less absolute. There is a certain common intuition, hardly whispered, among contemporary European artists, whatever their separate histories.

Today, the way to an understanding of Europe is through America (and vice versa), and the way to an understanding of European sensibility is no different. Each is implicitly the background for the other, through socio-historical circumstance, including not only their mutuality within that peculiarly metamorphic transcendent substance called 'Western Civilisation', but more particularly because they are major partners in 'information exchange', each always looking over its shoulder at the

other in what has become the quintessential activity of the Information Age. There is no way of being contemporary or current – carried along by the current – without being aware of what is happening elsewhere, especially in some other place that is implicitly assumed to be as important as one's own, if not secretly envied for being more important (or expected to be). Europeans have envied post-war American art, beginning with Pollock's trend-setting all-over paintings of the late 40s, and continuing through the 60s, with its fast-paced, highly innovative production (ranging from Pop art and Minimalism through Earth art and Conceptual art), and finally into the 70s, when a highly diversified, so-called pluralistic art scene (largely but not exclusively orientated to such social issues as feminism and the Vietnam War) was created. But at the beginning of the 1980s, with the *New Spirit in Painting* exhibition in London, and various other European, mostly German international, exhibitions, which retrospectively seem to have come hard on the heels of each other, Americans have envied (even hated) Europeans for their art's dynamic growth, and especially for its orientation towards memory. More precisely, its power of phylogenetic recapitulation to achieve a new ontogenesis, its desire and ability to delve into both the recent past of American art and the more distant past of its own art history, assimilating both into a new expressive (if not uniformly Expressionistic) art, was recognised

Mario Merz, *Objet cache-toi*, 1985, metal tubes, glass, clamps, twigs and neon tubes, igloos 800, 500 and 300cm in diameter

as pace-setting. Indeed, it was a major articulation of the Post-Modern condition, perhaps in a profounder way than Post-Modern American architecture. European historicism has come to seem very contemporary, and signals the fact that the present is no longer orientated towards a future – no longer as all-meaningful as it once seemed, for a variety of psycho-social reasons (not least of which is the collapse of belief in the Utopian promise of modernity) – but towards the past, discovered to be unexpectedly rich in possibilities. These can be realised by 'poetically' subsuming and synthesising the old modes of production and interest, to create a fresh sense of individuality and novelty. American forward-lookingness/ future-orientation, as it has been called, has been replaced by European backward-lookingness, or respect for the past (which of course always seems to have more dignity, to be more civilised, than the present).

From an American point of view, Europe has always emphasised, or rather meant, oldness, while America was the brave new world, the place of the infinitely expanding horizon of the future. Europe is the place of memory, masked and civilised by the *politesse* of art, but still peculiarly raw – perhaps, as today's

European artists seem to imply, more raw than the American wilderness, from which much American art implicitly took its inspiration. The Europeans know the past is not the dead horizon it appears at first glance to be. Paradoxically, the modes of civilisation – including artistic styles and interests – now seem fresher than nature. This is perhaps why the tide of art has become predominantly European, for Europe has always known how to live with ruins, how to work with and through the past, whose ghost often seems more living than one's body. America has assimilated European art information, just as Europe has assimilated American art information. Each keeps close watch on the other. But the European artist's response to information in general is essentially different from the American artist's response. The American tends to take it as an end in itself, as a structure in itself.

Information and facts are implicitly regarded as one and the same and, as the American typically says, the facts speak for themselves. The problem is to get to them. This remains so even with the widespread recognition of the relativity of fact. The facts are relative, but they must be the case, once a case has been made for them. They supposedly contain their meaning in

Jannis Kounellis, *Untitled*, 1988, sack cloth, iron and mixed media, 200x360cm

themselves. Moreover, the facts of the past are not related to with any depth by the Americans. They are not reworked, but sentimentalised, in Disneyland style. One cannot imagine an American artist seriously alluding to the American Indian heritage or Melville's dramatic vision of life in the way that Kiefer alludes to Hermann, the barbaric Germanic chief who defeated the Romans, or to Wagner's mytho-operatic vision. To carry this further, for the American, the bacon-strips of information-fact are allowed to fry in their own fat. They are then consumed for their own supposedly inherent testiness. In contrast, the Europeans, to continue the all-American metaphor, tend to fry the information facts in the grease of memory. This gives them an altogether different sense of the taste of the facts, that is, of so-called reality. And this is where the difference between contemporary European and contemporary American sensibility comes in seriously: they have a different sense of reality. (André Breton already said that the sense of reality was the issue of modern art). One can say, no doubt all too simply, that America, for all the difficulties of its current socio-economic situation, for all the pressure of predatory world-wide competition with it, remains optimistic, perhaps cautiously optimistic, but nonetheless forward-looking.

In Europe, for all its post-war prosperity and success, there is an ingrained pessimism, a kind of subliminal negativism, a certain sense of weariness and *déjà vu*, which informs the art. There it is often masked by black humour altogether beyond irony – and/or spiritual (reconstructionist/therapeutic) ambitions. There is evidence of both in Polke, Clemente, Dokoupil, Kounellis, the Poiriers, even Beuys, to mention only what seem the most exemplary cases. There is sometimes a pursuit of the mystique of 'memorableness' as an end in itself, to counteract the weight of historical facts. (I think this is the case in artists as different as Paladino and Kapoor, although it does not exhaust the understanding of their art.) And there is often a kind of insidious theatrical nihilism, nihilism in the garb of contemporary everydayness – a sense of the hollowness of things conveyed through the hollowness of representation, a kind of apathy of representation, an alienated representation (as in Richter and Armleder), which is nihilism at its most nostalgic and narcissistic.

The key point here is that contemporary European artists have a different sense of reality than American artists. The European

George Rousse, *Above*: *Untitled* (Paris, Bercy), 1985, cibachrome, 180x240cm; *Below*: *Untitled* (Geneva), 1985, cibachrome, 180x240cm

artists have internalised the modern idea of the relativity of reality with a vengeance. It suits their sensibility perfectly. Reality for them is inherently untrustworthy; for so history has been, notoriously. More particularly, contemporary reality is invariably understood in relation to past history. (The European instinctively feels there is no other way to grasp it, while the American tends to experience the present as a thing unto itself.) This necessarily changes the sense of both present and past reality. The future is less obviously real in contemporary Europe than in America, or rather, its reality is always tainted by the shadow of the past and the suspiciousness of the present. This is why I would say that the most general quality of contemporary European art – if one wants to make a sweeping generalisation – is lack of forthrightness, calculated equivocation, ambivalence of feeling and ambiguity of meaning, pursued as ends in themselves, rather than as the unfortunate fallout of circumstances. In this, contemporary European art shows how much it retains – has learned the lesson of – the so-called 'obscure' side of early European Modernism, or attempts to re-instate it, perhaps unwittingly. In any case, there is a new obscurity – not obscurantism – for all the Post-Modern sense of the past as 'clear information'. This new obscurity, with its feelings of intimacy and inevitability, is inseparable from endemic European pessimism, with its overtones of cynical self-enlightenment.

A paradox emerges from the contrast of the European and American sensibilities. If, as Baudrillard has said, the hyperreal is 'the generation by models of a real without origin or reality', or the establishment of a state of simulation, then we can say that the American world, and by extension American art, is more hyperreal than the European world. This is exactly because America believes in facts, in the form of information, that is, in hyperreal form. Facts are generated and administered by information systems, that is, models of fact. In Europe, facts are inseparable from memories; the past is unsystematic, or else the ruins of various systems. It is never as intact and closed as a system (of information). We are really badly informed about the past, and it is poorly administered. (Indeed, the past often seems more open, and more available for manipulative reflection, than the present. The rewriting of history is usually more complex and

evocative than predicting the future.) Thus, futility is built into the past, whereas in America, security is built into the past as much as into the future and present, because they are presented in information form, that is, as part of a system of simulated time, which is the American substitute for history and memory. There is no sense of inherent conflict between past, present, and future in America, but rather a sense of continuous development from one to the other. The equivocations of European art – sometimes brittle, sometimes poignant – reflect the conflict between the conditions of time. It is finally the different sense of time that is responsible for the different sense of reality in European and American art. European art today has a more haunted look than American art, indicating a different relationship with the past.

The preoccupation with both its substance and form is pervasive today, but the attitude to it – one might say the ideology of the past – is drastically different. Where American artists – such as those who simulate abstract paintings and the neo-Duchampian specialists in commodity objects (is their hyperreality or simulated reality simply an old irony in the Emperor's new artistic clothes?) – appropriate the past as a *fait accompli*, regarding it as a finished fact, the European artists are themselves appropriated by the past, which never stops unfolding and tightening its hold on the present. Their contemporaneity ends up belonging to the past, which shows not only the power of its hold on them, but the inseparability of their sensibility from it. It is not simply that Europe had to recover from World War II to repair its sense of autonomous identity, but that it had to recover sufficiently free to reflect on the recent past as part of its destiny, and to experience the past as an inalienable part of its identity. It had to recover a primitive sense of being possessed by an irreducible past to make new art. In America, identity and destiny seem much more predetermined, despite the fact that America has less of a (controlling) past than Europe. It is just because Europe unconsciously remains controlled by its past – and self-consciously knows it – that it has once again become the place where the possibility of profound, daring psychosocial awareness remains most alive, as is evident in its new expressive art.

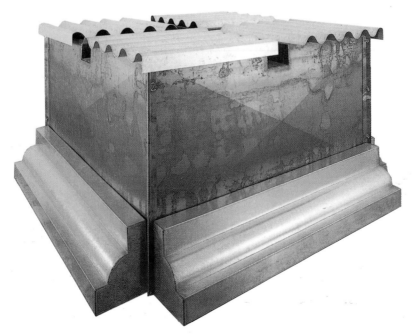

Susana Solano, *Estació Termal*, 1987, galvanised iron, 132x276x276cm

James Lee Byars, *The Golden Tower with Changing Tops*, 1989

ANTJE VON GRAEVENITZ
THE ART OF ALCHEMY

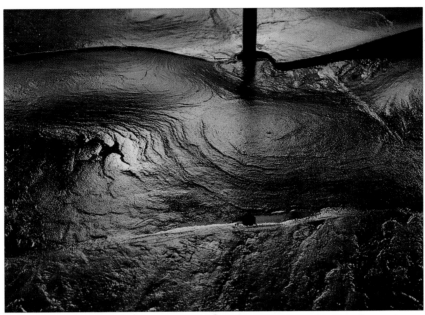

Giuseppe Penone, *Contour Lines* (detail), 1989, iron, glass and sand

In the 70s and 80s, artists have been especially occupied with two lines of thought. On the one hand they have hoped, through art, to achieve 'unity', meaning a conception of the clear and the pure, whether in thought or in life itself. Different art movements, especially Conceptual art, represented this idea. Conceptual art demands absolute lucidity of thought, absolute statements about man in

relation to nature and the cosmos, as well as clarity of the selected means – preferably texts and photographs, because one cannot conceal anything with these. Art concerning alchemy is also involved with the idea of unity and purification.

On the other hand, artists have been occupied with the opposing view that maybe 'unity' can never be achieved and that art enabling us to understand the invisible 'spirit' in the world does not exist any more. Relativity triumphs, as in for example the media which, in its, abundance of images, disallows any evaluation; or in physics which, with its theory of quarks and the black hole, derives from the idea that the world is reversible. This is shown by the lack of faith in the wholesomeness of psycho-analysis, assumed by Jacques Lacan in contrast to Freud.

A text by the German artist Jürgen Partenheimer appears symptomatic of these attitudes. In a hand-made book with linocuts, he printed the following: 'In his [Flaubert's] St Anthony, he re-interpreted the temptations as a vision, as a dream of limitless possibilities. The poor fool, the tormented anchorite, is freed from sin. The state of torment becomes a state of fulfilment. Values reverse themselves when we set them in motion: St George, for example, renounces his life and spares the life of the dragon [in us]. End of purification rites. The individual occurrence [the quantum leap] is no longer determined by its previous history. Contemporary scientific insights into the nature of

matter, space, time and gravity have opened up new perspectives for aesthetics. At the vanishing point of our ordered system we no longer perceive the transcending unity, clarity and simplicity of things, but rather the unpredictable contradictory way in which elementary simplicity is annulled [quarks].'

In addition to such analyses, one hears artists claim that there is no longer any unity between culture and society – an opinion that art historian Hans Sedlmayr had already stated in 1948, in his polemical book *Verlust der Mitte* (Loss of the middle). Recently the French philosopher Jean Baudrillard adopted and further expanded this line of thinking, the consequence of which he described as fatal. But this mentality is not in the mainstream of recent art. Artists involved with alchemy, if they ever refer to a lost world, believe in the power of creativity. The proposal of the presence of alchemy in recent art poses the question of whether art itself can be alchemy. Are the purposes and methods of art in accordance with those of alchemy or can one only speak about the adoption or incorporation of alchemic motifs and motivations in art? Why should artists strive for a marriage with alchemy or an incorporation of its motifs and motivations at all? Answers are not easy to find because alchemy, in a sense, is still a secret science. The concept is not exact enough to define; there is not, and probably never was, a common agreement about it, although one could say that alchemists equate processes occur-

James Lee Byars, *The Reading Society of James Lee Byars*, 1987

ring in nature with spiritual processes.

It is specifically this synchronisation of spirit and nature which distinguishes them from science. Moreover, alchemists want to instigate natural and spiritual processes, to influence them, and to be influenced by them, as wisdom and purification – their highest aims – are not learnable. The word 'alchemy' is of Arabic origin, derived from the first alchemist Chymes, later called Zosimus. In the 12th century, the term 'Al Khemia' entered Western Culture, signifying the secret black magic for which alchemists needed books and laboratories. As their doctrine remained accessible only to insiders, alchemy was often condemned as an hermetic science and witchcraft. This condemnation strongly increased at the beginning of the Enlightenment, when chemistry as the science of matter was separated from alchemy – for alchemy had much higher pretensions than chemistry. Because of its connection with art, it is necessary, in this context, to shed more light on these pretensions.

Alchemy is the doctrine that aims at producing the philosophers' stone – gold. Different metals are used to attain this. Fire is used to divide these 'base' metals into their separate components; these are then purified, mixed and ultimately fixed in the final stage as gold. This happens through seven processes: carbonisation, decay, dissolution, distillation, sublimation, combination and fixation. Each process is related to a certain constellation which exerts its influence on nature and man. During these processes the materials change in colour. There are three main colours: black (the colour of decay and carbonisation, the basis for frugality), white (purification), and red (the colour of cold and of blood, consequently of life). The alchemists' recipe consists of a language of signs, colours and materials with symbolic meanings which, when used in the right way, can lead to the 'Great Work'; the purification of the spirit by alchemical gold, also called 'elixir', the philosophers' stone.

The extent to which the alchemist departs from the aims of the scientist is clear. The alchemist always tries, by combining two elements, to produce a third, which in some sense should represent something new. It should therefore have a status totally different from that of the first two. Through the alchemical process, a transformation must take place of two known qualities into a new, preferably absolute quality, that of purity, which is not liable to decay. These are the qualities of gold, which the alchemist considers spiritual; because his own body belongs to the material world, it too must be able to acquire this essential quality of gold. Alchemists share joint goals:
– To gain insights about micro- and macrocosm.
– To demonstrate these by means of thoughts and images or exemplary processes.
– To recognise oneself and be purified in the 'Great Work' – to search for parallels between matter and spirit.
– To harmonise the struggle between the sexes (for example in an androgyne concept) – to recreate the world in an artistic, but not refined, shape.

Since the 19th century, classical alchemy, with its chemical experiments and old metallurgic recipes, was exchanged for artistic and philosophical methods. Letters, syllables, words, dream-visions, images, or the most diverse metaphors and symbols took the place of chemical materials. These materials, spiritual from the very start, through transformational techniques, combination and analogy, effect something new which could give a notion of the universe and help to achieve insight and wisdom. Once it was discovered that classical alchemy could be secularised, it became a suitable medium for all artists and thinkers who considered the exact sciences too limited a refuge. This applies more or less to all art, but alchemy by itself is not yet art and, in my opinion, art is only related to alchemy when the artists consciously apply these aspects in their works.

'I am interested in transformations', I was told in 1982 by the artist Joseph Beuys. 'Transformation is a basic concept. I am searching for the limits towards the religious and spiritual. A desperate attempt to preserve old knowledge in a spiritual way. As long as man fails to realise that money, in the sense of capital, and strictly analytic sciences suppresses his creative power, he is unable to develop . . . The quality of life', he continued, 'lies in asceticism, not in acquiring, since the latter leads to destruction of the consciousness of the future, of beauty, of art. The principle of possessiveness must disappear. Asceticism is very valuable. That is where the gold is – in relinquishing lies gold in a spiritual sense: that is where man's holiness lies.' He found an impressive image for this idea. In 1965, at the Galerie Schmela in Düsseldorf, he showed in a sort of *tableau vivant*, *'How to explain to a dead hare what art is'* ('Wie man dem toten Hasen die Bilder erklärt'). The explanation was not given rationally. His raised finger rather suggests the non-rational statement of saints on painted icons, which refer to 'Erleuchtung' (enlightenment), symbolised by the gold and honey on his head. Honey, in contrast to gold, stands for productive energy.

'Gold as capital', Beuys told me in the same interview regarding his connection to alchemy, 'that is inconceivable. What, then, is gold?' he asked himself and answered: 'To the alchemist it is a metal, the sun. In the alchemist doctrine of symbols, gold, like the sun, is the middle, in the heart, while desire comes from below and the head is above. Above are the higher forms of consciousness: intuition, inspiration and imagination. The heart mediates and the alchemistic gold is aptly placed there.' Beuys considered art not as the visual arts in the classical sense, but as a much wider conception; according to him art mediates between the consciousness of the inorganic world. During his performance at Lucio Amelio in Naples in 1972, he lay on the ground for four hours, rubbing a block of copper with oiled fingers. Next to him was a dry plant, whose Latin name, *vitus agnus castus*, was oriented in sulphor-yellow on a colbalt strip. This flower in the Middle Ages showed the hero Parsifal the way to the temple. *'Vitus agnus castus'* was also the title of Beuys' performance. It called to mind a statement of the first alchemist Chymes/Zosimus: 'Set to work and build a stone temple.' Could not the whole performance and not only the plant be seen as a symbol for the way to the temple? Yellow and blue, the sun and the moon, the male and the female element, Beuys as man rubbing the copper representing the energy-conducting female element: these are all symbols for the abolition of the struggle of the sexes. Beuys linked his own language to traditional alchemists and to Goethe and Rudolf Steiner. This, too, may be considered an alchemistic activity.

The Immaterial Gold

Just like Beuys' action as a searcher for the temple, the work of Yves Klein functions as an 'Anschauungsbild' (symbolic image) for the purification of the soul. On the 26th of January, 1962, Klein sold immaterial work to Dino Buzzati: 20 grammes of gold-leaf, in exchange for a check. Then as Buzzati watched, Klein scattered the gold into the Seine. On another occasion Klein repeated this activity and burned the check as well. This work has the programmatic title, *Session d'une zone de sensibilité pictorale immaterielle* (Session of a zone of immaterial pictorial sensibility). Like Beuys, Klein wanted to transform the gold into a special status of the soul, which he called the zone of sensibility. As a Rosicrucian, he was very conscious of the Parsifal myth: the legend of an untried young man, who must go through various ordeals before he is purified with the 'blue flower' which, according to the myth, showed Parsifal the way to the temple. Yet Klein probably did not intend all this too literally: 'The real blue is inside', he used to explain. In this way

97

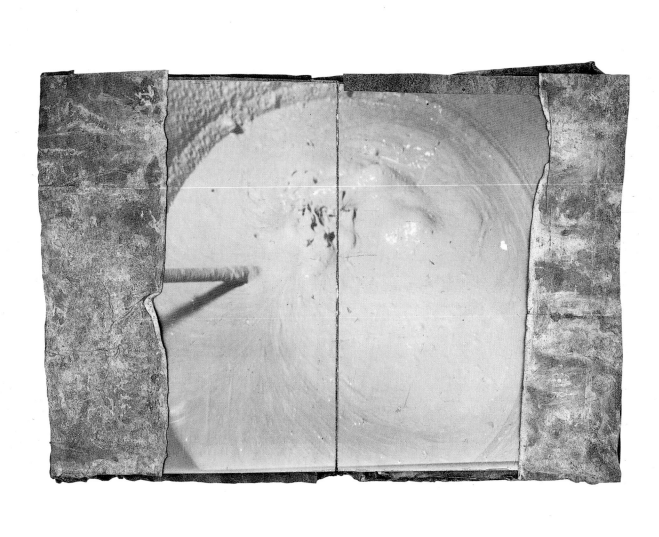

Anselm Kiefer, *Zweistromland, (The High Priestess)*, Book 80, 1985-89, original photographs mounted on treated lead, 74.3x54.6x7.1cm

his blue acquired the status of gold.

But not only gold is related to alchemy, other methods of making art among contemporary artists are intentionally related to alchemistic acts as well:
– Old symbols were taken up again by Beuys, Marina Abramovic & Ulay, James Lee Byars and Eric Orr.
– New symbols were added (Guiseppe Penone).
– Alchemistic operations and installations return by way of quotation (Terry Fox, Rebecca Horn).
– Purifying rituals are used (George Maciunas, Fox, Byars, Beuys).
– Instruments are presented which the spectator may use to understand the world in a better way (Dennis Oppenheim, Pieter Laurens Mol).
– Melting processes are set free to get new results for paintings (Sigmar Polke, Eric Orr).

The marriage of art and alchemy is possible in many ways. Because of the importance of the 'seven' for the trial and purification of the soul, I want to introduce the 'seven stages' as a possibility of bringing order to the phenomenon of art involving alchemy.

Seven stages

The first stage is that of emblems of the ego, such as the tree of life, the house, the tower and the column. The second consists of melting processes, the third of wishing machines – celibate machines; the forth stage is totally consecrated to levitation and the sixth to the formula: *unus ego et . . .* 'I am one inside me.' The alchemistic gold will complete the seventh stage. However none of the seven stages intend to reflect a hierarchy of subjects. Every work in itself finds the way to the highest alchemistic aim.

Emblems of the Ego

The first stage begins with the labyrinth, an old symbol to purify the ego. Without Ariadne's thread, representing memory, Theseus would not find his way out. In the beginning of the 70s, a lot of American artists such as Alice Aycock, Richard Fleischner, Will Insley and Robert Morris constructed mazes.

The tree of life is described by C G Jung as perhaps the most important ego. He explained how the alchemic tree in the Garden of Eden represents the immortality and knowledge of the highest universal power. The tree of life is also considered the inversion of a kind of womb. To the classical alchemist his oven or distiller

Yves Klein, *L to R*: *Requiem Blue (Re 20)*, 1960, 200x164.8cm; *Re 40, Bleu*, 1960, 200x150.1cm, both sponge and pigment on board

signified this earth, because he hoped that it could bring forth *athenor*, the philosopher stone. This motive returns in modern art: Giuseppe Penone drove an iron with Fibonacci-numbers into the trunk of a tree, hoping that in this, abstract and natural knowledge could grow together.

The tower is an old purification symbol which the alchemists adopted as *topos* for their seven stages of trials. Purification took place on the top floor. In 1984 the Danish artist Per Kirkeby, at the exhibition *Von hier aus* in Düsseldorf, built a high brick tower inside the exhibition hall, without a staircase or entrance. The imagination could only be stimulated by the suggestion of a tower-form. One of Kirkeby's books of poetry contains a text referring to his work. He describes a tower of a different shape, which one could enter without a staircase directly from the highest floor. 'There was a window, looking out over the sea. There he was alone, his head grew and grew until one eye entirely filled the window. The eye of the tower looked blindly over the horizon.' Kirkeby represents the ego as one who unites with the look-out tower. His eye is blind. Is this because he cannot see beyond the horizon, or because he only looks inside himself? Metaphysical anatomy arises from space in a symboli-

cal architecture occupied by body and spirit.

The column may have the same function as the labyrinth, tower and tree as a symbol for the ego. Byars, at *Documenta 8* in Kassel,1982, showed a golden column in the entrance hall which seemed to carry the spiritual entity of the whole exhibition.

Melting processes

Alchemical melting processes have already been mentioned; they are emphasised in the second stage. Both Anselm Kiefer and Sigmar Polke use melting processes in their paintings. Polke mixes chemical ingredients such as varnish, resin, acid and emulsions, as the old masters would have done, but he is concerned with suggestions of fortuity and surprise as unexpected forms develop. The titles of these paintings have also alchemical parallels: *Negativwert (alkor)*, *Negativwert 1 (Mizar)* etc. One painting is even called programmatically *Conjunction*. Anselm Kiefer used to carry out well-known historical themes from German history, integrating mythical stories from German culture into the imaginary landscape of his paintings. Nowadays he has given up the historical base. Since his visit to Israel, he conjures up Old Testament stories or alchemical histories of

Thérèse Oulton, *Tremolite*, 1989, oil, 167.6x147.3cm

creation, which he connects with the basic ground of his paintings. On the canvas, for example, a thick layer of molten, saturnine lead, resembling a rising cloud of air, melts with the thick paint in earth colours. The title of the painting, *Yggrasil* (1985), refers to the cloud of smoke that arose from the burning bush when God tried to convince the unbelieving Moses of his existence. Both painters focus on melting in analogy to alchemistic principles. On the one hand their paintings take the place of the experimental oven, yet on the other hand they are themselves the product – a transformation of the gold, which can come into existence only by looking and processing.

Celibate machines, wishing machines

Reflecting the spectator's desire for the *athenor*, Marcel Duchamp produced a complicated work, known as the *Large Glass*. It is a so-called celibate machine, which will confront the spectator with the third of the seven stages. Duchamp called it *La mariée mise à nu par ses célibataires, même* (The bride stripped bare by her bachelors, even). Does the bride signify Lady Alchemia or art? Although Duchamp wrote that he was influenced by R Roussel, the author of alchemical stories, he told Arturo Schwarz that if he had used alchemical subjects, it happened without knowing them.

The work was one of the most important sources for the art of Alice Aycock, who likewise in her sculpture constructed non-functioning machines. When I visited her in New York in 1980, she was working on the book *Anti-Oedipe* by Deleuze and Guattari. The concept of wishing machines as a counterpart to the actual machines of production which constitute industry, society and body, seemed to her to be applicable to her 'dream machines', which can 'produce' fears, joy and hallucinations. One work is entitled *How to catch and manufacture ghosts*.

Purification

The classical alchemist, too, was striving to produce, in machines or in his oven, a human soul as the ideal image of an androgynous person. This could happen if he was purified himself and had gone through every trial during the seven stages.

Many events from the beginning of the 60s consist of ritual affiliations of participants, who had to undergo purification rituals. In my opinion, then, it is no coincidence that Alan Kaprow, the pioneer of these happenings, considered purification rituals in modern art as 'the alchemy of the 60s'. The Fluxus movement took part in this, also: the apologist of this movement, George Maciunas, in his famous Fluxus manifesto, proclaiming that the great purification for society and culture is dysentery. As a solution he proposes melting. His word is 'Fuse' with which he puts social unification processes on a level with metallurgical ones. In the manifesto we find 'Purge the world of bourgeois sickness, intellectual, professional and commercialised culture.' Art was given the function of purifying the participant, but the participant had to play his part as well, in order to reach the high purpose. Joseph Beuys, too, always confessed to the ideals of Fluxus, and in his complex performance *Celtic (sinus cosinus)*, he used purgatorial actions: he washed the bare feet of his visitors and, finally, had himself baptised as well. The religious background of these purification rituals is evident. Beuys did not assume the part of Christ, but participated in his work of art, which represented a purification ritual in itself. According to Beuys a work of art must have the power to give people back something which they have lost. In Jannis Kounellis' and Anselm Kiefer's work, purification in the strict sense of the word is no longer relevant. Both artists represent the subject of purification in a symbolic way in their art, which rises like a phoenix from the ashes. Over a small place of sacrifice with ash and soot hangs a palette. Kounellis supports the idea that

energies from history must be understood and preserved to give man back his dignity. The rising of culture from the ashes of the past is his metaphor for a possible recovery.

Although Kiefer's work resembles Kounellis' on the surface, the accent lies elsewhere. He tests in himself and his art the value which history can still have for him. He does not proclaim the same message as Kounellis. He transforms loaded themes from history into his paintings, filters them and thus purifies them. Seen in full light it is carbonised paint which has combined with other paint. His winged palette rises above the black furrows of burnt paint. In this way it seems to be a conclusion of his whole activity as well as alchemic wishful thinking to attain the purgatorial effect of art.

Levitation

Kiefer and Kounellis connect the subject of purgation with the concept of levitation, the fifth stage of my discourse. Levitation represents the consequence of purgation – it means a liberation in the biblical sense as well. Yves Klein, on a Sunday in 1962, jumped from a high wall into the air, which he did not call air, but emptiness, 'le vide'. Although he publicised his jump, just like the visible blue of his monochrome paintings, it was meant as a metaphor for an inner state. Similarly the young Italian artist Marco Bagnoli ascended at sunrise from the heath in Holland in a hot/air balloon. This happened next to a spot where the faces of Bodhisattva seemed to rise from ground. The profiles of the Indian divinity were negative, as if the God had printed his face into the soil. For the spectator, who had been waiting for the spectacle since the dark early morning hours, the energy of the earth, transformed into fire and air, seemed to float away.

Unity

Midgard, to which the sixth stage of this story is devoted, develops by synthesis. Melting, purification and levitation preceed it, until Midgard – the unity, the essence of all this – could develop. It's worth recalling a performance of Marina Abramovic & Ulay which took place in Sidney as well as throughout Europe and America, entitled *Nightsee Crossing*. The two artists sat in front of each other for days at a long table, quiet, introverted, waiting, looking at and into each other and into themselves. First, they tormented their bodies; they actually became cold, stiff and suffered awful pains. Yet they felt themselves approaching a stage in which they could conquer all obstructions and begin to fly as if they had lost their body identity. At the most one can absorb their image and preserve it as an image of stillness and life. It represents a synthesis of the sexes, who nevertheless remain two human bodies, emphasised by two colours, similar to the spiritual unity of the 'chymic marriage' of the two sexes in the old distiller of the alchemist.

Gold

Nuggets of gold lying on the table during a perfomance by Marina Abramovic & Ulay were used as symbols for the *prima materia*, the only spiritual aim of their souls. Gold represents the seventh stage of this discourse.

The question still arises as to whether art can be alchemy. The classical alchemist tried to understand himself by working with material processes. An artist, on the other hand, keeps in touch with the outside world, aiming to communicate with it through his art. This is the main difference between the classical alchemist and the modern artist. The classical alchemist seems to be an individual mythologist, free from ideological dogmas. Contrary to the Modernist artist, the classical alchemist is not searching for a distant goal, but rather a nucleus within himself. With this aim his art may be a real alternative to Post-Modern art with, for example, subjects of 'emptiness' and 'consumption'.

ANDREW BENJAMIN
THE TEMPORALITY OF THE NEW

Fashion is the eternal recurrence of the new. Are there nevertheless motifs of redemption precisely in fashion? **Walter Benjamin.**

The new has a history. History, in addition to providing the new with a continuity, so that what is designated historically as the new forms no more than a harmless self-repetition, also works to construct a specific problem, namely history's 'outside'or history's other. This opens up the possibility of a space beyond the continuity of the new as history and thus as the historical. The new will still be linked to repetition since repetition rather than being overcome can only ever be reworked. Understanding the stakes of reworking will emerge from the attempt to clarify this link. The problem at hand however concerns the consequences of redeploying the new, of using it anew. In sum the redeployment amounts to moving the new from the frame of history in which it functions as a chronological marker – one with the potential to periodise – to the realm of interpretation. Once this move is effected, the immediate consequence is that it will demand a reformulation of time. Historical time will have ceded its centrality to the time of interpretation. This reformulation will concern what will be called the temporality of the new. Time here, if the move from continuity to interpretation is assumed, can no longer be expressed in either historical or chronological terms; *ie* dates or periods. Time, and the new, will form and comprise ineliminable elements within the actuality of interpretation itself.

The new, as part of interpretation, can be seen, already, to figure within a number of predetermined configurations. The new checks continuity; the new as opposed to the old; the new breaks repetition. Within the standard presentation of these configurations, and because the new is only present in them as a marker providing interpretation with the possibility of historical specificity, the components themselves remain unquestioned. Moreover the relation, which links and separates them, fails to be posed as a question. Placing the new within the realm of interpretation will mean that attention must be paid to the claim made by the designation new; *ie* the claim the new makes for itself. The constituent parts within the predetermined configurations will need to be clarified, as will the relation within which the contrast itself comes to be enacted. It is the relation that is, in the end, of greatest significance.

Within the actuality of interpretation, the new will always involve a claim made in relation to tradition. If the claim concerns the affirmed presence of the absolutely new then, though only on the level of intentional logic, this will both isolate and identify that moment or place at which tradition is not renewed.[1] In other words rather than its being a renewing of tradition the absolutely new will intend, in the sense that its logic will work toward, tradition's non-renewal. There is a problem at the centre of this understanding of the new. What is ignored is all implicit mediation that forms part of the designation itself. The new as the absolutely other is already mediated by its being the other. Alterity will therefore involve relation. The inherent presence of mediation brings to the fore that particular paradox of the new. (The new, now, of course, in contrast to the new as the absolutely other.) It is within the terms set by mediation and paradox that the new will come to be situated. It is, for example,

inevitable that tradition is both renewed and not renewed. This inevitability marks both the impossibility of the absolutely new while affirming the possibility of the new. Understanding the paradox does not hinge upon merely understanding the components of the predetermined configurations – old/new, continuity/ new, repetition/new – but the relation. How is relation to be thought? Answering this question will involve reiteration.

The claim of the new – a claim that must incorporate the claim to be the new – announces a relation. Within the claim, either of or for the absolutely new, a claim it must be added that has the same status as desire, the relation has to be cancelled. The necessity is binding. The absolutely new must appear as the singular event, one both isolated and isolable. An event whose time – whose now – must be thought in terms of a singular and unmediated present. Again the necessity is binding. Against necessity, in both instances, it must be recognised that the relation that is in fact announced is the one enacted within the denial of relation. The paradox is thereby compounded. Paradox also needs to be retained, thereby introducing a further necessity, for the singularity of the event must be sustained in addition; though not simply as an addition.

The singular event cannot be denied. Its singularity insists within the relation that denies absolute singularity but in which singularity comes to be enacted and maintained. Once again what is essential here is paradox. The singular event comes to be singular only in its not being singular. It is the relation that generates and sustains singularity. Furthermore it is the nature of the relation that is determined by the event. The event's relations, accepting all the complexity that this possessive entails, are themselves the enactment of tradition. Even though the specific form taken by its presence resists automatic generalisation. The result of this is that even though the claim of the new will always involve a particular relation to tradition, the relation cannot be separated from tradition.

The temporality of the singular event, when the event is posed beyond the parameters of paradox, is comprised of a present devoid of mediation. The question of time must be reposed to the extent that it can be argued that present with the event – though not within the event as though the event and the relation were constructed as a type of inside/outside opposition – are the relations that sustain it and which therefore mediate it. How will the temporality of this event be understood? Moreover there is the interrelated question of the nature of the concepts and categories through which this understanding is to take place.

The first thing to note is that neither the Bergsonian concept of *durée,* with its emphasis on pure becoming, nor a present construed as pure intensity can provide the basis for an adequate answer to this question if taken as ends in themselves. Nonetheless they gesture towards such a basis in that neither can account for repetition and thus are to some extent constrained to exclude it. Accepting repetition will allow for a connection to be established between paradox and time. What must be avoided is the either/or in which it would be argued that because the new cannot be reduced to the temporal moment, it thereby follows that the new can never be present, as the new, at the present. While it is inherently problematic trying to incorporate teleology into a projection – be it artistic or interpretative – whose aim is the new, it remains the case that a type of intentionality must be maintained. Retaining a conception of intentionality does not mean that intention is to be ascribed to an authorial subject. On the contrary it will form part of the project and thus pertain to its intentional logic. Displacing the centrality of teleology means removing the specificity that comes to be attached to the telos. Teleology contains 'motifs of redemption' once the teleological is reworked so that it becomes no more than pure project; a throwing forward whose force is internal rather than directional. Yet that internality will itself have or come to acquire direction.

This twofold connection between internality and direction is of fundamental importance. The 'coming to acquire' introduces – or rather reintroduces – repetition since it signals the work's own repetition within interpretation. The repetition of the work – its being given again – cannot be adequately formulated in chronological terms. Chronology would merely account for the site of its repetition. This on its own is not sufficient. What needs to be understood is that further element that sanctions repetition, namely the work itself. This is a complex problem since what is at stake here is the ontology of the work. The work is the site of an original heterogeneity.[2] In other words it sanctions its own repetition – a repetition involving difference rather than identity – within interpretation. Each interpretation will be a singular event, understood as actuality within potentiality. The singular event will however be marked on the one hand by the impossibility of the identity of actuality and potentiality, and on the other by relation. It is only in terms of relation that it is possible for there to be a repetition in which an event takes place for the first time. The reworking of the work is its coming to acquire a determination that is new. The recurrence of the work – recurring as an event – is not the eternal recurrence of the new but a paradoxical repetition in which the reworking of the work means the work's repetition both again and anew. Here the new figures within and as repetition.

Within interpretation the force of the paradox of the again and the anew resides, in part, in the relation that comes to be envisaged with tradition. Tradition is not a description of what has been. Tradition is not perdurable. Despite the fact that it seems to invoke a 'past' – even though it is a past oscillating between the differing though not necessarily conflicting determinations of history and nostalgia, tradition more properly involves dominance and futurity. It is for this reason that tradition can be given the working definition of a determination in advance. The practice of interpretations that work against dominance and the pregiveness of both meaning and propriety will involve a

repetition of a work – and thus the generation of an event in which a space is opened and a relation constructed whose determinations cannot be preordained. Once again what is at stake is internality, though an internality with exteriority rather than direction.

Even though the distinction is not absolute it is vital to construct and maintain, if only as strategy, the difference, adumbrated above, between works whose internality has direction and those works which come to acquire it through the process of interpretation and the action of repetition. In the latter case, as was noted, the new involves the paradoxical repetition of the again and the anew. The temporality of this process of reworking and repeating is provided, in part, by the Freudian concept of *Nachträglichkeit*.[3] Repetition becomes the new. The contrast here is with the singular event whose internality is such that the new no longer figures within, in the sense of being sustained by, repetition.

Repetition will figure. In this instance however it pertains to the repetition of tradition. This repetition is neither that of historical continuity nor is it the simple unfolding of dominance. Repetition in this instance involves the concepts and categories handed down by tradition and which determine meaning and understanding.[4] Because of this determination it gives rise to the trap of having to define the new in simply negative terms. The way this can be avoided is by refusing generality. There can be no single way in which the concepts and categories that mark out the possibility of meaning are shown by the presentation of a work, as an event, to be unable to incorporate its 'meaning' within their own terms. The limit, the moment where the question of meaning and propriety remains open, is the new. It is a strategy internal to specific works. The acuity of the problem such works create exists for philosophy. In addition to problems of meaning and understanding there will be the continual need to differentiate the temporality of fashion from that of the new.

Formulating the new in relation to tradition and to the conditions of possibility for meaning and understanding redefines the new in terms of the avant-garde. (It is, of course clear that this redefinition is reciprocal.) In both instances the specificity of the work is central. This is, in part, the reason why the project of the new – the avant-garde project – is not predictive. Prediction necessitates either generality or a form of artistic universality. The challenge that is presented by the new – the new in the sense defined above – because it concerns meaning and understanding, is finding a language, perhaps even a conceptual language, within which, what delimits the newness of the new can find expression. This is the reason why there must be experimentation within modes of writing. The new will demand to be addressed in different ways.

Notes

1 I have aimed at developing the concept of 'intentional logic' in 'Interpreting Reflections: Painting Mirrors', *The Oxford Literary Review*, vol 11, nos 1-2, 1989.

2 An original heterogeneity is a way of providing a description of an ontology of difference that retains the force of the ontological while not involving a commitment to Heidegger's 'ontological difference'. Difference, in the way that I have used the term, is differential. It thereby incorporates value. I have tried to expand upon these concerns in *Translation and the Nature of Philosophy*, Routledge, London, 1989; also in 'Interpreting Reflections: Painting Mirrors' (see above).

3 This key term within Freud's work provides a way of thinking through the concept of repetition. It has been deployed in similiar though different ways by Jean François Lyotard, *Heidegger et 'Les Juifs'*, Paris, Galilée, 1988, and Jean Laplanche, *Nouveaux fonde-*

ments pour la psychanalyse, PUF, Paris, 1987. The sources in Freud's own writings for this term are few in number. Perhaps the most important text is the neglected *Project for a Scientific Psychology*, even though Freud's formulations are problematic because of the uncritical adoption of a theory of energetics.

4 The role of concepts and categories needs to be explored in relation to Kant's conception of the understanding in *The Critique of Judgement*. The understanding, rather than being simply cognitive, can be made historical in the strict sense that it can function as an analogy for the operation of tradition. The new in this sense is linked to the sublime, not in terms of sublimity itself but rather as marking the limit of the understanding. This in turn would become the limit of tradition. I have analysed some of these issues in 'Spacing and Distancing', *Journal of Philosophy and the Visual Arts*, no 2, Academy Editions, London, 1990.

Mimmo Paladino, *Lonely Sun*, 1986, mixed media on wood

III

RETROSPECTION
AND THE POST-MODERN DISCOURSE

Robert Longo, *Untitled*, 1982, charcoal, graphite and ink on paper, 243.8x121.9cm

CHARLES JENCKS
THE POST-AVANT-GARDE

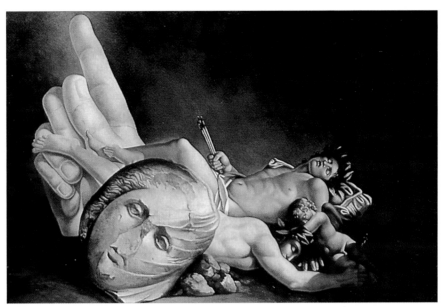

Carlo Maria Mariani, *It is Forbidden to Awake the Gods,* 1984, oil

The avant-garde is a curious term and idea; partly a military metaphor applied to the art and cultural worlds, partly a synonym and substitute for the more anodyne 'Modern' or 'Modern Movement', partly a sociological description of a patronless class of individuals. To some extent it is also a pseudo concept used to confirm the reputations of those who have arrived safely in the Vatican of

Modernism, The Museum of Modern Art in New York, that quasi-official institution which turns former acts of invention and destruction into fairly permanent icons to be studied, classified, and, on occasion, worshipped. The contradictions of this last situation have not escaped notice and now artists and critics ask themselves if the avant-garde really staked out new territory in the past so that one of their kind, Vincent van Gogh, should later have his previously unappreciated work exchanged for $40 million. $1.6 million for a Rothko, $2.2 million for a Jackson Pollock, $3 million for a Jasper Johns – the mass media keep us all up on the figures – Old Master Dadaists, Collectable Nihilists. And then another set of statistics: 50 new museums constructed in the United States in one year, 35,000 painters, sculptors and art historians graduating from American schools annually, Modernism accepted as the official culture of our time . . . Can the avant-garde, which has suffered so much disdain and disregard for 160 years, survive all this success and still be 'avant' anything?

Almost all serious critics think the avant-garde is dead as a result of absorption into the establishment and consumer society: if it has joined the centre, if it has made its peace with mass culture, if its ultimate goal is, when all is said and done, to be accepted into the mainstream, into MoMA, MOCA, or LACMA, then the avant-garde is really the Swiss Garde, or Salon Art of

our time. This is a verdict with which Robert Hughes, who has been studying Modernism and the marketplace, might agree:

> . . . although the 1970s produced its meed of good art, some of it very interesting indeed, the most striking thing now visible about the decade was an agreement that went on below the art itself: that Modernism, which had been the cultural bedrock of Europe and America for 100 years, was perhaps over; that we were at the end, as Hilton Kramer put it in a deservedly influential essay in 1972, of 'The Age of the *Avant-garde*'.

> By 1979 the idea of the *avant-garde* had gone. This sudden metamorphosis of one of the popular clichés of art-writing into an un-word took a great many people by surprise. For those who still believed that art had some practical revolutionary functions, it was as baffling as the evaporation of the American radical Left after 1970.[1]

But the question is obviously more complex and subtle than the simple death or life of the avant-garde. The 'death of Modernism' has been proclaimed this century many times and for as long as its Doppelgänger, 'the death of art'. A German book proclaimed its demise in 1907, and this didn't stop its multiple resurrections, nor the museums of the new built on its ashes. Like the Phoenix bird, Modernism seems best off just after it suffers a fatal blow and prepares for its next rebirth. One might even contend that its health depends on these ritual slayings which condition us for the next round of the cycle, the new movement which always promises to be fresh like an unknown future. The person who is tired of the avant-garde and its continual resurrections is, as they say, tired of life, of springtime and fashion, tired of continual change and business cycles: *ie* almost everybody today. How can we explain this paradox? By looking, briefly, at the four main stages of the avant-garde from the 1820s to the present, we can see how the word and practice have come, through a series of subtle alterations, to change their meaning entirely.

I The Heroic Avant-Garde

The phrase is of course partly French, but it has been adopted in many countries, notably English-speaking ones, and its primary emphasis is always on the notion of being 'before' – 'avant' other things. Thus the English 'avantalour' meaning 'one who goes before', or 'avant-peach', 'an early variety of peach'. Malory used 'avant-garde' in *Arthur*, 1470 – 'the Lyonses . . . had the avantgarde', and this sort of military usage extends up to 1796: General Stengel . . . commanded the avant-garde of Valence's Army'. All these usages are from the Oxford English Dictionary which, to prove it is aristocratic and *ancien*, actually avoids all the more contemporary meanings of the last 160 years, the only ones that actively concern us. These derive from the French Revolution and Henri de Saint-Simon's notion, formulated in 1825, of a unified avant-garde of artists, scientists and industrialists which would together create the future-positive – soon to be the science of Positivism. Saint-Simon, himself a former soldier, has the artist say to the scientist:

> It is we, artists, who will serve you as avant-garde: the power of the artist is in fact most immediate and most rapid: when we wish to spread new ideas among men, we inscribe them on marble or canvas . . . and in that way above all we exert an electric and victorious influence . . .
> if today our role appears nil or at least very secondary, what is lacking to the arts is that which is essential to their energy and to their success, namely, a common drive and a general idea.[2]

The 'common drive and general idea' was of course social progress; the march towards socialism which gave the avant-garde its direction and purpose. It also gave the artist and architect an important function as the harbingers of change *avant* the mainstream of society. Saint-Simon, as if to underline the Christian aspects of his message (and his own name) gives the avant-garde artists a priestly function:

> What a most beautiful destiny for the arts, that of exercising over society a positive power, a truly priestly function, and of marching forcefully in the van of all the intellectual faculties, in the epoch of their greatest development! This is the duty of artists, this their mission . . .[3]

Karl Marx was later, in the *Communist Manifesto*, to reserve this avant-garde role for the Communist Party, and many radical newspapers in France, after 1848, took on the title *L'Avant-garde* as an emblem of their political positivism. Even those opposed to communism got caught up in the military metaphor. The anarchist Peter Kroptkin, for example, gave the inevitable title to his Swiss magazine – something that was to directly influence the avant-gardism of Le Corbusier. One more quote from this first stage of the avant-garde may be given to underline its heroic, positivist role. It comes from Gabriel-Désiré Laverdant's book, *On the Mission of Art and Role of Artists*, published in France in 1845:

> Art, the expression of society, manifests in its highest soaring the advanced social tendencies: it is the forerunner and the revealer. Therefore, to know whether art worthily

fulfils its proper mission as initiator, whether the artist is truly of the avant-garde, one must know where Humanity is going, know what the destiny of the human race is . . .[4]

In other words Laverdant, Saint-Simon and Karl Marx would find today's avant-garde very *arrière*, just as they would find the subsequent split between art and politics into two separate avant-gardes a baneful situation. The split inevitably occurred in the 1880s with a Modernism which focused on each separate art language; the 'art for art's sake' which has remained one of the strongest of the avant-gardes to the present, with the writings of Mallarmé and Clement Greenberg among others.

Nonetheless the 'Heroic' avant-garde was the first and most important version of this changing institution and it gave direction to the efforts of painters such as Gustave Courbet and Utopian planners such as Robert Owen and Charles Fourier. It also led, when it marched on a social and artistic front at the same time as it did for about ten years – to the 'Heroic' period of Modern architecture in the 1920s; the work of Gropius, Mies and Le Corbusier. The Heroic avant-garde led society, or at least the professions, and the main-garde, or establishment, followed in its wake.

It's worth pausing for a moment to unpack this military metaphor a little further. If the Heroic avant-garde was to be out front annexing territory here and provoking outrageous skirmishes with the enemy there, then it was Serving the Destiny of Humanity, and its job was to be followed up by the main army, perhaps we should call it the *moyen-garde*, or *milieu-garde*, or best of all *centre-garde*, because this last metaphor gives a precise placement in front to the 'avant'. Can there be an avant-garde without a defined *centre* and *arrière*, without a Salon and Establishment, an Academy and Aristocracy? The Heroic avant-garde was itself to be the replacement for the older institution of the élite, with its intelligentsia, professionals and aristocrats. Thus its styles and virtues would be picked up by the rest of society: Le Corbusier and the Bauhaus would set the standards for mass production, the ideal types which would be endlessly repeated and thereby raise the level of mass taste; T S Eliot would 'purify the language of the tribe'; Eisenstein would reform the sensibilities of the film-goer as much as Picasso, Braque and Léger would transform and purify the visual codes of the public. Never mind, for a moment, that this never happened precisely the way they intended; the ideal was strong enough to carry ten generations of Modernists right up to the 1960s. It served to justify their experiments, their will to power, their endless housing estates and attacks on the academies of art.

2 The Purist Avant-Garde

This idea also paved the way for the second type of avant-garde, the Purist stage, because it provided a social pretext for making formal experiments with different art languages, at least on the level of analogy. Where the first ground-breakers could claim a potential social liberation, their successors could claim spiritual freedom: the heavenly city of artistic imagination liberated from previous convention in order to invent new worlds. And this formalist Modernism has proven much stronger and more lasting (though less interesting) than the first avant-garde. From Josef Albers to Frank Stella, from Theo van Doesburg to Peter Eisenman, from Buckminster Fuller to Norman Foster, from Modernist abstraction to Late-Modern formalism and technicism, the Purist avant-garde has dominated art and architectural politics from the 20s to the present and I am tempted to say, with others, that it is the only 'true' avant-garde there can be after the social/artistic one has died – the only one that stakes out new territory, conquers new languages and modes of experience. But I am not fundamentally concerned here with such incessant revolution for its own sake, and so will return to the last two types of avant-garde, of which one may deserve the epithet 'so-called', the other 'radical'.

3 The Radical Avant-Garde

The radical avant-garde of the 1910s and 1920s grew out of the attempt to overcome the final boundary; the dividing line between art and life. Where the two previous avant-gardes pushed into new social and artistic territories, the radical avant-gardes – the Futurists, Dadaists and Constructivists – sought to do away with all distinctions, all nationalities, all standards and professions (including in a sense themselves) and thus they were not only radical, but anti-avant-garde as well. Art would go out into the street, and the streets would be turned into art galleries, art would be life and life would become an artwork. Tatlin's machine art, particularly his Monument to the Third International, typifies this radical avant-garde and it's noteworthy that the German Dadaists of the time could interpret it with the slogan 'Art is Dead, Long Live the New Machine Art of the Tatlins'. The Constructivists, after the Russian Revolution, made the most radical assaults on the bourgeois separation of art and life epitomised in the institutional divide between the museum and factory.

The poet Mayakovsky and others proclaimed 'Down with Museums and Art! We do not need a dead mausoleum of art where dead works are worshipped, but a living factory of the human spirit – in the street, in the tramways, in the factories, workshops and workers' houses.' This attack on the institutionalisation of art within museums and the attendant notion of the autonomous work of art disconnected from society is the essence of the avant-garde for those materialists such as Peter Burger who write on the subject today.[5] It's easy to see why their arguments are persuasive: the art context does insulate the work of art, the art market and museum do change, however subtly, the meaning of a gesture and style. We can't look at a Julian Schnabel without thinking of the price tag and promotion apparatus surrounding it anymore than we can look at Norman Foster's Hongkong Bank without knowing that it is the most expensive Late-Modern building in the world. The mass media and marketplace have made materialists of us all and the only way to transcend this situation is to fully admit its implications and see how the artist and architect deals with this as part of the content of the work.

The extreme examples of this radical avant-gardism occurred first in the early 1920s and then again in the 1960s, with several Pop artists who attempted, in their words, to 'operate in the gap between art and life', close this gap or, like Andy Warhol, act as if it never existed, reducing art to a type of mechanised and stylised life. Warhol's gnomic utterances, 'I want to be a machine, machines have less problems', turned the whole positivist and socialist ethos of the avant-garde on its head; his admission that the ultimate content of his art was money showed that the old adversarial position of the avant-garde (as the alternative to mass culture) was dead. With Warhol and the 1960s, the period of the classic avant-garde as high culture came to an end as its critical and revolutionary implications were reabsorbed by consumer society, and the art market itself started demanding each season a 'new, improved shock of the new', or 'shock of the Neo'. One only has to recall Dwight Macdonald's notion of high culture as avant-gardism to see how it couldn't work anymore. In his 'A Theory of Mass Culture' written in 1953, he argues:

> The significance of the Avant-garde movement (by which I mean poets such as Rimbaud, novelists such as Joyce, composers such as Stravinsky, and painters such as Picasso) is that it simply refused to compete. Rejecting Academicism – and thus, at a second remove, also Mass

Culture – it made a desperate attempt to fence off some area where the serious artist could still function. It created a new compartmentalisation of culture, on the basis of an intellectual rather than a social élite. The attempt was remarkably successful: to it we owe almost everything that is living in the art of the last 50 or so years. In fact the High Culture of our times is pretty much identical with Avantgardism.[6]

With the Pop artists equating high culture with low, kitsch with the avant-garde, the old garde could no longer be 'avant' anything: rather it could reflect and play back mass culture on a different, aesthetic level. There was no room here, in Macdonald's phrase, 'to fence off some area where the serious artist could still function' – certainly nowhere safe from the voracious art market.

Just as devastating for the classic avant-garde was the counter-culture of the student movements, the protests against the Vietnam War, the activism of feminists and above all 'May 68', the *Evenements de Mai*, which made every Art Gallery Happening, every gesture of anti-art and performance art staged within the museum context look like amateur theatricals; an encounter workshop in a retirement centre located somewhere west of Phoenix, Arizona. The critic Harold Rosenberg saw immediately the damaging implications of the May Events for those who were trying to sustain an anti-art avant-gardism and he wrote about it in *The New Yorker* so that lessons would not be entirely lost on the centre of the art world. He quotes Michel Ragon:

> During the events of May and June, 1968, culture and art no longer seemed to interest anyone. Drawing the unavoidable conclusions, the museum curators closed their cemeteries of culture. Infected by this example, the private galleries locked their doors . . . During the May Revolution, the city once again became a centre of games, it rediscovered its creative quality; there instinctively arose a socialisation of art – the great permanent theatre of the Odéon, the poster studio of the ex-Ecole des Beaux-Arts, the bloody ballets of the CRS [police] and students, the open-air demonstrations and meetings, the public poetry of wall slogans, the dramatic reports by Europe No I and Radio Luxembourg, the entire nation in a state of tension, intensive participation, and, in the highest sense of the word, poetry. All this meant dismissal of culture and art.

The death of art has been declared for half a century, but this statement, by the French critic Michel Ragon, forecasts what will replace it. Against art, Ragon poses the political demonstration as a superior form of creation: the public event becomes the model of aesthetic expression. Whatever the merit of this view, its effect is to discredit the anti-art artist, who in demonstrating the death of art has continued to present himself as its heir. From Mondrian to Dubuffet, this has been the century of 'the last painter', whose formulas of negation promised to defy further reduction. Painting divided by zero, however, proved to equal infinity: art might be coming to an end, but there was no end to anti-art. Now the whole game is being put into question not by works of art but by collective action that, in Ragon's phrase, simply 'dismisses' it.[7]

May 68 produced what was called 'Modernism in the Streets', a 24-hour Art Opening cum Happening which was in some ways more creative and spontaneous – at least while the food and petrol lasted – than what was occurring in the lofts of SoHo. But as we know, this radical avant-gardism of political art didn't last much more than a month, after which the art market and politics returned to their old ways. In retrospect it's obvious that the world's political, cultural and economic systems can overcome most shocks, most business cycles and recessions, accommodate most political and artistic activity directed against them; they are all much stronger than the 60s dissenters had predicted. Indeed these systems thrive on dissent, criticism, cycles of destruction and near-collapse; both capitalism and its cultural world need these catalysts as their life blood.

It seems to me, and this is of course more speculation than conventional wisdom, that what is called the 'modern world' depends essentially on production and destruction cycles and that Modernism mirrors quite faithfully this eternal swing of the pendulum, this 'transvaluation of all values' in Nietzsche's terms, this annihilation of the fixed, the valued, the already achieved. The three avant-gardes I have mentioned are like an aggressive multinational out to capture new markets, never content with what it has already done, always intent on the next challenge; 'innovate or die', continually change or dry up, continually destroy in order to create. I'm told that in Foster's Hongkong Bank they changed one third of the layout and organisation last year and envisage such continual cycles of renewal in the future. If that restructuring is the reality of international finance today, it is also reflected directly in the production of art and architecture.

The negative consequences of this have been expressed very poetically by Karl Marx in *The Communist Manifesto*. Before I quote the well-known lines which have implications for the idea of the avant-garde, I should declare a debt to Marshall Berman and his important work on Modernism, called after Marx's words *All That is Solid Melts into Air*, because it is Berman who has shown us how much of a Modernist Marx really was and even, to stretch a point, how much he admired the dynamism and self-realisation of the bourgeoisie. Of course Marx was out to sink capitalism and like the typical son of the bourgeoisie hated his class, but in these attitudes of love/hate he was not unlike the typical avant-gardists of the last 160 years who have sought to overthrow their immediate predecessors, their father's generation, as they realise their own unique style and message. Karl Marx wrote of the continual revolution, or avant-gardism, of the bourgeoisie:

The bourgeoisie cannot exist without constantly revolutionising the instruments of production, and thereby the relations of production and with them the whole relations of society. Conservation of the old modes of production in unaltered form, was, on the contrary, the first condition of existence for all earlier industrial classes. Constant revolutionising of production, uninterrupted disturbance of all social conditions, everlasting uncertainty and agitation distinguish the bourgeois epoch from all earlier ones. All fixed, fast-frozen relations, with their train of ancient and venerable prejudices and opinions, are swept away, all newly formed ones become antiquated before they can ossify. All that is solid melts into air, all that is holy is profaned and man is at last compelled to face, with sober senses, his real conditions of life, and his relations with his kind.

While this incessant destruction is partly nihilist, as Marx and Nietzsche were to recognise, it also liberates enormous potential for creativity and self-realisation – the development of each individual and society as a whole. It reminds us that Thomas Jefferson, after enjoying the self-realising potential of the American Revolution for his own generation, wanted to guarantee the 'right of revolution' for each future generation, something that hasn't quite occurred in the political world, but does exist in the capitalist economy and the art and architectural markets.

It was the architect and theorist Adolf Loos who at the turn of the century connected the notion of the bourgeoisie with the style of Modernism. Loos, like so many 19th-century writers, lamented the absence of an authentic culture comparable with those of the pre-industrial past. Whereas previous ages had their integral style and set of values, the present was lost in eclecticism and copying: while the aristocracy was confident about its traditions, and the peasants naturally followed slow-changing conventions, the bourgeoisie, who were wallowing about at sea, naturally produced and consumed a superior form of kitsch. Therefore, Loos concludes, if the bourgeoisie is to discover its own authentic culture and style, it must do so in utility, function, efficiency – in the great, austere monuments that the captains of industry were creating, unselfconsciously, everywhere: bridges, skyscrapers, and engineering works.

This interpretation of Modernism as authentic bourgeois culture is not, as far as I know, formulated as such by Loos, but it is suggested throughout his writings. It's not an interpretation which is likely to find wide assent since the middle class have a dynamic self-image and a conspicuous dislike of the bourgeoisie as a class (one definition of the middle class is that it won't recognise itself). There are different attitudes one can take towards this evasion and loss of self-identity. The Modernist and Late-Modernist attitude is often to adopt a working-class style – a stripped and tough industrial mode that now graces every chic restaurant from Tokyo to Los Angeles. Tom Wolfe, in his amusing caricature of Modernism, *From Bauhaus to Our House*, rests his entire case on this single idea and it's not surprising how much juice he can squeeze out of it: the

. . . Bauhaus style proceeded from certain firm assumptions. First, the new architecture was being created for the workers. The holiest of all goals: perfect worker housing. Second, the new architecture was to reflect all things bourgeois. Since just about everyone involved, the architects as well as the Social Democratic bureaucrats, was himself 'bourgeois' in the literal, social sense of the word, 'bourgeois' became an epithet that meant whatever you wanted it to mean. It referred to whatever you didn't like in the lives of people above the level of hod carrier. The main thing was not to be caught designing something someone could point to and say of, with a devastating sneer: 'How very bourgeois'.[8]

So we come by way of Karl Marx, Adolf Loos and Tom Wolfe, an unlikely threesome, to the conclusion that Modernism is the natural style of the bourgeoisie (even if disguised in blue jeans and I-beams) and the implication which follows, that the avant-garde which drives Modernism forward directly reflects the dynamism of capitalism, its new waves of destruction and construction, the yearly movements and 'isms' which follow each other as predictably as the seasons.

4 The Post-Avant-Garde

But this situation has changed in the last ten years, not because the bourgeoisie and capitalism have 'melted into air', but because artists, architects, critics and the public have begun to understand these dynamics and have taken up a new position, what I would call, perhaps rather predictably, the 'Post-Avant-Garde'. This new stage of the institution is obviously quite different from the previous three – the Heroic, Purist, and Radical avant-gardes – because it doesn't try to conquer new territories: for the old 'shock of the new' of Duchamp, it substitutes the new 'shock of the old' of Mariani.

The territory that the Post-Avant-Garde discovers is the entire old landscape and it is calculatedly shocking insofar as it's upsetting the taboos of the Modernists – perhaps none so important as the image of the bourgeoisie triumphant and enjoying itself. Ricardo Bofill, for instance, takes the social Utopianism of Fourier and builds those 'heroic *phalanstéres*' which were meant to transform the life of the working class as 'palaces for the people': it's incongruous and blatant perhaps, but no more so than Palladio designing Villa Rotondas, and other church/temples, for patricians: or the mansions of the American South which are based on the same appropriations of religious forms.

Most Modernists and even Post-Modernists dislike these works because their classical and bourgeois imagery is so obvious, but ironically the people who live in them often find them preferable to the Modernist solutions offered at the equivalent price. The 'machines for living in' of Le Corbusier, the mass housing based on abstraction and the machine metaphor, have not been embraced by the working class, which was meant either to like them, or improve its taste and learn to love them. Post-Modern architecture, more than Post-Modernism in the other arts, is faced with such clear failures of Modernism as the bi-monthly blowing-up of inoperable housing estates, and this is why it has faced the 'death of Modernism' so directly. Modernisation, the destructive/constructive forces of urban renewal and capitalism are nowhere so apparent as in the environment.

The Post-Avant-Garde thus not only acknowledges that it is bourgeois, but in so doing recognises class-based tastes, and other tastes as well, as valid in themselves. Hence its defining eclectic style, hence its philosophy of pluralism and participation, hence its strategy – articulated by the Venturis and others including myself – of designing partly within the codes of the users.

This aspect of current art and architecture is discussed by Howard Fox in the exhibition and catalogue *Avant-Garde in the 80s* under the category of 'Community, Shared Values and Culture'. Here, as elsewhere, he is a shrewd and wily fox arguing that the present avant-garde is like that of the past because it is concerned with many of the same issues – except in opposite ways. One by one the clever Fox shows that the avant-garde of the 1980s has cancelled all the avant-garde checks of the past 160 years. It leads to the question: 'why then call it the avant-garde?' It reminds me of the definition of a reproduction: 'A reproduction is exactly like the original except in every respect'.

What, then, are the other defining characteristics of this Post-Avant-Garde? It has a new relationship with society now, an expanded audience of different tastes and cultures. Its art is perceived from many differing points of view at once, so it is inevitably ironic and multi-coded, like the work of R B Kitaj and Robert Longo, providing several discontinuous interpretations and based on multiple perspectives, different vanishing points. Narrative, local harmonies and iconology have returned, but they don't, as in the pre-Modern past, point to a single solution, to a unified world-view or metaphysics.

In this sense Post-Modernism is still partly Modern, acknowledging the discoveries of the famous triad, the Old Testament figures Marx, Freud and Einstein – as well as supplementing them with the New Testament prophets – Lévi-Strauss, Chomsky and Foucault. A common figure, or motif, in

Post-Modern architecture shows this new metaphysics quite vividly and one can find parallels in art: the return to the absent centre, the centre which could not hold; the return to the circular plaza sited in the heart of the city, which is meant to give the kind of place centredness – lacking in modern urbanism. Arata Isozaki, Michael Graves, Ricardo Bofill, Charles Moore, James Stirling – virtually every Post-Modernist – provide these gathering figures, these enclosing squares, these enveloping rotondas, these centred cities – but then leave the centre blank, an indication of the void at the heart of society, or the lack of a suitable icon to place on the high altar. They provide the necessary social space for the public realm to come into existence, they celebrate and contain this space with a beautiful and permanent masonry, but then leave it up to an agnostic society to provide the final touch; the sculpture, painting, or artefact which will give it precise definition. Much Post-Modern painting shows the search for this missing centre and thereby, as in architecture, the primacy of the rhetorical figure, 'the presence of the absence.'

To conclude I would return to our military metaphor and ask how much can be salvaged. The Post-Avant-Garde comes *after* the previous three and so this term is quite precise in its description of placement: in fighting terms it is not the front-line, but the second echelon, not the *corps d'élite,* but those who come onto the battlefield afterwards, to mop up. The great strength of the Post-Avant-Garde is to recognise what its predecessors couldn't admit to themselves; that it is a small part of the powerful middle class which is indefatigably transforming the world in ways that are simultaneously destructive and constructive. It doesn't seek to hide this self-knowledge, or pretend it can lead the working class or overcome the contradictions between life and art, the programmes and pretensions of the previous avant-gardes, and in this modest self-recognition lies its particular kind of authenticity. It is realistic about the limited role open to self-elected élite in society: it may set standards, define what's relevant for different professions, but it doesn't march on a wide common front, as the avant-garde did in the 1920s, because there is no enemy to conquer except itself – on a huge scale. And this is the telling joke or revealing paradox of the Post-Avant-Garde: it doesn't exist as an avant-garde because it is everywhere and nowhere, dispersed throughout the world as a series of individuals, and yet still a loosely shared cultural movement among those who come 'after' the previous battles. All the avant-gardes of the past believed that humanity was going somewhere, and it was their joy and duty to discover the new land and see that people arrived there on time; the Post-Avant-Garde believes that humanity is going in several different directions at once, some of them more valid than others, and it is their duty to be guides and critics. No doubt we need a good word for this loose institution, this pressure group and set of groups that now operate in the world village, that communicates quickly and effectively with each other across continents: 'cultural élite', 'intelligentsia', 'interest group', 'leading professionals', 'clerisy' – none of these work so I fall back on the partly inadequate label of my title. At least its locational metaphor is extremely accurate.

Notes

1 Robert Hughes, 'Ten Years That Buried the Avant-Garde', *Sunday Times Magazine,* December 1979-January 1980, p18.

2 Henri de Saint-Simon, *Opinions littéraires, philosophiques et industrielles,* Paris, 1825, quoted in Donald Drew Egbert, *Social Radicalism and the Arts: Western Europe,* Alfred A Knopf, NY, 1970, p121.

3 *ibid,* pp121-2.

4 Quoted from Renato Poggioli, *The Theory of the Avant-Garde,* Harvard University Press, Cambridge, Mass, p9.

5 Peter Burger, *Theory of The Avant-Garde,* translated from the German by Michael Shaw, University of Minnesota Press, Minneapolis, 1984 (original text 1974, 1980).

6 Dwight Macdonald, 'A Theory of Mass Culture', *Diogenes,* No 3, Summer, 1953, pp 1-17, reprinted in *Mass Culture and the Popular Arts in America,* ed, Bernard Rosenberg and David Manning White, The Free Press, NY, pp59-73.

7 Harold Rosenberg, 'The Art World: Confrontation', *The New York,* June 6, 1970, p54.

8 Tom Wolfe, *From Bauhaus to Our House,* Pocket Books, NY, 1981, p17.

Two Brothers, 1987, oil

R B KITAJ
TWO PAINTINGS: PREFACES AND POSTSCRIPTS

Two Brothers

The whole art of Kafka consists in forcing the reader to re-read. His endings, or his absence of endings, suggest explanations which, however, are not revealed in clear language but, before they seem justified, require that the story be re-read from another point of view. Sometimes there is a double possibility of interpretation, whence appears the necessity for two readings. This is what the author wanted.   **Camus**

For many years, this painting was called *Bub and Sis*. It depicted a lesbian couple and was inspired by a picture-story about Times Square, which I've kept from the old *Life* magazine. Then I painted it over in black.

The new picture is about two brothers I got to know almost 30 years ago. I was a student at the Royal College of Art and I used to lunch now and then at a cheap Polish restaurant at South Kensington called Dacquise. It's still there and still cheap. One day I sketched two men at a nearby table speaking Polish to each other. They noticed me and after a while, as they were leaving, one of them came to my table and asked if I would show him my sketch, which I did. He said he loved art and gave me his card which said 'Count Martinus a Grudna Grudzinski' and under that: 'Fine Art Consultant.' They were quite old brothers, remnants of Ander's army, who lived (and died) a few doors from the restaurant. To make a long story short, the Count appeared at my degree show and bought a life drawing. I visited them irregularly in their large dark flat. The Count lovingly kept a picture collection including Sickert, Corinth, Menzel, Polish painters I didn't know and unknown artists like myself. His brother kept small birds – he is clutching one in my painting while the Count is looking at a Matisse-like Polish painting.

For many years this painting was called *Bub and Sis*. It depicted a lesbian couple and was inspired by a picture-story about Times

The Caféist, 1980-87, oil

Square which I've kept from the old *Life* magazine. Then I painted it over black.

The new painting is about two old brothers I knew almost 40 years ago. They lived together in the same rooming house, in the 18th district (Währing) of Vienna, as I did when I was a 19-year-old student at the Art Academy in the Schillerplatz. The fat one was a poor painter who had a Matisse-like style as you can see in my painting. He had been a student at my very school along with Schiele, whose work he hated. Somehow, through thick and thin, he had survived as a painter. They painted and lived and kept small birds in a single large room. My landlady told me they were Nazis. I didn't tell them I was a Jew because my landlady, Frau Hedwig Bauer, was a dear old (Gentile) friend of my Grandmother and I didn't wish to cause her trouble so I ignored the two old men. I was courting a Christian girl and my life was overflowing. The awful thing was to have to share a bathtub with the bastards.

The Caféist, 1978-1987

I am a Caféist. So is Joe Singer, who is at least ten or twelve years older than I am. Here is Joe in 1987 in the café called Le Central at the east end of the rue Blondel in Paris. A Caféist is one who prefers his own company, alone, in a café, with the life spinning around him, having nothing to do with him. The Caféist writes and sometimes furtively sketches in the café. He prefers cafés in 'low' districts, like red-light areas – such as Le Central where the Caféist rests his bones before taking to the streets yet again. Joe may be drinking coffee but at Le Central it is my own habit for 35 years now to drink hot chocolate while the local girls rest up before going out in all weather to work. One's habits are changed with the advent of AIDS and besides, the Caféist is not young anymore and the café seems more delicious a waystation. This painting began in the late 70s as a scene in a New York brothel I used to like on 3rd Avenue which is now closed. When it shut down, I began this picture, leaving the left hand side almost intact and overpainting the rest. Such places as Le Central have given me many ideas for painting and I owed it this picture.

These two texts are from R B Kitaj's book, Hints for Young Painters (Prefaces and Postscripts) *published by Thames and Hudson in 1989.*

Dein goldenes Haar, Margarethe (Your Golden Hair, Margarete), 1981, oil, emulsion and straw, 130x170cm

'Black milk of daybreak we drink you at night
we drink in the morning at noon we drink you at sundown
we drink and we drink you
A man lives in the house he plays with the serpents he writes
he writes when dusk falls to Germany your golden hair Margarete
your ashen hair Shulamith we dig a grave in the breezes there one lies unconfined.'
Paul Celan, *Todesfugue* (Death Fugue), written in a concentration camp in 1945

ANDREW BENJAMIN
PAINTING WORDS: KIEFER AND CELAN

There is a line of painting. And yet what is painted in being painted and in becoming words, differentiates itself from painting. The technique of the same breaks with itself in becoming painting; breaking while remaining painting. Is it thus that painting can work with itself against itself? Furthermore there is the related demand that relation comes to be rethought, with the result that such a rethinking may cause relation to be taken as central. In Anselm Kiefer's painting *Your Golden Hair Margarete*, the line written into the frame also works to frame. (Despite the necessity of the 'also', this work – the line's work – is neither a simple addition nor a supplement. Work here attests to the anoriginal plurality of the line when construed as an event.[1]) The words cut the furrows – cutting them by cutting across them – thereby providing another horizon. (This 'another' while denoting an addition is a further presentation within an already existing plurality.) The painted words work therefore in different ways.

The difference is both announced and maintained by the combination of painting and words. It is this combination that effaces the possibility of a reduction, within any putative interpretation, of paintings to words. The line in this painting, *Dein goldenes Haar Margarete*, (Your golden hair Magarete), is in addition (again an addition which resists the import of a simple addition) to its being a line, an as yet to be specified citation, the painting's title. The problem of names and titles thereby ensues. Here, this problem will remain by being introduced – perhaps reintroduced – within citation; the other site of naming.

The presence of the line is, on one level at least, unproblematic. It is taken from Paul Celan's poem *Todesfugue*.[2] (It will be seen that the singularity of this 'it', the line, is already, from the start, open to question). The citation, within the already given frame, raises quite specific questions. They pertain to the site of citation. The site is, of course, the framed area. However, as has already been indicated, the words also frame. These words, the line, occur five times in the actual poem. What therefore has been cited? Which one – which instance – comes to be sited in the painting? The difficulty of answering these questions is not derived from any epistemological shortcomings or hindrance. Indeed the contrary is the case since the setting of a limit to any particular frame of questioning is in itself significant. A significance that is neither delimited nor enclosed by the established limit. The emergence of limits works therefore to open citation thereby indicating that there is more at stake here than a simple repetition. Furthermore, a consequence of this opening is that there can no longer be either a direct or unproblematic answer to the question; which line has been cited? While it may appear, as a question, to be apposite, its pertinence is lacking because its force depends upon its having been formulated within the frame established by the logic of identity. The question intends to pick out a single answer. Its scope is limited from the start.

If it were thought that all that was at play within the general frame were words and their repetition – the intended singularity – then the repetition in question would involve the repetition of the same. (Care must be taken here for while the 'same' may include equality it can never be reduced to it). This particular construal of repetition has its sources in what could be described as a formalised Platonism. It endures as that element of the Platonic tradition within which that conception of mimesis proper to the dialogues (proper in the sense of intended) remains as a determining and structuring influence. What such a conception of mimesis will always involve – involvement as consequence – are the problems that come to the fore within the attempted 'giving again' of that which had already been given. (The mimetic structure does not necessitate the presence of the Platonic 'idea', for it involves the work of an already abstracted logic of mimesis). The problem stems, as the formulation indicates, from the posited centrality of the image. The image is articulated within the terms set by the ontology of stasis; here involving the assumed singularity of identity. In other words the image, when taken as a remove, opens up the problem of its own authenticity. This can itself only be guaranteed if the relationship between the image and its source is rid of either the plurality or overdetermination, be they potential or actual, that will jeopardise the work of homology; *ie* repetition of the same within the reign of the Same.

Even after having moved from repetition structured within the terms set by the Same and thus which demand a repetition that is the same, to a dynamic repetition, presentations still occur. In broad terms it remains the case that there is still a giving. However there is a different occurrence, for now what is given is the affirmed presence of the same and different. (Presence as that co-presence marking the complex simultaneity of the event.) The introduction of an event whose plurality is marked by irreducibility becomes part of the work of the reworking of repetition. Moreover the positing of this irreducibility alludes to, perhaps even invokes, the threat that was always inherent in the interarticulation of image and mimesis. Here beyond the range of this threat and thus the work of identity and the repetition of, and in, the same – the deferral of its reign – there is the redolent presence of the poem *Todesfugue*.

While it anticipates an argument to come, the work of Celan's poem can nonetheless be described as the enactment of a repetition working within the abeyance of similitude and thus beyond the sway of the domination of the Same. Its being that enactment means that it eschews firstly any straightforward formulation of the logic of identity and secondly any rigid distinction between form and content.[3] The poem thus demands that both within and as the act of interpretation, the question of identity and the stakes of repetition come to be reposed. It is this demand which figures here in terms of both the problem of citation and the subsequent location of that problem within the frame. The citation becomes a repetition of the site of repetition. The difficulty arises here not from having to provide a formulation for the relationship between the line and the poem but from the location of the line within and as part of the painting.

Provisionally, Celan's poem situates a contrast between two forces; two moments that become history. One is marked by the name Margarete and the other by the name Shulamith.[4] It is these two names which are present as either titles or figure as part of what is framed within a number of Kiefer's paintings undertaken

Margarethe (Margarete), 1981, oil and straw, 280x380cm

in 1981. (Is what is at stake here painting as an intended meditation on poetry?) The complexity of the proper name is already apparent. The proper names have a specific and unique referent on the condition that it names in never just that referent. The propriety of the proper name is maintained to the extent that it enjoins a type of paradox. Here the presence of proper names raises the complex question of what they name from the moment they are at work within the poem and in the paintings. The complexity is reinforced once it is recognised that as names they also function as titles. It is thus that the name is irretrievably, if only formally, doubled.[5]

Within the poem what the names mark out is only fixed in repetition. If one is the figure of Germany and the other is the figure of the Jew then such a description only works if these figures are understood as an integral part of the poem's rhythm. At first the names are contrasted, then in the final two lines they abut. What they do not form is an integrated whole. Their irreducibility figures in the poem in terms of the oppositions between life and death, and then, between solidity and smoke. It is also present in the contrast between 'golden hair' and 'ashen hair'. This contrast only introduces an inseparability in the sense

that it is impossible to consider the history of Germany independently of the Shoah. And yet the Shoah remains as the event that works to check all events because of its absolute singularity. A singularity that in being maintained and thus repeated works to open that singularity beyond itself. It is thus that the contrast and inseparability of Shulamith and Margarete means that to the extent that they are apart they form a part. It is precisely in terms of the apart/a part that the words forming part of what is framed as well as the combination of oil, straw and emulsion can be understood. The latter is not just the presence of mixed media. It signals a more significant and radical division within the frame. Furthermore while in paintings such as *Your Golden Hair Margarete – Midsummer Night* and *Margarete* do not incorporate either the figure or the name of Shulamith, she is there in the burnt straw, or in the dark and ashen markings. Her presence does not demand representation. The interplay of these two figures is captured in an important way in *Your Golden Hair Margarete*. Looking at how this works will open a way towards the words. The words which are in addition, the title.

In its most simple presentation this painting is a landscape; the furrows depicting the field move toward, and away from, the

Dein goldenes Haar, Margarethe – Johannis-Nacht (Your Golden Hair, Margarete – Midsummer Night), 1981, oil, acrylic, emulsion and straw, 130x160cm

painted horizon. On one side are a group of houses. The juxtaposition works to reinforce the presence of the field. The furrows are cut by words, by the presence of golden straw and by large black marks. One of the latter is applied such that it borders the straw. The reciprocal description would of course also be true. Before moving on in this description, it is essential to note that the problem of representation and how history can be represented forms a vital part of Kiefer's project. It is a project that is depicted, projected, in and as painting.[6]

The landscape is the field of history. It is the inscription of the place of history into the painting and as painting. If history is not just the recitation of events, then the presence of the field is Kiefer's response to the question of how the event of history is to be represented. History as the field of repetition. A repetition that breaks within the dominance of the Same by the repetition of landscape where that repetition is contemporaneous with the impossibility of the field's being reduced to a simple enactment, repetition, within the genre of landscape. The frame becomes therefore the field of irreducibility and thus the site of anoriginal heterogeneity. The frame resists simplicity.

The straw and the black marks are part of what is framed, are part of the furrows in that they cross them and yet are apart from the furrows. Again, the straw, is part of the painting's work and yet it is neither painted nor is it paint. Its presence complicates the canvas. The straw plays an integral role but only on the condition that it is not, in any sense of the term, part of painting. Its presence is enacted within the logic of the apart/a part. The straw and the black marks do not come to have representational, perhaps even symbolic force in terms of themselves but only in relation to the words. They do not in any straightforward sense therefore either represent or function as symbols. The words work to inscribe the concerns of Celan's poem into the painting, as part of the painting, such that the relation that is thereby established between all the elements within the frame works to picture the co-presence of Germany and its other within the field of history. The Germany in question is not an element of a tradition that can be denied or displaced. Not only is this rendered impossible by the interplay of apart/a part, it is also marked by the furrows, the place. They designate the field of renewal. However the site of renewal is not new it is the working over of what is given. Renewal in this sense is not the new but the co-presence of the again and the anew. There cannot be one

Gefallene Bilder (Fallen Pictures), 1986, emulsion and photograph on cardboard, mounted on lead, 102x141cm

without the other.

It is the line, in opening a field of repetition by introducing the play of repetition that drives the work of the painting. The words in being a part yet apart also open the possibility of a presence that eschews the distinction between the literal and the figural and thus displaces by reincorporating – reworking as reincorporation – the strategies of representation and mimesis. What is at stake therefore is the image beyond the image; painted words.

Notes

1 I have tried to develop the term 'anoriginal' in relation to interpretation and in particular the interpretation of paintings in art, see *Mimesis and the Avant-Garde*, Routledge, 1991. I have given further philosophical elaboration in *Translation and the Nature of Philosophy*, Routledge, 1989.
2 I have alluded to the relationship between Kiefer and Celan in 'Kiefer's Approaches', A Benjamin and P Osborne (eds), *Thinking Art: Beyond Traditional Aesthetics*, ICA Documents, 1991.
3 The relationship between form and content becomes extremely complex in relation to repetition. Repetition is both form and content, however the consequence of this 'identity' is that the only residual force these terms may have had is finally effaced.
4 In this instance I have only dealt with the paintings that 'concern' Margarete. Those in which Shulamith is a named presence are left out of consideration.
5 The problem of naming and titles has been addressed in greater detail in 'Present Remembrance: Anselm Kiefer's *Iconoclastic Controversy*', in *Art, Mimesis and the Avant-Garde*.
6 In this regard careful attention should be paid to *Gefallene Bilder,* 1986. The importance of this work means that it warrants detailed analysis. It forms part of Kiefer's more general preoccupation with images and pictures.

———— * ————

The High Priestess

Zweistromland (The High Priestess), 1985-89, 200 lead books, two steel bookcases, glass and copper wire, 426.7x792.5x91.4cm

'More a bulky sculpture than a library, this work alludes directly to some objects by Kiefer which are inspired by the eagle-winged form of the church lectern – an expression of the ambiguity of object, form and material analogous to that of the lead books which he has incorporated in paintings . . . Apart from such heterogeneous materials as dried peas and black human hair, which serve to point the contrast between the organic and the inorganic, the contents of many of the volumes consist of photographs modified by the application of chemicals, acrylic paint, wet clay and other materials . . . The subjects of these photographs are of many kinds. Very often they are views of the earth from the air, often dominated by clouds. There are also other elements such as water or earth and stones. The geographical range runs from Israel, by way of various parts of Europe, to South and North America. The sites of antiquity alternate with such features of contemporary civilisation as cities, railway tracks, factories, bridges, and the like. All this is consistently shown in a context of decay, dissolution and destruction . . . Kiefer's twin steel bookcases, with their burden of lead books, thus assert a form of syncretism. On close consideration it becomes apparent that Kiefer finds artistic truth at the point where the past and the present interpenetrate (as form) and interact (as content). This is not simply a matter of rehabilitating what has been repressed and forgotten, or of finding the future foreshadowed in the past: it is an intuitive process, which traces the external forms of ancient legends back to a nucleus of constants which the artist would certainly never think of categorising as eternal certainties. On the contrary: in such a context, he would prefer to speak of eternal uncertainties, or permanently open questions . . . History, for Kiefer, becomes "a material, like landscape or paint". He reflects a great deal "on religions, because science gives no answers".'
Armin Zweite

ANDREW BENJAMIN
REPEATING THEMES
Notes on Haacke, Kiefer, Beuys

The poetry of Paul Celan frightens – frightening because of wounds which both haunt and work within his poetry. In *Todttnauberg*, the poem written after his encounter with Heidegger, the words announce a hope, 'einer Hoffnung'– a hope that within the confines of the poem is linked to the yet to be revealed. The confines, the place, the 'Hutte', are overcome by the work of poetry itself. These words, 'eine Hoffnung', signal more than the simple possibility that Heidegger's past, his commmitment to National Socialism would be discussed, at least announced, and in being said, in being uttered, would come to be acknowledged. In this singularity the hope, realised, would mean that the wound had been noted. That it was not does not mean that hope had been dashed. Hope endures. Hope becomes linked to a disclosure to come. Its force however will lie in the future; a future that will remain haunted not by the actions of one man but by the singularity of the name Auschwitz.

There is therefore a deeper wound, one that this name inflicts on language. Auschwitz works to check history, thereby philosophy, while at the same time being the event that language fails. Auschwitz has wounded language and in so doing would seem to have robbed it of its redemptive character. The scar endures. How is the fright of language – its displacement to be understood? This question can be posed with equal force in relation to both poetry and painting. In other words it is a question that inheres in the Western philosophical tradition's conception of art and knowledge. It is, in other words, a question striking at mimesis and representation. At work within all of these 'concepts' or 'categories' of thought is time, the time of the past, and the past in the present. The future attends. The wound remains. The ghosts haunt, frighten, out of place and therefore in place.

The frightened presence of wounded language is haunted, scarred. The marks of history, of the passing of time, force a reworking of the means by which the wound and the ghosts could be, again, represented. All will change while remaining the same. The landscape remains a landscape and yet it differs. The event causes it to differ from and within itself. It is, perhaps, this conception of

Frighten, v to throw into a fright, terrify . . . drive away out of (place etc).

Haunt, v t frequent (place) frequent company of (person) (of thoughts, memories, etc.) visit (person) persistently or frequently: visited or frequented by ghosts.

Scar, n (Fig) abiding effect of grief etc; mark left by damage; v t mark with scar.

Joseph Beuys, *Hasengrab*, 1962-67, mixed media

'*Show your wound.*'
J Beuys

'*You cannot paint a landscape after tanks have passed through it.*'
A Kiefer

repetition, with difference inscribed within it, that will bring about a redemption of redemption. This raises the important question of whether this will mean that hope itself will have been saved. Will the wound have been healed? It is in the attempt to locate answers to this question that a divergence of strategies between Beuys and Baselitz on the one hand and Kiefer and Haacke on the other, can be located.

These proper names, while unique in that they serve to pick out both 'authors' and individual works are at the same time only markers. They serve to locate particular strategies within painting. The split also identifies a similarity. All of these painters use art to question explicitly and not just implicitly, the possibility and function of art. The mode of questioning, while different, nonetheless points to the centrality of the aesthetic and thus of art itself and thereby links the aesthetic to the political. Exploring these connections, links, splits and differences is made possible here by concentrating on time. The time of repetition will become time politicised. The possibility of an original repetition will not heal the wound. It will mark – scar – its having been overcome: thereby redeeming redemption.

The time of Hans Haacke's recent work *Und ibr habt doch gesiegt* is in its very complexity of enormous importance. The work involved a repetition of the original 'Nazi victory column'. The ostensible difference between the original column and the one created by Haacke was the addition of a list of the dead from the Austrian province of Styria. It read in the fractura script often utilised by the Nazis: 'The Vanquished of Styria: 300 gypsies killed, 2500 Jews killed, 8000 political prisoners killed or died in detention, 9000 civilians killed in the war, 12,000 missing, 27,900 killed'. This is not a simple addition. The power and strength of the work, while stemming from, does not lie in the irony of the juxtaposition. The way in which repetition works here demands not just a rethinking of the categories and concepts through which evaluation would take place, but a reconsideration of the event, the occasion, and thus time.

Fractura script was not used on the original monument. And yet its use would have been compatible within the stakes of the first occasion. Fractura script could not have been used to announce the aspirations of National Socialism. At least not those aspirations that would have demanded the death of gypsies, Jews, etc. Fractura could not announce the truth about itself. It was a style inscribed within a specific project. Its occasion – its time, was delimited from the start. What is at stake then in Haacke's use – reuse – of it to announce the truth about National Socialism? What event is taking place? How is the history of this event to be understood?

The importance of the event is linked to the recognition that the wound – the wounding of language and art, the wound that Celan understood to be almost fatal and that Beuys wanted to be healed, derives its force from a

'All writing is crap.'
G Baselitz

'As a result of coming to life again through language we would inflame our land too; we would be able to consumate a process of healing this soil where we were born.'
J Beuys

Time, n duration, indefinitly continued existence, progress of this viewed as affecting persons or things; . . . conditions of life . . . occasion.

Above and Below: Anselm Kiefer, *Märkischer Sand V (March Sand V)*, 1977, double-page photographic images with sand, oil, and glue, mounted on cardboard, 62 x 42 x 8.5 cm

'Peut-être s'est-il produit dans l'histoire du concept de structure quelque chose qu'on pourrait appeler un evenement si ce mot n'importait avec lui une charge de sens que l'exigence structurale – ou structuraliste – a justement pour fonction de réduire ou de suspecter. Disons néansmoins un 'événement' et prenons ce mot avec précaution entre des guillemets. Quel serait donc cet 'événement'? Il aurait la forme exterieure d'une rupture et d'un redoublement.'
J Derrida

specific conception of language and signification. As such the wound remains but must now be incorporated within an original repetition that involves a change in the stakes of language and repetition. Limits are established and yet ghosts live on, the haunting remains; haunted, it is however the nature of its endurance that needs to be examined. Haacke's strategy begins with the recognition that re-presentation is impossible. There cannot be that particular movement that depends upon the giving again of that which had not been presented; absence to presence. The impossibility must be linked to the very real possibility of presenting again; a presenting that it not a re-presentation; but a repetition that incorporates originality within it. The repetition of the victory column does not simply mark the presence of the past in the present; it bears witness to the past without succumbing to the belief that history can be reincorporated in its truth and thus forgotten. Memory and history depend upon present remembrance. This is itself a strategy articulated within a conception of language/object/event that is located beyond the nihilistic oscillation between loss and presence. The column and the use of fractura are part of this process.

The interplay of time and repetition is also at work in Kiefer's landscapes. Here the intrusion of the 'tank' must be understood beyond its simple literality while, of course, incorporating the reality of the tank having been present. The force of Kiefer's claim resides in the 'cannot'; 'You *cannot* paint a landscape after tanks have passed through it'. Here the negative neither negates nor interdicts. Kiefer has painted what for all intents and purposes are landscapes. Tanks have been incorporated into some of the paintings. In addition there is general preoccupation with geography, perhaps as the place of history, that does not necessarily involve the actual representation of a landscape as in the sculpture *The High Priestess* (*Zweistromland*). Here however the question must concern the meaning of the 'cannot'. Once again what this question brings to the fore is repetition, linked in this instance to difference within repetition; repetition as difference. With regard to landscape there are two types of repetition involved. The first is the repetition of the genre and the second is the specific repetition. Kiefer does after all refer to actual locations (eg, in the painting *Icarus – March Sands*). His paintings take specific referents. If the 'cannot' is given its full force then the paradox to which it attests must be taken as central to the possibility of his art – its conditions of possibility – as well as inherent in the presentations themselves. The paradox, it can be argued, concerns the relationship between history and mimesis. The paradox, which works as much in titles (eg, the stakes of *The Iconoclastic Controversy*) as it does in actual presentations, articulates that relation to mimesis and representation which while recognising their presence displaces their centrality and thus refuses to allow them to dominate either the painting's own presentation or the reception proper to that presentation. What is at play in this particu-

'When asked to provide a statement to accompany the proposal for my piece, Und ihr habt doch gesiegt, in the catalogue of Points of Reference 33/38, I wrote: "And you were victorious after all" the Nazis proclaimed, full of pride, on the red fabric with their eagle and swastika, which decorated the Mariensäule in Graz on July 25 1938. They were referring to themselves. 50 years later, I hope we can make sure that the cheering will turn out to have been premature.'
H Haacke

Hans Haacke, *US Isolation Box, Grenada, 1983*, 1984, wood planks, hinges, padlock, spray painted stencil lettering, 244 x 244 x 244 cm

'I tell stories in my pictures in order to show what is behind the story. I make a hole and go through. I use perspective to draw the viewer in like a bee to the flower. But then I want the viewer to get by that to go down through the sediment.'
A Kiefer

'To my mind, art is the only possibility of making a connection between disparate things and thus creating a meaning . . . I see history as synchronous, whether it's the Sumerians with their Epic of Gilgamesh or German mythology. As far as I am concerned the old sagas are not old at all, nor is the Bible. When you go to them, most things are already formulated.'
A Kiefer

lar form of 'propriety' is a difficult and complex problem. Within it redemption becomes linked to affirmation.

The displacement of mimesis and representation means that his work can still mark the horror of destruction, be a witness to loss, while itself not marked by the now futile attempt to represent; where that attempt is advanced in terms of a repetition in which the *same* dominates. The possibility of representation and this type of repetition, one governed by the *same*, has been displaced from the start. What emerges as central is an understanding of memory and history in which temporality is complex and where the past can never be one (or won) within the present. The relation to history takes place in terms of what can be called present remembrance. The strategy at work in its presentation, its effectuation, is original repetition.

The ghosts still endure. Language marks wounds; however language, presentation, artistic activity, remain possible. What vanishes are the illusions of domination, totality and the absolute giveness of representation. They have been checked by their attempted realisation within history as the attempt to determine history. They emerge as illusion. This emergence is not an emergency for art since it can be attributed to the possibility, at the present, of realising, of releasing, the paradox that is central to mimesis and which in the displacement of mimesis works to rework the relationship between the aesthetic and the political. The landscape attains its full horror and force precisely because of this paradox.

Beuys is right to emphasise the relationship between capitalism and war. He was correct in identifying the failure that occurred, and still occurs, in relation to the actual experience of the work. The trap lay in his identification of the redemptive power of art as working on and through the individual.

Redemption will involve the affirmation of paradox, of heterogeneity coupled with the displacement of the centrality of mimesis and representation. At play here are the means in terms of which interpretation, the visual arts, politics, etc, can come to be rethought and in being rethought are thereby repeated again though now the repetition will involve originality. The work of Haacke and Kiefer can, in part, be located within this movement.

Anselm Kiefer, *Cauterisation of the Rural District of Buchen*, 1975, oil, charcoal, and glue on 20 strips of burlap, bound, 60 x 42 x 8 cm

'When we start work . . . we always have a huge sack of culture on our backs.'
A Kiefer

'The cause of two world wars lies in the enslavement of the spirit under the state and the capitalist economy.'
J Beuys

Joseph Beuys, Untitled, *1963*

Georg Baselitz
Pandemonium Manifestos

Nachtessen in Dresden, 1983, oil, 280x450cm

First Pandemonium Manifesto
(November, 1961)

The poets lay in the kitchen sink,
body in morass.
The whole nation's spittle
floated on their soup.
They grew between mucus membranes
into the root areas of humanity.
Their wings did not carry them heavenward
– they dipped their quills in blood,
not a drop wasted writing –
but the wind bore their songs,
and those have shaken faith.

The poets are still throwing up their hands. Point to changes? Bitterness, impotence, and negation are not expressed in gesture. TILL IT HURTS! With a final, finite truth pouring out. No truck with those who can't wrap art up in a SMELL. I have no kind word to say to the amiable. They have proceeded by art historical accretion, they have ruled neat lines under things, they have practised mystification with all the passion of a collector. The survivor's beds are not unmade – remnants of the last housework stuffed under the bed – the gelatinous threads have not become visible, the unfruitful troubles derided. The rest of history is instances.

We have blasphemy on our side! They have escaped their sickbeds. Their simplifying methods have swept them onto the crests of the waves. The ice beneath the foggy maze is broken. They are all frozen stiff – those who believe in fertility, those who believe in it – those who deny their pens and those who revere them. Fiery furrows in the ice, flower-like crystals, criss-cross icicles, starry sky torn open. Frozen nudes with encrusted skin – spilt trail of blood. The amiable are washed up, deposited as sediment. Faces that the moon pulls, in perspective, in the rivers, faces into which waste water drips. The toad that licks up the singers' spittle. Glowing crystal mountain. Homer the water of thine eye, in the mountain lake. Caught in the curlicues of the manuals that invented the method . . .

The seat of all unfruitful religion. Piles of squatting background monks, spread out in tiers, rigidly staring. In me there is a dead-end slide, the longing for Grecian columns, the addiction to excess, the Mannerist's addiction to excess, a tangle of tendrils and artifices, coldness and devotion – it is always enforced love. Because revulsion often overcame me without warning, I took – and still take – delight in sullying my own moments of innocent openness. Flat-chested and lacerated, I assail the hollow spaces. It has turned into impressiveness. Another procedure that shame demands. Shame is not Situationism, it is the slide into the abyss, it is frightening, it is mob delusion, it is a relapse into the pubertal ooze. Euphoria deepens abysses.

Second Pandemonium Manifesto
(Spring, 1962)

Negation is a gesture of genius,
not a wellspring of responsibility.

. . . Irreconcilable with cognac and sober-fastidious democratic contemporaries. Asiandom of the Season. Now the membrane borrowed from the sacrosanct surface, vibrating canvas (lending sexual maturity a helping hand), lovingly violated. Ripped away, the last skin, the last simile. On, far on, into the white quick. Look good in boxes, all the heads, the poets, confusion of profusion. Lightening without God into bare woods, body of mine born into clearest water. Fearsome darkness into the ice crystal of one and only truth. Up floated twisting celestial updraught to the final mission.

I am of invisible extent. Systematic mortification of the regions without sensation (grading off) into a single lapse of time. The infinity that blows from my mouth. I am on the moon as others are on the balcony. Life will go on . . .

HEINRICH KLOTZ

GERMAN PAINTING

The Transition from Abstraction to a New Objectivity

Bernd Zimmer, *Rapsfeld*, 1980, tempera on paper, 70x100cm

Art is an important early signifier of breaks in the trend, a precursor of changes extending beyond art into our everyday lives. In the 70s and 80s, while art did not undergo a revolution, a change in direction nevertheless did take place. Critics have interpreted this change in terms of a farewell to the spirit of progress, to social responsibility and enlightenment. The pendulum has swung back, they

argue, bringing with it a new conservatism, irrationality and mysticism. Instead of belief in the future we now have nostalgia, instead of technical perfection an artificial patina. Post-Modernism has betrayed Modernism.

But such an interpretation is far too facile and cannot be justified, if only because many of the innovations that are determining art today refer to the early 60s and were part of the spirit of change that characterised that decade of space exploration and student revolt. Indeed, Baselitz, Lüpertz, Penck, Polke, Richter and Kiefer – probably the most prominent painters in Germany today – appeared on the scene as early as the beginning of the 60s. Their work suggests that they are not only continuing the Modern movement, but that they have enhanced it with a new objectivity.

The first signs of a return to the object in German painting coincided with the emergence of Pop art in the United States at the beginning of the 60s. In Düsseldorf, Sigmar Polke began to paint his autotype pictures of banal everyday themes and Gerhard Richter created his first blurred paintings, ennobling the snapshot of the amateur photographer.

At the same time, Baselitz, Lüpertz, Penck, and later Immendorf and Kiefer, began to create their own mythologies, while Hödicke and Koberling in Berlin were preparing the ground for a new painting. It was a rich and varied scene, which progressed

without the public taking much notice of it; for unlike Pop art, it did not demand attention. During the early 60s painters such as Baselitz, Lüpertz and Hödicke remained isolated, while the Zero group with Uecker, Piene and Mack dominated the field. Abstraction had certainly not come to an end, and triumphed again with the work of Graubner and Gierke. Only when the new decade of the 70s began was the tradition of Modernism increasingly called into question and doubts began to arise concerning its orthodox doctrines. Only then did critics begin to discover the art of Baselitz, Lüpertz, Penck and Immendorf. Indeed, these artists have only really come to be appreciated since about 1980, when a new generation of painters, the so-called 'New Wild' or 'Neo-Fauve' artists, appeared on the scene with an intensity of colour and expressionist gesture that aroused much interest, drawing the attention of a broader public. Even the least perceptive of commentators then realised that Germany had possessed a new painting since the 60s, a form of painting that simply ignored the later manifestations of Modernism, namely Minimal and Conceptual art; for the white canvas had catapulted itself away from the consequences of the Modernist theories.

The point had been reached in art when the great potential of abstraction inevitably seemed to be exhausted and, in view of the new possibilities that had become available through the media of film, video and photography, the question had to be faced as to

Markus Lüpertz

Triptychon: Harlekin mit Raucher, Harlekine mit Schrank, Napoleon, 1984, oil, 3x320x10cm

'I am only interested in painting, never in the themes. If they see something they recognise, they think, now he is painting harlequins of all things. Perhaps they may also feel that I have done them better, differently, or in a new way.

'Art is something great, and politics is not great. Art is something divine; and what is closest to God is a great work of art. Great art rises above everything and is on the way to eternity or endlessness. Art stands between God and life. To show that there is alwas something better, something greater and more beautiful that what is real, than life, than death, than fear, that is why there is art. 'Once there was a long, broad path which led to abstract painting. At that time the public was highly intelligent and able to appreciate abstract painting. Now we have a history of downsliding in the approach to art. There are an awful lot of people who haven't got a clue and still concern themselves with art. Objective painting was rediscovered for them. There is no necessity in art to return to objective paintings. To speak of the apple of knowledge, that is, abstract painting – once one has eaten of it, one stays with it forever. 'I have not gone back to the object. I paint things that are such banal objects, that remain so far removed from themselves through my way of transmuting them, that they are abstract again.'

interview with Heinrich Klotz, 1989

whether painting was in fact a medium capable of expressing the realities of modern life. Artists had been searching for new forms of expression in Happenings, Fluxus and Performance art, moving away from the flat canvas into real life. Joseph Beuys had always confronted the pupils at the Düsseldorf Academy who still saw themselves as painters with a certain irony; he challenged them not to continue clinging to the canvas but to be more enlightened, to take art into life, to abandon the traditional fields of art and to break down the boundaries between the aesthetic and reality.

However, Beuys never extended his approach to the radical conclusion that Allan Kaprow and John Cage demanded, namely to identify the meaningless flow of life itself with art. For Beuys, 'action' retained its symbolic, deeper meaning; consequently the Fluxus movement, in which he played a key role from the early 60s, remained caught within the aesthetic fiction. Thus, Beuys' actions such as *Coyote* and *Titus Andronicus* essentially retained the theatrical character of a performance.

These actions could not be marketed as art objects, and again and again he attacked the organised art trade. The Conceptual artists followed the same direction in refusing to produce a material artwork, indicating the possibility of one only by means of a concept translated into words. The work of art is thus suggested through formal approaches rather than through a given form. In a conceptual sense, they went far beyond what could ever be realised; but at the same time they were unable to foresee that ultimately a work of art translated into the written language, or an artform implied through an outline of ideas, would in turn become a marketable object. Moreover, art had become a force of the imagination and of association, and all these attempts to withdraw from the art market had finally resulted in the negation of a sensually perceptible art. The approach of Marcel Duchamp had become the formative gesture, and the last act of the artist was to relapse into total silence.

While the gestures of refusal became saleable documents of contemporary art, the negators themselves overlooked the fact that anything made by man can become a marketable object; that ultimately the fixed idea can become a document of art and can be sold as a commodity. And finally, the consequence of this formal withdrawal was signifying the end of art.

The other alternative, again eliminating from the work of art any form of sensuous appeal to desire, led to the creation of

Rainer Fetting

Night of the Pelicans, 1987, oil, 99x129cm; *Durchgang Berlin*, 1988, oil and sand, 250x220cm

'I think it is a cliché to see painting as a performance, a cliché of Berlin artists. Somebody like Salomé, for example, comes from performing and he also talks about his painting in terms of performance. I never do that. Critics try to relate my paintings to other Berlin artists but I have never thought like Salomé, or Middendorf, or any of the others. Sometimes there's a correspondence, but everybody has his own background. Painting requires already enough concentration and does not leave you the time to perform. What may have been seen in my movements as dancing is really nothing but my concentration developing the image by moving from the colour buckets to the canvas and away from it to view the image from a distance, then back to the colour buckets. It is an intense and irregular rhythm, but it is just painting.

'When I paint, there is first the idea of an image. In order to obtain the best result, I just use my experience of painting, which could be based on my experience of Abstact Expressionism, or of Turner, or my own experience. There is a certain beauty in dripping paint, especially if it fits the spirit of the painting itself, as a formal or aesthetic content. But it would be boring to repeat what the Abstract Expressionists have done; I try to make something different.

'I'm all for loosening up, and not always doing the same, with the brush. So I do some etching, and some sculpture, I make movies, to make it more interesting. I just go after my own moods. Doing sculpture is another challenge for me. It demands a different energy. You don't always want to make your hands dirty with colour and confront a white, empty canvas. You want to dig in mud or clay, let

something grow between your fingers, distort it, twist it, let it grow again, go around it and see it from above and underneath. There is a different approach of energy.

'I have just bought a new loft in New York and I have got a great view. To get even better views, I am having windows cut, to get a more panoramic view all around. New York is already a good image by itself, and so if I paint it, I become a part of it. I don't think philosophically, I just enjoy the view; there is tension in trying to paint the city. Maybe I have philosophical thoughts, we all know those aspect of alienation, yes. But creating an image is more like the creation of a great movie. Life is the script and tradition, the screen. Paintings should not only come from reading old books but also from dealing with the present and looking into the future.'

interview with *Art & Design*, 1989

Minimal art. To perceive the beauty of an object in its most reduced state, and to escape from the spectacle of the form itself, became the strategy of artists who aimed to counter with silence a society blinded by superfluity. Sol LeWitt installed a few plywood cases, Carl Andre put square steel plates on the floor and Gerhard Richter painted grey pictures. The colour grey, into which all other colours merge, spread out as a uniform surface, extending beyond even Rauschenberg's black and white pictures. For while Rauschenberg limited perception to the shadow of the viewer moving in front of the white canvas, Richter's grey removed even the shadow itself.

However, all these artistic experiments, which characterised the 60s, had lost their vitality by the 70s. The demonstration of art theory could not be visually exploited for long. When some German painters ceased to follow Modernist theory, returning to figurative and abstract painting, not only was the historical continuity of Modernism called into question, but critics argued that this new painting signified a regression into long obsolete positions; it was termed Post-Modern.

Since around 1978, *Die Neuen Wilden* or the New Wild painters of the Federal Republic of Germany have been trying to

revive the medium of painting and to defend it as a relevant and artistically credible medium. Not only have they ignored previous attempts to undermine the art market, but they have moved away from the essential manifestation of the Modernist aesthetic, namely the art of non-objectivity.

These painters reversed the argument for pure abstraction and instead sought to re-establish the object in painting. A well-known painting by Bernd Zimmer, *The Field of Rape*, illustrates this. A large yellow area covers about two-thirds of the canvas. The artist has applied liquid paint to the canvas to form a large flat plane, a technique resembling that of the American Colour-Field painters, allowing the pigment to drip and smear, forming a certain preliminary structure. It is the narrow strip of blue on the upper edge of the painting, together with the two brown triangles on the upper right, that transform these colour fields into an objective painting. It becomes a landscape. Brown fields and a blue sky also affect the yellow, transforming the large area of colour into a field of rape. Zimmer is not simply resurrecting illusionistic painting in this work; rather he articulates the return to objectivity through abstraction. Allowing flatness to remain, as Greenberg demanded of Modernist painting, he does not use

Karl-Horst Hödicke, *Flagge (o du mein Brandenburgerland)*, 1985, synthetic resin, 200x300cm

traditional devices of perspective to establish illusionistic depth; rather he establishes a perspective that relies on the viewer's ability to mentally transform the colour fields into a receding landscape that stretches back into a fictional world scene. Fluctuating between objectivity and abstraction, the ambiguous effect prevents illusionism and, at the same time, directs attention to the 'subject'. The abstract composition rearranges itself into a context of regained meaning. Form and colour are not working for themselves; they are taking on shape, describing a blossoming field of rape under a blue sky. There had never been such a painting before, and in its return to objectivity it is still progressive, for it has provided a new aesthetic experience which neither abstraction nor objective painting could offer.

Bernd Zimmer was one of a group of painters which also included Rainer Fetting, Helmut Middendorf and Salomé. Their work was shown to a wider public for the first time in 1980 in the *Hoftige Malereí* (Wild Painting) exhibition at the Berlin Haus am Waldsee. Unlike other artistic groups formed at about the same time in Hamburg and Cologne, these painters incorporated direct experience into their themes. They depicted their own urban life experiences centred around their personal existential problems. Salomé, for instance, translated the subjective experiences of homosexuality, right down to a revealing confession, into a pictorial theme. Middendorf and Fetting explored life in the best cellars of the 'New Wave' scene, using singers, drummers and dancers as subjects for their pictures. Direct experience, almost without reflection, was continued on the canvas. Such paintings were in marked opposition to the detached exercises, empty of subjectivity, of late non-objective painting and the geometric calculations of the Constructivists. The confessions of the ego, unacceptable in painting for decades, now celebrated an untamed comeback. This new naïvety was all too easily misunderstood as impertinent and obtrusive, but at least the New Wild painters were in sharp contrast to the outmoded theories of Conceptual and Minimal art. A new sensuality was asserting itself on the slippery floor of late Modernism.

Although the term *Die Neuen Wilden* may initially have been applied in a derogatory sense, it did reflect the spontaneity that characterised these paintings. Fetting's hand with the stick beating down on a drum and Middendorf's gothic singer holding the microphone like a fetish, his 'natives of the big city', their bodies swaying in the red light, for whom the beat cellar is the

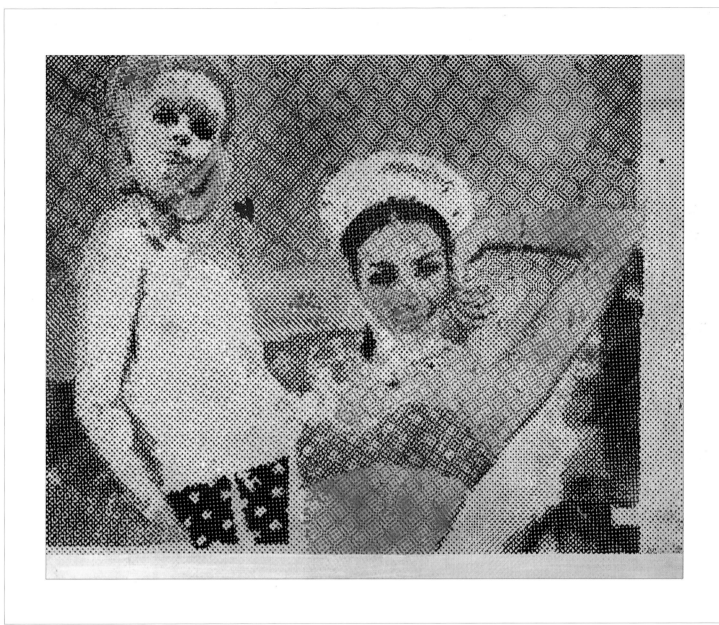

Sigmar Polke, *Freundinnen* (Girlfriends), 1965-66, oil, 150x192cm

centre of the world, elevated the direct experience of life to the level of a confession.

The Cologne painters, centred around the figures of Walter Dahn and Jiri Georg Dokoupil, reacted in a very different way. While they corresponded to the Berlin painters in celebrating the brushstroke as an act of painting, they nevertheless remained more distanced from their ego in their choice of subject matter. Dahn, who worked closely with Dokoupil from 1981 to 1983, sought the elementary, irrational aspects of life in a primitivism that rejected high culture. In that respect, he remained close to his teacher, Joseph Beuys. He broke through the tradition of controlled, calculated primitivism and, through his technique and subject matter, he expressed his contempt of culture. On a smeared background he set his motifs, clumsy and distorted by a gluey paint: a man eating a broom, a drunk whose arm has become a bottle, an emaciated smoker's leg bored through by burning cigarettes. Dahn made every effort to paint in an unbearably primitive way. Nevertheless, these early pictures with their technical understatement and trivial subject matter signified a breakthrough in the resurgence of representational painting.

The Hamburg Wild Style painters, including Werner Büttner, and Albert Oehlen, most of them pupils of Sigmar Polke, sought their legitimisation in pictorial themes that were either cynical, critical or nonsensical. Büttner's *Vandalised Telephone Boxes* and Oehlen's *Be True in Honour, Slow in Flight, Work Hard and Love Well* are painted unbearably badly. Nothing is worse than vandalised telephone kiosks which the authorities have covered with black and yellow marker tapes to indicate that they are out of order. Oehlen's *Be True . . .* is another work which employs a theme that is unworthy of painting and denigrates art. These desolate pictures, which deny the value of art and are badly painted, are pictures that, to use the inverted logic of Büttner and Oehlen, will promote art. 'Indicate right, turn left' is the motto for these painters, as they mock those who seek meaning and sharpen humour to a critical spearpoint; they are not going to spend any more time hoping for reactions from the public. Criticism can become blunted with use, while amusement at so much superstition remains.

Büttner and Oehlen have made the banal the centre of their thoughts. They have interpreted the world from a marginal position, turned mindlessness into a higher meaning with wit and

Helmut Middendorf, *Hochbahn Skalitzerstrasse*, 1987, synthetic resin, 162x130cm. 'Painting today formulates what other media cannot . . . If the unspeakable could be shown by other, better means then painting would be meaningless. If I knew a better form I would work on another level. Painting is not justifiable in itself, and I find painting for the sake of painting totally boring.'

unmasked this higher meaning as mindlessness. For Büttner, the picture signifies a plea for peace and is conceived as a metaphor for disarmament. To have the freedom to arrange things as meaningfully as this and to allow them the rare aura of colour is the privilege of the artist; pictures of this kind are proof enough that a narrative art can produce valid metaphors and should no longer be disregarded as just the latest development in art history.

The art historical event of the late 70s and 80s has been the return to representational painting. But for many critics of the Post-Modern movement, this signifies a relapse into an obsolete past. The forward gaze, as it appears, has been exchanged for a glance back. How can art want to be again what it has already been? But does that simple manoeuvre of turning backwards not correspond to the real movement of history? Paintings such as Zimmer's *Field of Rape* have only become possible today. In describing the breakthrough of the depictive as Post-Modern, we must also say, as the new painting shows, that the Post-Modern movement is more than nostalgic. Indeed, the emergent tendencies toward a neo-historicist painting, which have not been discussed in this essay, are showing signs of a regressive pressure of repetition manifest in the multiplicity of languages characteristic of a growing pluralism. This recreation of the Arcadian landscape with contemporary stage-set figures is only understandable as an exaggerated reaction to an exhausted Modern movement, a declamatory surprise effect. We are in the company of a child that is stamping its foot and doing the opposite of what is allowed: a rapid act of liberation from an over-powerful moral constraint. Such reactions ease the constraints for a time, but they lead nowhere and at best have only symptomatic value.

The way in which art is presented in Germany today is part of the history of art, and today art is largely produced for museums, many of which have unexpectedly become the focus of an expanding leisure culture. The popularity of art reflects a change in attitude by the public at large; the enjoyment of art is no longer the exclusive privilege of the wealthy, educated classes. The great influx of visitors to museums of 20th-century art indicates that the rejection of modern art has largely disappeared. The avant-garde has became the daily bread of many.

Much as the popularisation of the art museum has increased the political relevance of these institutions, their public appeal has also become the indicator by which their success is measured. Was the Nolde exhibition in the Staatsgalerie in Stüttgart with about 280,000 visitors more successful than the Ad Reinhardt exhibition in the same space which met with little response? Some of the exhibitions which have been of major importance for the development of contemporary art, like the 1984 Sigmar Polke retrospective in the Kunstverein in Cologne, were failures in terms of popularity.

The great museums have become expansive enterprises. The Metropolitan Museum in New York, for example, has four million visitors a year, 15,000 sponsors and a staff of 6,000. Public relations offices have now become the central switchboards for modern cultural life. Standing somewhere between the populist impressario and the imaginative producer, the exhibition organisers have the task of presenting the artworks. Mistrusted on the one hand because they relativise art by putting it within a specific context, on the other hand they are called upon to create some sort of order amid the multiplicity of thematic contexts.

But the success of modern exhibition policy and skilful presentation cannot disguise the fact that the end product is essentially an entertainment, reducing the exhibitions to the same level and blurring the powers of critical and public distinction. The decision between a reserved form of art presentation and a stimulating experience has to be made when the museum is being built. Moreover, the architecture of many contemporary art museums has become independent; the demonstrative character of the buildings dominates the art. It is not surprising that artists such as Markus Lüpertz vehemently demand a museum in which architecture is subservient to art:

> Everywhere museums are being built, art museums. This would be both honourable and necessary if there were no art. The classic museum should have four walls, upper lighting and two doors, one by which you go in, one by which you go out. That simple principle has unfortunately had to give way to art – the art of architecture. Architecture should be great enough to present itself in such a way that art is possible within it; it should not be so demanding as to displace art or even worse, to use it as mere decoration.

A R Penck, *G.B.I.*, 1988, oil, 51x76cm

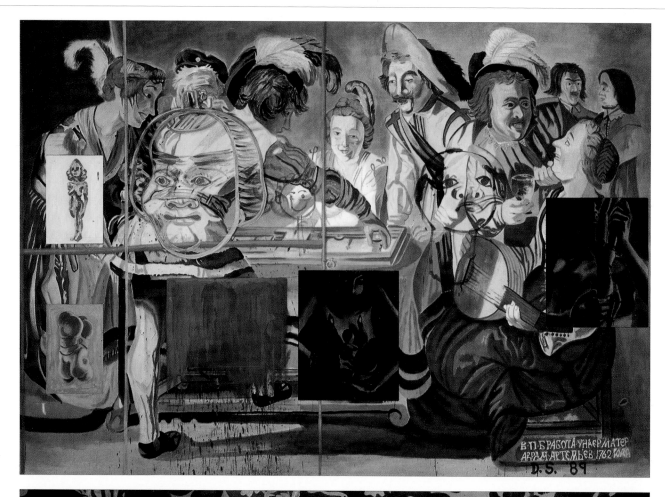

Above: *Tiny in the Air*, 1989, acrylic and oil, 238.7x345.4cm; *Below*: *Vagrant*, 1989, acrylic and oil, 238.7x345.4cm

DAVID SALLE
AN ART & DESIGN *INTERVIEW*

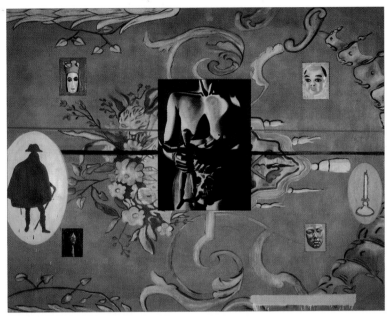

To the Bar, 1989, acrylic and oil, 254x330.2cm

Held by Dan Cameron to be 'the sole painter of his generation to have brought appropriation onto a grand scale', David Salle describes his background in Conceptual art and his move to painting in the late 70s. He also discusses some of the latest sources of his imagery – from 18th-century tapestries to Japanese puppets – touching upon the controversial critical reception his work has always received.

– Recently, critics have discussed the sense of accelerated history pervading the contemporary art world, the market's insatiable demand for the new and the tendency for new artists to be instantly analysed and exhausted by the media. As an artist who, as Robert Rosenblum recently commented, has gained an historical status in the context of new art, how do you respond to these market demands?

Well I think that just the opposite could be argued. If you look at the exhibitions of the high-visibility New York galleries last season, what you mainly find are dead artists or a fixation with, one might say (although I hate these terms), a 'fetishisation' of certain artists such as Roy Lichtenstein, Andy Warhol, Jasper Johns, all of whom I love and admire but who are not exactly accelerated discoveries.

– Your 'signature' is instantly recognisable: the juxtaposition and layering of fragmented, disparate images, appropriated from a number of sources, which recall the techniques and representations of art history and the mass media.

I don't have a signature. I have some kinds of propensities and some kinds of interests. But I have no interest in the mass media. In fact you probably won't find any of my images in the mass media. Critics have no idea what they are talking about when they relate my images to those found in magazines or any other mass media; it's just another example of critics quoting each other. I

abhor the mass media and it's not even something I'm interested in thinking about, never mind quoting from.

– So in that sense you're very different to artists such as Jeff Koons, for whom the mass media plays a central role.

An interesting lesson about art is that in a sense it doesn't really matter what your starting premises are; all that matters is the result. I don't know if I'm all that different to Jeff; statements are just statements and shouldn't be dwelled on.

– In your new canvases the images seem to be more heavily painted and the quotations from art history are juxtaposed to quotations from your own paintings. One critic interpreted this as a desire to attain 'old master' status; can you comment on this?

I'm ambivalent about the ageing process, so I don't think that being an 'old master' is my desire. There have been cycles of images that appear and reappear in my painting. But I don't know why this should be seen as self-conscious, self-referential quoting. If it were, I don't know what the real meaning of that would be. It's all these assumptions about paintings that drive me wild; it's just superficial, critical jargon. What we're talking about is hostile critics with a predisposition to make a case for something which they will always be able to do, regardless of what I do or don't do, and regardless of what I say or don't say.

– Were you aiming to challenge the modes of representation with

your visual juxtapositions and layering of dislocated images, and did you anticipate the strong critical response?

I never anticipate any response whatsoever.

– You studied at Cal Arts under the guidance of John Baldessari. What influence did this background in Conceptual art have on your development as an artist and on your concept of the artistic process?

My background is in art and has always been in art. The historical moment when I attended university just happened to coincide with the moment of the ascendancy of Conceptual art. It would have been impossible not to have become aware of it, or even inundated with it. Anyone who was conscious of art in 1969, 70, 71, couldn't have avoided the ideas and intentions that the Conceptual artists were involved with and if you have that anarchistic bent of mind, as I did and do, it would have been impossible not to have been intrigued by it. But I never saw myself as a Conceptual artist.

– When you talk about your anarchistic disposition, were you attempting to undermine artistic conventions and conceptions?

I think that anarchy simply refers to not belonging to any one party. It refers to the idea that human beings can determine their own lives or fates without assistance from political organisations.

– Were you preoccupied at that time with the idea in art, with questioning concepts and assumptions?

It's really a sensibility rather than a specific idea or anything else. As such I don't think it is something that is specific to the Conceptual artist, but is something that is part of the history of Modernism. It isn't simply confined to the late 60s and early 70s. It picked up a lot of velocity at that time which is appropriate when you consider the sociological and political environment in which people had to operate in those years. It's neither surprising nor untoward that young people, particularly in the late 60s and early 70s, would have been thinking about all these kinds of things. It didn't mean the end of art, nor did it mean that we were trying to do anything in particular other than what we felt at that moment.

– What made you decide to go to New York?

I don't have an answer for that. I thought I wouldn't be so alienated, but of course when I got there, I felt just as alienated as I had in California.

– Can you comment on your collaboration with Vito Acconci at that time?

Well, I knew him and I did a couple of things for him. I put together some tapes and some exhibitions. He was a very interesting person to be around at that time.

– And when did you begin to concentrate on painting?

It started around 1976, but I don't really know if I was exactly thinking of painting *per se*.

– Were you more involved at that time with the thought processes behind your paintings, the selection and juxtaposition of images, than with the act of painting itself? Did you feel at all 'distanced' from the medium?

I would never break up painting into those component parts. Painting has nothing to do with theory or with some notion of 'anti-theory'; it's just about making something worth seeing. That's all that matters.

– Do you do any preparatory thinking and organising, in terms of the selection and arrangement of images and the insertion of panels into the main canvas, before beginning work on the actual painting?

No, I just begin. It's all completely intuitive. I never have a preparatory drawing or anything like that. It's all improvisation. The real way of working has so little to do with what anyone talks about.

– Did your arrival in New York coincide with that of Julian Schnabel whose large-scale canvases gained the attention of the art world in 1979 when he exhibited with Mary Boone?

I came to New York in 1975. I met Julian a bit later.

– Was there an immediate response by dealers to your large-scale painted canvases which, rather than undermining the commercial gallery, were very 'saleable' works of art?

Well, we were making large paintings for a very long time before anyone thought they might be saleable.

– How did people respond to your paintings, in which fragmented images, though identifiable, were arranged and juxtaposed in such a way as to challenge and frustrate interpretation?

I think my art was seen as a problem and still is.

– Were you conscious of reacting against the art of preceding generations?

Yes and no. But it's never that simple. I was of course heavily influenced by certain major painterly achievements of the past.

– Are there any particular artists you would mention in this context?

I was interested in Roy Lichtenstein's work, and that of Jasper Johns, both artists who have come to represent the American kind of 'hard modern'. You can't simply say that *x* is a reaction to *y*. It's partly continuity and partly discontinuity. It's more to do with the resonances than with action/reaction.

– How do you see your paintings in relation to Pop art? Do you share the same concern with questioning and challenging concepts and modes of representation?

Well, that is an aspect of advanced art, whether it's Pop or any other form of art. In my opinion, not to have that component is just retarded, but whether it takes the form of Pop art or not is insignificant. Pop was really only possible as a manifestation of a particular generation. A painting, painted by someone else ten years later is not the same painting.

– Do you see your art as a manifestation of the late 80s? Your use of dislocated images could certainly be related to the experience of the modern world and the continual bombardment of media images and information.

I can only imagine the world as it is. You might say that's part of the modern world and of course it has influenced me.

– Do you see yourself as 'inventing' or 'rearranging' visual language? And is the concept of new art important to you? I'm thinking here in particular of your tendency to appropriate images.

I don't believe an artist can't invent any more. The new, the idea of making something new, is incredibly important and always will be. My work is obviously new, otherwise people wouldn't be reacting to it in the way that they do. Painting has always involved appropriation. You can go back to Watteau and find that his paintings involve the reshuffling of existing images which were to a large extent cliché images at that time. Watteau didn't invent them, but he did arrange them in such a way that his paintings were incredibly 'present', and disturbing. It has been said about cinema that there are only 26 movie plots, but why do some movies strike us as being new or ground-breaking?

– Your images have been read as 'signs'; have the writings of Baudrillard interested you at all?

We invented all that stuff long before Baudrillard came along in America. I think that the ideas of Baudrillard were things that we instinctively came to realise even when I was at Cal Arts; it was completely understood already. To see Baudrillard come along 15 years later and put it into words and to hear people claiming that it is new has been a little bit startling.

– Your images bear no recognisable relation to each other, they appear arbitrarily selected, ambiguous in meaning – a puzzle that can never be solved and yet continually challenges the viewer to interpret it. Are they arranged with meanings and associations in mind?

Every sophisticated artist's work has real themes in it, purely formal themes, and mine is no exception. But just what those themes are I can't tell you.

– Your images of women, at times fragmented and lacking individual identity, have been a controversial aspect of your art, primarily because the meaning is ambiguous and your own attitude ambivalent. Are you criticising the representation of women or condoning it in some way? Why is it so open to interpretation?

I don't see what I do as criticising or condoning. That is something for other people to do. As in any dramatisation, you have to work with what is the case, not what ought to be the case.

– But you seem to be representing a very limited view of the way in which women are represented today.

Well you can't do everything. It might be limited but most people's work is limited. I don't think it is about being fair; it's about making something that does something. It's not a public opinion pole. In fact it's not about opinions.

– But your paintings represent a subjective response to the world and to the representation of the world?

It is complicated to know where the world leaves off and where representation begins, where you leave off and someone else begins.

– Artists such as Barbara Kruger, Jenny Holzer and Cindy Sherman, who work in new media, have cited the large painted canvas as the historical domain of the male artist. Are you conscious of that?

I'm aware of it. Once again, one has to work with what's there.

– Do you think art should aim to be socially or politically conscious?

I don't think that it should be anything in particular.

– Your images of women are frequently painted in black and white. Is this an allusion to photography? Are they ever portraits?

Yes they always are. In my mind they are specific, particularised and expressive.

– Do you employ sources for your images?

It all comes from somewhere. The invention is not on that level, it is on another level. One of my sources is a Japanese puppet's head from 1670 which is still in use in BunRaku theatre. A lot of these images have to do with theatre, with different forms of theatre. This is a particular BunRaku head which is called *split head* and is used for a specific theatrical effect. It's a kind of tragi-comic character in the repertoire of the BunRaku. The character's head is actually split open with a sword and falls down. It goes from tragedy to comedy. It is quite funny in performance.

– What are the sources for your male figures? Are they taken from paintings?

Not from paintings but from tapestries, although the original tapestries were probably based on paintings.

– There are several recurrent images in your new paintings – the ring, the bird, etc. Were these canvases conceived as a series?

No, but as I said images appear and disappear; it seems fairly normal to me.

– Do you welcome the individual's interpretation of your art?

I don't think about it.

– Do you think it is possible to define new art in international terms? And do you see your art as a particular reflection of American culture?

There is more than one America. America is not as homogenous as most European cultures are, or in the way that Japan is. So who the real American is, is hard to say. I don't know what I am, although I'm certainly not European.

Young Krainer, 1989, acrylic and oil (two panels), 213.3x264.1cm

Sandro Chia, *Hand Game*, 1981, oil

ITALIAN TRANSAVANGUARDIA

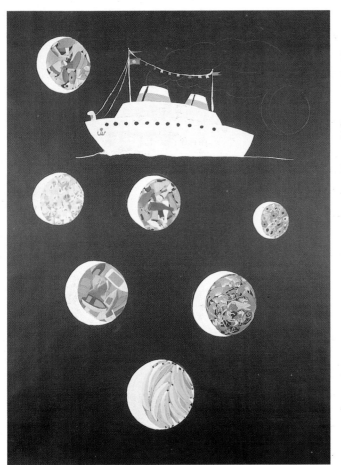 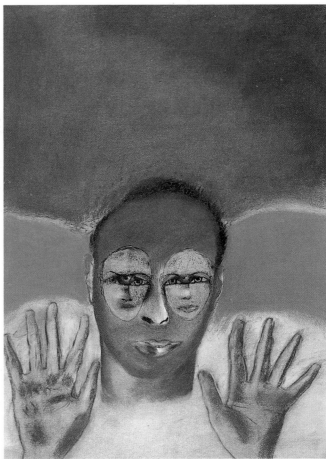

Francesco Clemente, *L to R*: *Emblems*, 1978, mixed media, 198.7x152.4cm; *Italy*, 1983, pastel on paper, 71.12x45.72cm

The Transavanguardia can be seen both as a break from as well as a continuation of what had gone before, namely Conceptualism and Arte Povera. At the start of the 80s, there had been much talk of a return to painting. Painting as a tradition had never died, for example Baselitz in Germany or Lucian Freud in Britain, but critics quickly picked up on renewed interest in a saleable art form with its rich yet accessible meaning and instant aesthetic appeal. It was striking, undemanding intellectually with a strong emphasis on the self – the artist individual as hero – and the physical presence of a large painted canvas as opposed to the dematerialisation and 'hands off' approach of Conceptualism. Artists such as Sandro Chia, Francesco Clemente, Enzo Cucchi and Mimmo Paladino quickly became international art stars, synonymous with 80s success and the art market boom.

Labelled by Achille Bonito Oliva in *Flash Art*, 1979, the Transavanguardia sees the artistic language as an instrument of transition, of passage from one work to another, from one style to another. Thus it looks backwards and forwards at the same time with a wide range of reference, reaching back into the subconscious both to primitive instinct and received tradition. Its position in history is therefore not fixed, it is a nomad position opposed to the evolutionist linear theories of artistic development (*Linguistic Darwinism*) adopted by the post-war avant-guarde. It is a crossing of the experimental, rational notion of the avant-guarde; it sees art as catastrophe, as unplanned accident.

The return to painting was regarded by many as a 'sell out', a negation of hard won modernist principles. It was certainly a reaction to the obscure language and the strange, evocative combinations of untraditional art materials which characterised Arte Povera. Although both movements shared the archaeologising, the fragments of history and mythology – which appeared also in artists such as De Chirico and Savinio – with the Transavanguardia, there is no sense of confrontation with the present, no hint of cultural provocation.

The work of Chia is epitomised by a sense of bravura and technical self confidence; his artistic heroes being Michelangelo, Titian and Tintoretto. His imagery invariably features the artist himself as a child or as a man. Using watercolour and fresco, the main force behind Clemente's work is psychological, explorations into the self, the depths of which he sees as the source of the creative urge. Paladino draws on imagery as varied as African cave painting and Byzantine mosaics to Joseph Beuys. His paintings and sculptures are full of images of ritual, silence and also death. Cucchi's dark expressionism reflects similar concerns to northern Europeans such as Kiefer with his evocations of the end of civilisation.

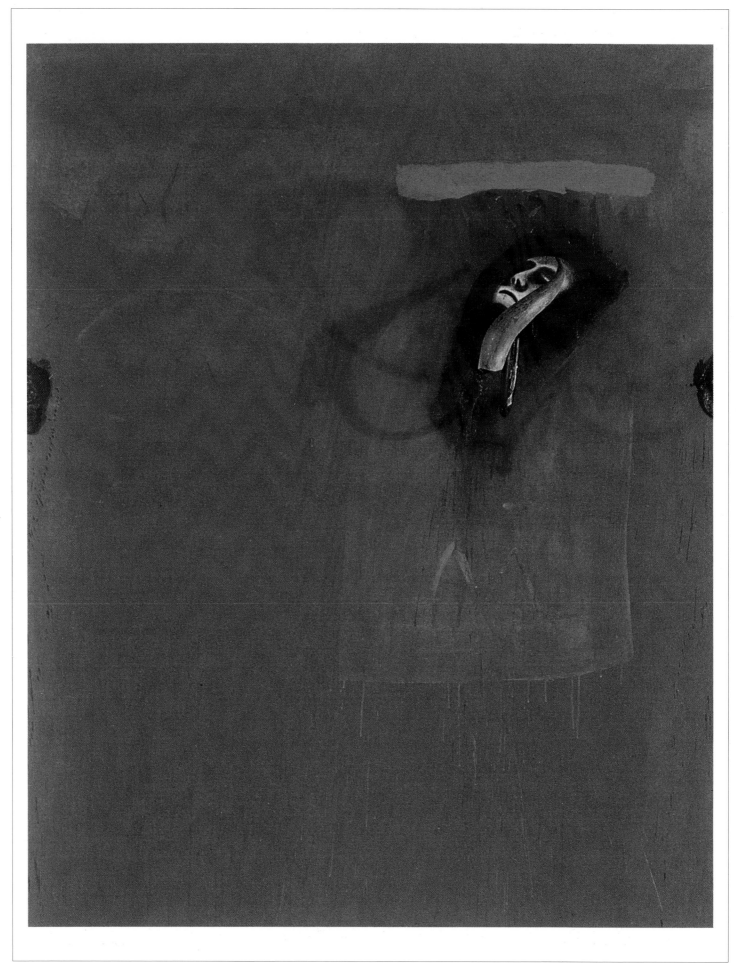

Mimmo Paladino, *Untitled*, 1987, oil

Enzo Cucchi, *House of the Barbarians*, 1982

Barbara Kruger, *Untitled (You are not yourself)*, 1983

IV

NEW CONCEPTUALISM
AND THE POLITICS OF ART

Jeff Koons, Peter Halley, *New York Art Now*, Saatchi Collection, Sept 1987, installation view

MICHAEL COMPTON
POP ART II – JEFF KOONS & CO

Haim Steinbach, *dramatic yet neutral*, 1984, wood, formica, wicker baskets, footballs, 96.5x118x44.5cm

While leafing through recent art journals, I noticed more articles on Jeff Koons and Andy Warhol than on any other artists. The simultaneous dominance of two such figures is plainly no coincidence, nor has the resemblance of a certain art of the late 1980s to Pop passed unremarked. One curiosity is that, although this art has been extensively reported, it has not yet acquired any stable name. I shall

therefore refer to it as 'Pop Art II'. The failure of a name to emerge probably has to do with the fact that this art is recognisable by a sort of theory associated with it rather than by a style or look, a theory that relates equally to a form of abstract art, 'Neo Geo',[1] and to 'Neo Pop'[2] – the art of appropriation, transformation or simulation of commercial products. The neatest example of the common ground is Peter Halley, both as writer and painter.[3] To oversimplify, Halley seems to argue that abstraction is the vice of capitalism; that abstract art is a manifestation of this, as are the control circuits of electronic machines. Therefore, as a means of deconstruction, he has painted simulations of abstract pictures that also resemble circuit diagrams.

In Britain the theory of the information environment, covering both abstract and what were later called appropriationist manifestations, flourished in the late 50s when the metonymy on control system circuitry was also employed as a means of visualisation. Robyn Denny, Dick Smith and Ralph Rumney made a maze-like installation in *Spaces*, 1959, modelling social control. The irony is that the interest in circuitry, which had emerged some years earlier in the group that formed the seed bed of Pop art (Hamilton, Paolozzi, McHale, Alloway, Banham etc), was based on the notion that it exemplified a non-Cartesian geometry called 'topological' and that this, being used to represent feed-back loops and other homeostatic systems, was a

metaphor for the humanisation of science and even perhaps of society. Halley's pictures of circuitry represent, of course, neither the flow of information nor the actual circuits (whose three-dimensionality and sheer complexity might weaken his rhetoric), but rather elements of circuit diagrams of the sort that were familiar to amateur electricians in the 30s. By using such an archaic analogue he produces a striking picture, one that may imply condemnation of Mondrian as well as Stella, but at the same time he weakens his political argument. The interdependent network of a more complex cybernetic model would have been a better image of the structure of control in a society that he hopes to attack. He also weakens his argument by laying himself open to the charge of complicity twice over: that is he paints a picture which is in the first place exceptionally marketable, being assimilable by the élite as a witticism, and secondly one which is abstract in both its superficial appearance and in the sense that it overlooks the reality of its target in order to reduce it to a scheme capable of being commercialised. To the former point he may be able to reply that the enemy must be infiltrated to be subverted, but the only answer to the latter can be that no realism is possible in a radically corrupted world.

Halley's pictures were no doubt painted in complete ignorance of any British antecedents in the late 50s and early 60s, and arose in a very different global and local context. They resemble more

145

Ashley Bickerton, *Atmosphere #2*, 1989, mixed media

closely some of the diagrams of control drawn and published by Steve Willats in the last 20 years, with whom Halley does share some of the same culture, that is the ideology of the New Left. In his magazine *Control,* Willats has published articles by himself and others that testify to a late Marxist or late Socialist view of social structure, but his work is often preoccupied by the gaps in the system which allow people to create their own sub-cultures within it. He takes on some of the optimism of those who thought that the development of the cheap video camera, photocopier and offset printer in the late 60s would open up the possibilities of a participatory democracy and the by-passing of the mass media.

In the 50s, a preoccupation with semiotics flourished in the group around Hamilton, who were concerned with the phenomenon of mass and international culture. The source of that concern was affection for certain of the products, rather than hatred for the class that was blamed for producing them. Nearly all the people involved were (as we would say later) 'committed' socialists and all were very well aware of the economic structure that generated their material, but they saw in their use of it a form of opposition, both to the class system as a whole and to the intellectual élitism of the mandarins and Marxists. To them it was a manifestation of working-class culture, or rather a network of interconnecting sub-cultures with which they identified themselves, demanding kinds of skill in consumption. I don't recollect that, in those optimistic days, the exact nature of the mechanisms by which the educated responses of the consumers would affect the output was fully worked out. Certainly the idea that, if one understood, one would neutralise an advertisement, either on the psychoanalytic or on the demystification (deconstruction) model, was not entertained. That would have implied the unreality of working-class ideas and desires at a time when they felt strong and did not wish to be excused for their tastes nor to be told by experts what to think and feel. Rather, it seemed to be supposed that the output of objects and images was so vast and various that individuals and particularly groups could define their identity by selecting within it. As consumers, they certainly felt that in such fields as film, advertising and packaging, the creators, sensing public response, would respond in turn by producing material that would be ever more sophisticated, couched in a form of wit playing on the knowingness of the consumer. The subsequent history of certain media, including advertising and fashion, have shown this view to be, at least to some degree, justified.

Nevertheless, for the last 20 years in Britain and for longer in France, such a view has been regarded as dangerously naïve. The late Marxist criticism of Barthes is roughly contemporary with that of Alloway and Banham and shares a semiotic approach to the phenomena of mass culture. However Barthes combines a mandarin moralism with his Structuralism, onto which his followers have often grafted the recurrent continental anti-Americanism. He does not speak from inside the culture with which he often deals, but rather from that of an intellectual élite educated to rule. He is among that group of mainly French intellectuals – Sartre, Lévi-Strauss, Marcuse, Foucault, Lacan, Derrida and now Baudrillard – who, together with older figures whom they have restored to attention – Gramsci, Adorno, Benjamin etc – have been quoted everywhere in writings on art. Benjamin's elegant and passionate essay on the effect of the mass reproduction of works of art must be the most cited text of the last ten years, especially in the United States; and yet it is a *jeu d'esprit,* having little basis in research, inaccurate in its day and falsified as a prediction. What then is the charm of such a text? One charm at least may be that though revolutionary in spirit, it deals with a matter on the fringe of fundamental matters, but close to the concerns of the art world. The belief that we no longer live in a world of objects but one of signs allows a

preoccupation with the media to be redefined as the fundamental matter, with the result that an alibi for the failure of the revolutions of 1968 is achieved.

A common factor in all this writing, borrowing as it does from Marx, Freud and Saussure, is that people do not have control of what they say and, even, that they do not understand their own words. The mandarins' own texts are generally long, complex and difficult to understand. They are based on research in libraries, not in the field. The authorities cited in the footnotes are rarely ones that support the argument by substantial evidence; rather they support it by indicating a pedigree of equally insubstantiated judgements. That is to say, they exhibit the characteristics of an élite sub-culture which shows off its membership by footnotes and professional jargon, the equivalent of the fan's badge or sticker. The art writers who follow them show the same characteristics in exaggerated form.

This hostile phase of the relationship of art to the mass media is exemplified by another Englishman, a writer and an artist, Victor Burgin. His writing is full of such citations as Peter Blake's Levi jacket is of fans' badges. The message these convey is the same as that which is explicit in his text: how to be both an artist and politically committed to the Left. Alloway had called for 'descriptive study of particular aspects of the popular arts. Only after this has been done can we assess the status and role of the mass arts in our lives in the way that trigger-happy aesthetes and arm-chair educationalists are prematurely attempting'.[4] 20 years later Burgin wrote: '*we* first examine those *codes* and practices *we know de facto* to be *mass-consumed.* It is these *codes* which enshrine the *dominating ideology* and it is these *codes* which *are to be deconstructed'*.[5] The nastily authoritarian tone of this quotation is not altogether typical of Burgin, although the style is; words displaying membership of the sub-culture are in italics. Burgin's principal source for the association of semiotics and Marxism (also Freudianism) is evidently Barthes. Barthes' own mention of this issue in the first introduction to *Mythologies* (1957) is relatively unaggressive: 'I wanted to track down, in the decorative display of *what-goes-without-saying,* the ideological abuse which, in my view, is hidden there.' In the long essay at the end of this book, Barthes shows that he believes that the 'myth' can be annihilated by decipherment, but he leaves unclear the extent to which such deconstruction can be communicated to others. The principal effect of the work of what he calls the mythologist (*ie* demystifier or theorist of myth) is to set himself apart. That is, he seems to take to himself the myth of the avant-garde bohemian driven by a pure moral imperative but reduced to speaking in sarcasms.

Burgin does not appear to have these doubts. Demystification or deconstruction is carried on by him as straightforward techniques of Left-committed work. If he does not imagine himself changing everyone's way of seeing, at least he is demonstrating his membership of the party. In what may be identified as his works of art as distinct from his writings, we find illustrations of his written theses: combinations of images and words constructed according to principles which, following Barthes and others, he finds in the commercial art that he believes carries bourgeois ideology. However the signs are altered by interpolations and combinations in order to deconstruct their actual or imaginary prototypes. I think that Burgin underestimates the ambivalence of his own products as a result of his own too complete identification of photography with (written) language and too great faith in the scientific validity of his sources. Since they can only be correctly interpreted as deconstructive by those who are attuned to a socio-structuralist sub-culture, they serve more to ratify a myth than to demystify it. The work of Barbara Kruger, which somewhat resembles his, carries ambiguity much further, reflecting the self-

ALLAN McCOLLUM

Surrogates on Location, 1982-89, photograph from TV

'My first impulse was to make only one painting and exhibit it over and over again, to create a sort of archival object – like the government's Bureau of Standards maintains the standard "inch" in platinum. But this solution eliminated the possibility of exchange transactions – and how could a thing represent an art object if it couldn't be bought and sold? I ultimately decided to use a single but repeatable image, one which I could vary minimally in size and proportion, but which remained essentially the same: a frame, a mat and a black centre.'

artist's statement

'Before I ever actually made any *Plaster Surrogates*, I was always seeing them on television, on the walls behind the actors. But they were only fleeting images, like accidents of light, or mirages. What I was recognising, I guess, was an image which was only just potentially developing inside my head. So when I ultimately began to physically create these objects, to cast them in actual plaster, and to produce them by the hundreds, it was always very mysterious to me which image I might honestly point to within this chain of representations as the *original* "surrogate".' 'Considering the range and potency of the feelings we all have for industrial production, it continues to be a surprise to me that artists never want to utilise industrial production in their work. They will *allude* to the mass-produced object, through imagery, but

deconstruction of, I suppose, Derrida, but relying on the much greater currency, substance and urgency of feminist thought to give force to the attack.

The 70s and 80s saw the importation to the USA of many of the proponents of late Marxist ('new') art history, of Structuralist and Post-Structuralist criticism, and of their books. Their ideas have taken an ever stronger hold on the sub-cultures of art and on the mutually reinforcing courses of universities and colleges. This has taken place during a period in which there seems to have been a slight decline of their influence at home in France, Germany and Italy, so one may suppose such critics to be following the market. At any rate, like any other intellectual group, they have ratified themselves by mutual publication and citation, by making appointments in their power, by directing fields of study and so forth. Their writings seem to have become more didactic.

Their value for universities whose sponsors may not sympathise with their Left politics or comprehend their jargon, may very well be that their methods, and particularly the strategy of crossing-breeding paradigms, act as a fertiliser of publications. The same possibility exists in the field of fine art. One of the principal generators of new forms during the last century and more has been the absorption into art of sets of concepts and devices (paradigms) taken from other disciplines, especially the sciences. This fertility has been strongest when comprehension has been partial, mediated through popularisers and sociable conversation. The reason may be that anyone who fully understood a scientific theory would also understand its necessary gross distortion in being converted to visual art (since art cannot express such concepts as probability, verifiability, repeatability etc). However, in the last 50 years, non-scientific thinkers – those who combine the roles of moralist, prophet, litterateur and critic – have become even more influential: Marx, Freud, Benjamin and all the Analysts, Existentialists, Structuralists and Post-Structuralists. Their ambiguities, contradictions, unverifiabilities and opacities render the incomprehension of artists and critics (which does exist) unnecessary and their distortions relatively undetectable. Their cult words can be applied to any artist, snippets of theory can justify any style, and a generalised representation of their position any practice. None of this is to be seriously deprecated (except to the extent that it produces boring art criticism).

Plaster Surrogates, 1989 (1982), installation at Serpentine Gallery, London 1990

not through any actual replication of thousands of things. In our era, we have great powerful ambivalence towards large numbers. We're afraid of how there is more in the world than we can ever know or understand, more human souls than we can imagine, and so forth: hordes of people, hordes of machines, hordes of information. But we are also completely infatuated with exaggerated quantity, with the possibility of abundance and plenitude, with wealth, and with our fantasies of perpetual fecundity, and so on. It's amazing that art completely stands aside of all this drama, preoccupied with its own scarceness, with its own uniqueness. I think that possibly we create art the way we do in order to *avoid* our feelings about these issues.'

interview with Selma Klein Essinck

'I think that there must be something false about the desire to look at a picture; it couldn't possibly be something we are born with. It must be something we grow into, like the way a dog comes to desire such a strangely contrived activity as being taken for a walk on a leash . . . My paintings and drawings don't serve a proper function – how could they? They're only representations, props, and surrogates: not real paintings at all. If I can engineer this charade the way I want, I think I can transform the seemingly innocent act of looking at art into a slightly nightmarish duplication of itself.'

artist's statement

Artists can make play with this situation. In an interview with the critic Pincus-Witten,[6] David Salle deftly avoided his interlocutor's attempts to frame him in the sub-culture defined by the mandarins and assumes an almost Warholian elusiveness. I attribute this principally to the usual unwillingness of the artist, once he has gained an audience, to be pinned down by the critic. However it may also have to do with the subtly changed estimation of Warhol among many intellectuals, which has made him a more possible model. In his 1989 MoMA catalogue essay, Benjamin Buchloh could not quite bring himself to present Warhol as a hero of the deconstructive Left but he certainly did not see him as a mere Capitalist Realist. Warhol's pictures seem to me to short-circuit the problems of realism and authenticity; they instantly conjure up people, objects and stories whose reality is guaranteed by familiarity and feeling, even though the production of the image is without perception or passion. The instantly perceived richness of the end-product is often set in opposition to the pathos or banality of the source. All the same he leaves a track to be followed under the guidance of his own attribution of his choices to us, everyone else. The first feet seem to be those of the consumer whose trace is the popularity of the image; the next are those of the chimera 'journalist-reader' whose track is the coarse half-tone screen of newsprint; the next are those of the artist-connoisseur – the tracks are the evidences of paint and canvas, of flatness etc, the very matter of Greenbergianism. On the surface is the trace of marketability – the brilliant colours, the assorted sizes, the near repetitions etc. All these traces are superimposed so that one is the subject or image of the other. In the Pincus-Witten interview, Salle argued that his works brought together the images of high art and pornography. He said that pornography has a peculiar character of reality in that one knows the object of desire was seen by someone. Fine art, on the other hand, is open textured so that seen at a distance, it distinguishes itself as just art. But Salle's images of art are often very real, heavily painted, while his pornography is blurred or over-enlarged so that its reality is underplayed. He recognises the reality of the feelings of those who object to it, while insisting that his work is not about popular imagery but is autonomous and deals with the mechanics of fine art and popular art, which, one may presume, are part of his subject matter. Pincus-Witten invokes the name Pinter in his title, no doubt to signify his unease at the lack of shared assumptions between himself and Salle, but does not seem to recognise that the practice of incomprehension is itself a means of functioning within a sub-culture, one that is very familiar in the art world, which is a sub-culture of self-definition and conflict. At any rate, by depriving his interlocutor of the cues he expects while mentioning elements of familiar topics, Salle provides an analogy to his own painting with its recognisable motifs but, as he says, 'no story'. He offers only a structure of contiguity and superimposition, opacity and transparency. These, together with the traditional contrasts of high and low art, representation and abstraction, reference and autonomy, again identify him, to members of the sub-culture, as one of themselves. Comparing Salle's paintings with those of Richard Hamilton in the late 50s and Warhol in the early 60s, which share some of the same constituents, we see that Hamilton emphasises the degree to which the response to image fragments is conditioned by the culture (but expects an expertise in this response on the part of the consumer), while Warhol's imagery (car crashes, electric chairs etc) is like that of Salle's pornography; at some point it was seen as real, unconditioned. But of these three only Salle can rely on a response that deals with the issue of high and low art, money, the possibility of individual self-expression, the nature of the medium, etc, in terms of the Marxist, Freudian, Structuralist, Post-Structuralist sub-culture. The work of ordering the expectations of his consumers has been done for him by artists like Haacke and Burgin. This allows Salle, especially in the context of other, much more obviously associated (committed) artists, to play down his own 'argument' and to let it emerge from ironies.

Artists like Jeff Koons, Haim Steinbach and Ashley Bickerton, can assume a response still further conditioned to this culture and, within it, to the writings of yet another French sage, Jean Baudrillard. Insofar as I can understand this critic (who is much easier to read than Lacan or Derrida, more like the Barthes of *Mythologies*), he has deconstructed many of the basic assumptions of his own culture, while retaining an unaccounted-for faith in the triumph of a Socialism, undefined in what I have read. In the essay which is most quoted in the context of art,[7] Baudrillard uses the term 'similacrum'. This is introduced in an epigraph fictionally attributed to *Ecclesiastes*. It reads: 'The similacrum is never that which conceals the truth – it is the truth which conceals that there is none'. Baudrillard's writing proceeds by some types of falsehood characteristic of his sub-culture, particularly the aberrant use of words without suitable redefinition. This allows the use of several senses of such a word and so the creation of a false syllogism; one is constantly reminded of the theorem in logic that a falsehood implies everything. The equivocal expression of Baudrillard's morality and reality make it difficult to judge the substance of any influence he may have on artists, but he does supply them with words to play with. Halley, to whom I referred at the start and who bases ideas on those of Baudrillard, seeks to avoid complicity with his own world by producing a similacrum of a work of art: it looks like a work of art but it isn't one, or rather it is one after all, because it's a similacrum.

The critical reception and promotion of this art is marked by an equally equivocal sense of reality and value. It seems to have taken three forms from the start. One form shows some enthusiasm for the work but makes a point of mentioning the dealers who have sold it and the collectors who have bought it, for example Jeffrey Deitch[8] and Brian Wallis.[9] A second form, closer to the late-Marxist sub-culture, shows less enthusiasm and more scepticism, even when published in the catalogue of a definitive exhibition dedicated to the work, and not as magazine articles written from the outside, specifically to condemn. Two 1986 articles by Hal Foster and Thomas Crow,[10] seriously question the deconstructive power of the work. A more openly hostile critique of this art is that of Donald Kuspit,[11] who argues that art that concerns itself with the media is inherently collusive with the power of the media. His position is more closely allied to the psychoanalytic tradition, but he shares with many other critics the view that artists ought to be attacking the dominant authority, what he calls 'the evil internalised in us', but he considers that 'their throwaway conscience [is] incomplete . . . anti-authoritarian but also non-humanistic'.

Other writers, sharing the view that artists should be changing the world by attacking its visual language are convinced in varying degrees of the political effectiveness of Pop Art II. They include David Joselit, also in *Endgame*,[12] Michele Cone[13] and Dan Cameron.[14] Lynne Cooke[15] seems to beg the question of complicity[16] versus effective deconstruction; she collages a sort of quote from Foster in the article cited above: 'For Foster, for example, the crucial question is whether they "defy the 'social progress' of commodification" whether they stand outside rather than collusively reflect "a process of acculturation that reduces all expressions to a commodity, all events to a spectacle"' and later cites the work of Steinbach as giving the impression that when 'every object is reducible to the status of a commodity, then every commodity is an object', so conforming to Foster's thesis. But of course whether or not a work of art is presented as a commodity is not a key to whether it defies Foster's 'social process'. She implies that to raise the question is enough to constitute the political act. Foster himself leaves open the question of whether the art is genuinely subversive.

The denizens of the Capitol, banks, boardrooms and advertising agencies are showing no signs of alarm, but the issue of the power of art, that is its power to affect change in society, that change called for by Marx himself and quoted by Kuspit, is an issue that appears overtly or by implication in most of the writings of Pop Art II. It is argued that the multiplication of galleries, museums and private collections and of the attention given to artists, shows that those artists could have or do have power, but the writers regret that this power is mitigated by the weakness, that is the collusiveness, of an art that deals in the terms of the enemy and its unwillingness to produce a new realism. Jeff Koons is explicit in seeking to re-empower the artist and to take advantage of the position he is given and to exploit every vehicle of popularity in his work (like Warhol).

Koons has also exploited opportunities to be interviewed for the art press. The cultural background of these interviews is both that of the sub-culture which I have mentioned repeatedly and that of the object of its obsession – the world of galleries, museums, collectors and the vehicles of communication between them. Koons' remarks seem sometimes to reflect more the language of one, and sometimes more the language of the other of these two contexts. In a joint interview with Allan McCollum,[17] he speaks as a deconstructionist, although with little of the jargon: 'I don't seek to make consumer icons but to decode why and how consumer objects are glorified' and 'the show is about how (the upper) class controls the class structure by propounding, through information, the desire for luxury and abstraction above people's level of education.' Allan McCollum speaks in a similar vein, though his devices are more narrowly those of the artworld: 'Art is clearly used as a means of exclusion in the sense that a class consolidates its identity by developing certain aesthetic values and collecting certain types of objects . . . Even the museum, ostensibly a public institution, is a powerful instrument of exclusion, one whose pernicious dominance in governing the general reception of art I attempt to defy by trying to produce more art work than most museums have in their inventory. I address the commercial gallery in a similar way by reducing the artwork to a sign of itself: a sign not only as an object-in-the-world, but also as a particular kind of commodity'. It is not clear whether in this interview Koons and McCollum are prompting each other to take the deconstructive line or whether Salvioni or some contemporary circumstance influenced them. In another interview,[18] McCollum expresses his criticism in a psychological frame: 'An effective work of art can render out of us anxieties we never knew we had, and in turn mediate the repression of these anxieties in an orderly, socially acceptable way. It is the expectancy of this transformation that I am trying to effect in the viewer, without offering its fulfillment.' He believes that 'vast economic powers . . . work to intimidate us from above, creating the insecurity and feelings of helplessness' which unnecessary products are designed to displace.

Haim Steinbach[19] offers a positive solution: by dissolving the hierarchical differences between objects, he hopes to break down those between people or classes. Koons asserts similarly that his art will create equilibrium and a sense of security: 'These objects will not be looked at in a contemplative way, but will only be there as a mechanism of security. And they will be accessible to all, for art can and should be used to stimulate social mobility

. . . every citizen will be of the blue blood . . . the individual will exist in a state of entropy, or rest, and inhabit an environment decorated with object art that is beyond critical dialogue . . . For the lower class and middle class (my art) will lead to a state of rest: for the upper class it will lead to an unprecedented state of confidence . . . There will be no losers'.[20] Equilibrium and confidence are among the themes of Koons' work; the former expressed, for example, in the floating basketballs, the latter in the familiar images and devices and in the richness and precision of materials, as well as in the lack of interference with the outlines of his objects. He is scrupulously legal in his transactions, as much with powerful companies as with craftsmen. He speaks more often of the relationship of the upper to the middle class than of either to the working class and claims to 'believe in advertisement and media completely. My art and personal life are based in it'.[21] In short, although speaking at much greater length, he is playing the role of Warhol, the artist who, more than any other, taught the world to see that, if the medium of the painter is paint and canvas, the medium of the artist (Koons says he is not a sculptor) is himself in the art world.

Notes

1 Ross Bleckner, Peter Halley, Sherrie Levine, Philip Taaffe etc, all consecrated in Whitney Biennials 1987 and/or 1989 and, except Levine, in the Saatchi Collection, *New York Art Now*, 1987.
2 Ashley Bickerton, Jeff Koons, Allan McCollum, Haim Steinbach etc, all in Whitney Biennials 87 and/or 89 but the last, and in the Saatchi Collection.
3 Peter Halley, 'The Crisis in Geometry', *Arts*, Summer 1984.
4 Lawrence Alloway, *Ark* 17, 1956.
5 Victor Burgin, 'Two essays on Art Photography and Semiotics', 1976.
6 Robert Pincus-Witten, 'Pure Pinter: An interview with David Salle', *Arts*, Nov 1985.
7 Jean Baudrillard, 'Simulacra and Simulations', 1983, abridged in *Selected Writings*, ed Mark Poster, 1988.
8 Jeffrey Deitch interviewed by Matthew Collings in 'Mythologies: Art and the Market', *Artscribe* 57, April 1986.
9 Brian Wallis, *A Product You Could Kill For*, New Museum of Contemporary Art, New York, June 1986.
10 Hal Foster, 'Return of Hank Herron' and Thomas Crow, 'The Future of an Illusion, or The Contemporary Artist as Cargo Cultist', both in *Endgame*, Institute of Contemporary Arts, Boston, June 1986. See also Hal Foster, 'Signs Taken for Wonders', *Art in America*, June 1986 and Thomas Crow, 'Versions of the Pastoral in Some Recent American Art', *American Art of the Late Eighties*, ICA Boston, 1988.
11 Donald Kuspit, 'Regressive Reproduction and Throwaway Conscience', *Artscribe* 61, Jan-Feb 1987. See also 'The Opera is Over', *Artscribe International*, Sept-Oct 1988. Sidney Tillim makes a similar case in 'Ideology and Difference', *Arts*, March 1989.
12 David Joselit, *Endgame, op cit*.
13 Michele Cone, 'Readymades on the Couch', *Artscribe* 58, June-July 1986.
14 David Cameron, *Art and its Double*, Fundacio Caixa de Pensiones, Barcelona, 1986.
15 Lynne Cook, 'Object Lessons', *Artscribe* 65, Sept-Oct 1987.
16 This issue is the specific topic of a debate including six of the artists mentioned in footnotes 1 and 2, moderator Peter Nagy, 'From Criticism to Complicity', *Flash Art* 129, 1986.
17 Daniela Salvioni, 'McCollum and Koons', *Flash Art* 131, 1986-7.
18 D A Robbins, 'An interview with Allan McCollum', *Arts*, Oct 1985.
19 Holland Cotter, 'Haim Steinbach: Shelf Life', *Art in America*, May 1988.
20 Giancarlo Politi, 'Luxury and Desire: an Interview with Jeff Koons', *Flash Art* 132 Feb-March 1987.
21 Jeff Koons interviewed by Klaus Ottman, *Journal of Contemporary Art* I No 1, Spring 1988.

Jeff Koons, *Ushering in Banality*, 1988, polychromed wood, 96.5x157.5x76.2cm, edition of three

Buster Keaton, 1988, polychromed wood, 167x127x67.3cm

JEFF KOONS
THE POWER OF SEDUCTION
An Art & Design *Interview*

Jeff Koons, *Ilona on Top (Rosa Background)*, 1990, painting on canvas, 344x366cm

Interviewed in London towards the end of 1989, on the occasion of his talk at the ICA, Koons reflects on his commercial success within the consumer-dominated art world of the 80s. Seeing the influence of the mass media as exercising a positive effect on the artist's power to communicate and seduce an audience, he discusses issues such as exploitation, political effectiveness and the concept of the new.

– Glancing through the abundance of 'Jeff Koons' interviews and statements from the 80s, the issues constantly under discussion range from art as a commodity, the art 'industry', the power of the market, political effectiveness and exploitation, to advertising, information networks, communication devices and entertainment. Do you see your art primarily in these terms?

My own interests are in many of the areas which you mention. I believe that it's very important for art to be effective in communications. For a very long time art has not been very effective and artists have not taken the responsibility to communicate. Of course, when anything like this occurs, when one political network or one industry defers its responsibility to communicate, other industries that do feel responsible and are ambitious will take control of that industry. We've seen this occur with the advertising industry and also the entertainment industry; they've been much more effective in communication than the fine arts. I would like to do everything possible to assist in returning this responsibility to art, to manipulate and seduce an audience and to communicate effectively with them. In doing so, it's a responsibility not only to exploit oneself, which one must do – artists must exploit themselves – but to exploit others, to communicate with them in order to meet their needs and to be the great communicators.

– When you talk about communication and effectiveness, what ideas are you aiming to communicate and in what ways are you as an artist being effective?

First of all I've been very interested in trying to help liberate people so that they can participate in social mobility; social mobility and education is always a dialogue within my work. My art is really there to help keep people out of equilibrium and to enable them to participate in mobility. My work tries to embrace everyone, to educate the lower classes in how systems work and how one can be effective within a system, thereby giving them a chance to exploit themselves.

– So, by appropriating familiar images from the mass media, from advertising, pop music etc, images which break down the boundaries between gallery-exhibited art and everyday consumerism, you are aiming to communicate to a mass audience?

I believe in using imagery that is familiar. I hope that people will be able to embrace my work and to communicate with it. I hope that somewhere I will break down a wall so that they will participate and just give in to the image, saying 'Okay, you know you've got me.' Even if they are very resistant, at some point they will let their resistance down. My work tries to describe what the parameter of life is. I want it to have the sudden sense of familiarity because it is not about formalism. This is not subjective art, it is very objective, and in this aspect I want my pieces to really erase themselves as far as form is concerned and

the amount of space they take up. They're really about everything that is just invisible, that's in the air, that's ephemeral perhaps. It's about things that people are maybe familiar with in a post-card shop or just in some aspect of their life.
– And by confronting viewers with familiarity, you are forcing them to abandon their inhibitions about art and about what art 'should be'?
I'm trying to help liberate people, to remove inhibition and to let the individual be as loud as possible, to remove people's fear and guilt and to let them know that all the great things in the world-to-come are already here. Nothing new is ever going to come here, it's just going to be the transformation of what is already here. It's like making a new chemical compound, it's putting different associations together and really great, wonderful things appear. Only the things that will come are already here and if people look they will be able to liberate themselves and will realise that ultimately their state of being is becoming. Everything is here and everyone can just become.
– While your aim is to communicate to a mass audience and to break down social barriers, the inevitable criticism is that your art isn't in fact accessible to a mass audience; it is exhibited in commercial gallery spaces so that, rather than communicating to the child in the street, for example, you are only really seducing the fashionable art-going élite.
Although my dialogue is above all with the adult community, the child in the street is a living human being and represents our future. I absolutely want to be having some dialogue with our future. I embrace these people just as I would embrace someone who is much older, who is part of a generation that has preceded my generation. The dialogue is the same. I try to function within my art and the vocabulary is really about eternal things. I'm not interested in the surface of things and certainly not in fashionable trends or anything of that kind. I do not involve myself in that sort of thing. I'm involved in what my ideas are and in what I think is important to myself and I try to lead in the best manner that I can.

My interests are very tied up in my own vocabulary. I'm interested in trying to liberate art, in trying to make artists ambitious again so that they take on the responsibility to participate and to assist in breaking down some of the walls so that they can experience their own culture. Artists don't want to show that they're victimised and of course one must be victimised to be able to absorb one's culture and to participate. And one also has to take the responsibility as far as leadership is concerned. It is about governing and communicating and one must communicate in any way that is possible. My work will do absolutely anything to communicate. My work will say that it is speaking in any dialogue the viewer wishes to hear, just to be able to start a communication. I believe that once a communication process starts, my political intent will be transferred to the viewer.
– In your conscious manipulation of the mass media and your attempts to seduce an audience by displaying familiar consumer objects and ready-mades in the context of a commercial gallery, to what extent have you been influenced by the example of Warhol and the Duchampian concept of art?
I am absolutely a product of Marcel Duchamp; I come out of the Duchampian period. So did Andy. Andy is like a child of Marcel and I'm like a grandchild of Marcel. Of course Marcel was the one who, mostly along with Braque and Picasso, liberated everyday things and the use of collage, be it newspaper or some other material. Marcel introduced the object into art and Andy followed through in the use of that object. However, one of the things I so respect in Warhol isn't so much his use of the familiar and the ready-made, because Marcel had already ploughed through that, but rather it is the aspect of sexuality in his art.

Warhol was able to communicate intellectual information, not through a cerebral process, but through a sexual process and this is why I have so much respect for Andy. As far as my own role is concerned, I believe that I started to add to the Duchampian philosophy and to create a new ground when I did my work called *The New*. This was an encased work displaying vacuum cleaners for their newness; that is displaying an object for its integrity and for being brand new. It dealt with the negotiation between the animate and the inanimate, with the positive aspects of the animate alongside the positive aspects of the inanimate. It's part of reading something that's in a position to be immortal; it's a kind of ultimate state of being, of being eternally new. My work continues to deal with ultimate states of being.

As far as participating in the media, I believe in total co-ordination. It's very important to do everything one can, not to hurt oneself but to be able to help oneself. In a political power situation, to be able to communicate with people through the media is wonderful. The media is a phenomenon of communication, that is something that should be embraced, whether you're using aspects of envy or whatever to communicate and stimulate the public. It's all very positive and you must use everything that's available to the best of your ability. I think that the intent of the media is to communicate and to deliver the information at hand. Of course nothing's ever that perfect but I don't think that working with the media is any form of compromise at all. I think that it is very positive.
– Frederic Jameson has described the New York art world in terms of 'perpetual change', highlighting the transience of artists operating in a market that is constantly demanding 'the new'. Is there a need for artists to 'liberate' themselves from the commercial system to a certain extent?
I think that artists must deal with this situation and I think that it is very important for young artists to be able to defend their independence from the system. One has to understand the system, to be independent of it, or to participate with it. You always have to be in control. If you feel that you're not in control of the situation, then you have to be able to divorce yourself from it. A lot of artists feel too insecure, particularly if they have had success without ever having being able to claim their independence. I've been very lucky in that I did claim my independence.

I participated with the art system when working with galleries such as Mary Boone, although I didn't enjoy the experience that much because it wasn't really a time when my ideas could penetrate. There is a network and once this network of dealers and writers and critics and collectors starts to focus on one area, then they just want to concentrate on that one area for quite some time, to digest the information that's there. I realised that my ideas were just not really going to have a chance to participate at that moment and, instead of sitting on the sideline and moping, I decided to go out and take care of my own work. I didn't have to participate in the commercial art world. I had a responsibility to my work. I worked as a broker down on Wall Street to support my art. My work was expensive to make but I had a responsibility to continue making it. In this way I was prepared, when the environment was better, to have my political stage. The environment at that time was looking in a different area. However much I might have yelled 'Hey, look over here!', at that moment it was too focused on something else. But as soon as I could see that the environment was changing and looking for something new, I showed my ability to lead.

The art world is by no means unique from other professions such as acting or stockbroking. One can rise to a certain level of notoriety and then fall; that happens everywhere. But of course if artists are good, then they can maintain themselves and can continue to participate.

I think I have done substantial work which has helped contribute to the culture since 1980 when I did my encased works. After my encased works, I did my equilibrium work and after my equilibrium work I did my first stainless-steel *Luxury Degradation* show and after that I did my *Statuary* show which has the *Rabbit* piece and others like it, and after that I created my *Banality* exhibition, so I think I've got a pretty good decade behind me. Warhol had one great decade and I've already had a good decade. But I still have a lot to say. I don't believe in the idea of creating an 'end-all' state and making a finished product that is so great and so wonderful. Art to me is about becoming, it's about what Jeff Koons can become and how evolutionary I can be within myself at the present time.

– When you talk about your past decade, there is a sense of constant and self-conscious change, of continuously coming up with something new. Was it in any way a self-conscious stategy of change and novelty, or does it appear so only in retrospect? How did these ideas come about?

I get bored easily, but change is not something I set down on a piece of brown paper and say 'What do I do next? Now I should do A B C because this is popular with this critic'. It's nothing like that. My work is about resonance, which is increasingly at the heart of my work. I'm focusing on something as intensely as I possibly can, to reach to my limitations; my aim is then to exploit that idea as much as possible and then to liberate myself from it. I always demand to be able to liberate and divorce myself from what I've done previously. It's been my own self-interest, my own growth and ideas, and this enables me to focus intensely. The only reason I do editions, editions of three, is so that I can then have enough work to place politically, and to communicate those ideas. Those ideas then have a political platform and I can liberate myself from them.

– As you talk, there is a sense of detachment towards your art, a certain objectivity. Does this arise from the fact that, while the ideas and concepts are yours, the actual works are manufactured by others, according to your instructions, as was the case with your recent polycromed wood and porcelain pieces? Do you feel that sense of detachment from the creative process, a certain distancing from the materials, and do you see your work primarily in terms of production and industry?

When I go into production, of course I generate the ideas for the work. All the editing takes place before I go into production, so my work is extremely edited. After I go into production, I produce an exhibition. It's not as if you can walk around and say this is a strong piece, this is a weak piece; there's a small range of good and bad work because of the way it's produced and the expense involved. It's an intense focusing down that takes place. As for the distance, I've always tried to keep a certain physical distance from my work so that I would not get lost in the subjective. I'm very interested in the objective, in meeting the needs of the masses and in having art deal with things that are important to everyone, not what I dreamt the night before, or how I feel subjectively about this or that, but in trying to communicate far more with the mass consciousness. However, I'm in control of every aspect of my work. Once the idea is generated, then I find people who can exploit what I'm interested in. If I choose an individual to make a porcelain nude of a woman for me, they must be able to have sexuality in themselves and to be able to exploit it out of themselves. Therefore I can use them within my work and anticipate them because they will exploit that aspect of themselves. I am in control of every aspect, of form, size, colour; there's not one little detail that is not a Jeff Koons detail. I choose the production people specifically for the skills that they have and for their own ambition of self-liberation.

– So in that sense your art is an industry, with large numbers of people working to realise an individual's idea or vision?

It's politics. If I myself were to make a 'Michael Jackson', I'd

still be learning to make porcelain. All through art history, since the Renaissance, anybody who has been politically ambitious has never spent all that energy just to do one project. If you have ambition, you cannot do anything on a large scale by yourself, you would get so little done within your life. I get everything done exactly the way I want it; there is not one detail that is not articulated by myself. I am not that detached, in a way I am closer to what I want to accomplish, and that is to be able to communicate and to have my political platform.

– Why have you chosen art as the medium to gain a political platform and to communicate? Surely the medium of film, for example, which reaches a larger mass audience than art, would be more politically effective?

Or just the media itself? These are wonderful areas and I think that actors too are great liberators. They are able to show people little nuances of life or voids that people can live or participate in to expand the parameters of life. I think the most important thing an artist can do is to be able to remove inhibitions and to let people live, to try to show them that the parameter of their own life can be much greater. That's the most exciting thing one can do. I'm an artist and I intend to remain an artist. I don't intend to be an artist who becomes a filmmaker and tries to get into a different area. Art can be absolutely anything, art can become commercial fine art, it can become just the film industry, it can become anything. It really is the most liberating industry to be involved with.

– Surely you would expand your potential for communication by taking your works out of the context of the commercial gallery and contemporary art museum and by making them more accessible to a wider audience?

The system of art can also change and transform and it must change; it's a growth process and I don't intend to abandon it. I want to liberate it and to make art something other than what it is. I would like to increase the parameters of art. I believe in embracing other areas and using them, but I really have no intention of leaving art. I really believe in liberation, and I'm not politically going to change camps.

– You have claimed to 'believe in advertisement and the media completely', saying that 'My art and personal life are based in it'. Do you see interviews as a form of advertising?

Right now, I'm in the process of physically transforming my body.

– Your body?

My body. Just to be able to have the body to effectively do my work, I work out seven days a week, an hour and a half to two hours a day.

– Have you ever considered performance art?

I think that all aspects of life are a performance. I'm really not too interested in this title 'performance art' because I think it got framed and labelled in the 70s in very boring and defined areas, just as people think of political art in terms of some activist movement trying to save trees in Brazil or a woman's place in art; it's all so defined. As soon as you have a definition of the political activity that's taking place, you're limited in scope. I don't like to participate in that manner and that's the way I think performance art has acted.

– So, like Warhol, you believe that art is inseparable from life, and that life itself is a performance?

I think this idea goes past Warhol. We have only to look at the great philosophers throughout history to see that life and activity are one and the same thing.

– You have been quoted as saying 'I don't seek to make consumer icons but to decode how and why consumer icons are glorified'. Can you elaborate on these ideas?

The work that I did from 1979 to 1982 dealt with appliances, with this negotiation and seductiveness which some types of objects have and their presentation of the new. I always thought that this was looked upon by critics and the public in a feminine manner. I used vacuum cleaners because they are sexual and also anthropomorphic, they are breathing machines, they are lungs, and they have sexual connotations to them, it's to do with the apparatus that they are made of. Every one of those pieces is labelled 'new', like *New Hoover Convertible*.

I've tried to show that consumerism also has a dark side and that's what my tanks are about. They are very masculine aspects and it's a form of liberation. We have to maintain this clean, pristine look, so I went into all my darker colours, my bronzes, the dark browns, the blacks, the steel bands, the tanks, the black basket-ball players. I never alienate sex from my work. I never just do work directed in a feminine manner or a masculine manner. In the *Equilibrium* show there were objects which were extremely feminine such as the bronze snorkler which is very like the *Venus* or the *Olympia*, very provocative when seen from the front, even though at the back it is very masculine. Even one of my Nike posters had a woman in it. Of course, going through my work, it's not about consumerism, it's about desire and temptation and it's about needing those desires. But I'm not making a dialogue that you are what you buy or anything like this. I really don't deal with that.

– *In aiming to 'decode' consumer objects, are you drawn to the theories of deconstruction at all?*

I've never read any of those theories. All this information has already been incorporated into society and it's in the mass consciousness of everybody; so I don't understand everyone jumping on that band wagon. My work tries to perform much more on the frontiers of things. I don't read books. I create from the very base bottom of things. My works are not made out of clay, they are not made out of wood, they are not moulds of things, they are commodities. What *New Hoover Convertible* is saying is that everything's here, all the inclination is here, it is really wonderful. The best colour to me was actual colour, like the colour on the side of a vacuum cleaner is actual, real colour; it's more real than painting. *Two Ball 50/50 Tank* is about social mobility, social equilibrium, either/or, being or nothingness; it's a political idea, that's what the tanks are about. Half this tank is filled with water, half is empty, that's wet/dry. See the side of that vacuum cleaner, is that dry? Either/or, being or nothingness. I go through ultimate states of personal being into ultimate states of personal being.

– *So you are not critical or cynical about consumerism?*

I'm not cynical at all, I'm self-cynical. I look at every imperfection in myself and I go to my inner depths. I don't point the finger at society, I believe in generosity. Saying that art is a vacuum, which is an underlying idea here in that the emptyness of the space is being made visual, I don't think that's really cynical. I think that it's saying that change just has to take place and I'm just looking to lead and to give direction to the object.

People expect certain needs to be fulfilled by objects, by material things. It's like a store, people talk about a store of value, but also a store of emotional needs etc. To me consumer objects still have meaning. I'm not interested in emptying out, I'm not pessimistic and I don't believe that everything is dead and that things don't have meaning. Things do have meaning. I'm an optimist and I embrace everything for what it is and I love things for what they are. Materialism is a store and it is a supplement for things which people are not receiving in their own lives and if you stress that to people, you help them to realise that these are manifestations of things which they are really not getting out of their own lives. I believe much more in liberating, so that people can live as intensely as possible, to help break down their inhibitions and to participate in life.

Cicciolina is a great liberator. She's absolutely one of the best artists in the world and a great seductress. She's a great communicator. She is the eternal virgin displaying the ultimate states of purity and innocence. I'm being extremely sincere about the communicative power of Cicciolina. She meets the needs of the people. She's one of the greatest artists and politicians alive. When I say one of the greatest politicians, I mean someone who has been able to formulate and to create a vocabulary of her own ideas in a way that is very, very productive. I think that she is taking herself and becoming as much as she possibly can become, which is something phenomenal. She has become eternally pure and this is a phenomenal thing, it's amazing, it's a great art, a tremendous art and it liberates what the parameter of art can be. She can take you to Hell and back to Eden, who else can do that?

– *How do you respond to different readings and interpretations of your work?*

There's a tremendous layer of context within my work, so I doubt that a person would read something into it that is not there. Whatever it may represent to the viewer, my work morally accepts that and just wants those things to come out in the work. My last show, the porcelain or wood figures and nudes, was about trying to serve the bourgeoisie, to remove their guilt and shame so that they would be able to liberate themselves and have the confidence to become the new upper class. It was to remove their guilt and shame at being. They should be baptised in banality and move forward, embrace who they are, embrace their past, accomplish and become what they must.

– *By exhibiting your kitsch sculptures of St John the Baptist, Buster Keaton and Michael Jackson in the same show, you seemed to be placing religion and popular culture on the same plane of banality and consumerism. Was this your intention?*

My intention was to show that religions have changed and that there are always transformations. I am a very, very spiritual person and I believe that spirituality is very, very necessary in the life of an individual. But I was representing a new religious stance, a new spirituality, and in this case an authoritarian figure to baptise in banality was St John the Baptist. I also have Christ there too. Christ was there as Buster Keaton on the back of a pony, but a very small pony, very optimistic for a journey but very unprepared. Michael Jackson was there as the symbol of a contemporary Christ, one who has been baptised and who is now performing effectively as a great liberator and doing anything that is necessary to be able to communicate. He has embraced aspects of who he is, and has been baptised in banality.

– *So you see these works as being very positive?*

I see them as spiritual, very, very, spiritual.

– *And do you believe that the majority of viewers see them in that light?*

I think that, at least on a subconscious level, they understand the spiritual aspect to the work, that there is a vision and a mission. I think it's evident that at times I present myself as John the Baptist and also as the Saviour within the work itself. I also believe that having John the Baptist there was like saying yes, I want to assume leadership and responsibility and I will do things to afford this level, things that I can't do with my limitations but there are greater things to come. My show was like a baptism signifying that there are greater things to come.

– *You seem to be, not only the artist, but also the representative and spokesman for your work. Would you describe yourself in these terms?*

I believe that I am a smoke-screen for my own art and I am closest to its core. I don't believe in the role of the critic, the spokesman. If critics have so much to say and so much that they believe in, why don't they go out and do it? They shouldn't tell artists that they should do this activity for them; they say things like, 'Oh you don't make your own work Jeff, you have other

artists make it!' What do you think the critics think their position is? That they come up with these ideas and then they leave artists to generate these ideas in a plastic art form? You know, I feel much more that my responsibility is to communicate the ideas that I'm interested in and to wear my own shoes and my own clothes in this world, rather than another man's or woman's.
– *So are you in a sense undermining the role of the critic?*
No. I'm interested in being myself and in following my own political ideas and aspirations rather than someone else's.
– *Do you feel that you are also undertaking the role of the dealer to a certain extent by promoting and advertising your own art through the media?*
Not advertising, but politically communicating what my intentions are. That of course does involve aspects of promotion and everything else that's been involved in any political platform since the beginning of time. Just as in mating calls, one is showing one's feathers; is that advertising? Of course. The preening of one's chest, is that promotion? Of course.
– *Jean Baudrillard has discussed contemporary existence in terms of the 'ecstasy of communication', an ecstasy that is 'obscene'. What effect do you see the current obsession with media communication and information-networks as having on the individual?*
I am not anti-media, I am not anti-information. I think it's very positive. I believe in absorption. I think that there are certain aspects of the quality of life that continue to change and transform themselves and I really believe in evolution and in moving forward. He's being cynical, he's being a pessimist. To me, information has made my quality of life so much better, it has helped to educate me; it has not ruined my quality of life. The media really is a great liberator, it's a great educator. It's not always perfectly okay, but I think that its intentions are really to relay information.

Television is only one aspect of the media, we have the news networks, we have the advertising industry with images which can really penetrate people and show levels of abstraction, we have all different forms of news and newspapers. Even though the story may be short, at least there is a point and it shows people that there is a larger world outside. We can help them to participate in the world and to be involved with activities which they would like to be involved in.
– *You have described your work in terms of 'unobtainable states of being'. Can you elaborate on this?*
Everything is obtainable, there is nothing that is unobtainable and what is so wonderful is to embrace the obtainable but still to strive for what is unobtainable. That's what all life, all consciousness is about, it's not an end-all state. It's about becoming and trying to achieve the impossible. Perfection is non-existent, but striving for perfect states I think is absolutely wonderful. Everything is accessible. Nothing is unobtainable.

All commodities are negotiable, everything is negotiable in that way and is absolutely obtainable. If somebody really wants something, they should liberate themselves and go out and do what is necessary to get it. I do not believe in the pursuit of luxury, I think that you end up giving up your chips, you give up your economic power base to someone else. I do not believe in that. But if that is really what an individual wants he can do it, he can get it. There's nothing that can hold an individual back.
– *And do you believe your art succeeds in communicating that?*
I think so. You know I've become one of the leading artists in the world. Isn't that wonderful?
– *And you believe that you can have anything if you want it badly enough?*
If people want things, absolutely. But you have to really want it, you can't just think you want it. If you would right now give everybody what they think they want; if you gave everyone the

position they thought they wanted, you would find out in a period of time that everything would dwindle and the political power situation would go back to the people who have it now. The people who don't would have given it up because they don't really want it. The people who want things receive them because that's what they want; they are out there doing everything they can to achieve it, to work in that area and to assume that responsibility.
– *And what is it that you really want?*
To become the most that Jeff Koons can become.
– *To realise your own potential?*
Absolutely, to become what my limitations allow me to become, so that I can participate in a revolutionary process with myself and with society.
– *How do you view the work of other contemporary artists, such as Julian Schnabel for example, who has also become extremely successful by manipulating and seducing the audience of the 80s? And how do you respond to Neo-Expressionist artists, including Schnabel and Anselm Kiefer, who are more physically involved with the medium itself and are less objective, less distanced from their art?*
I have a tremendous amount of respect for Julian and Julian's position in the art world. I like his work and he presented himself as someone with a lot of confidence which I think was very, very good for the art world. I like the operatic aspect of Kiefer's work very much. Kiefer's a seducer and I like that and I think it's very good. I also think that my work is expressionist; it's just not subjective expressionism, it's objective expressionism.
– *This issue is called* New Art International. *Your work seems to be very much involved with American culture. Do you see yourself primarily as 'an American artist'?*
I am trying to create a work that transcends cultures. I am an American artist but, since 1986, I have been making my work in Europe. Europeans can respond to it in the same way as an American can. They will define new answers. But it's really made to transcend cultures, to be really global work.

I see myself as an international artist, but I am an American and I have been influenced for most of my life by that, although recently I have been more influenced by European culture. I think that the basic philosophy, the very core of my work, this negotiation between animate and inanimate, is probably very Eastern. Don't you see a little parallel with Kiefer, who did so much based on Judaism while I present myself very much in the manner of one of the heavy-weight prize-fighters, using the political back-bone of Catholicism and Christianity? I know where some of my power base is from and where it's collected, but I'm showing that I can also participate and try to expand and bring other people into this vocabulary of art. I don't just have to use a base in Judaism, for example, I can use a base in Catholicism and Christianity.
– *Do you think that art is about creating something completely new or do you see it more in terms of redefining and rearranging existing images and ideas?*
I think it is about the things that are new, but all that energy is already here in the world; we can't generate new energy, it just doesn't exist. So it is about the transformation and recollecting of things and this is the way that everything has participated throughout history. Nothing has ever come in from the outside of this universe. So I believe in new things, I don't believe in repeating the past, or that everything is just a constant repetition, but it's like creating a new chemical compound. Up to this point, the world may have only seen, let's say, two types of chemicals combined and all of a sudden, with those two types of chemicals, you bring in one other compound and you have a whole new, different material. Its properties are totally different from the properties that existed with only the other two.

SHRIEK WHEN THE PAIN HITS DURING INTERROGATION. REACH INTO THE DARK AGES TO FIND A SOUND THAT IS LIQUID HORROR, A SOUND OF THE BRINK WHERE MAN STOPS AND THE BEAST AND NAMELESS CRUEL FORCES BEGIN. SCREAM WHEN YOUR LIFE IS THREATENED. FORM A NOISE SO TRUE THAT YOUR TORMENTOR RECOGNIZES IT AS A VOICE THAT LIVES IN HIS OWN THROAT. THE TRUE SOUND TELLS HIM THAT HE CUTS HIS FLESH WHEN HE CUTS YOURS, THAT HE CANNOT THRIVE AFTER HE TORTURES YOU. SCREAM THAT HE DESTROYS ALL KINDNESS IN YOU AND BLACKENS EVERY VISION YOU COULD HAVE SHOWN HIM.

Jenny Holzer, offset paper poster from *Inflammatory Essays*, 1979-82, 43.2x43cm

BROOKS ADAMS

'INTO THE WORDS'

Thoughts on A Forest Of Signs

Barbara Kruger, *Untitled*, 1989

'Photo: Ceci est la couleur de mes rêves' (Photo: This is the colour of my dreams) reads the inscription on a 1925 painting by Joan Miró, seen recently in The Dada and Surrealist Word-Image *at the Los Angeles Contemporary Museum of Art. Taken figuratively, the Miró seems to anticipate the feeling and content of* A Forest of Signs – *the large group show of contemporary artists, many of them*

working with both photography as well as word-and-image, that was recently on view at the Temporary Contemporary. The Miró, using a single patch of dreamy blue in conjunction with the hand-written phrase, expresses, in a seemingly effortless way, the poetics of modern revery. It does not insist on a 'crisis of representation' as the *Forest of Signs* show did; in fact, it rather breezily seems to imply that no such crisis exists. The Miró does draw our attention to several conundrums, such as the fact that this is a painting of a photo and not a photo itself, or that words function somewhat differently from colour, or that the idea of a black and white photograph in the 1920s cannot quite be equated with the colour blue, that epigone of both Symbolist and Surrealist dream states. But none of this is experienced as 'crisis', and, neither, I would maintain, is much of the work included in *A Forest of Signs*.

According to Richard Koshalek, Director of MOCA, the show focused 'on the central artistic issue or "crisis" of our time: the meaning of art in a media- and consumer-influenced era, and the meaning of representation within this art. The title of the exhibition refers to the "forest" of signs and symbols that define contemporary culture: the flow of images from films, billboards, bus benches, magazines, television and art itself that are with us daily. These images have come to represent a new reality in their own right – a reality that we seek to enter and imitate in our own

lives.' In her catalogue essay 'Art in the Age of Reagan: 1980-1988', Mary Jane Jacobs (co-curator of the show with Ann Goldstein) points out that: 'the relation of today's art to consumer society is perhaps even more complicated that that of the Pop artists. The subject now is not a product pulled from a grocery shelf, but art itself as a product for sale. Appropriating techniques of commerce and advertising for the content, mode of fabrication, and presentation of the work, artists are playing with strategies of both the business and art worlds that have combined forces in so many ways over the past decade. As a result their work stands somewhere between criticality and complacency.'

Now whether any artistic issue can be considered central to the global concerns of today is highly debatable; the very concept of centrality suggests a colonialist approach, or better yet, a neo-colonialist approach to art and to art criticism. It strikes me that the meanings of art are always multiple at any given moment (and for any given viewer), and it also strikes me to call any artistic issue, even in quotation marks, a 'crisis' is pushing it, to say the least. Whether it be a flashy polychrome sculpture by Jeff Koons, or an incisively funny paperweight by Louise Lawler, or a strangely inscrutable narrative by Larry Johnson, which proves difficult to read because of the jazzy colours it is printed in, the contemporary art in *A Forest of Signs* all represents a sold link to art of the past, be it the Baroque art

Installation view showing works by Jeff Koons and Robert Longo

that has so clearly influenced Koons, or the 60s dot paintings that seem to inform Johnson's photographs. The obvious links with 70s Conceptual art, discussed by Anne Rorimer in a catalogue essay 'Photography – Language – Context: Prelude to the 1980s' have prompted many people to call this kind of work 'neo-Conceptualist' or even 'neo-70s'. Many have made the point that the exhibition was visually impoverished, in fact, that 'this was the show you didn't even have to see in order to review it'. Yet to my eye, there was plenty to look at in *A Forest of Signs*. In fact, many artists' decisions to work site-specifically produced works of unique impact at the Temporary Contemporary. The show was full of amazing *coups de théâtre,* such as Jenny Holzer's soaring wallpapered stripes of brilliantly coloured pronunciamentos, which formed a backdrop for Allan McCollum's equally breath-taking tabletop display of 10,000 individually cast, peach-coloured plastic hand grenades. The installation also had a subtle visual logic to it. The gridded order of Holzer's placards played off the implicit organisation of McCollum's objects, not to mention the soft grid structure of Gretchen Bender's mammoth *People in Pain,* a series of heat-set vinyl panels illuminated with the white neon titles of every movie that came out in 1988. Thus,

for better or worse, these works make use of 60s Colour-Field and 70s grid thinking – changing and, in a sense, historicising it in a hip and knowing way. Holzer uses the grid structure to break down any hierarchical readings of her work; we can scan it top to bottom, side to side or a panel or a sentence at a time.

The issue of legibility is a complex one which deserves some discussion. Do we enjoy Larry Johnson's gay narratives any less because they are hard to read? Isn't the difficulty part of the content? Or how about if we just enjoy the Jenny Holzer for the colour of the stripes, Richard Prince for the neo-Ed Ruscha palette, or Sherrie Levine for the framing and faux-wood grain-ing? So common have most of these works become on the international art circuit that we are almost obliged to look at only one level in them per viewing, or rather, to look for a new level of meaning at each viewing if we are not to become impossibly jaded. Thus much of this work can seem to take on the monotony of 'official' art. Yet to read a part for the whole, especially in the enormous pieces of Bender, Holzer and McCollum, makes for a kind of necessary visual synecdoche – one might even call it a survivalist synecdoche. This kind of fragmentary visual experi-ence never seems to bother us when we're looking at ancient

Installation view showing works by Allan McCollum, Jenny Holzer and Gretchen Bender

sculpture (where some parts are usually missing) or Impressionist painting, with its radical croppings of figures and landscapes, and it certainly doesn't bother us when we're watching TV.

As for visual fragmentation, Jeff Koons' polychrome sculpture *Woman in Tub,* with its sawed-off head, can be made to seem like the latest model in a venerable tradition of sawed-off sculpture, beginning with ancient ruins and extending to Degas' bronzes. Similarly, Louise Lawler's mysterious photograph of museum floorboards which reflect Frank Stella's protractor paintings on the wall might even have a subliminal source in Gustave Caillebotte's *The Floor-Scrapers* (1875), not to mention Sylvia Plimack Mangold's 70s paintings of floorboards and mirrors – one of the many ghosts of recent art that flicker, seemingly unnoticed, through *A Forest of Signs.*

Many of the artists in the show seemed to be preaching a new American sublime of absolute size and sheer number of parts (*viz* Holzer's and McCollum's installations), and the size of the TC allowed some artists to work especially big. A more traditional landscape sublime was evident in Jack Goldstein's early 80s panoramic paintings of lightening fields, themselves seemingly dependent on an old *Artforum* cover of May 1980 illustrat-

ing Walter de Maria's *Lightning Field* at work in New Mexico. Coming at the end of the 80s, a renewed fascination with the sublime, and the overpowering effects of artistic or natural scenery, may be one road out of sterile, art critical casuistry.

The exhibition also espoused an architectonic sublime – an art of building signs that uses very simple, reductive, visual means to express some readily understandable architectural function, with a new, expiatory or Utopian twist. Ronald Jones' very expensive-looking stone floor pieces, which embed the plans of American internment camps in the floor of the Temporary Contemporary for what seemed eternity, struck me as an almost pharoanic enterprise – one which nevertheless has roots in Carl Andre's 60s and 70s floor pieces, as well as more anonymous and popular monuments such as the celebrity footprints at Mann's Chinese Theater. Jones' piece was intended to remind the public of crimes perpetuated against the Japanese during World War II. Matt Mullican's signs and symbols, on the other hand, often seem to be postulating some *Brave New World* city planning on a par with Le Corbusier – only now with an ironic edge. Mullican's signs are all immediately legible and comprehensible, which sometimes makes them less than fascinating.

Above: Barbara Bloom, *The Reign of Narcissism*, 1988-89, mixed media installation; *Below*: Mike Kelley, *Pay for your Pleasure*, 1988, installation view

And Richard Baim's slide show *Turn of the Century* captured the feeling of the world's fairs past and present, expressing a nostalgia for the future that was also one of the hallmarks of the show.

The paradoxical use of photography was clearly a binding element, insofar as none of the artists seem to practice photography as a fine art. Barbara Bloom's inclusion of her dental X-rays and horoscopes printed on to fabric which was used to upholster faux-period chairs in her Neo-Classical room called *The Reign of Narcissism* constitutes a novel, or perhaps a very archaic, use of photography. Bloom almost seemed to be taking us back to the era of daguerrotypes, and her signed handkerchiefs on sale in the bookstore were a nice neo-Victorian touch. Christopher Williams' decision to label his black and white photographs of old glass flowers at the Peabody Museum with the names of countries that currently practice terrorism had a kind of Baudelairean logic to it; these really did become 'Flowers of Evil', an idea already implicit in Robert Mapplethorpe's photographs of 'fatal' flowers. Like the biting commentary behind Bloom's temple to the self, Williams' photographs become updates on the *vanitas* theme in Dutch painting, exposing the mortality, and in this case, the terrorism, behind seemingly pretty and innocent images.

Many artists seemed obsessed with the aura of the page, be it the intense charisma of printed stationery, newspapers, or even hand-written letters. Stephen Prina's decision to reprint a 1969 Lawrence Weiner word piece *A Translation from One Language to Another* on 61 pieces of specially designed stationery in as many languages (58 of which were exhibited in a long line at the TC), deals not only with appropriation but with a kind of endless theme and variation of a simple 'module' of language (Weiner's original piece). Here Prina literally incorporates one of the father figures of Conceptual art into an 80s corporate letterhead from the Berlitz translation house in Woodland Hills, California that produced the project. All of this seems doubly ironic in light of the current revival of interest in Weiner's work, which in the late 80s can summon up images as unlikely as Dutch landscape in its succinct 'horizons' of words.

Prina's appropriation also brings to mind the pranks of Marcel Broodthaers, the Belgian poet and Conceptual artist, whose retrospective at MOCA provided any number of toney European precedents for the work in *A Forest of Signs*. Broodthaer's anodised aluminium version of Mallarmé's poem *A throw of the Dice* (1969), expressed as so many abstract bars of a certain length, seems particularly prescient of Prina's works, which often deal with the masterpieces of world art in terms of their relative dimensions. This kind of super-dry Conceptual wit would, no doubt, have been appreciated by Broodthaers, whose *La salle blanche,* a reconstruction of the artist's apartment in Brussels with words painted all over the walls, became at MOCA *the* 70s precedent *par excellence* for *A Forest of Signs*. Indeed,

coming across a small image of a dog looking at a dolphin floating above him in *chien souffrant de la solitude* (dog suffering from solitude) of 1975 with the caption, 'Die Crise? . . . Ein Traum' (The crisis? . . . A dream), I was reminded once again of that epithet 'Art in the Crisis of Representation' and was tempted to see in the Broodthaers a solution, or at least a precedent, for the problems that *A Forest of Signs* posed.

At its best, the show offered many such paeans to visual literacy. Mike Kelley's *Pay for your Pleasure,* a rainbow bright corridor of famous artists' and writers' portraits and their quotations on how art is somehow above the law (for example Jean Genet's 'I want to sing murder, for I love murderers'), worked like a refresher course in graduate school high seriousness. Yet, by adding artwork by the so-called 'Freeway Killer' William Bonin at the end of the corridor as well as a donation box at the entrance, whose proceeds went to Local Victims' Rights Organisations, Kelley brought real-life concerns into the sacred precinct of high art. Here for once we seemed to encounter a genuine crisis of representation for, without the donation box, Kelley's piece might seem to extol crime as well as romanticise real-life murderers. Yet for all its so-called dire subject-matter, this piece, not unlike the Miró, could be experienced as an upbeat, joyful, even celebratory rite of passage. As in the Holzer, the zowy Colour-Field stripes belie the dour sentiments expressed. Like it or not, Kelley's veritable spectrum of a corridor has as much to do with the conventions of Minimalist painting, California light art and Bruce Nauman's corridor sculptures of the 70s as it does with Baudelaire's *Flowers of Evil.*

Kelley's piece, like Bloom's, succeeded in creating a mini-environment, a kind of museum-within-the-museum, that in fact becomes a simulacrum of the museological experience, such as we also find in Broodthaers' work. His *Musée d'Art Moderne, Départment des Aigles* (Museum of Modern Art, Department of Eagles), a vast Conceptual project that entailed loans of art and curiosities on the subject of eagles from museums around the world, seems to announce the spirit in which so many artists in the show are working today. As Broodthaers noted in a famous quote, explaining how he became an artist: 'I, too, wondered if I couldn't sell something and succeed in life. For quite a while I had been good for nothing. I am 40 years old . . . The idea of inventing something insincere finally crossed my mind, and I set to work at once.' Yet even this posture of insincerity does not exactly cause a crisis of representation. It may cause a crisis of conscience, as it seems to have in Kelley's case, but then again, it may serve as yet another rallying cry for the artists in *A Forest of Signs*. Many of them succeeded in creating just this sort of fictional, one-person archaeological cabinet, or rogue's gallery – much as if the TC were some sublimely Brontësque, deserted English country house that we had discovered – chock-full of dusty 1980s memorabilia.

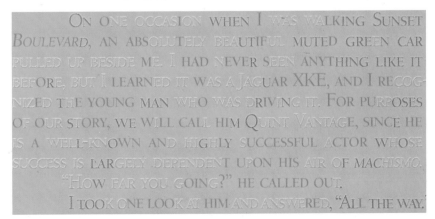

Larry Johnson, *Untitled (I had never seen anything like it)*, 1988, Type-C Print, 115.5x228.6cm

Nelson Mandela 70th Birthday Tribute, London 1988, show design by Fisher Park, London, *L to R*: Malangatana Ngwenya, *The Eyes of the World*; Jenny Holzer, *When Someone Beats You With A Flashlight You Make Light Shine In All Directions*; John Muafangejo, *Hope and Optimism*; Sue Coe, *A Clean Sweep*; Keith Haring, *Untitled* (flanking the performance area); Ralph Steadman, *The Struggle is My Life*.

   This benefit rock concert was conceived as a celebration of the 70th birthday of the world's most famous political prisoner, Nelson Mandela, whose recent release, witnessed by millions worldwide, has once more placed him on the central stage of international politics. The set, devised by Jonathan Park and Mark Fisher, stage designers for the Rolling Stones, illustrated the theme of the concert with artworks given by international artists opposed to apartheid. These and other key images were enlarged and used to decorate the arena frontage and stage. The concert was presented at Wembley Stadium in London on 11 June 1988 to a live audience of 72,000 and to a worldwide television audience of 500 million in 63 countries. Major rock'n'roll bands, including the Eurythmics, Chrissie Hynde, UB40, George Michael, Whitney Houston and Dire Sraits with Eric Clapton, and many other artists – a total of 300 performers – played during the ten-hour concert.

THOMAS LAWSON
GOING PUBLIC

As I sit down to write this I have just completed a huge public commission for a temporary installation on the outside of one of the main centres of local government in New York City. Stretching for about a third of a mile, this billboard/mural will encircle the Manhattan Municipal Building for about five years during a major renovation project. Painted in a declarative style using a limited, but very bright, range of colours (derived from the orange and blue of New York's flag), the painting inserts itself forcefully within the daily life of that part of the city that houses the enforcers of government – this is where you must come for a licence to marry, build, do business; the Police headquarters are in the area, as are the offices of the FBI, the Immigration Services, the Customs; so are those other branches of the law, the courthouses and gaol. Within this framework my goal was to open the possibility that ordinary citizens might want to reconsider aspects of the official representation of the city proffered by the authorities. The imagery I worked with is all developed from New York's civic statuary, an archive of power frozen in a past time that keeps women safely allegorical and minorities all but invisible. A panoply of men in period and contemporary costumes, arms flung about in the gestures of impassioned rhetoric, is caught between the close-up faces of staring children and laughing women. The men, mostly New York politicians repeat themselves absurdly as they adopt the official postures of power. The women and children are simply repeated, to emphasise their absence elsewhere.

I'm hardly the first artist to become interested in intervening in public space, nor have I been alone in moving away from the restricted confines of the art market in recent years. Indeed quite a few of my generation, artists who began with an investigation of the structure of meanings articulated within the privileged space of the art gallery, have been shifting attention to the actual spaces of the City. We have been steadily moving from a private experience shared by a few, and equally ignored by the many, to a larger, more inclusive, and definitely social interaction. We have all done billboards, bus and subway posters, and other forms of transitory public art. Since it is unlikely that any of us seek fresh air and sunshine in the name of art, it seems safe to say that what is going on is a widespread effort to recast art production as an activity of social meaning. As Declan MacGonagle, putting together the First Tyne International, has said, we are facing 'A New Necessity'.

The old necessity was precisely to return attention to a market structure that had been willed into invisibility. In the early days of the Neo-Expressionist boom, the idea of this work as subversive was pretty tenuous; by the time Jeff Koons was in full swing it had become risible. But over a decade ago, in that now unimaginable period before Reagan, Thatcher, or Kohl, the last-gasp *avant-gardist* work of Conceptual and Post-Minimal artists had succeeded in isolating art from all but its own discourses. A concentrated self-examination had exposed the ideological underpinnings of a certain subculture alright, but in the process left most people disinclined to care. To many of us then it seemed that our elders had brought art very close to being a meaningless activity in the least exalted way, and that it was imperative to try

to reconnect to the larger world. Two congruent strategies emerged in this attempt, both necessarily rooted in what we understood to be current dogma.

The first was a calculated return to the use of images – 'recognisable imagery became the favourite term of the professional packagers. This imagery was recognisable because it was taken – or 'appropriated' to use another then fashionable word – from sources in the mass media, with the intention of raising questions of meaning within the broad scope of cultural representation. Simply put the question posed was: if we know what these images are, if we in fact recognise them, do we then know what they mean? Since the answer is almost certainly negative, we are suddenly face to face with a kind of crisis concerning the apparatus we use to construct our daily lives. Asking this question in relation to both art and mass media proved to be quite liberating, opening up new territories for exploration, and re-opening some that had been apparently closed. Of the latter, of course, the most prominent was the issue of painting, that old bourgeois practice so thoroughly discredited in the 70s. Indeed the re-emergence of painting was, at the time, the most energising of options, containing the most possibility of creative contradiction. The hand-made work foregrounded the problem of subjectivity raised by all appropriationist work, and did so while reasserting the importance of sensuous pleasure. It thus saved appropriation art from being merely a bureaucratic continuation of fundamentalist Conceptualism by other means. It must also be said that some of the pleasure of the new painting derived from the knowledge that its very existence infuriated so many of our mentors and teachers of the previous generation.

The re-emergence of painting as a legitimate working method also facilitated the second strategy of the moment, the decision to place art once again within the arena of the market. In retrospect this always risky strategy has proved a disaster, leading down a path of increasingly diminishing possibilities for continuing to make interesting art. At the time, however, a deliberate return to the marketplace seemed an obvious way to begin wooing the attention of a wider public pretty much conditioned by a rampant consumerism to consider only things offered for sale. We thought we could do this and engage in some clever ironies at the same time. Even now it is hard to say there was any alternative, since it was precisely because appropriationist work was concerned with the whole idea of the spectacle of consumption, that it was bound to face that spectacle head on.

What I am saying, then, is that the desire to re-insert art within a meaningful social discourse in the US of the late 70s, inevitably meant that the new work had to concern itself with a context – the art market – that artists tend to view with ambivalence. Almost from the beginning this idea of a reactivation of the marketplace as a context in contention became a disputed one. It was very much an art concept, not a thoroughly articulated strategy, and so there was no real understanding of how quickly the flow of money would replace the flow of ideas. Marketing overwhelmed discourse as the art world moved into the hyperreal world of product promotion and star creation. Money talks, but it rarely allows anyone a word in edgewise, and soon the only topic

Thomas Lawson, *A Portrait of New York* (detail), 1989, billboard/mural, 2.4x518.2m, Manhattan Municipal Building, New York

discernible in the work on display in the galleries and in the magazines was money itself.

Sensing this incipient problem many artists, notably many women artists, rejected this model of activity, preferring a more directly political mode of operation. Jenny Holzer, for instance, sought out a different audience by carrying out a campaign of small-scale billposting throughout Lower Manhattan at around the same time that David Salle was insinuating his painted manifestoes into SoHo galleries. Of a size that spoke of an economy that was both necessary and right, her handbills listed, in alphabetical order, a cacophony of statements that, taken together, defied all logic. The confidence of these *Truisms*, statements of personal belief and public knowledge, is shattered in the confusion of their ridiculous contradictions. Coming across these anonymous warnings on a broken-down wall in the East Village, or, later, flashing on an electronic signboard at Caesar's Palace in Las Vegas, a shopping mall in Philadelphia, a sports stadium in San Francisco, one recognises a staginess, even a kind of hysteria. The voice of authority is made as urgently unbelievable as that of a crazy person. Holzer's dire stream of language, in its electronic proliferation throughout the public spaces of modern life, denies the possibility of a personal voice by seeming to insist upon it.

Taking a somewhat different tack Barbara Kruger attacked the problem of self-representation by developing a very distinct persona through the idiosyncratic voice of her writing. Advancing at high speed, this voice pushes hyperbole to the limit as it displays a position in relation to the fantastical world of television and the movies. It is a voice by turns sympathetic, amused, outraged. Descriptive aphorisms – the incessant shifting of attention from subject to object and back, the sense of detail as an index of the absurd, the referencing of present insults to a history of their return appearances in popular culture since the 40s – provide the structure upon which Kruger builds everything, from her column in *Artforum* to her large photo/texts. The latter, presented in galleries and as billboards on the street, work through the disjunctive placement of mostly sentimental images recalling a particular vision of domesticity with a typographic riot aimed at shattering the complacency of such images which are of women, but not for women.

One of the side effects of a triumphal Reaganism has quite clearly been the return of a kind of State art, an art that glorifies

Gran Fury, *Kissing Doesn't Kill*, 1989, panels on New York bus

the *status quo*. For some time conservative forces have been fashioning a theory of the end of history, a blueprint for cultural totalitarianism that also gives believers permission to ignore the cries for betterment from those shut off from Reaganite prosperity. This theory obviously dovetails nicely with the passive radicalism of Baudrillard, providing the purveyors of advanced art with a handy way to stay up to the minute and yet upset nobody. Scepticism of progress has been turned into a convenient denial of its necessity. Throughout the decade, opposition, in politics as much as in art, was rendered marginal, and from that enforced marginality began to gain strength. By the latter part of the 80s, a new sense of urgency had re-ignited the desire for an engaged art.

The return of an alternative to market-driven art is hardly news in itself, after all it provides convenient cover for those who fail to make a killing as much as an honourable position for crusaders of the avant-garde spirit. What is more remarkable during this period has been the growing desire to place these alternatives in public space with the intention of stimulating public discourse on the nature of the society we have and want. After much talk, and little to show for it, political artists in the United States have

been faced with a realisation. Simply making pictures of outrages and abuses, even using more so-called advanced techniques than painting, is not a particularly effective tool for political change. Indeed, given the co-optive power of mainstream culture, such pictures function in opposition to the artist's intentions by masking a social reality with the veneer of tender-hearted concern. Political art, relegated to a stylistic option, becomes nothing more than the ineffectual bleating of an élite whose job it is to show the human face of entrenched power. In the wake of this prolonged discovery, politically motivated artists have begun aggressively seeking more combatatively discursive methods of working.

In many ways the richest of these experiments have been carried out by Group Material, a small, and changing collective that organises large, bewilderingly inclusive exhibits in art spaces and public spaces. The point has been to open up discussion of contemporary cultural life in the US, on as many levels as possible. Many diverse contributions are solicited, from artists, well-known and not, politically correct and not; from non-artists, people in the work force; from school children. The material collected is then displayed in highly self-conscious

Barbara Kruger, *Untitled* (Your body is a battleground), 1989, photographic silkscreen/vinyl, 284.5x284.5cm

formats: heavily designed, one might even say didactically designed exhibits; newspaper inserts, poster campaigns on public transport. The framework of the show then gives what is shown its focus. Thus a project in which 100 people provided posters for one line of the New York subway system seemed to get around issues of violence, domestic and political. Another project at the Whitney Museum of American Art, a project that foregrounded American consumer objects against a wall of popular art and artworks from the Lower Manhattan art ghettos, addressed the oscillation between conformity and diversity that fuels cultural debate in this country. In their most ambitious work to date Group Material took over one of the galleries of the DIA Foundation for several months in 1988 in order to open a debate on the issue of representation in democracy. Four separate exhibits were organised, *Education and Democracy*, *Politics and Election* (to coincide with the Presidential and Congressional elections), *Cultural Participation*, and *AIDS and Democracy: A Case Study*. All four exhibits provided diverse information in a designed, but welcoming environment with plenty of seats, tables, printed and video-taped information. There was art in abundance, from figures as unalike as Leon Golub and Peter Halley. There was also plenty of non-art and bad art. During each segment of the project, various meetings and discussions were held, and by the end a publication planned. The series was successful in opening up possibilities; differences and inadequacies were displayed alongside unexpected moments of strength. The entire debate was problematised, with no practice or artist put forward as having a lock on truth, or even effectiveness. Group Material's contribution, then, was to provide a context in which the context of art could be aired and discussed, an open-ended context free of the imposed certainties of quality or the politically correct. They provide a blueprint for what we must hope for in art in the coming years as the unfolding crisis in the East inevitably creates a response in the West.

Not that a cultural crisis has not already gripped the West. We know too well the tightening grip of the forces of reaction, the increasingly homogeneous production approved for mass consumption, the hot breath of official and unofficial censors seeking scandal with anxious prurience. Western culture is a battle zone, a fact only too clear to those working on the frontline of AIDS awareness. To date, some of the most effective attempts to bring art production back into the mainstream of public policy discussion as a potent element in the creation of cultural self-representation have been the zap-attacks of ACT/UP and the poster campaigns of Gran Fury, both collectives that are as much, if not more concerned with AIDS activism as with art. But not all the activity I'm thinking about has been so pointed, or even so anonymously collective. Of equal importance are Kryzstof Wodizcko's exemplary interventions, nocturnal attacks on the very bastions of entrenched power, or the poetic disjunctions of the billboard works of Jessica Diamond or Felix Gonzalez-Torres. It is not the case that art must now become a species of agit-prop, or at least not that alone. It is the case, however, that artists who continue to hold themselves clear of contamination from the world at large are condemning themselves to an increasingly unforgivable irrelevance. There can be no strictures on how to connect, only that we had better. This is the new necessity.

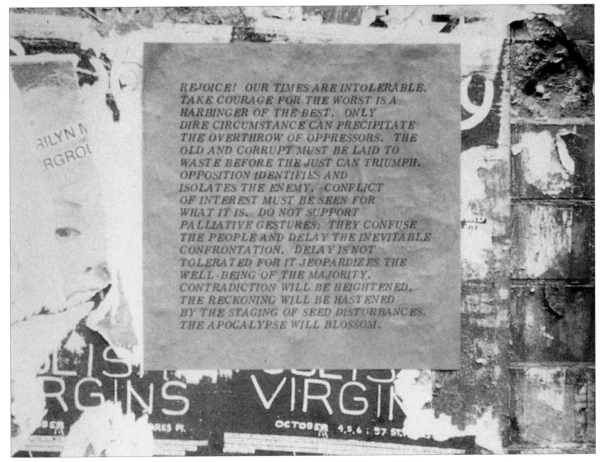

Jenny Holzer, *Inflammatory Essay*, 1978-79, Lower Manhattan

Jenny Holzer in the American Pavilion, Venice Biennale, 1990

JENNY HOLZER

SPACE, LANGUAGE & TIME
An Art & Design *Interview*

Installation view, Solomon Guggenheim Museum, New York, 1989-90

'I see space and it looks like nothing and I want it around me.' **Laments, 1989**

– *I would like to begin by focusing on the question of context, and its significance in determining the conception, transmission and reading of your texts. Having gained critical and public recognition for your street-poster aphorisms and electronic billboard messages which operate within a commercial 'non-art' context, to what extent did the transition from public street to the spatial confines of a gallery or museum affect your thinking?*
For the most part, all the writing can function in both situations, in public places as well as in museum spaces; although when I did start to do more museum exhibitions, and when I began to use stone, I let myself ramble a little more. I did things that were not only longer but also were a little more complicated, because I knew that I was more likely to have the viewer's attention for a greater period of time. But I would still say that ninety per cent of the work is designed to function well in both settings because, hopefully, the main interest of the writing is the subject matter, and these issues are interesting in or out of art museums.
– *To what extent do the spatial dimensions and limitations of a gallery or museum enhance the visual and psychological effectiveness of your messages, transmitted as dislocated, fragmented texts of red, green and yellow light, physically 'enclosing' the viewer within a confined and darkened space? Does the ability to 'confine' the viewer increase the power of your art to psychologically affect or alter the viewer's state of consciousness?*

One factor would be the element of time that we have just discussed. When people are coming to an art space they are a little more willing to give additional time to what I am presenting. The other thing that I enjoy when I'm working indoors is that I can change the entire environment. I can, for instance, make the room completely dark, which works well for the electronics, and for spotlighting individual texts on the stonework, and I can make a total experience that's not just comprised of the content of the writing and the act of reading. It's the visual experience, the physical experience, of being in a room that sometimes seems to turn upside-down, or pulse, or have reflections, or any of those things that I can do when I have complete control. It's for the mind and the body.
– *You have acknowledged a debt to the writings of Samuel Beckett, and certainly there seem to be analogies in the treatment of language, the use of anonymous, disembodied voices to communicate a sense of dislocation, alienation, loss of identity and extreme states of detachment and fear. Would you agree with this analogy?*
I think that my relationship to Beckett is mostly one of being a fan! For whatever reasons, I do attempt some of the things that he realises, probably just by virtue of being in the modern world that he anticipated so well. One thing I can say is that I like to use reduced language, spare to the point of almost being nonsense. Beyond that, he operates at a level of skill far above mine.

Laments, 1989, installation view, Dia Art Foundation, New York

Laments, 1989, installation view

Laments, 1989, installation view

– In the controlled conditions of light, darkness, space and time, with texts materialising from a black void, you seem to be creating a theatrical experience for the viewer. Do you see your installations in terms of theatre?

Not so much in terms of theatre, but I would say that I use some of the same things that people in theatre do, to evoke basic human responses, from dramatic lighting, to movement, to the content. It's intended, not to be like theatre, but to be effective. Somebody the other day was talking about how I've redone painting, in terms of the colour, light and line. And again, it's not so much that I want to do 'modern paintings', it's just that people respond to the colour, the lights, and so on. And it's not a homage to a certain discipline, be it theatre or painting; it's just that I want people to use their eyes and their minds, and a lot of the same aesthetic or formal rules apply. I'm not trying to do work that would refer to either painting or theatre. I would just like it to be primary experience.

– Are there any other writers or artists who have influenced your treatment of language and spatial context?

I was aware of people like Joseph Kosuth, who didn't make objects. I like that very much. And Daniel Buren, who does things in public for people to puzzle over; and Lawrence Weiner I also like very much. I always have trouble with that question because I admire so many different kinds of art, you know, Leonardo comes to mind. But it's fair to say that, once I learned about them, I liked Conceptualists. So when I started studying them I'd say, 'Yes, that's right!'

– Have you been influenced by Roland Barthes and his conception of language as a system of signs?

A little bit, but not so much by the signage, more just by his practice of looking at society at large, to learn more about culture. That kind of tendency I admire and would emulate, more so than anything about semiology.

– In your installation Under a Rock *at the Barbara Gladstone Gallery in New York, 1986, which you have referred to as 'My Temple of Doom', to what extent were you responding to the confined space and context of a commercial gallery?*

I was doing an installation for a specific space, but it was immaterial whether it was a commercial space, or whatever. It was for that *physical* space that the installation was made. So it was specific, not in terms of the content, but in terms of the form that the installation took; in other words, what went where and how many benches there were and where the electronic signs should be placed. The content was determined, as always with my things, by whatever's going on in the world, whatever I'm particularly afraid of, whatever I find contemptible, or whatever I think is wonderful. Sometimes, for a public situation, I'll choose or write texts that I think are suitable for that setting; but in general, in a public or in an art space, my content is only about what's happening in the world. I tend not to like self-referential work, like 'it's an art space, so I'm going to make art jokes', or 'fight the commercial system by being in it'. I find that beside the point. But about Gladstone, that was one of the first times that I did an installation that was born in an interior space to begin with, and didn't just involve transferring public things and trying to make them look OK.

– What thoughts determined the combination of the LED (light emitting diode) texts, transmitted as an unremitting stream of perpetual instants, with the same words inscribed in stone, repeating and consolidating the dislocated language fragments? Were you exploring the visual and linguistic effects of sign and language, and the significance of time and continuity on the reading of a text, which in this context is more complex and poetic, transmitting a greater sense of anxiety and violence, and a more personal, apocalyptic message?

I wanted to play with a number of things, one being the contrast between high-tech and ancient materials, the sign and the stone, and I wanted the experience of the two ways of reading to be very distinct. There's a great difference between trying to follow the signs – it's just light, it doesn't really exist – and tracing words with your finger in the stone. And I kind of liked showing the same text in two different ways, to make that text repetitive and insistent. Sometimes it was as simple as just getting sick of wondering whether the signs were going to work. I knew that the stone would just sit there and function. Also I suppose, too, that I liked the connotations of the stone, not its being an art material, but something cold, ancient, permanent. You know, if you get into an apocalyptic mood, you want to write on stone so that something you thought will remain. I like that, played off against the high-tech that is very pretty and almost represents the sort of trouble we are getting ourselves into. I like the electronics too because they almost seem to be like thoughts – they move so quickly, they seem to be the electronic impulses that make up your mind, they represent the way a thought moves around your head.

– The combination of new and timeless media was repeated in Laments, *at the Dia Art Foundation in New York. To what extent did the architecture of the vast warehouse space determine the conception and realisation of the work?*

This was a process similar to that at Gladstone. Again, from the beginning, I designed a show specifically for a space. I went to Dia a number of times and came up with the idea of having the stones and the signs. I figured out how to place the signs around the room so that the space would seem vast. But at the same time, by turning the lights off, the space would disappear. You couldn't see the walls, you would be aware that the room was large, but you couldn't quite tell where it ended and where it started. And then I wanted to have a contrast between the big open room and then the more closed and claustrophobic sarcophagus chamber.

– With the columns of moving, fragmented light and texts materialising from darkness, and the 13 'voices of the dead' inscribed into the granite and marble surfaces of stone sarcophagi, the experience was described by a number of critics in terms of silent theatre and visual music, a rhythm of alternating colour patterns and words in light, punctuated by periods of complete darkness. Did you see the environment in these terms?

In terms of the silent theatre, I would go back to what I said before, that I wanted to evoke basic human emotions through visual means, not as a reference to theatre, but to create some of the same effects that theatre does. The analogy to visual music I like. When you write the programmes for the signs, because you're dealing with time, it gets to be something like writing music; you need crescendos, you have to have quiet parts, you need to have variety, but you also want recurring themes. It is something like structuring a long composition. It's funny, I'd never really noticed this until I started putting the programmes together. It's partly like doing a piece of writing but, because there's movement and time, it is like music too.

– Was the combination of electronic and stone texts also a means of situating contemporary issues such as AIDS within the context of timeless fears of death and insanity?

Yes, to give them the weight they deserve.

– Would you say that the Guggenheim installation in New York signified the greatest challenge for you in terms of operating within an existing architectural space? One critic wrote that you were having to contend with 'the forces of the architect's ego', namely the theatricality and the spatial dimensions and limitations of Frank Lloyd Wright's design.

It was very hard, but I knew that, if I did it right, it could be great. I love the museum, but I have always thought that it should be

Selections from *Truisms*, 1977-1986, Caesar's Palace, Las Vegas

Selections from *The Survival Series*, 1983-85, Times Square, New York

Installation, 1987, Candlestick Park

handled as a space for installation rather than as a traditional museum. For example, when Beuys did his show, and put things all around the ramps, it was much more effective than a painting show. But when I had the chance to do it, I have to admit that I was stumped for a long time. It took a while before I figured out that it should be something very, very simple, and that to a certain extent, it would have to go with what was there. What Wright made was a gift, if you can deal with it properly, and then your work *also* has to be strong enough to stand on its own.

– So did you conceive your spiralling signboard of electronic words as existing in equilibrium, in the form of a dialogue, rather than in contention with Wright's conception?

Yes, that's what I had hoped for, that it wouldn't destroy his building, which is grand, but at the same time, I didn't want the museum to destroy my work. Both could do what they really wanted and hopefully would enhance each other.

– Would you say that you were also exploring the more abstract relationships of language, light, colour, space and time?

I wanted to have many variables functioning optimally. I wanted to have as many things working as possible, up to the point of it being ridiculously confused, purposeless and grotesque.

– Peter Schjeldahl described the experience as like being 'inside the head of somebody probably insane'; is this how you conceived it?

I wanted it to seem that way. I wanted the signs to go along and make sense from time to time, but then just spiral out of control. It seemed reasonable for modern life. And then I suppose the fact that the signs are round makes you imagine being inside someone's skull, and again, as I mentioned before, the electronics make you think of the statements as ideas, which sometimes are sane and sometimes aren't.

– In your recent Venice Biennale installation, how did you come to terms with the context, architecture and interior space of the neo-classical American Pavilion?

I wanted to do something that would look well in the building and would also nod to Venice; but at the same time I wanted something that would be appropriate for my work. So, for research, I went to a number of different churches and palaces. I wanted to find, not only materials, but also forms that were right for Venice, and I came up with the native red and white stone, the diamond-shaped tiles, the neo-classical benches, and the stone floors that act as reflecting surfaces. Those were the things that seemed proper for Venice and that didn't argue with the building.

– So you were very aware of communicating to an international, rather than a purely American sensibility?

Certainly, I used a variety of languages, which I thought was appropriate because Venice is an international city. And even though neo-classical architecture obviously doesn't belong to the United States, it is part of our tradition; it's both familiar and exotic to me. I hoped that the floors and the benches would make sense and would seem logical to Americans and to Europeans, as well as being site specific. Those were considerations when making the piece. Of course, I had to do things that were particularly interesting for me, and those were the electronic signs, the programmes, the lightening-fast changes, the content, the nonsense and endless other things.

– The transition from the visually silent and contemplative rooms, darkened and empty except for the inscribed Italian marble floors and neo-classical benches, to the spaces transformed by electronic media and fragmented light, is again a theatrical experience involving space, language and time. Did you conceive the initial rooms as 'mediators' in terms of the context and the language?

In terms of the installation as a whole, I knew that you needed to have a restful area to contrast with the sign rooms. It's a space for 'the before and after', firstly because you don't know the

electronics are coming and you need to sneak up to them, and then it's a place to recuperate when you have been in the wild sign room.

– One critic described them as 'waiting rooms', which corresponds to the atmosphere of suspense and anticipation that pervades them. And an analogy has been drawn, once again, to Beckett's Waiting for Godot.

I did plan them as waiting rooms. Again, I was thinking about how much of contemporary life, in the nuclear age, is waiting for the bomb to drop, waiting to die of AIDS, or waiting for some fool to go to war and kill everybody. So this seemed to be, not only representative of what life is like, but also an OK way to structure an exhibition.

– The floors and benches instantly call to mind Venetian church interiors, and there is a sense of time, solidity, continuity, silence and contemplative thought in these rooms; yet the texts seem to signify a loss of faith, a fragmentation and a dissolution of belief. I'm thinking of language such as 'Flee the Church', 'Dissect Myth', 'Forget Truths', 'Restrain the Senses'.

It depends. The text on the white benches, even though there are a number of black thoughts, is I think, on balance, optimistic. The *Inflammatory Essays*, which are the red benches, are indeed wild and hot, but even these, for example 'DON'T TALK DOWN TO ME', I see as the under-class saying to the overlords, 'get off my back or die'. It's kind of an optimistic thing. And the other one, 'SHRIEK WHEN THE PAIN HITS' – is an anti-torture text. Again it's resistance. On the floor tiles are the clichés which voice a number of different opinions, that hopefully don't cancel each other out. All seem equally true, if you give everybody's voice equal weight. They're as much an assertion of individual truths as a breakdown of all belief systems and despair.

– In the darkened room with 12 vertical electronic signs and a red stone tablet set into the floor, the inscribed and transmitted text, one of fear and aggression, is in the first person, the voice female. To what extent is the text autobiographical, and does this signify a change in your writing?

It's not autobiographical *per se* but I used a number of experiences and feelings that I've had since the birth of my child. But I'm not the narrator. I just found it to be more effective in the first person.

In the final room, the contrast between the solid reflecting floor and the LED texts, aggressive in terms of the language and the medium, enclosing the viewer and creating a sense of dislocation, spatial disorientation, and confusion, is physically overwhelming in its effect on the viewer. The reading of the texts veers from the disintegration of the body and the environment, to the misuse of power, greed, death and murder. The room has been described as an 'electronic cage of language', the viewer bombarded with words, information and moving lights, and repeatedly plunged into total darkness.

I wanted it to be extremely violent, again because I think it's representative of what's going on, not necessarily in your or my room at any given moment, but at the same time some place else, something like that is happening, be it an individual act of violence or a war. I want to be truthful in my work; I have always been scared to death and furious about violence, so it is often my subject, and I want it to be so, not just in terms of what is written, but in the actual experience of the installation.

– One critic described the blackness in terms of a negative, pyschological space, detached from the existing architectural context and signifying an expanded threshold of consciousness. Is this how you see it?

I hope it's a psychological space.

– What was the public and critical response to this installation?

The most interesting responses were to the 'mother' text. A lot of women and some men would come to me and say everything from how they had lost a child and what it was like, to how similar thoughts had occurred to them, to this was why they had never had a child because they didn't want to worry about or feel these things. That was genuinely uncomfortable and moving for me.

– *What was the public response to the street posters, the airport and station signboard messages, T-shirts, and television projects, works that extended beyond the confines of the official 'art space'?*

I wasn't there long enough to get a complete picture of the response, but apparently a lot of people noticed them and, in my walking around, I would see people looking and reading and scratching their heads. And I heard from some teenagers who saw the spots on television, that people found them intriguing.

– *Why did you decide that television would be an effective medium for your texts?*

It seemed like a logical place to go after the electronic signs; because there's an enormous number of people who are just staring at it, and it works well the same way as the electronic signs do in that it's an official medium, and when you put

something on that's counter to people's expectations, you get the element of shock and surprise that I like people to have when they encounter my pieces.

– *And do you think that these works, operating within familiar, 'non-art' spaces, are more successful in terms of communicating your messages to a mass audience than those works confined within the space of a gallery or a museum?*

I like doing both. What I feel currently is that I very much enjoy public space for some of the reasons we just discussed, namely the element of surprise that you get when my stuff is juxtaposed with everything, from commercial advertisements to official pronouncements. I like my stuff falling in the middle of all that. I also like doing art installations in which I control every aspect of the environment and can do many things for the eyes.

– *Finally, in being selected to represent the United States at the Venice Biennale, do you see your work as reflecting current artistic and critical thinking in the USA?*

Some of it! I think there has been interest recently both in installation works, pieces that are not just discreet art objects but that take on an entire environment, and in works that have specific 'real world' content. So in that sense, yes.

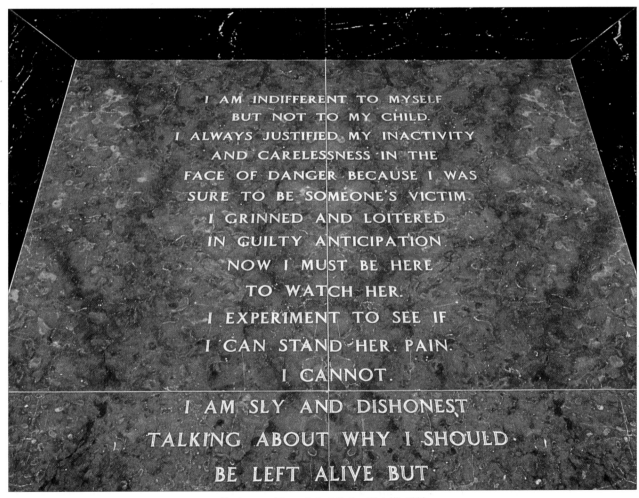

Venice text, Biennale installation (detail), 1990

———— * ————

Object Relations (2nd panel), 1989, mixed media, 185.5x124.5x4cm

VICTOR BURGIN
A NOTE ON MINNESOTA ABSTRACT

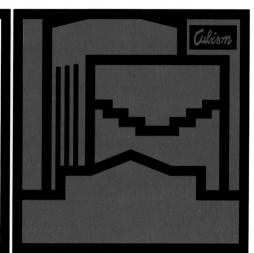

Minnesota Abstract, 1989, linotronic print, 7.7x23.3cm

In the summer of 1989, I was invited to make a work in the 'Twin Cities' of Minneapolis/St Paul. This was not the first time I had received such an invitation: I have also made site-specific works in response to commissions in Berlin, Lyon, Grenoble . . . and more recently, Boston and Adelaide. I have always tried to make a visual representation of what I might call an 'apprehension' of the place

to which I've been invited. There is no word for it today, but if I were in the 18th century I might have spoken of my attempt to give image to the 'genius of the place'. Over the years, psychoanalytic theory has become the critical tool I use most often in trying to understand the mechanisms at work in visual representations – from classical painting to modern advertising. Freud's original discovery – the foundation stone of psychoanalysis – was that thoughts we find painful, or otherwise cause us anxiety, may be repressed and thereby made unconscious. The unconscious thought however is likely to return to us in a disguised form. For example, the repressed idea, or memory, might return as a seemingly inexplicable physical symptom, or as an apparently nonsensical dream, or in the form of a slip of the tongue or some other error, or as a joke. I'm becoming increasingly interested in the idea that we encounter the 'return of the repressed' not only at the level of the individual, in the speech and dreams of that individual, but also at the level of the nation, in its various cultural products. The histories of many nations contain painful and discreditable facts. Great Britain, at the end of the 19th-century, at the height of its power and prestige, probably preferred not to remember the extent to which its great wealth had been derived from the slave trade. A painful fact of American history is that the United States is founded on an act of expropriation, in which the indigenous peoples of the North-

American continent were systematically deprived of their lands. This fact had been brought to my mind earlier in the summer when I spent some time in Vancouver, and visited a part of the city which had been returned to native Americans as the result of a land-rights case. It was perhaps inevitable that it should be on my mind when I visited Minneapolis. Here, I was presented with an environment in which the repressed images and names of native Americans constantly return: on labels of products on supermarket shelves, in corporate logos, on automobiles . . . and so on.

Shortly after I arrived in Minneapolis, the Sunday July 23 edition of the local *Star Tribune* newspaper carried a story headed, 'Historian finds names of Minnesota's forgotten Indians'. Although it was a local story, concerning the Twin Cities, the story came from an outside agency, the Associated Press. It was based on information supplied by Virginia Rogers, working for the Minnesota Historical Society in St Paul. The part of the story which caught my attention read:

> The US government created the 837,120 acre White Earth Reservation in 1867, intending that all Chippewa Indians be relocated there. As enticement, the government offered 40 acres of land for every ten acres cultivated . . . for nearly 20 years the Chippewa who relocated to White Earth fulfilled government expectations, farming quite success-

fully. In 1885, however, white settlers on adjoining Red River Valley lands adopted a resolution demanding that the reservation be opened to white settlers ... For the next two years, Episcopalian Bishop Henry Whipple lobbied Congress and the administration on behalf of White Earth Indians. All of Whipple's efforts were in vain: by 1982, just 1,952 acres remained in trust.

The name 'White Earth' reminded me of the name 'Little Earth' – a Federal-sponsored 'HUD' housing development in the Twin Cities occupied mainly by native Americans. Since the project was built, the care invested in it by the people who live there, together with a changed market situation, has turned what was originally assumed to be a strictly non-commercial housing project into an attractive, potentially profitable, 'investment opportunity'. Today, official mismanagement of Little Earth has brought it to the point where the project is in danger of being taken from the people who now live there, and sold to private interest – and this in spite of the scandal over alleged massive frauds perpetrated by HUD officers during the Reagan administration. The *Star Tribune* story about White Earth concludes: 'White Earth prospered until people outside the reservation realised that the Indians had rich resources in trees and farm land ... Then they legislated the reservation nearly out of existence.' It seemed that history was threatening to repeat itself: what had happened then to White Earth could happen now to Little Earth.

The famous 'first rule' of psychoanalysis is to say what first comes to mind. I try to apply that rule when I work. Structurally, the work represents a *condensation*. Freud observed, 'The dream is laconic by comparison with the interpretation'. A dream image, or a fragment of the analysand's speech, may serve as a cross-roads where several paths of thought intersect. The ideas are packed into the relatively small space of the image. In Freud's terms, such images are formed by a process of 'condensation'. This is the way I plan my images – as condensations. In this work, the image in the central panel is built of elements derived from logo-types which make 'Indian' references: *Mutual of Omaha; Detroit Bank and Trust; Continental Airlines*. The following buildings are cited, in St Paul: *Minnesota World Trade Centre Cathedral of St Paul; Minnesota State Capitol*. In Minneapolis: *IDS Center Tower; Piper Jaffray Tower; Normandy Inn Best Western*. For me, new to the Twin Cities, these are the buildings which seemed to give a distinct signature to the skylines. I based the shapes I used on sketches and Polaroid photographs taken in the street. These shapes went through several stages and evolved into forms which made me think of the work of Stuart Davis. I was living near the Walker Art Centre. On one of my visits to the museum I checked to see if they had a Stuart Davis painting in the collection. Sure enough, they did. The title – *Colonial Cubism* – seemed too much of a gift to ignore: Western-European colonialism had always advanced through the building of forts, followed by cities; literally cementing itself into place. Davis' painting is unusual in that it does not contain the elements of writing he usually incorporates into his work. I therefore took it on myself to draw the words in the title of Davis' painting, 'forging' them in his own characteristic style. The colours? 'Legally' expressed market relations were the alibi which turned 'expropriation' of native American lands into the more respectable 'purchase'. So, for example, in 1803, through the 'Lousiana Purchase', the United States bought almost 900,000 square miles of new land from France. A few square miles of this parcel, lying west of the Mississippi River near its confluence with the 'St Peters' (later, 'Minnesota') River, later became part of the Twin Cities. For this reason the colours of my panels quote the red, white and blue of 'Old Glory' in a format which more directly evokes the 'Bleu, blanc, rouge' of the French *tricolor* – much in evidence in the Bicentennial Year of the Declaration of the Rights of Man.

I use computers to make my work. Does this make me a 'computer artist'? No more than it makes someone who uses a pencil a 'pencil artist'; no more than a painter is a 'paint-brush artist'. To make this work I used an Apple *Scanner* digitiser to feed my drawings, photographs and other image-fragments into my computer. You can think of the scanner as the input end of a zerox machine; on the output end, instead of hard copy, you get an 'image-file' consisting of binary digits. Next in the production-line from the scanner was an Apple *Macintosh 11* computer, with a colour monitor. This machine allows me to edit and manipulate the scanned image in a variety of ways, and also to draw images directly to the screen – depending on the particular software, or 'programme', I use. I also scanned my own pencil drawings into the computer in order to be able to further modify them while retaining the original. Today – in so-called 'desk-top publishing' – the Macintosh computer has virtually taken over from traditional methods of page lay-out for publications, from simple brochures all the way through to substantial books. The 'Mac' is also increasingly coming to replace traditional dark-room techniques for the manipulation of photographs. The photograph is now scanned into the computer, where such operations as contrast and colour control, burning and dodging, cropping, and so on, are performed on screen. There's no need to stand in the dark, up to your armpits in toxic chemicals. For proofing my drawings I used an Apple *Laserwriter II NT*. You can think of the Laserwriter as the output end of a photocopying machine, with a computer bolted onto it to receive and translate the information coming from the *Mac 11*. There are basically three sorts of printer available: *Dot-matrix printers*, such as the Apple *ImageWriter 11*, produce 'screen resolution' images – 72 lines of dots per inch ('dpi') – acceptable for text but not satisfactory for graphics; *Laser printers*, like the Apple *Laser-Writer 11 NT*, produce 300 dpi – adequate for low-budget 'cheap and cheerful' printing jobs, and for proofing graphics; *High resolution printers*, for example the *Linotronic*, can produce up to 2450 dpi (6,002,500 – dots per square inch). Linotronic machines are extremely expensive, but Linotronic output is available at moderate cost from service bureaus. The final colour separations that I sent to my silk-screen printer in New York, together with colour sketches and other instructions, were Linotronic prints.

I called the finished work *Minnesota Abstract* as it draws on elements abstracted from Minnesota history, and includes a reference to the Stuart Davis 'abstract' in the Walker Art Center. As I began by saying, the work was an attempt to sum up, 'condense' in an image, some of the perceptions, thoughts and feelings which came to me in the Twin Cities. Work didn't stop there. The historical parallel to be drawn between 'White Earth' and 'Little Earth' seemed worth pointing out in public. I took the central graphic element in *Minnesota Abstract* and combined it with a text – set in parallel columns – based on the *Star Tribune* story and what I had learned about the HUD housing project. Through the agency of a friend in Minneapolis I asked a native-American organisation to check my text, and changed it in line with their suggestions; they gave their approval to the finished design. This piece was made for the street rather than for the gallery – designed in black and white, and in 'US Letter' format, so it could be cheaply reproduced on a photocopy machine. I asked the organisation which had invited me to Minneapolis to help me print and distribute the 'street work', as they had expressed an interest in 'public art'. They declined, worried about embroiling themselves in a controversy that might affect their funding (this was the summer of the Jesse Helms/Mapplethorpe furore). The Minneapolis critical monthly journal

Artpaper had, independently, already offered me their back-cover as a site for the 'street' piece, and I had designed another version to fit their 'tabloid' format – it appeared in the October issue; *Artpaper* ran off extra copies of the page for posting in the streets. All of this illustrates what is, for me, one of the great advantages in using a computer – a lengthy process had gone into the making of *Minnesota Abstract,* but once the elements had been stored in computer memory I was able to quickly restructure them in response to changing circumstances.

I've explained something of how I came to make this work. Is my explanation of the decision-making process the 'meaning' of the picture? No – I've had this confirmed many times in the past when other people have found meanings in my work I was not myself conscious of. Moreover, I've said nothing about the 'affect' of line, form and colour. (I tend to agree with Wittgenstein – 'whereof we cannot speak, thereof remain silent'.) Unlike my essays and talks, and my occasional works for the street, my works for the gallery are not constructed in the form of an explanation. I distinguish 'gallery work' from 'public work' primarily by the form of address it involves – a relatively 'open' structure which allows more freedom of association to the viewer (although what one is asked to associate *about* is strongly indicated). The word 'public' conceals a complexity of heterogeneous audiences, with various reading protocols and competences, situated within different institutional contexts, which in turn imply their own particular frameworks of 'legitimate expectations', and so on. In navigating such complexity I am guided by the old adage: 'form follows function'.

Office at Night, 1986, mixed media, 183x244cm

———— * ————

Untitled Film Still #35, 1979, black and white photograph

CINDY SHERMAN
BEHIND THE IMAGE
An Art & Design *Interview*

Untitled Film Still #47, 1979, black and white photograph

Presented here with a selection from many different periods of her work, Cindy Sherman discusses the thought processes behind her solitary images of women, from the early passive images which appear to manipulate the viewer into the position of voyeur, to the later more active roles she plays in imitating poses from old master paintings with often ludicrous, horrifying or humorous results.

– Do you have scenarios in mind when working on a picture? Are there narratives you construct around the character, which may help you, as the actress, get into a role?
Generally speaking, yes, I do have scenarios in mind when I'm setting up an image, although a full or even partial narrative is not usually worked out around it. You could say I've worked out a basic plot for the image to function on, at least for me, while I look into a full-length mirror placed next to the camera to help me really 'get into character'. I might imagine that I'm making eye-contact with someone outside the camera's gaze, for example, but I'm not thinking of who or why.
– Do you ever photograph more than the one particular pose that is shown in the still, for example, the woman about to lie down rather than lying down, or about to open the envelope rather than reading the letter, as she does in the photos?
Very often, especially in the black and white works, I shot a variety of poses for one scene, and even used several versions from the same 'character' in exhibitions etc. (This is particularly true in the outdoor, 'location' shoots, where I was moving around more and guiding whoever was actually clicking the shutter. These were the only occasions when someone else was even present while I worked, much less taking the picture.)
– Your film-still characters often seem 'still' – in a contemplative mood or waiting for something to happen. How do you feel about

the idea of the woman as a bearer of meaning rather than someone involved in action – causing movement, progression, disruption?
Perhaps it was characteristically the male counterpart in the older black and white films, that I was emulating from the female standpoint, to be the cause of whatever action was to affect the female. I never thought of the woman in question as a 'bearer of meaning', but then I never analysed the characters I was portraying. My intentions were to suggest very little so that viewers could make up their own, hopefully *very* diverse, narratives. This might account for the contemplative, even expression-less mood; the ambiguity suggesting something about to happen.
– How did your interest in photography develop? Was it something that grew after studying film or fine art?
I studied painting/fine art but became disillusioned with it once I learned about truly contemporary art such as Conceptualism and Minimalism. Performance art, as well as film, had probably the most influence on me, although I never thought to make performances. Right from the start I only used a camera as a means to an end, because photography, *per se*, never had a direct influence on me, except peripherally through the media.
– Are you interested in film theory? Do you find that your ideas for your Untitled Film Stills *come from a love of film or an interest in film critique, or are these inseparable in your photographic project?*

Untitled #122, 1983, colour photograph

Above: *Untitled Film Still #4*, 1979, black and white photograph; *Below*: *Untitled Film Still #32*, 1979, black and white photograph

Untitled #98, 1982, colour photograph

Untitled Film Still #37, 1979, black and white photograph

Untitled #224, 1990, colour photograph

I am not interested in film (or any other) theory. My film stills come out of a frustration with having had certain role models with which I had, I suppose, a love/hate relationship. The 'film still' was merely a device I could relate to because of my interest in films and because I could suggest a narrative without really having to commit myself to one.

– *Given that you dress up for various roles in your photographs, is this something that you have ever done or been tempted to do in the flesh, as a live performance?*

I still have no interest in performing live.

– *Photography has the ability of questioning the original versus copy as exemplified in your work where the viewer knows you are photographing yourself as someone else. Here the original, or origin of the work, is difficult to pinpoint. Do you see art in this way too, with the impossibility of the artist being original, and distanced from the world he is dealing with, as well?*

Yes, I think it's impossible for true originality to exist in art/life and art that tries to distance itself from the world (such as pretty, decorative art) becomes in the end petty and banal.

– *Doesn't showing the viewer scenes she/he has probably already seen in films, adverts and on television reinforce the way women have been used to being seen? If so, how far can repeating familiar stereotypes criticise the perception of woman as seen object?*

I've been criticised by feminists in the past for reinforcing negative stereotypes of women just as you describe. It's been suggested to me that I put statements on the wall next to the photos, or captions underneath, to hammer the message into those who can't see the irony. I felt that by exposing these stereotypical characters of mine to much more ambiguity in their surroundings and expressions, I could subtly subvert the 'intention' of the 'male gaze' (as the camera's view-point has been called in this case). In other words, and perhaps this is only possible in seeing the works as a whole, if the viewer is looking for a titillating peek into this woman's privacy, I hoped to put the viewer on the spot and make them feel uncomfortable, perhaps in recognition of their expectations. On the other hand, I've recognised that not all viewers are that in tune with their feelings or reactions and that since the work is ambiguous and open-ended, it allows for a broad spectrum of interpretation, some of which I will detest or reject.

– *The human figure is always central to the work. How much does the background, whether it be country road, skyscrapers or hotel lobby, have on the person within this landscape?*

With the black and white work, the background only became integral to the picture when I shot outdoors and then, depending on the location, sometimes as much the subject as the 'model'.

– *Do you consider your work as forming some part of an autobiography in as much as the photographs are your pictorial critical record on how a female is viewed and that you, the subject, also become the seen object for the observer to view?*

The work is in no way autobiographical. I do not see 'myself' as being 'seen' in any of these works. The characters are always the 'other' and that other is always different. I am trying to explore characters and situations that are unrecognisable and unfamiliar to me personally, although perhaps very familiar to someone else, or familiar to me through, again, the media.

– *Was photographing yourself as other characters, and albeit in very different types of work, a project which you had decided to undertake in the early stages of your work?*

Although I began using myself in the work from the start, in 1975, I never projected a long-range plan of how my work would progress. I think I'd have been surprised to know then that I'd still be doing it today. However, I don't intend to be doing it 15 years from now either.

– *Were you aware of or influenced by feminist criticism that was being formulated while you were studying photography? Has your attitude towards various theories changed over the years and are there any that you use as tools in your work?*

I was never influenced by any specific or general criticism and continue to be ignorant of the theories, although I'm amused when my work is applied to them or vice-versa; neither do I write any criticism myself.

– *Can you see yourself moving away from the purely pictorial to include statements and language or is there no room for language in the work as the body, being so central to it, encompasses any statement within it, so that language does not need to be uttered.*

Actually, I'm not using the body exclusively now, and in fact I've done several series without central figures and certainly without myself. But, I'd never incorporate language into my work as I'm much too awkward with it.

– *The work of Kruger, Holtzer and Kelly in particular springs to mind; not in comparison or contrast to you, but because, to refer to my previous question, they incorporate words into their work. Do you feel, however, that your work relates to their's at all, or indeed, other women artists working today?*

My work relates to the artists you mention but in different ways for each one. I think that there are so many different women artists working today that we hear about (finally) that, I'd have to say, some I can relate to and some I can't – just like male artists.

– *Are there particular photographers and artists who have influenced you?*

Goya, Borges, Bierce, Sanders and performance art, in general, as well as Douglas Sirk.

– *By appropriating old master paintings into your work, you seem to be photographing, focusing on, a tradition of painting and poses that have a very still quality about them in their gravity and solemnity. Do you think they have a similar narrative vein as the* Untitled Film Stills *in that they have a scenario around them – caught in a pose in the middle of a story. How do you see these as continuing on from the earlier work?*

Yes, I think there is a similarity in the *Untitled Film Stills* and the historical portraits. Perhaps that's why I only did about 35 of them and realised I needed to go on to some new direction which I'm trying to do. For this reason, I see no point (for my sanity's sake) in my comparing the two.

————— * —————

ALTERNATIVE SPACES
IN NEW YORK

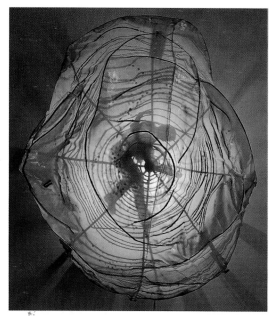

Jonathan Kessler, *Parasite,* 1984, mixed media construction with lights and motors, 111.8x119.3x58.4cm;

Artist's Space

Artist's Space, conceived in 1973 as an alternative to the commercial gallery system, was created to expose the work of unaffiliated artists enabling a more radical, New York-based art scene to develop. Concerned with 'the activity of art itself' and apolitical, Artist's Space has played a significant role in art of the 80s, exhibiting the early work of, among others, Koons, Salle, Holzer and Kruger.

Artistically, the era between 1973 and 1983 was characterised by the idea that there were many kinds of art being made, experimentation in many forms, but no single predominant style. There was a feeling of dissatisfaction combined with anticipation as to what ideas would become the most appropriate and expressive and which would characterise contemporary art. Artist's Space had a definite hand in creating the situation and crystalising ideas that were to become the identity of art of the 80s.

At the inception of Artist's Space, the existence and purpose of alternative spaces were only beginning to be recognised. Seemingly, they had come about in response to the relative inactivity of new art; alternative spaces were founded mainly by artists for places to exhibit their own works and those of other artists they admired. In New York, some SoHo area galleries featured the work of younger artists, but most were showing the work of nationally or internationally-known artists. This situation provided a dramatic backdrop for the artists exhibiting at Artist's Space, throwing their efforts into high relief, so that a more radical, New York-based scene could develop. Artist's Space itself has never functioned as a meeting place for artists on a day-to-day basis, but it has functioned as a place where multi-disciplinary activity could take place. It has never evinced a political position or any philosophical cant, but rather is surprisingly democratic and is only devoted to the activity of art itself.

The significance of Artist's Space has extended beyond any of the separate disciplines it encouraged. It has supported painting, sculpture, music, dance, film and performance art. It has provided an atmosphere which encouraged artists to take chances and to realise ideas – to create what seems almost impossible.

Artist's Space is not easily categorised. It is not a funky-anything-goes space. It does not take an anti-materialist stand. It is not aggressive. It is not angry. It is simply alternative. Interestingly enough, the work exhibited in it does not come out of nowhere, it has precedents, like all interesting art does and those precedents are somewhat easier to trace at Artist's Space than perhaps at other alternative spaces because of the original artists-nominating-artists policy. Often the older artists would nominate their students or someone who had come to their attention through apprenticeship. Looking at this relationship gives us some idea of the stimulus and historical perspective affecting these young artists. The artists who began to show at Artist's Space in the mid-70s were not artists who belonged to the traditions of the 60s. They were not Pop artists, they were not Minimalist, they were not necessarily Conceptual artists. They were artists who wanted to make art in the spaces between these definitions and they wanted urgently to have a place to exhibit it. These artists who exhibited here were mostly products of training in other American cities during the late 60s and early

70s. They grew up with the attitudes that they had learned in school toward using traditional media and realism or Abstract Expressionism or hard-edged painting of some sort. They also were looking at the recent work of the process-oriented, anti-aesthetic, post-minimal artists who were using new materials. It was the latter of this group which seems to have mostly inspired artists showing at Artist's Space to work directly using installations and then subsequently with images taken from the media.

Linda Cathcart

The Alternative Museum

The Alternative Museum is the first museum of contemporary art founded and operated by artists in the history of the United States and the only one dedicated to art with a socio-political content. I wanted to demonstrate that museums could be established by artists themselves, not just by very affluent individuals such as Guggenheim, Getty etc, and that the average person can become responsible for his or her own socio-political environment. I believe the general public thinks of museums primarily as warehouses and showcases for works of art. We are taught to believe that this is the sole responsibility of a museum, and that museums exist as a form of élite entertainment for the educated, for those who have studied art and art-history courses. But people forget that museums also have a tremendous social responsibility. Such responsibilities tend to be put aside, because many of the relevant socio-political issues are disturbing to staff members who have to stimulate public dollar support from people who might disapprove of issue-oriented presentations.

Education is the primary role of the museum; staff must therefore become more responsible in selecting exhibitions and not merely succumb to predominating tastes. For example, museums which interact with the art world tend to pander to the tastes of collectors, dealers, critics and artists who are thought to be in vogue; if a painter becomes popular, everyone wants to show him. I don't find many museums giving the public what they don't expect to see, or what they don't already know from visiting commercial galleries. Such a museum would never show an exhibition which contains provocative content which sectors of the public would rather not know about. This attitude is not an example of social responsibility on the part of a museum.

New museums should have opinions, for by presenting exhibitions with an opinion, dialogue is created. Moreover, museums have another responsibility – it's called leadership. But to lead one must really believe in something.

Most museum exhibitions are oriented solely toward the dominant American culture with the implication that other Americans of non-European descent must adapt their interest to the main cultural group. Social responsibility in this case means equality in consideration and presentation. It also means going out of your way to understand the needs of all the American people.

When I say 'social' I have to include 'political'; and indeed the economic as well. There are many exhibitions that could confront socio-political issues – religion, sexuality, morality, poverty, economics, politics – but other museums refuse to handle such content.

Although we are dedicated to contemporary artists, I think of the relationship as a partnership. On the other hand, if there were no museums, there would probably be a lot fewer artists. Artists do not work in a vacuum; they must have walls on which to hang work. And since commercial galleries are more about commerce, the artist does need a place in which to explore new ideas.

The Alternative Museum devotes itself in particular to mid-career artists. With the young artists commanding more and more attention, the older artists were stopped in their tracks by economic factors and lack of recognition; they were left out. The Alternative Museum took on the responsibility of bringing these artists back into into spotlight, devoting a catalogue to discussing their career – past, present and future. Likewise, there are a number of artists making work with strong political content who were unable to find a serious space in which to exhibit. We decided that someone had to provide a forum for this work and we became recognised for assembling exhibitions which have a strong socio-political content. Everyone else wants to show the Meyer Vaismans and the Cindy Shermans, but we don't . . .

Geno Rodriguez (from an interview with Roger Denson)

Exit Art

EXIT ART, founded in 1982 by Jeanette Ingberman and Papo Colo and situated on Broadway, New York, is an art organisation concerned with exploring multi-cultural, multi-disciplinary issues in contemporary art through critical presentations and publications. Concerned with 'The right of culture to change itself' and 'The right of history to have opinions', the purpose of EXIT ART is outlined as follows:
– To provide a context for understanding the art of the Americas as we approach a new definition of our continent through an appreciation of the transcultural changes and challenges occuring in our society.
– To provide a different historical perspective on the culture by establishing a substantial dialogue among diverse backgrounds and aesthetic values in contemporary art.

– To organise comprehensive one-person shows of mid-career artists who have not received critical attention or exposure and through catalogues with critical essays to place their work in an historical context.
– To educate the community in the diversity of art realities: the parallel histories which exist in our contemporary culture.
– To document artists whose works are difficult to categorise or exhibit either because of their content or manner of working, and to make this information available to a larger public through exhibitions and publications.
– To work with individual artists to sponsor and produce special projects including: installations, record albums, print portfolios, performances, films, special edition books, etc.

———— * ————

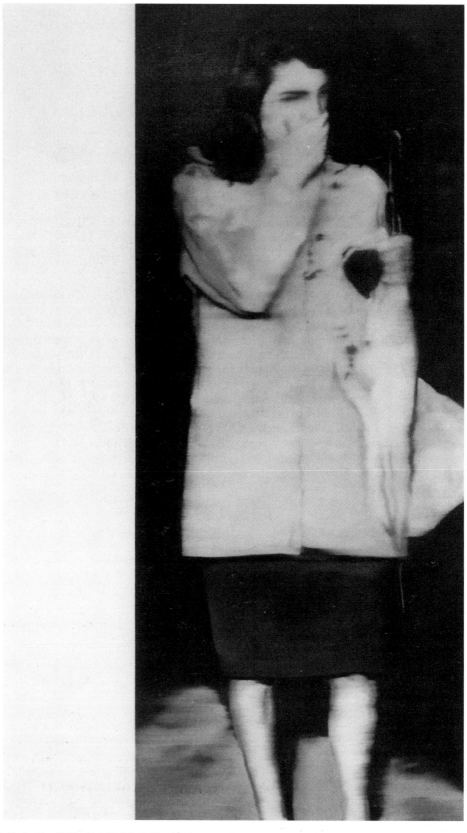

Woman with Umbrella, 1964, oil, 160x95cm. 'I painted all the time, sometimes with a very bad conscience. I painted to find out what painting can still be and can still be allowed to be. It was an act of defiance, to paint although it seemingly led to nothing . . . I protected myself from being tied down, I won the freedom to do what I want – to try out anything I like, and not to be labelled for the art market. Although you can be very successful with a label, because you are easily recognisable. But you can manage without it. Now this slight confusion has become a sign by which I am recognised . . . In using banal snapshots for pictures I wanted to establish the quality of the photos, that is, what they have to say. I wanted to show the things that are always overlooked in a little snapshot. Snapshots are not thought of as art, but if they are transported into art, they take on a dignity and they are regarded. That was the point, or it was the concern, if you like, in using photos.'

BENJAMIN H D BUCHLOH

RICHTER'S FACTURE

Between The Synecdoche and the Spectacle

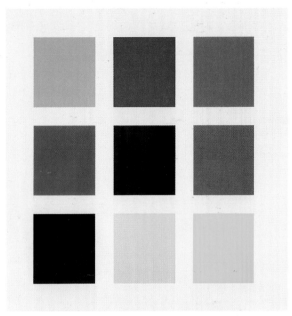

Colour Chart, 1966, enamel paint, 70x65cm

Mechanical and organic aspects of the painterly procedure – these are two oppositional terms between which Modernist painting has shifted since Manet with ever increasing radicality and exclusivity. Whenever the seemingly mechanical aspect of the application of pigment on canvas – the brushwork as labour, the brushstroke as fragmented unit of a repetitious activity – was emphasised

and foregrounded, the approach was cyclically hailed or condemned (dependent on the ideological investment of the critics and audiences) as the end of painting. Whenever the apparently organic aspects of painterly procedures and materials were re-instituted – brushwork as gesture of symbolic liberation of unconscious forces, the brushstroke as the immediate tool and record of expressivity – this was again cyclically and with equal fervour of conviction condemned by the opponents as a betrayal and falsification of the means and the tasks of *Modernist* painting (see for example Cézanne's critique of Van Gogh as a 'madman') or it was celebrated – as is currently again the case – as a recovery of the ties between the aesthetic, the emotional and the sensuous experience against the positivist rationality of the Modernist approach to the practice of painting.

While the extremes of this dichotomy might have been less pronounced in the actual work of the painters than in the claims of the critics associated with a particular reading of painterly procedures (compare Rosenberg's interpretations of Pollock with those of Greenberg and his followers) it seems nevertheless appropriate to address the cyclical nature of this opposition: the various claims that have been associated with it in order to clarify some of the underlying conditions in Richter's recent series of large-scale gestural 'Abstract Paintings'.

Already in 1886 the critic Félix Fénéon had observed the mechanical nature of painting in Seurat's work and he had explicitly distanced it from the traditional values in painterly performance such as *patte* and the bravura of *facture*.

Monsieur George Seurat is the first to present this new painting in a complete paradigm. Wherever one examines his gigantic painting *La Grande Jatte*, it spreads out in a monotonous and patiently speckled surface, like a weaving: actually here "the hand" is superfluous and tricks are impossible . . . Let the hand be numb but the eye be agile, aware and knowing; be it on an ostrich, a bottle, a wave or a rock, the manoeuvre of the brush remains the same.[1]

Fénéon's statement – or rather – Seurat's art indicates that the procedure of painting had come under increasing pressure of examination and competition: that of the laws of optical science and colour theory as much as the pressure of the new tools and technologies of representation-production, lithography and photography. But pressure also in a more metaphorical understanding. This becomes apparent when he compares the painting to a tapestry weaving; the competition of the manual craft process of designing, producing and finishing a representation with the increasing presence and domination of mechanical production processes in everyday-life. 40 years later, André Breton voices once again the same critique of the pictorial production process when he argues that '. . . painting tends to glorify the hand and

St James, 1988, oil, 189x244.8cm. 'Until the 70s there were intellectuals who dared to say what is good and right and what should be different. In a way we are being abandoned by society. You can see from the academies, from any exhibition, any review in the art magazines how art is received. It is accepted uncritically, and the attitude is "get on with it, anything you do is interesting". That was not always the case; probably it has to be like that for a time, to prevent art from being inhibited. I am sure criteria will develop when we know what we need, what is right for us.'

nothing else. The hand is the great culprit, how can we accept to be the slave of our hands? It is unacceptable that the hand, that painting, are still on a level today where writing was before the invention of Guttenberg.' [2]

In the face of photography and mechanisation the facture of painting was increasingly confronted with a question of its proper competence and authenticity, a reflection process that found its penultimate theorisation in Greenberg's theory of Modernism. Richter's so-called 'Abstract Paintings' – a series that originated around 1976 and has since undergone a number of subtle transformations – has elicited on numerous occasions, in particular with American viewers, the question concerning their historical place and their aesthetic attitude. Responses range from arguing that his attitude is that of the quintessentially Post-Modern painter (since 1962) to the argument that his paintings look more than ever like second-rate and third-generation Abstract-Expressionist painting (Hans Hoffmann is mentioned or Hyman Bloom). While the first reading would suggest that paraphrase and citation, parody and repetition are the tropes and the modes of Richter's painterly rhetoric, the second, obvious but telling misperception wants to suggest that his is the dilemma

of a latecomer and virtuoso simultaneously: to have mastered a craft and a skill at a moment in history when the practices of meaning production have already moved on to other necessities, requiring different techniques, and where the meaning produced by the belatedly acquired virtuoso performance generates an empty speech.

But Richter's language is neither one; he is not the omniscient author-painter who commands the past practices of painting with ease and subjects them at will to the needs of the present (the cynicism of certain so called Post-Modern architects for example), nor that of the obsolete, but convinced practitioner of a craft whose moment of rediscovery has not yet come (like the rediscovery of obsolete Neo-Expressionist and figurative modes of painting emerged in the late 70s against all normative aesthetic logic). The obvious answer to resolve this dilemma would be to argue that a supreme irony is at work in Richter's painterly production, yet any attempt at looking at the 'Abstract Paintings' must reveal to the careful observer that irony is not Richter's mode of thinking and painting any more than it is the mode of Ryman's work for example. The series of 'Abstract Paintings' emerged, according to Richter's own testimony as a

St Andrew, 1988, oil, 189x244.8cm. 'What strengthens me is the certainty that painting is not a strange hobby; it is a fundamental human activity, and so it has qualities that can be distinguished and identified. If a number of people look at pictures, and most of them have the same opinion of which is best and which is worst, that for me is confirmation that we all have the ability to recognise quality and understand painting. And that also confirms me in the certainty that despite all the errors, painting can in principle make manifest our best, most human and most humane qualities.'

response to the series of large-format monochrome grey paintings that were produced by semi-mechanical painting procedures (rollers, sponges) in 1975. Richter has commented upon the series of the grey paintings as '. . . the most complete ones which I could imagine'. And further he said that the grey monochrome paintings were for him:

> . . . the welcome and only correspondence to indifference, to a lack of conviction, the negation of commitment, anomie. After the grey paintings, after the dogma of "Fundamental Painting" whose purist and moralising aspects fascinated me to a degree bordering on self-denial, all I could do was to start all over again. This was the beginning of the first "colour sketches", conceived in complete openness and uncertainty under the premise of "multi-chromatic and complicated" which obviously meant the opposite of anti-painting and of painting that doubts its proper legitimacy.[3]

Thus it seems that Richter, in 1976, abnegated his previous stance of being one of the most radical painters of the European neo-avant-garde; a painter who had challenged with each series that he initiated the received ideas about painting in general, as well as those about his art in particular, by confronting his viewer on each occasion with a *volte face*. But this time, so it seemed, the conversion of 1976 was not one that remained immanent to the parameters that had been established since 1913 as the critique of the institution of art by the means of art production. Now those very ideas about a pictorial practice of self-reflection and self-referentiality were explicitly rejected when Richter said: '. . . there is no colour on canvas that means nothing but itself and nothing beyond it, otherwise the *Black Square* by Malevich would just be a silly coat of paint.' While Richter seems to reject the aesthetic positions of the 60s which clearly had also been his own, it is revealing that he refers to Malevich in the discussion of the implicit meanings of monochrome painting – the first painter in the long and complicated history of monochrome paintings who associated the decision to paint a monochrome central pictorial figure with a spiritual and metaphysical explanation while already his immediate successor, Alexander Rodchenko detached programmatically any spiritual or metaphysical meaning from the first truly monochrome triptych that he painted in 1921. Richter's emphatic assertion of the *meaning* of painting – as opposed to his previous attitude that he once characterised as that of an 'anti-painter' would prohibit thus a reading of his paintings in terms of either supreme irony and detachment or that of a critical assault on the practices of painting that was clearly an aspect of his practice during the 60s and early 70s, when the refusal of meaning, the denial of the artist's role and its traditional implications were at the centre of Richter's concerns.

While we have no reason to assume that Richter would have changed his attitude about painting out of sheer historical opportunism – at an early moment incidentally, since in 1976 the subsequent reversal of pictorial aesthetics was still difficult to anticipate – at least two major projects, the 'Mirrors' from 1981 and the mural-sized yellow 'Brushstrokes' from 1980, would already complicate if not outright contradict Richter's claim to have assumed a traditionalist position with regard to the assignment of meaning to pictorial structures. Furthermore it is important to understand the process of transition which led to the new polychrome gestural paintings that resemble the attempt of other earlier artists to convey emotional, spiritual or psychosexual meaning through semi-automatist, highly gestural, non-representational modes of painting.

Richter has descibed that transition as the phase in which he produced what he called 'colour-sketches' and he gives us a reason why he identified these small paintings (by now considered as fully autonomous valid paintings) as sketches: '. . . I called them sketches to make them harmless in order to be able to continue working in that manner . . .' These sketches were subsequently subjected to a technical process of reproduction and scale differentiation that has become the essential working procedure for the mostly large-scale gestural 'Abstract Paintings' that Richter has produced since 1976. In two instances the full range of 'meaning' inherent in the technique – as specific to the tradition of Modernism it is the technique and the process of production that transform the conventions of reading and seeing and it is in this transformation that the work's 'meaning' is operative – has assumed exemplary significance in Richter's work that opens a perspective on the 'Abstract Paintings' as a category of work in general. The first being a project from 1978 when Richter decided to photograph one of these 'colour-sketches', unstretched in various positions and from various angles on a chair, or as he described it:

In the summer of 1978, I took photographs of the surface of an oil-sketch on canvas . . . The photographs were taken from various sides, from various angles, various distances and under different light conditions. The resulting photographs were organised in two versions; one, the sequential order that is presented here under the covers of a book, and a second version which is presented pictorially in grid form . . . [4]

The second instance, structurally comparable, yet technically different, was the production of the two architectural murals commissioned for a public institution. The two paintings, entitled *Zwei Gelbe Striche (Two Yellow Brushstrokes)* measure 190x2,000cm and are the largest paintings that Richter has yet produced. A single yellow brushstroke is minutely reconstructed through photographic details. These details are subsequently assembled to form a large composite image of a giant gesture of the painterly act through photographic projection onto the various canvas panels by a laborious transfer process of molecular painterly elements.

This process of mediation of an original, direct and *organic* painterly activity (organic in the sense of the traditional definition of the symbolic sign that supposedly renders an unmediated and substantial presence of the transcendental experience) through the various stages and practices of a mechanical construction of a pictorial sign (the photographic recording of the presumably original and immediate trace of expression, its transfer and enlargement, the change of scale and that of pictorial execution) is the manifest subject of Richter's 'Abstract Paintings' (in the way that Lubov Popova said in 1919 that '. . . facture was the subject of painting'). While it differs from the two extreme examples that we have quoted, the process of structural transformation in the 'Abstract Paintings' remains essentially the same, even if the result of the investigation is another painting (rather than a photographic grid of a mural-sized architectural decoration). The 'Abstract Paintings' therefore provide us with immediate insight into the contemporary conditions of painting; to exist between the irreconcilable demands of the spectacle and the synecdoche and it is this dialectic that determines the reading of the 'Abstract Paintings'. As the work fulfills these two historical requests simultaneously, it unfolds an infinite range of combinations and future tentative reconciliations of this dialectic while it rehearses at the same time a recollection of the past potential and devices of painterly practice. Richter's paintings constitute a memory of the past of painting (when gesture could still engender the experience of emotional turbulence, when chromatic veils credibly conveyed a sense of transparence and spatial infinity, when impasto could read as immediacy and emphatic material presence, when linear formation read as direction in space, movement through time, as operative force of the will of the subject and when composition and successful integration of all of these elements into painting constituted the experience of the subject. Even though we are aware of the fact that the often very ominous titles of Richter's 'Abstract Paintings' (unlike his previous method of identifying his paintings laconically by subject of representation or by colour) are randomly chosen, it is perhaps not purely accidental that the *chef d' oeuvre* of the 'Abstract Paintings' so far (certainly the largest, a triptych measuring 295x675cm) is entitled *Faust*. After all the literary adaptation of the mediaeval legend in the early 19th century is still one of the grand visions and utopian designs of what bourgeois identity and individuality could be and should become. As a vision of governance and control, self-loss and passion, commitment and moral responsibility, extreme subjectivity and simultaneous devotion to the construction of society, the figure of Faust has haunted the 19th- and 20th-century artist (certainly in Europe in works such as Mann's) as one of an identification that could no longer be fulfilled or even approached, as it seemed. The totality of the vision, the centrality of the human subject had long ago lost their historical credibility and had been increasingly replaced by the necessity for the fragmented vision, the restriction to the detail, the critical negation of the aesthetic's function to provide transcendental compensation for a secularised society. It was the plight of the Modernist artist to provide the representation of truth in the guise of those reductions and strictures, and Modernist painting is a history of the increasingly radical exclusion of all plenitude and totality, of all symbolic and organic completeness of expression and identity, it is the history of self-purification and self-imposed limitation of means, foregrounding the technique and the device, purging of subject matter and emphatic presentation of the synecdoche as the ultimate mode within which visual truth could be constructed and imbued with historical credibility. What the practice of the synecdoche (in the tradition of Realism) promised was a form of resistance and opposition against the totality of myth in the mass cultural forms of representation that governed everyday life: the spectacle of consumption and the consumption of the spectacle. Richter has explicitly referred to the hermetic nature of painting as a strategy of resistance against the dominance of consumption when saying that '. . . painting is the creation of an analogy for the invisible and the unintelligible, which should become figure and should become accessible . . .

Gerhard Richter
18 Oktober 1977

 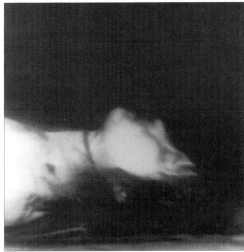

L to R: *Gegenüberstellung (1)* (Confrontation), 1988, 112x102cm; *Tote* (Dead), 1988, 62x62cm.
'With his cycle of paintings representing the events of October 18, 1977, Gerhard Richter recalls an experience which has fallen prey to a greater extent to psychological rather than actual political repression: the Stammheim corpses, the demise of the Red Army Faction.
'. . . these paintings are continually reformulating the question of what attitude it would be appropriate to adopt towards them. On the one hand, they escape the consensus view that art has nothing to do with "reality"; on the other, they insist that – as paintings – they should be distinguished both from reality, *and* from the photographs on which they are based. This forces the viewer to make the impossible decision between distance and proximity, through which he can become aware of his attitude towards the subject represented and the nature of representation itself in its various forms.
'. . . As it has ceased to be the primary medium for the social production of images, and is not only competing with but rather outmoded in compari-son to photomechanical reproduction, Richter uses his art less for the production of what would assert themselves as "new" pictures than to reflect on pre-existing images. The distinction between pain-terly "signifiers" and photographic "signifieds" produced by this process has a subversive quality. It stresses the fictional character of the reality indi-rectly conveyed, and thus restores to painting – which has allegedly become obsolete since the arrival of the new medium – its critical function, in both senses of the word.'
Stefan Germer, Paris, 1989
'Photographs are practically nature. We get them pushed through our door, nearly as undistorted as reality, only smaller. But we want to see these terrible small pictures. They save us a lot of public executions, perhaps even the death penalty. We have a craving for such things.
' . . . I don't think they are any worse than pictures, just different, – more direct, more emotive, more intimate . . . I would say that the photograph generates horror, whereas the picture of the same subject evokes sorrow. That would come very close to my intention.
'. . . the public ambitions of these people, their non-private, impersonal, ideological motivation. And then the tremendous force, the power of an idea to the point of dying for it. This was for me the most impressive and inexplicable aspect.
'. . . We are capable of pity solely in limited quan-tities: to a great extent, we avoid pity whenever we can. This surely has a purpose, connected as it is with a strategy of survival. But when you realise the degree to which we avoid compassion, how we look on with dispassion whilst hundreds of thou-sands starve to death or are tortured or beaten – and we don't bat an eyelid – that's no longer an indifference justified by the need to survive, that's worse than killing. In reality we are all to blame . . . I consider every type of belief, from astrology to every higher religion and all greater ideologies, superfluous and life-threatening. We have grown out of these things; we should develop a new strategy to combat misery and injustice, war and catastrophes.'
Richter, in discussion with Jan Thorn-Prikker, 1989

Good paintings are therefore incomprehensible . . . They are incomprehensible so that they cannot be consumed and remain essential . . .'

If Richter's current 'Abstract Paintings' have been defined by him as a programmatic departure from the dilemma of his grey monochrome paintings in 1975, they have to be seen as a dialectical negation of the former's implications. Thus abnega-tion of the purity of means and the self-reflection of procedure, would imply the embracement of the spectacle and the renewed mythification of painting, ie, that from now on gesture did no longer mean facture, but it meant emotional experience on display for others, that colour meant no longer chromatic relationships, their interaction and scientific intelligibility, but it meant from now on again the simulacrum of spiritual space.

'Polychrome and complicated' were the terms that Richter used to identify the qualities of the paintings with which he wanted to be engaged, yet he did not mention that they would be mediated through changes of scale and photographic technology, that their 'facture' would be shifted from the immediate to the constructed, that the catalogue of pictorial devices – the memory of painting – would assume suddenly the dimension of a manifestation of the conditions of spectacle within the practice of painting itself, that it would betray the heretofore unknown degree to which the pursuit of the Modernist high art of painting had already assumed its historical share to exist in the culture of the spectacle itself, as the one practice that remained outside of the totality, it had become its most precious domain.

Notes

1 Félix Fénéon, as quoted by Paul Signac, *D'Eugène Delacroix au Néo-Impressionisme*, Paris, 1911, pp133 and 167.
2 André Breton, as quoted by Jacques de la Villeglé, *Des Réalités collectives*, exhibition *Dufrêne, Hains, Rotella*, Stuttgart, 1971.
3 This and all following quotations by Gerhard Richter cited in Heribert Heere, *Gerhard Richter – Die Abstrakten Bilder: Zur Frage des Inhalts*, exhib cat *Gerhard Richter – Abstakte Bilder 1976-1981*, Bielefeld/Manheim, 1982, pp9-20 (my translations).
4 Statement by Gerhard Richter, '128 details from a picture: Halifax 1978', *The Nova Scotia Pamphlets*, Vol 2, Halifax, 1980, p65.

Gerhard Richter, *48 Portraits*, 1971-72, photographs, *Above*: details, *from above L to R*: Thomas Mann (1875-1955), Franz Kafka (1883-1924), Albert Einstein (1879-1955), Nicolai Huntmann (1882-1950), Patrick Maynard Stuart Blackett (1897-1974), Louis-Victor de Broglie (1992-1987), photographs, each image 70x55cm; *Below*: installation of 48 plates, each image 70x55cm, Museum Ludwig, Cologne.

IRIT ROGOFF

DOUBLE VISION
Politics Between Image and Representation

Jorg Immendorf, *Brandenburg Gate-World Question*, 1981-83, height 330cm

Struggling up the interminable flights of stairs of one of Berlin's old apartment houses, I interrogate
a friend about the prevalent cliché that German art is more overtly politically engaged than any of its
European counterparts. My friend seems to agree with this assumption and claims historical
conditions for its emergence, primarily the legacy of the Lutheran Reformation and the subsequent

need for justifying cultural pursuits via their ability to express redemptive and socially critical projects. He even quotes chapter and verse from Werner Hoffmann's exhibition catalogue of Luther and his epoch at the Hamburg Kunsthalle a few years ago concerning the instructive potential of art. This explanation leaves me stranded mid-staircase in a state of great concern over the mythical construction of national cultures and national heritages. Had Adorno not already warned us that '. . . the ideal (*national/cultural*) suffers at the expense of the idealisation. The fabrication of national collectives . . . is the mark of a reified consciousness hardly capable of experience. Such fabrication remains within precisely those stereotypes which it is the task of thinking to resolve.'[1] And what of the so called 'political' nature of this art? Are the mere appearances of Swastikas and ruins, crematoria chimneys and barbed wire fences, signs invoking a recent political past, are they reflective images of politics or analytically oriented representations of politics?

In a recent discussion of Claude Lanzman's film *Shoah*, theorist Gertrude Koch makes the following differentiations:

Authenticity as a criterion indeed encompasses many forms and genres. Yet it unmistakably opts for a Modernist aesthetic which aims at expression rather than communication. If the affirmative aspects of the metaphysical and/or theological imputation of patterns of meaning to mass

annihilation can be linked to a premodern aesthetic, there are on the other side of the scale, the unresolved aporias of autonomous art. The latter obtains its power from the theory of the imagination, the notion of art as idea or image (*Vostellung*) rather than representation (*Darstelling*), expression rather than illustration. The imagination claims its own autonomy; it can project, annihilate social existence, transcend it to become radically other, while allowing the speechless, hidden substratum of nature in the mute body to reappear. At first glance, the autonomous freedom of the imagination, which does not allow itself to be confined by any concept of meaning, seems far less burdened with the tendency to suffocate, through affirmation, the claims to expression made by the oppressed and the tormented.[2]

The stereotype then can be subjected to a closer analysis taking into consideration the conditions and materials of the objects' origins. Alternatively it could also be interrogated for its constitutive, as opposed to reflective, qualities, thus entering into the discourse on representation and allowing that visual culture in all its forms can construct and circulate new meanings within the wider political culture. Certainly the uniqueness of a German tradition must be examined for ways in which it positions itself *vis à vis* other contemporary cultural manifestations, not simply through a reading of its autonomous, substantive meanings.

In certain works of the past decade such as *48 Portraits* (1972), Gerhard Richter internalises the inherent tensions between image and representation into the body of the work itself. *48 Portraits* is a modern photo-album, made by the artist for the German pavilion of the 1972 Venice Biennale, and featuring the great men of Western, Modernist culture.[3] The grouping of 48 individual canvases executed from old photographs in black and white, focuses on the representation of history as a form of sorting and collecting in the making of encyclopaedic taxonomies. At the edges of the work issues of difference, of minority cultural traditions arise – the subjects of the portraits are all great men, all representatives of a great Western tradition. Many of them are also Eastern Europeans, others are Jews, many have been subjected to racial defamation and persecution, to exile and to various forms of exclusion. Richter features the canon of European culture, masking, throughout this fictive college album, the differences and exclusions practiced by the very culture they are now perceived as representing. It masquerades as an illustrative work, emphasising its authenticity and factuality through its form, through the formal conventions of a document. The subtext of the work however is precisely its own deceptiveness, its ability to construct some visual representation of history that in fact functions purely in the realm of representation, constructing meanings, lineages, chronologies and coherencies as it makes its way in the world. Equally it expresses an unease concerning the position of this culture to other European cultures whose representatives are included in this grouping. The tensions between inclusion and exclusion are then in relation to national cultural narratives as well as to personal biographies. This struggle against the imposition of cultural coherence in all its forms seems to be at the heart of many of the most potent of contemporary German artistic practices. These practices in turn are engaged in a dialogue with state cultural policies and subsidies, with the constant revising of historical narratives taking place throughout the culture and in the consistent struggle between the transcendent vs the critical functions of culture.

Pitting critical artistic practices against the cultural policies which facilitate them is the core of the following discussion. As such it is not, in any way, an attempt to place a value judgement on the quality of the Federal Republic's state cultural subsidy or on the efficacy of the principles put forward by the Constitution and by the 11 länder and the numerous municipal authorities which administer these policies in West-Germany. On the contrary, the commitment, the wealth and the range of these activities are the envy of Europe and the pride of post-war reconstruction within Germany. What this analysis can do however, is to provide us with an exceptionally interesting set of historical circumstances and responses which form spheres of direct cultural engagement and which look back over five separate phases (phases unique to modern German history) of disjuncture and the ensuant efforts by policy-making bodies and spokespersons, at a rhetoric of continuity.

This attempted analysis is founded on the premise that there exists a reasonably coherent hegemonic ideology of culture. It maintains that this ideology is in turn formulated into cultural policy as well as into various other realms of cultural understanding, self assessment and cultural representation. At the core of this dominant ideology lies the desire for cohesion, collectivity and continuity of cultural practices. Furthermore this analysis operates on the premise that the clearest indications of what this hegemonic ideology of culture stands for are perceptible through its policies of cultural subsidies.

The inherent tension between this dominant ideology, its policy of cultural subsidy and their interaction with artistic production are what constitutes the divisive and embattled nature of culture itself. What I intend to look at in this brief discussion are the ways in which all of these engage with one another in the form of a critical interrogation. This is attempted through the elucidation of some of the main characteristics of the policy itself and through a discussion of a few examples of the work of Hans Haacke, Gerhard Richter and of Jorg Immendorf. In looking at this equation via three separate responses we are also distinguishing between three radically different perceptions of culture which are represented by the three sides of this equation:
a) Hegemonic ideology sees culture as constructed through 'The Informing Spirit' of an entire bourgeois way of life and supporting its universal, humanistic aspirations.
b) Haacke as representative of critical Modernism demands that culture be viewed as a representation of the whole social order in which artistic and intellectual work would be seen as related products of an order primarily constituted by other social activities.
c) Immendorf in the anti-cohesive vein of Post-Modernist posits culture as a *signifying system* through which the social order is communicated, reproduced, experienced and explored.[4]

In order to attempt this we must begin by characterising the main tenets of the dominant post-war West-German cultural ideology. I would like to suggest that it is dominated by a concept of the collective nature of the project at hand and that its main ambitions lie in the direction of the restoration of a culture that had been decimated from the inside, the wide-scale dissemination of this restored culture and finally an emphasis on its unifying properties. If this is the case then obviously one of the main issues we would need to address is the way in which the past constructs the present in ways that differ from the notion of 'tradition', a concept that has long dominated methodologies of cultural history.

As the polemical focus of my argument I would like to make the highly unpopular observation that a thundering silence concerning a critical analysis of NS fascism and its cultural activities has lain at the heart of the previously described hegemonic ideology of culture, up until the 1980s. By this I do not mean a visually codified investigation of the way in which the past constructs the present. There have in recent years been numerous examples, both cynical and serious, which have launched an interrogation of the communicative nature and validity of representations of history.

This does not mean an interrogation of what was visible and represented but of what was silent and absent; for example the peculiar nature of a patronage system in which continuously over the century whole schools of art appear and disappear at will, while much of the institutional infrastructure remains. A system, which in its efforts to gain an autonomous post-war identity apart from East Germany has ended up collapsing the concepts of nation and state into one cultural entity. Silences and absences also exist beyond debates concerning inclusion/exclusion into the realm of privileged artistic selection; the degree to which NS condemnations and exclusions construct today's inclusions and valorisations; ie what was brought back into museums after the war, what is put forward as representing German art throughout the century etc. (The implications of this within a contemporary international market situation are quite amazing!)

My interest then, is beyond the conditions for artistic production and onto this production's interrogative engagement with the understanding of culture as its main subject matter via an increasing refinement of its own mediated relationship to a materialist reality. These are set in the context of recent concepts of cultural policy and subsidy in the Federal Republic and their critiques. In an explication of West German Federal cultural policy during the late 1970s, optimistically entitled 'Culture for All', Hilmar Hoffman, one of the architects of this new post-war policy, explained why it must enter a new phase in the 1980s:

The new phase has come about with the recognition that the strategies pursued until then in 'Democratic Cultural Policy' (which worked under the concept of 'Culture for All') have become inadequate. These had mainly been preoccupied with the democratisation of supply by making access easier, by offering art and culture in unusual places and with the use of pedagogical aids. Now that the democratisation of art and culture itself, which largely began in the museums, that is; the inclusion of the problems, desires, interests and needs of the public at large in the production and distribution of the arts and of cultural institutions has been recognised as a major task, the public is not satisfied with being told: 'That is art, look at it and come to terms with it'. They want to feel that art has something to do with them, they want to see their own problems and hopes reflected in it.[5]

There are two main lines of criticism of democratic cultural policy in West Germany; firstly the argument from the Left that *culture for all* must be replaced by *culture by all*, that is culture or art that includes a wide-scale representation of diverse social factors in its various modes of production. However, as Hoffmann states, democratic cultural policy has also come under debate as a result of attacks from the conservative side: in the education system, in scholarship and in the traditional attitudes of cultural institutions, it is old privileges, restrictive interpretations of democratic principles and introverted value judgements which have once again become predominant. These arguments are aimed at casting doubts on the legitimation of a democratic cultural policy which has attempted to take on any new and responsive forms.[6] Concurrent with these two sets of criticism we also find in the 1970s, the decade immediately following the student movement inaugurated in 1968, the emergence of a new form of artistic representation which also has an interrogation of patronage and subsidy inscribed into its formulation. These speculate on the objectives of sponsorship, its inherent and ignored exclusions, its service in the promotion of national myths, on the collusions between public and private funding and the resultant conferral of cultural legitimacy on both the state and individual patrons.

Historically, then, how did culture become a focal point for a public debate of this scale and magnitude, initiated by official Federal and regional policies and debated by every facet of establishment and alternative public spheres in West Germany?

To begin with we have to look very briefly at the nature and the dominant patterns of post-war patronage. Of these the most fundamental is the principle that culture is predominantly publicly subsidised. This public patronage and encouragement, or intervention, within and beyond the conditions of the market are viewed as a matter of general public policy and are integrated with other facets of that policy. This institutional public subsidy, which in 1986 amounted to approximately DM five billion supports over 1,000 museums, 2,274 Adult Education Institutes, 97 theatre companies in 198 locations, 65 music and opera theatres, 83 orchestras (exclusive of 12 radio TV orchestras, choirs etc), 700 music schools and academies, 7,123 libraries and so on and so forth, on a permanent basis.[7] Aside from these institutional subsidies there are also several hundred prizes, stipends, festivals, temporary international exhibitions, arts associations, cooperatives, clubs, galleries, an international network of Goethe Institutes, academic and artistic exchange programmes, foundations sponsoring research and production all of which are publicly funded. Similarly numerous programmes now exist for the funding and promotion of films, which had previously not played a major role in the post-war reconstruction of culture for obvious historical reasons to do with their manipulation as propaganda during the National Socialist era and conse-

quent devaluation as an artistic form within traditional cultural hierarchies.

Through these numerous different avenues, modern patronage in West Germany has therefore been reconstructed as state subsidy. A secondary consideration in the execution of state subsidy views regionalism and local authorities as better able to gauge the needs of the different communities and social groups at a grass-roots level. Within this are the beginnings of a recognition of ethnic, racial, generational and gender differentiations within the potential public of cultural activities.

Private patronage of course exists, although the main tendency until quite recently, has been for it to keep a very low profile. Such patronage is presently supporting some 25 museums and 27 theatres, numerous temporary exhibitions as well as academic research projects and artistic bursaries on a scale unknown anywhere else in Europe. As such the various private initiatives now constitute approximately 12 per cent of the overall cultural subsidy. Whereas it is very difficult to assess precisely the amount involved in overall cultural subsidy by Federal, regional, local and other authorities aside from the institutional support mentioned earlier, it does nevertheless appear that these different activities involve sums of approximately DM ten billion per annum. Both the scale of the funding and the diversity of its sources make this the most active and highly endowed cultural subsidy policy in Western Europe.

Where, then, within this veritable paradise of universalist aspirations, well endowed cultural subsidy and autonomous activity, are the areas which called forth an interventionist stance from the Left in the wake of the student movement of 1968 and its concomitant critique of culture?

Even progressive and unconventional cultural politicians such as the aforementioned Hilmar Hoffmann, failed to address an analysis of the underlying meanings of culture beyond that of a worthy panacea for a destroyed and agonised society. In all of the documents which discuss the facilitation of cultural activity, no critical model is ever advanced in which culture is equated with power, whether liberal or authoritarian. The nature of objects and what they uphold or represent is not part of the cultural debate and instead their history and their distribution take precedence over everything else. The second missing element is that of history. The formulations of the specific cultural policy from which I have quoted above have assumed a certain new-born status, conceived after the moment known as 'Stunde Null', the 'Zero Hour', which lasted between 1945 and 1949, between Allied occupation and the formulation of the Federal Republic's constitution. The critical nature of the moment and the spirit of its creation have therefore, at least overtly, absolved it from a discussion of precedence and of historical continuity *per se*. It is important to realise here that the issue of immediate history is a fundamental but unspoken factor going far beyond the practical need for the wholesale replacement of a lost, dispersed and mutilated culture. Part of the conceptual interrogation put forward by contemporary art works is related to the rhetoric of cultural unity and wholeness which has long had a hold on German debates on internal politics and cultural aspirations. From the mid-19th century onwards a fundamentally conservative historical yearning for unity and continuity has battled continuously with the disruption and change brought about by the onslaught of Modernism. Be these the disjunction of Bismarck's imposed unification, the upheavals of large-scale modern industrialisation and urbanisation, the trauma and destruction of two world wars or the geographical and political divisions and conflicts of the post-war era, they have all had counterparts in cultural debates based on conflicting views of history as continuity or disjuncture. Whereas it is traditionally the conservative factions who supported and articulated a cul-

Hans Haacke, *Homage to Marcel Broodthaers*, 1983, installation details, *Above*: oil painting/velvet rope, *Below*: photomural

tural discourse emphasising continuity founded on traditional modes, these convictions have also encompassed certain inbuilt dichotomies. For example, both Völkish idealism and National Socialist cultural ideology contained within them a curious balance between pragmatic progress and regressive nostalgia.[8] Within contemporary ideological discussions this same debate has focused on the notion of the 'Sonderweg', ie the divergence of German historical development from that of other Western countries. For our purposes the centrality of this argument hinges on the way in which the past is perceived to construct the present and to dictate the ideological terms of reference for any reconstructive project. Whenever historical continuity is mentioned in relation to cultural policy, it is described in terms of the continuity of a tradition of regional sponsorship that survives unabated through the Wilhelmine Reich, the Weimar Republic, Nazi Germany and the present Federal Republic of West Germany. In reality there are other levels of debate concerning continuity, such as the legacy of mass consumption of culture pioneered by the National Socialists, access to which was equated with such fundamental needs as the supply of proper housing and accessible motor cars.

The recognition of the historical factors at play within cultural policy formulations leads in turn to the recognition of the legacy of history as a constant reminder of a divided heritage; the physical division of country, communities and families between East and West Germany and the fact that existing collections, monuments, landmarks or linguistic practices have had little or no continuity. Beneath all the frantic activity that constitutes cultural rehabilitation, what Adorno has called 'the testimonies to the historical process' had very deliberately been lost.

The reception of these cultural policies by the artists working within it, if not under its direct auspices, has provided us with several further modes for its critical interrogation. Hans Haacke and Jorg Immendorf are two such artists who have continuously taken an interventionist stand in cultural politics and who have, in differing and opposite ways, addressed themselves to a critique of those elements constantly missing from official cultural policy. For Hans Haacke, the concept of nation is a quasi-mystical entity which he totally rejects. Instead of the traditional concept of nation, he substitutes that of the State which he conceives of as the conjunction of institutional and industrial power and their manifestations. It is evident that these industrial and institutional powers construct authoritative legitimation through a variety of cultural manifestations which include the accoutrements of high culture.

The marketable status of objects and the role they play within the constantly conflicting modes of public and private patronage are a major theme of Haacke's work. In 1974 Haacke was invited to create a piece for the Wallraf-Richartz museum in Cologne as part of a collective celebration of that institution's 100th birthday. Here was an institution that had been through the gamut of German cultural history; staunchly conservative in the 1890s, increasingly liberal and internationally oriented in the 1920s, penalised and robbed by National Socialist cultural policies in the 1930s, rehabilitated in the 1950s and actively engaged in purchasing back its former glories.[9] Haacke, ever a true commando of culture, chose to mark this celebration through an investigation of the evolution of artistic market and patronage practices and their ultimate autonomy from the objects which initially motivate them. The result was Manet-Project 74. As the object under investigation he chose Manet's small and humble studio sketch of 1880, Asparagus Bunch. As the painting changes hands its price increases and so does its status; it enters the art market through the circles around the painter himself and soon gains the status of a commodity. Through the work's odyssey in the world of dealers and collectors, transformations in the artistic

forum are chronicled such as the interconnections between the dealer Cassirer and the painter and Secession president Liebermann in plotting the course of the importation and exposition of French Impressionism in Germany at the turn of the century. In the subtext of these particular portraits is located the awareness that these activities formed the basis for paranoid claims of an international Jewish conspiracy which was monied, élitist and hell bent on cultural internationalism as can be seen in its efforts to gain an audience for French painting of which Manet's sketch is a coveted example.[10] The next panel in the series documents the fascist era as the painting immigrates with its Jewish owner Käte Riezler, daughter of Max Liebermann, to America and becomes an emblem of European culture in exile. Its return to Germany as the triumphant and vastly expensive symbol of cultural continuity was engineered by the Chairman of the governors of the Wallraf-Richartz museum and its financing aided by his numerous non-cultural economic activities. In the final panel we find the conjunction of humble work, awesome price, a museum board of trustees incorporating some of the main industrialists in the Ruhr area, and a board chairman who was closely involved with NS financial institutions[11] building upon one another to gain cultural legitimacy.[12] Haacke has here constructed a case history which forms the basis for contemporary cultural practices. He has also pointed that such historical self consciousness accommodates a certain in-built duality since by compensating for the past's cultural policies a certain authority is gained for the present cultural activities.

Nowhere has the facade of autonomous and publicly sponsored cultural democracy been more challenged than in the case of the collector and patron Dr Peter Ludwig dubbed by Haacke 'The Chocolate Master'. This industrial giant whose fortune has been founded on chocolate has single-handedly challenged the entire public patronage structure through the combined forces of philanthropy, cultural authority (both he and his wife hold doctorates in Art History and therefore have scholarly as well as financial authority) and political acumen. While none of these are particularly unique or astonishing characteristics it is their effectiveness in constructing irrefutable facts of an autonomous cultural patronage in the face of the massive public subsidy that challenges the realities of cultural democratic practices. To begin with, what are the specific business practices which both fund and benefit from the cultural activities as documented in Haacke's piece The Chocolate Master finished in 1981.[13] Under the brand names of Regent, Van Houten, Lindt and several dozen others, Ludwig gained ownership of much of the German and Central European chocolate market, as well as substantial enterprises in Canada and the US. His main factories which employed approximately 7000 workers at the time, had a ratio of 90% women to 10% men of whom approximately 65% were foreign Gastarbeiter, who have neither German nationality and possess only limited civil rights.'The company maintains hostels for its female foreign workers, in which three or four women share a room, on its fenced factory compound in Aachen, as well as in other locations. It is reported that women employees living there who give birth have to leave their employment since the company has no day-care centre or other facilities for children or alternatively have to give up their child for adoption. Workers are checked at the end of each working shift via searches conducted by other employees in authority, presumably for missing chocolate bars. In the series of panels documenting these conditions Haacke has combined three levels of imagistic and contextual representation relating to contemporary economic practices. On one level he presents a documentation of the women's living and working conditions within the Ludwig chocolate empire. At another level he invokes the spectre of advertising, illusion and public image, although still in relation to the industrial product, by illustrating in detail the cheap and gaudy display boxes and by focusing on the way in which it is disseminated to the public through advertising. The conjunction of these elements in the panels traces the process by which industrial effort has been transformed into illusion and artistic effort into commodity, the one gratifying the other; what Walter Grasskamp has so aptly called 'information magic'. In the next two panels the third level at which this work functions is introduced through the following texts relating to the financial incentives offered by tax exemption to collectors and philanthropists: 'Art Objects on Permanent Loan are Exempt from Property Taxes' and 'Through Donation a Spouse's Payment of 35% Inheritance Tax is Avoided'. Through these exemptions and concessions we find industrial and commercial practices employed for the supposed advancement of cultural practices while in fact creating yet another realm of civic and national authority for the patron. This has been achieved in the following pragmatic ways; permanent loans to the Wallraf-Richartz museum in Cologne which has now become the Museum Ludwig and where Dr Ludwig also holds the position of adjunct professor of art history. The founding of the Neue Gallerie Ludwig collection and the Sauermondt-Ludwig Museum in Aachen, location of his main chocolate factories, and where he has been awarded the freedom of the city and chairs several important municipal committees. Other projects are permanent loans to the National Galleries of both East and West Berlin, Kunstmuseum, Basel, Centre Pompidou, State museums at Saarbrucken and Mainz and several dozen others. His Mediaeval art collections are housed at the Schnutgen Museum Cologne, the Couven Museum Aachen and the Bavarian State collections. Since Haacke has produced this work in 1981, Dr Ludwig has also engineered the conversion of the Baroque Palais Lichtenstein in Vienna into the city's museum of contemporary art, housing parts of his own as well as the city's collections and staffed by a German director and several other staff members of his choice. Similarly he has founded an ambitious international foundation which is intended for art-historical research, the promotion of Eastern European art and the coordination of buying and loan policies to public institutions. Haacke's detailed exposé serves to locate Ludwig's economic and cultural practices against a patronage policy which is opposed to them in theory but which has endorsed them indirectly through an emphasis on ever increasing scale and distribution. This contradictory endorsement results, according to Haacke, from the lack of a built-in critical apparatus focusing on an analysis of what is being disseminated, what it represents and how it is characterised. Certainly Dr Ludwig himself has been aware of the implications of the conjunction of information documenting his activities and the critical analysis put forward by Haacke's work since he has tried to buy the work on at least eight separate occasions without success.[14]

In several recent works, he examines in representational terms the cultural ramifications of international power play. Like the aforementioned series of portraits by Richter, many of Haacke's projects deal with the problematics of cross-cultural positionality, with histories mediated by multinational cooperations, universalising exhibitions, international marketing campaigns and other strategies which obfuscate the conditions of cultural and industrial production. *Homage à Marcel Broodthaers* was completed for *documenta 7* and he said of it: 'The Reagan piece dealt with a highly charged political situation, the deployment of a new generation of nuclear missiles with potentially horrendous consequences. In the subtexts you find 20 allusions to the myths of power and art and to the waves of conservative painting engulfing *documenta 7*, the exhibition for which the piece was made.'[15] The piece itself is divided into an oil painting of President Reagan in a haughty and defiant pose and executed in a

manner reminiscent of *juste millieu* paintings with their licked and sealed surfaces. This is installed opposite an immense blown up photograph of a German anti-nuclear demonstration; popular political manifestations and the representations of power engaging in direct conflict within one work. Furthermore they are divided by a plush red carpet and a red velvet rope, the trappings of distancing in both political officialdom in separating the political dignitary from people and in high museum culture where it serves to distance the spectator from the precious object. The work functions to some extent in tandem with an earlier piece dealing with the conjunction of media power, political power and cultural power, the Reagan portrait, *'Yes, my son collects unemployment too! REAGANOMICS'*. Though in this instance it is a manifestation of populism rather than of high culture. The picture appeared after the *New York Post* carried on 14th October, 1982, a photo of Ron Reagan Jnr standing in a dole queue and quoted him as saying 'I spoke with my mother before I signed on and she OK'd it'. For Haacke, language is the combined code for both political rhetoric and advertising which are used to support and reaffirm one another; here he uses the affirmative mode which emphasises the populist stand of the former President. The fact that the policies of Reaganomics were antagonistic to the welfare state and have imposed greater hardship than ever on the unemployed, are rendered obsolete in this image by the shared burden of parenthood. The text is in turn superimposed onto a tinted photograph of the kind put to use by businesses trying to project a trustworthy image. But it is not only the echo of an advertising mode within business practices, it is also an artistic mode in service of the homespun populist image. Those of us who are affectionados of *Dallas, Dynasty* and other assorted soap operas will remember that in the so-called den of the Ewings of Dallas and the Carringtons of Denver there hangs a large, tinted photograph of the entire clan beaming at the spectator. Through these we are reminded that despite the plots, counter plots and dastardly deeds which these relatives seem to inflict one upon the other *ad nauseum*, they are nevertheless an affirmation of the ideal of togetherness and The American Family. The plots are simply the normal everyday workings of capitalist endeavours which do not negate the unity of the family in the same way that the divisive ruthlessness and the home-spun populism of Reagan do not negate the unity of the nation behind him, captured in a piece of advertising cum art.

As is often the case in Haacke's work different media, such as photographs, gilt frames and red velvet carpets in this case, represent differing political forces and simultaneously maintain an open discussion between the work and the context in which it is exhibited. When the political context is delineated to encode both a superpower struggle and the local response to its manifestations; the proliferation of nuclear arms, the subtext of cultural politics is immediately linked to it. In the case of the Reagan piece exhibited at *documenta 7*, we have a recent history in which West German cultural policy for museums encouraged the buying of American Abstract Expressionism and its related practices as part of an aspiration towards taking part in an international movement whose artistic expression dispensed with narrative and therefore with specific traditions and differentiated historical narratives. The historical moment for which this piece was created was somewhat ludicrously characterised in 1983 by the cover of an American art magazine with a banner 'Europe is Back!'[16] Haacke's response makes it clear that for his part he will not succumb to an illusion that several groups of narrative and representational painters who have captured the dynamic end of the art market actually constitute a true cultural autonomy and an independence from superpower hegemony. Instead he strives to find visual codifications for the conjunction of cultural subsidies and market forces with a policy which aspires towards re-entry into the Western family of nations and which functions within a sphere of external political pressures.

Over the past two years the silences at the heart of all these engagements have become increasingly audible, and a greater boldness to confront and articulate the precise reasons necessitating such an elaborately autonomous cultural subsidy, can be discerned. The recent attempt to rehabilitate the sculptor Arno Breker, an artist beloved of Nazi officials at all levels, has met with a vociferous and organised opposition by the combined forces of radical artists and the popular press. It was however Haacke's experience at the 'Styrian Autumn' festival held in Graz in 1988, which best encapsulates the deep internal contradictions of the tension between image and interpretation in contemporary German art. Werner Fenz, curator of the public art section of the festival, called 'Points of Reference' had designated the Column of the Virgin Mary at the heart of the city as one of the 16 points of reference which would allow for public art projects which would confront history, politics and society in historically sited spaces. The precise description of both the project and the event following it are best left to the artist:

> Fenz designated the Marienstule and its surroundings as one of the 16 'points of reference'. According to photographs of its transformation into a Nazi Victory column, I had its appearance of July 25, 1938, reconstructed for the Styrian Autumn. The only difference from the original was an addition around the base. Listed, white on black ground in the factura typeface preferred by the Nazis, were 'The vanquished of Styria: 300 gypsies killed, 2,500 Jews killed, 8,000 political prisoners killed or died in detention, 9,000 civilians killed in the war, 12,000 missing, 27,900 soldiers killed'. Facing the obelisk, on the spot where in 1938, a wall of large swastika flags served as a backdrop for the Nazi dignitaries addressing their uniformed audience, I had a billboard erected to hold 16 posters. With a Swastika in the centre of each, the posters carried, in white factura on a red ground, the inscription 'Graz – City of the People's Insurrection'. Pasted into the middle of the swastikas were facsimile reproductions of documents of the period . . . The 16 posters with documents from 1938 were torn down frequently and had to be replaced . . . Out of view of the guard, about a week before the closing of the exhibition, on the night of November 2nd, my memorial to the victims of the Nazis in Styria was Firebombed.[17]

Following the arson, the commemorative monument was itself commemorated extensively in protest at the forces attempting to repress memory. The title of Haacke's piece was taken from the Nazis themselves who in 1938 claimed triumph over their earlier failed putsch in Vienna in July 1934. Haacke sought to make concrete that '50 years later we can make sure that their cheering will turn out to have been premature'.[18]

It is with such visual explorations and codifications of history as a continuity of disjunctions, so noticeably lacking within the official formulations of Federal cultural democracy, that Jorg Immendorf enters this sphere of response to the formal reconstruction of culture. As formulated in his vast series of paintings entitled *Café Deutschland* which stretch from 1979 to 1985, these provide the final, cultural phase of 'coming home to history', to borrow Thomas Elsaesser's phrase.[19] Immendorf had started out as one of Beuys' students at the Düsseldorf Academy and was an active participant in the 1968 rebellion launched against that institution. His own alternative formulation, the 'Lidl Academy' (*lidl* being a phonetic rendition of baby talk) provided a forum of cultural innocence without the constraints of inherited value hierarchies and stripped of their main organisational tool and most refined representation ie mature adult language.[20] Having launched back in a deconstructive project

aimed at erasing the inherited values of culture it eventually became possible for Immendorf to launch forwards into a new form of confrontation with the conceptual analysis of inherited values, culture and history.

Although at its outset German Federal cultural policy was essentially pragmatic and preoccupied with the codification and distribution of the artistic product and Immendorf was essentially a radical preoccupied above all with deconstructing the authority of that very same culture, they seemed to have arrived at their own formulations of 'zero hour' albeit from opposite points of view. As the events of 1968 and their spontaneous and optimistic populist impulses hardened into the terrorism of the 1970s, framed on the one side by the hysterical right-wing reaction to the *Baader-Meinhof* tactics and on the other by Willy Brandt's *Ost Politik* of national reconciliation, it became increasingly clear that history was the only forum which could explicate such disparate and conflicting manifestations. While Immendorf painted the 30 odd canvases known as *Café Deutschland* the Federal Republic erupted in a series of publicly organised exhibition projects under such titles as *Art in Resistance, Art in Exile* and *Art and Collaboration*. Simultaneously the literary establishment embraced the work of Heinrich Boll, Günther Grass and Siegfried Lenz as acceptable voices of the recent past and a huge film project was embarked upon at whose centre lay the attempt to examine the past as a sign system from which present day popular myths and responses were codified.

The series of paintings which he embarked upon in 1976 attempted to amalgamate every strand of the emergent discourses on Germany's past, so that the concept of a new beginning linked to a historical moment could be nullified. His meeting during that year with Penck, the East German, served to both add another dimension to the political discourse he was constructing as well as to give it another artistic personification. From this point on almost all of the paintings incorporate into their space both past and present, both East and West; all emphasised the 'artist', in the dual personification of Penck and Immendorf, as the lynchpins of this historical discourse and all embrace a social, racial, political and gender plurality. Immendorf's discursive space of history in *Café Deutschland I* (1978) is located in a combination of the traditional alternative space of artistic activity, that of the Café/Cabaret/Disco depicted as an intensely centrifugal and hallucinatory dive, lit and coloured with a garishness which points to the artificiality of a dream space. At its centre we find Immendorf and Penck trying to traverse the division imposed by the Berlin Wall; Immendorf thrusts his hand through it while Penck is reflected in ghostly fashion in the chrome column behind his head next to an even ghostlier vision of the Brandenburg Gate, the emblem of yet another decisive historical moment. The figures themselves are framed by two columns of war emblems relating to the Fascist and Communist heritages but formulated in the timeless idiom of the totem pole; part myth and superstition, part historical data. In the background we find Immendorf on the dance floor engaged in frenzied jiving under the emblems of a nationalist past; the German Eagle and the Swastika, while his own image reflects the schizophrenia of the legacy he has inherited by dressing as part Fascist officer and part 60s revolutionary. He appears for the third time in this painting in the depths of the bar where clad in a leather jacket he embraces a naked woman. Here again we find a duality inscribed into the image which is equally a representation of sexual freedom as well as a condemnation of sexual consumption as a pornographic market practice.

Each of these images puts forward a pictorial discourse of the duality and contradiction inscribed in both conformist and critically responsive positions. On the one hand all of these dualities seem to indicate a world in a constant tumult of critical

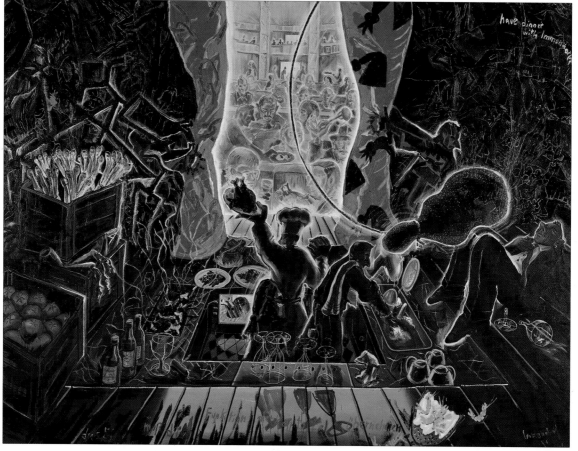

Jorg Immendorf, *Above: Café Deutschland I*, 1978, oil, 282x320cm; *Below: Das Bild muss die Funktion der Kartoffel Übernehmen*, 1988, oil, 300x400cm

ideological conflicts which in turn are not exempt from their own banality or clichéd and conformist representations. Simultaneously however, they are also the representation of a hankering after a unity of historical purpose and the negation of a collective need to escape forwards. Immendorf seems to site these within what is clearly to him a system with no prevailing ideology.

This checking of attitudes within the discursive space of painting is continued in another version of the *Café Deutschland* series entitled '*Let's Go to the 38th Party Conference*' (1983), which works to reinstate the full spectrum of political ideologies within this discursive space of history. These are represented by the figures of Lenin, Trotsky, Stalin and Hitler, the readership of Pravda confronting those who wished to ride the flying horses of mythology which are dropping down to earth everywhere in the painting; the materialist tendencies versus the mythologised symbols. These are however political emblems which he evokes via easily recognised, coded references. To them are added reflections on the reception of history by the anonymous populous; the cloth-capped worker, the leather-clad thug and the spiky-haired punk waitress. All of these are incorporated together into one space which constitutes the history of the present culture. The artistic modes which Immendorf practices in the making of these works also reflect attempts to integrate conflicting opposites into a working relationship. The size of the paintings for example, all of them between two and three metres square, contain an emphatic reference to traditional history painting while at the same time referring to the particular brand of Socialist Realism which was being evolved in East Germany. On the other hand the simplified forms of the actual painting incorporate the lessons of clarity, legibility and accessibility gleaned from advertising and the media and consequently confirm a commitment to the Modernist project and its aspirations.

Similarly the space depicted or rather, delineated, tends to include certain round, proscenium-like, circles which focus the multitude of activities around a stage or a dance floor. Nor does Immendorf attempt to represent his efforts at accommodating several different histories within one frantic space, as in any way successful. In works such as the one discussed above he and Penck inhabit the foreground of the painting, crawling on the floor – felled by art. For all of their painterly and narrative bravura these paintings succeed in maintaining a speculative quality since they do not make claims on behalf of preferred accounts or the feasability of historical coherence. In fact one senses that Immendorf is inscribing a similar dichotomy into the actual representational idiom he is employing since both the

supposedly regressive act of reference to the past in which he indulges himself as well as the operatic quality with which he does so, are negated by the fact that he has no theory of history to present through this construct. Similarly there is a deeply ironic subtext to the overtly political/historical one in which he speculates on the holy status of culture and the importance attributed to its desecration. The jiving, writhing, assaulting and assaulted figures he portrays are placed in the opulent splendour of a theatrical set thereby rendering the act of cultural presentation, an empty gesture. It is obvious that the flying horses, the heraldic emblems of recent history and the ghostly and distorting deep purple glow of the painting are invoking the spectre of Wagnerism. Even the dead bodies of the protagonists in the foreground are reminiscent of a dramatic/operatic convention. It is similarly clear that this spectre is not being utilised for its aura of splendour but precisely for the seduction of gesture inherent in the attempt to package and present a cultural project. By placing the emblems and personifications of conflicting political ideologies within one discursive space, Immendorf proclaims his insistence that they are co-existing constitutive factors within present-day realities; neither choice nor exclusion being truly possible. By ironically placing them within the frantic and lavish environments he creates, he also expresses his own doubts concerning the tendency to invest culture with healing properties.

The artistic and discursive practices of Haacke and Immendorf differ radically from one another although their points of departure share certain principles relating to the social and political project to which engaged art is committed. While Haacke has continuously investigated both the status of cultural authority and the representation of art as commodity, Immendorf has formulated a concentrated attack on convenient histories and their celebration by culture. Furthermore, he has done so in artistic modes which in themselves interrogate the ability of culture to serve as a panacea, since his lavish and opulent cafes are the scene of nightmares populated by cultural emblems.

Nevertheless the discourses which they have both been expounding have served, in differing ways, to offer a critique of an apparently ideal and enviable public cultural policy. Both of their art shares an investigation of the fact that this policy could not articulate its terms of accountability much further than a self regulating market forces dynamics of production and consumption. In formulating these questions into major cultural issues and providing a new set of visual representations of them, both Haacke and Immendorf have in fact constituted them as a new set of discursive signs within this culture.

Notes

1 Theodor Adorno 'What is German?', trans T Levin in *New German Critique*, No 36, 1985.

2 Gertrude Koch, 'The Aesthetic transformation of the Image of the Unimaginable', *October*, no 48, Spring 1989, pp17-18.

3 Jurgen Harten, *Gerhardt Richter*, Dusseldorf Kunsthalle, 1986, pp44-45.

4 Categories adapted from Raymond Williams, *Towards a Sociology of Culture*, London, 1981, ch 1.

5 Hilmar Hoffmann, *Culture for All – Support for the Arts in the Federal Republic of Germany and in the United Kingdom*, Proceedings of Colloquium held at the Goethe Institute London, June 1980, p52.

6 *ibid* p58.

7 Statistics quoted from Andreas Johannes Wiesand, 'KulturPolitik – Kulturförderung – Kulturwirtschaft', in *Deutschland – Porträt einer Nation*, vol 4, 'Kunst und Kultur', 1986, pp37-56.

8 For a discussion of the internal ambiguities of regressive cultural policy under the National Socialists see introduction to Jeffrey Herf, *Reactionary Modernism – Technology, culture and Politics in Weimar and the Third Reich*, Cambridge, 1985.

9 Gerd von der Osten and Horst Keller eds, *Kataloge Des Wallraf-Richartz Museums*, Vol I in cooperation with Rolf Andree, Cologne, 1964.

10 See Peter Paret, *The Berlin Secession – Modernism and its Enemies in Wilhelmine Germany*, Boston, Harvard UP, 1981.

11 See Benjamin H D Buchloh, 'Hans Haacke – Memory and Instrumental Reason' in *Art in America*, February 1988, pp97-114.

12 For full documentation of Haacke's 'Manet-Project 74' see *Hans Haacke – Nach allen Regeln der Kunst*, Neue Gesellschaft der bildende Kunst, Berlin 1984, pp10-23.

13 See *Hans Haacke – Volume II*, Tate Gallery, London, 1984, pp42-65, also Brian Wallis (ed) *Hans Haacke – Unfinished Business*, New Museum of Contemporary Art, NY, 1987.

14 *op cit* p42.

15 Interview with Haacke by Jeanne Siegel 'Leon Golub/Hans Haacke, What Makes Art Political?' *Arts Magazine*, NY, April 1984, p110.

16 See also editorial 'The "Return" of European Art' *Art in America*, September 1982, p6

17 Hans Haacke 'Und ihr habt doch gesiegt', *October*, No 48, Spring 1989.

18 *op cit* p83.

19 Thomas Elsaesser, *New German Cinema*, Rutgers University Press, NJ 1989.

20 For documentation of Immendorf's work to date see Harald Szeemann in *Jorg Immendorf*, MoMA, Oxford, Ulrich Krempel in *Jorg Immendorf*, Kunsthalle Dusseldorf, 1983 and Picture documentation in *Jorg Immendorf*, Kunsthalle Braunschweig, 1985.

Within and Beyond the Frame (detail), Oct-Nov 1973, work *in situ*, John Weber Gallery, New York

DANIEL BUREN
SIGN AND CONTEXT
An Art & Design *Interview*

– *Your materials have remained constant since 1965 – vertical stripes of canvas or paper, industrially produced, alternately white and coloured, or alternating stripes of white and transparent plastic. What determined your choice of this vertically striped and coloured material?*

What I should first of all say is that the 'material' which I have been using continually since 1965 was never chosen to be used for so long, nor was it planned for some foreseen project. It is through constantly renewed experience that it is used today and this has occurred for many reasons, none of which imply that it will be the same in the months or years to come. I started to use material with white and coloured stripes purely by chance when I noticed that this particular material had all the qualities and characteristics which the painting I was doing at the time couldn't bring together. Choosing this material made me take a decisive step towards clarifying the subject I wanted to put forward; to show simultaneously 'painted' painting, and that to which the painting is applied and how. Consequently the work progressed; the striped cotton material evolved into other materials which took on the same 'pattern'. It was first of all printed or silk-screened onto paper, then onto cellophane, then sticky-back plastic, then painted onto glass, then wood, steel, stone; then it was engraved and sanded, sewn, stuck, cut etc . . . The only constant elements are the spaces between each stripe, which, since the beginning, have been 8.7cm wide with a maximum/minimum play of 0.03cm, the alternation of one white and one coloured or transparent stripe and the way that, placed on to vertical surfaces, the direction of the stripes is always vertical. If they are on the floor or ceiling they obviously have no predetermined direction. The choice of verticality is due to the wish to avoid the least possible 'accident' in the reading of the work, to leave a foreign 'mark' on the support or on the worked space and to 'say' as little as possible. Put horizontally for example onto a vertical wall, the 'dialogue' between the two opposites already says more than the mix of 'vertical on verticality'. Moreover, man is an upright, vertical animal and it is to him that the work is addressed first of all.

– *By reducing the medium of painting to its minimum in terms of visual communication, do you conceive your canvases as neutral 'signs', as being 'worth nothing' in an autonomous sense, yet focusing attention on and questioning the context of art, the spatial and temporal conditions under which the work is exhibited?*

Exactly, and in any case, your question leads me further – thanks to the material we were just talking about – to discuss the possibility of reading a place and making a place read. Is it a real space, or simply a wall before which to read or to decipher an object produced and defined as a work of art? Indeed, it is because the 'sign' used is not, in itself, the carrier of any particular or specific meaning that it can take one on, in a way that is both precise, original and different each time, according to the way it plays once it is applied and used. The vertical stripes – and I can never stress this enough – do not show themselves as first themselves, they are never autonomous, but are always primarily seen in relation to . . . , in contact with . . . , in conflict with . . . , in harmony with . . . , perturbed by . . . , defined by . . . , constructed on . . . , made with . . . , defining this . . . , defining that . . . , etc.

– *How significant is the context of an artwork in terms of how the work is viewed and the message transmitted? Do you see the artwork as being subordinate to the site, its visual effect and message determined by its context?*

In most cases, there is a conflict between the context of the work of art and the work. I think that this is where a fundamental inadequacy can arise, to the misguided impediment of art historians and other critics who never talk about the context and generally behave as if either the reception place came 'from itself or as if it didn't exist. The reason that this block occurs regarding the place is understandable, but start thinking about it and you will see that the whole of Western art history needs rethinking. For one thing, you will notice that very often the work is subordinate to the site and to its context and that its message is completely twisted for the benefit of whatever (visual) discourse dominates at the time. Site and context are used here in their wider sense: architecture, the cultural importance and accumulation – or not – of different works, price of the work, etc. This is not necessarily serious as long as one doesn't believe in the autonomy of the work of art in general and as long as one ceases to apply the exclusive viewpoint that a hypothetical autonomy could give. Most works of art, having been formed in the real or feigned ignorance of their constraints, can only be appreciated on condition that one totally ignores the context and the place in which these works are presented. This is of course from where the arguments for art for art's sake, the autonomy of art, etc, stem.

– *When operating* in situ, *what characteristics of the site do you examine (the surrounding space, the architecture, the arrangement of rooms, windows, stairs, lighting, etc)? Does each site represent a new challenge in terms of the situational conditions?*

It's very difficult for me to answer this as I do not have, nor do I apply, a system. Absolutely everything, from the architecture to the collection if there is any, from the time of year to the outlook and attitudes of the gallery director can be the beginnings of a work. For these reasons, every new place allows for a new work, or at least has the potential for one; something I might add that can be triggered off by the same place when one is working there for the 2nd, 3rd, or even the 10th time.

– *How important is time in the context of your exhibitions? In what ways do you dictate the temporal conditions? How important to you is the notion of the temporary, as opposed to the permanent?*

Time is as important for me as the place. Moreover the two are totally inseparable. Obviously, time is not a notion that is always as perceptible as the object produced in time. Besides, space time is a space that is far more unforeseeable than the 24 hours in the day that materialise it. Space time is like a gas! Both are compressible and elastic. From there, the notions of temporality and permanence are nothing less than subjective. And to begin in

Sans Titre (detail), 1966, paintings on different fabrics with white and coloured stripes, L'atelier-cave, Cité des Fleurs à Paris

a general way, what is the permanence of works of art in general, that is, works whose goal, whose highest aspiration is to be eternal? Compared to the history of humanity, what remains of it is very meagre indeed. Compared to the history of the universe, the art history which has reached us is less long again than an exhibition visible for only two months and then disappearing, in relation to the artist's total life's production. Now, for everyone, the history of art is eternal and a two month exhibition is temporary. These notions of the temporary and permanence hold little interest for me. What does interest me is the appropriateness at which one can arrive as regards the relationship of a work X makes, and the time of its material existence. For example, the appropriateness of a piece of work which has to be carried out for a duration of two months, between the time it takes to create it, its price and the time it takes to destroy it. When I say appropriateness I don't mean that there must be one only and perfect appropriateness. What I mean is that all the parameters that I have just indicated for a work which has to be seen for two months will 'colour' and will induce the understanding of the work. The greater or more extreme the distortion, in relation to all these parameters, the more the discourse which the work will open will be obliterated by these tensions. I'll give you two examples to clarify what I've just said. On the one hand we have a work made with extremely fragile materials which deteriorates quickly and which provokes – even because of its fragility – great admiration. The artist allows its sale, and we then see the irony of all 20th-century art which consists of preserving what are technically speaking 'unpreservable' pieces in museums. The museum must make an effort in the way of money, care, etc . . . in order to preserve something that may not want to be preserved. On the other hand, I can give you certain works by Christo as concrete examples. Here we have an activity which is an uphill struggle, occasionally procedures which require years, millions of dollars, hundreds, even thousands of people for the preparation and logistics of the work, all of which will last a few hours, a day or a fortnight at most. In these two examples, whatever the work might intrinsically signify, the extreme distortion between their time of being seen and their time of production will produce a discourse on that very distortion. Unless it is not wanted, such a discourse is extremely damaging in relation to the work itself. As for myself, I think that each work, as it is physically limited by a place on which it depends and simultaneously transforms, must

Permutations 7 days – 6 replacements – 7 colours, 1973, work *in situ*, Halifax, Nova Scotia, Canada

be coherent with the exhibition place. Therefore I would say that my work is neither *a priori* ephemeral, nor permanent, but flexible and different according to the length of time it is being exhibited. The *Place des Colonnes* at the Moderna Museet, which was shown for some three months, was in wood and fabric and the whole thing was destroyed after the exhibition. The *Deux Plateaux* square at the Palais Royal in Paris, which has been there for some ten years, is in marble, cement and steel. According to the criteria which I apply to my procedure, the opposite is totally incoherent.

– *Are the light conditions under which a work is exhibited another factor that determines the perception of art? Is this the thinking behind your 1974 installation* Transparency, *in which attention is focused on the gallery windows?*

Of course light determines the way in which a work is perceived. I personally prefer natural to artificial, electric light, the main reason being that artificial light in museums and galleries is average, if not totally mediocre. Natural light is on the whole better, but institutions generally do their best to camouflage it. I have worked a lot with light in many different opposing ways. The exhibition you have just mentioned is one example.

– *By disrupting and 'interfering' with the conditions under which an artwork is perceived, are you criticising, commenting on, questioning, or simply rendering visible (in a neutral sense) the factors that determine the way in which art is seen? Lyotard has described your work as 'struggling against the "boundaries" imposed on vision by the art institution'. Would you agree with this statement?*

If I can view my work objectively, I would say that this is true, it has happened and continues to happen in successive phases. Lyotard's comment also seems absolutely correct.

– *In* Within and Beyond the Frame, *installed inside and outside the John Weber Gallery in New York, in 1973 and 1978, were you questioning and dissolving the boundaries (signified by the window) between the art institution and the public street, or were you drawing attention to the difference involved in the perception of an artwork according to its context? In the context of the urban street, did you see the suspended canvas as a sign, comparable to a street or advertising sign?*

Here again I would say 'all at the same time!' If the interior and exterior are put in relation to each other, this opens up a series of questions and paradoxes that this piece would certainly open as

Above and Below: Del colore dell' Architettura (Partie I: Pittura sopra pittura) (detail), June-Oct 1988, Galerie Tucci Russo, Turin

well. On the other hand, made identically (with the same elements renewed in five-year intervals) they accentuated other differences (while remaining quasi-identical); for example the internal transformations of the gallery (the disappearance of all the windows facing the street as if by chance!) and the extraordinary transformation of the area itself, *ie* Soho. As for the second part of your question, I would say that even if, installed as the piece was, it made a sign, this could in no way be confused with an advertising or street sign. At best – or worst – the exterior part of the work might make one imagine washing on a line, washing that one might see in the area, but in courtyards, never out in a public space.

– *The advertising billboard, situated in an urban street context, has also been the context for your art. In installations such as* Position-Proposition *(Mönchengladbach, 1980), were you questioning the effects of visual communication and the sign, in the context of art and commercial advertising?*

It's true that advertising billboards have often been of use to me. It was even the first exterior medium that I used in my first experiments outside the studio at the end of 1967. I found this medium extraordinary, they were real 'paintings' in the town as

regards their format and framing. On the other hand, what I found less extraordinary was that it permitted me – without permission of course! – to work directly and without any kind of guilt. This partly answers your question. I used a medium reserved for advertising and/or political slogans on which to apply/glue something (covering it in a fragmentary way or completely) which also said practically nothing, neither as an image, nor about the author, nor about his intentions. It was in complete contrast to advertising, but also as visible; generally well-placed and in the centre of town. If one wanted to extrapolate somewhat, these actions 'said' nothing; by completely mutilating or camouflaging the text and images which were on these billboards, they criticised the advertising which was on them by nullifying them. It is a limited gesture against the emission of all these mercantile slogans in everyday life, a 'plastic' reaction against society, or a sort of 'cleaning' of the image at the level of the city. I think this idea exists somewhat in the museum, even when it concerns the works within it. In no way does it have to do with a visual competition with advertising signs; on the contrary, although on their own ground, it is a completely paradoxical, even contradictory discourse.

Above and Below: 4 couleurs pour un patio (details), June-Aug 1988, work *in situ*, Porin Tadeimuseo, Pori, Finland

– Steps, both in the street and in the gallery or museum, have acted as a recurrent context for your art, in works such as Up and down, in and out *(Chicago, 1977) and* 99 escaliers *(Spolète, 1981). What is the thinking behind these temporary installations? are you again questioning boundaries and oppositions, marking what is often an 'invisible' functional context, as is also the case in* 90 chaises *(Venice, 1980)?*

Firstly, these propositions are not always 'ephemeral' or' temporary'. For example – and this completes one of my previous answers – *Up and down, in and out, step by step* is a piece that was finally bought by the Art Institute of Chicago. What were they buying? What were they preserving? They were buying a piece that will exist (1) as long as the Art Insitute remains as it is and as long as its architecture keeps the same characteristics as those which allowed the entry of this work; and (2) this piece will really 'exist' for as long as it is shown, which is true for all works forming part of the collection of a museum as well as the work in question, if they are not presented, nor 'existing' in the reserve. The museum only preserves a 'usage' which allows it, according to the instructions, to 'reconstruct' the work when it sees fit. With each work of this kind, a number of rules are enacted and accepted by the buyer. For example, here, the colour of the piece could never be the same more than once. Every new presentation will be another colour. The museum must also keep a record with a sample of every colour used as long as the museum functions. Other clauses indicate that for example no one can ever replace this piece with a photograph, drawing or text of it. It therefore can only be reconstructed or not exist at all. To my knowledge, this piece, made in 1977 and bought by the museum around 1981-82, has never been reconstructed to this day!

The idea of using risers of steps came to me for a variety of reasons. One was the discovery of spaces, which in this instance were extremely important and significant. For me, those spaces where the work in general is not expected to be seen are as interesting as those which are reserved for works of art, namely picture rails. One of the other reasons is that which consists of visually marking a place which 'signifies' when it would only want to be necessary, even ornamental. Indeed, it's not for nothing that a certain type of museum allows its collection to be seen only after one has climbed a series of steps just before the entrance and then in the interior. This obligatory 'climb' towards

7 bouquets dans Vienne (detail), July-Aug 1988, work *in situ*, Vienne, France

the work says a great deal. At Spoleto, the reasons are very different. Seeing the incredible amount of different steps, marking them signals one of the characteristics of the city, contrasting architectural differences which are read far better by the user if visually underlined. The chairs in Venice were concerned with something different, even though there was a similarity regarding their exclusive connection with the context in question. Indeed during the Biennale, when they were set up, the organisers decided to forbid any work to be done outside the buildings, in order to take the opposite course to what they had been doing for the last ten years. As a response to this new regulation, I decided to use the chairs that were in the cafeteria of the International Pavilion, chairs which were by definition in the interior and exterior of the buildings: a supremely unexpected space at which many people sat without even realising that it was one of the exhibited works. Relating to this one will notice that many of my works are ambivalent, above all those which utilise places, spaces or objects which function in a certain way or for certain reasons. In all these cases, the functions of the place, the space or the object, are respected.

– Lyotard sees your art as an 'inquiry' or 'experiment' that 'exists in locating the conductors' that affect the viewing process, defining them in terms of oppositions: 'inside/outside', 'present/absent', 'now/before-after', 'durable/ephemeral', etc. Do you conceive your work in terms of oppositions; and have Lyotard's philosophical texts affected your thinking and writing in any way?

I don't consider my work in terms of oppositions even if I am forced to say that very often the questions asked and my way of solving or answering them opens the door to a series of paradoxes. As for J F Lyotard's texts, I wouldn't be able to say to what extent they have affected or could affect my work, but they undoubtedly do, along with certain others like Gilles Deleuze and Blanchot etc, which form part of the basis and are indicators of my thought and sensibility.

– In your recent installations, you have 'intervened' in the space and structure of the museum or gallery, deconstructing the contextual fabric of the exhibition space (Venice, 1986), or completely covering the walls of a gallery (Los Angeles, 1990). Does the latter work signify the most recent direction in your thinking?

It's impossible to answer this question. Is the reason because the development of any work is not linear? I would say that it is very jerky and proceeds by incessant comings and goings. A detail of a work from 15 years ago (a detail which didn't seem especially important at the time or which completely escaped me) may be the principal 'theme' of a work made today. There isn't therefore one direction towards which I will be conscious of reaching (even if it exists despite myself), but many directions at the same time which are successively taken up, abandoned, taken up again, etc.

– Are there any artists whose work has influenced your thinking and practice?

Of course. The list would be long and the degree of importance of each name would be different. There are those whose work I admire but of whom I think that no influence is visible or exists in my own work. The opposite is also equally true. There are artists whose work and attitude I detest, yet who are a great influence as they serve as boundaries for exactly that which should never be done; they're even there for one to avoid going completely wrong. Their influence is therefore paradoxically extremely important. I won't give you names as I could only, given the time, give you a list without explaining the particular reasons pertaining to each of the people named. As much as I think we can draw lessons from reasons, they can also quite simply be stupid.

– What relationship exists between your installations and your writings; do you see them as two distinct disciplines? Do you see the written text as another factor instrumental in controlling the viewing process?

I have already explained that and I would briefly say that my writing and my visual work are two totally different, separated disciplines. For me, visual work always initiates and allows if the case arises, a reflection of a written type. Never the contrary. However, once the text has been written, I think – even if that wasn't the first intention – that it can help, if not control the visual process of the work. But it can fade on the one hand to the texts that nobody wants or which are not useful on the subject of the work, and on the other hand attempts to counter-balance those that are often difficult to digest, products of habitual criticism. Only in this sense are they an attempt to control other's texts which are by definition uncontrollable.

Following and to be followed (detail), Dec 1978, work *in situ*, Galerie Peter Nadin, New York

Paolo Laudisa, *Untitled*, 1988, oil

ANTONIO D'AVOSSA
CONCEPTUAL ANALYSIS
Young Artists in the 80s

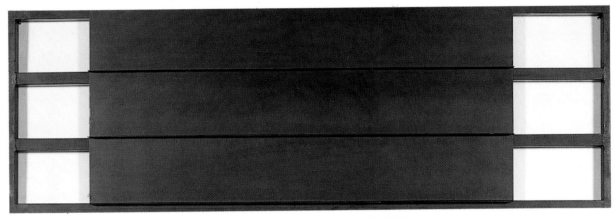

Carlo Guaita, *Paesaggio*, 1989, iron, 60x180x7cm

Arte Povera, Minimalism and Conceptualism are the main art-historical experiences that young Italian artists are turning to most frequently and with renewed interest today. This does not mean that we find ourselves once more in a revival of quotations from the past as happened with the Transavanguardia. The gaze of Italian artists of this most recent generation is not the kleptomaniac's

gaze, although it is simultaneosly reflective, slow and quick. It is a look at ideas and not gestures, that is, an uncertain look towards the questions of the genesis of the work of art which return to the control of space and of reality in its occurrence as a reduced presence.

Any analysis of the full spectrum of artworks by the recent generations of Italian artists cannot avoid looking at the success and international rise of the Transavanguardia. Sandro Chia, Francesco Clemente, Enzo Cucchi, Nicola De Maria and Mimmo Paladino, the protagonists of the great season of the Transavanguardia and of international Neo-Expressionism, became the principal points of reference for young Italian artists of the early 80s. The return to traditional painting and sculpture imposed by the practices of these artists has however brought with it the dangers of a sort of 'trashcan' following which has seen three successive waves of the Transavanguardia pass by. Figurative nomadism, stylistic eclecticism, wild expressionism which were the expressive styles in the Transavanguardia have with the academicism of its followers become areas of perversion, fulfilment and pictorial orgy.

Now the new generation of Italian artists, growing tired of this facile way of making art, is changing direction and moving towards a renewed need for rigour of design and away from Expressionism. Over the last year the end, therefore, of the

Transavanguardia and the beginning of a new situation has become gradually more obvious, marked by the resumption of analysis and mental attitudes towards making art today.

Even the location of the art market and centres of artistic activity have undergone a notable change. The birth of new galleries in the great centres, which prefer to work with young artists promoting them in the marketplace, the growing lack of interest in exhibitions put on by the large Italian galleries and the increasingly close attention paid to the work of new galleries, especially in Milan, Turin and Florence, must all be noted. Thus the primacy of Rome as the nerve centre of Italian art, which has lasted since the 60s is also waning, giving way to a situation which reveals young Roman artists, with some exceptions, as backward and conservative compared to what is happening at the same time amongst artists in Milan and Turin. At the front line of this change of generation are new galleries such as Marconi 17, FacSimile, De Carlo, Le Case d'Arte, Grazia Terribile, Studio Guenzani, Piero Cavellini, Studio Casoli and Diagramma in Milan; V S V, Weber and Paludetto in Turin; Carini and Vivita in Florence; Lidia Carrieri and Il Ponte in Rome; Lucia Scalise in Naples; new critics (often linked to art journals and who bring to the front the work of the young artists who work with the new galleries) and, finally, of course, the new artists themselves.

Augusto Brunetti's work is both 'povera' and Minimalist at

Marco Mazzucconi, *Paisley*, 1987, cut iron 150x180cm

the same time. He works on a geometric scheme exalted by compositional modularity. The use of 'poor' materials and their repeated assemblage across modules of square forms installed along the courses of the exhibition space renders the work extremely analytical of its relationship to external and internal space. The geometric repetition put into action suggests a solution to the changing/constant and continuous/discontinuous relationships.

Maurizio Camerani creates his video installations through the casual use of solar panels. In this way, in the inner workings of the piece, there is a kind of internal circuit that does not permit the image to invade the technical sphere. The video work is therefore in perfect equilibrium with both its container and support. In his work, there is a tautological equation which is fundamental in the overcoming of the old way of organising video-sculpture. His work is a unique example of this within the Italian art scene.

Silvio Wolf uses the photographic medium to create a virtual re-presentation of light. His work is the result of a project which is spacial and temporal at the same time. The visual icon is the light itself, its own imprisonment. Eventually, the adjustments of

a binary system make his project, from the point of view of the construction of the image, a true analysis of the icon-figure and of its debate, by resetting the instrument that brings it to view.

The influence of the installations of the 'poveristi' is very marked in the work of Mauro Folci who combines sheets of glass with forms worked in iron. His objects, with a technological foundation, have the capacity to shift effects towards the form-content bases of architecture: wood, stone and clay. Putting these elements into action suggests the volume of the transparent medium (glass) as the space to make sculpture in the difficult matter of the concept of volume. The glass in his work thus becomes the object and subject of the reality of art as we see it every day.

Carlo Guaita constructs structures in iron to delimit the physical space of his work, which he calls 'additions'. Their Minimalist origins are obvious even with chance modification. The elements of the construction rest against the wall or the floor and are controlled on the base of the serial combination. There is an order which recalls the logic of geometric abstraction in its denial of every linguistic spontaneity. Finally, there is almost the capacity to affect the postulates of the sculpture suggesting a

Mauro Folci, *Nel perimetro della negazione l'idea al cubo*, 1989, wall painting, steel, slate, 230x230x85cm

strategy of transgression and play on ratios, balance and modular progression.

Massimo Kaufmann is the most acclaimed Conceptualist on the entire Italian scene. His work is raised in lack of concern with materials for the surrender an idea of analysis of the linguistic conventions of creating art. The constant use of weights and measures suggests the standard cultural convention of the unit of measurement as the mental space which accompanies aesthetic judgement in the terms of the practice of art. It is work which marks itself as reflective of paradox and rhetorical representation. Paolo Laudisa makes painting a meditative exercise. The stratification of the colours often accompanies the folds which the canvasses seem to construct. All this is in a pictorial process which marries design and sensitivity; its basis clearly analytical towards the instruments of picture-making.

The traditional materials of picture-making (canvas and frame) and sculpture (wood and cement) are used by Saverio Lucariello to depart from every recognisable scheme of painting and sculpture. His work, certainly among the most unusual, shares the intention of great architecture which empties and fills space, organises and disrupts it, to reconstruct instead a directionless journey through the transparency and solidity of the materials.

Marco Mazzuconi has deliberately chosen to utilise the inexpressiveness of abstraction and is indifferent to which medium he uses in the elaboration of his project. All the elements already exist, from the brandnames of merchandise to the floor of a mosque, from the writing to the ranges of colours, all that is needed is their material and mechanical articulation in a regular presentation of the object constructed in this way as sculpture in iron or as film glued on sheets of aluminium.

Gabriele di Matteo investigates ways of overturning the structure of the common perception of the image. The choice, what is withdrawn, enlargements, repetitions, all seem to retain, yet change the meaning of the original image. The image in turn is removed from its original placement through the use of a scanner-chrome. Images of paintings, engravings and photographs of their graphic reproductions, when spaced out or changed in scale, begin to assume a different perceptive impact. The concept of simulation is thus substituted by a sort of death of the image.

With the work of Alfredo Pirri one can see the first Italian example of a modification of art towards a new constructive

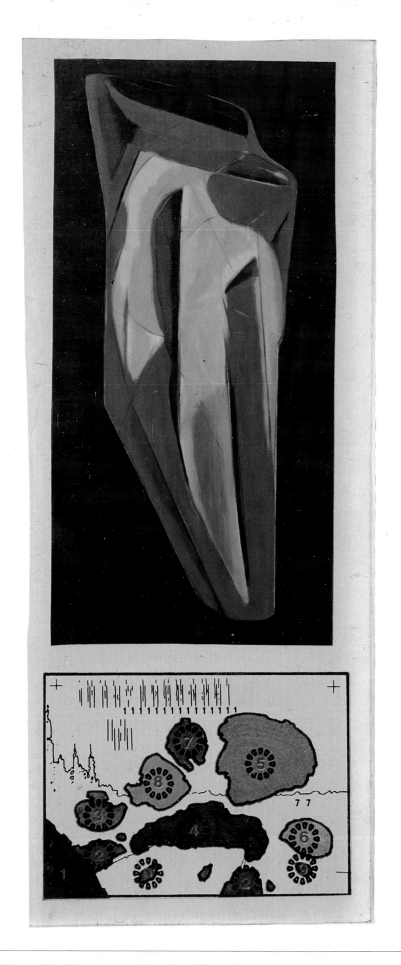

Michelangelo Tomarchio Levi, *Of the Distance and the Dispersion*, 1988, acrylic on board with elements in steel and polycarbonate.

analysis. His work is characterised by the enigmatic figure of the circle and the use of painted wood in its formal synthesis of smooth surface barely touched by the signs of painting. In this sense, he constructs the figure of the circle as in an art which finds itself in the fundamentality of forms. His recent works suggest instead repeated but not modular reflection on the places of the effect. The breaks-frames turn inside themselves to colour the walls against which the form rests. With this work we enter into the sphere of overcoming Minimalism and Conceptualism.

Michelangelo Tomarchio Levi discovers the possibility of an organic development of subterranean energies to technological order through his repetition of form in painting. His constructions, whilst suggesting technical schemes are totally emptied of iconic references and present themselves as such in an extreme combination of a painting and sculpture, but always in the emptiness of making and in the fullness of the practice of art meant as the development of an idea.

We cannot exclude from this survey other artists who work in similar directions defined by attitudes of analysis, mental and material. These are young artists who are changing the image of an Italian art that has been wrapped up in a pictorial orgy of Neo-Expressionism. They also come from situations different from the Roman one, they present themselves as the most precise trend in young Italian art. Stefano Arienti has fixed his ideas on folded paper; Fausto Bentasa presents works which lie between neo-geometry and Neo-Conceptualism; Luigi Carboni organises his installations with painting and warm materials; Manlio Caro-preso constructs chance volumes and forms with sheets of aluminium; Antonio Catelani analyses the uncertainty of the space which holds his sculpture; Daniela De Lorenzo organises repeated structures on the variations of volumes; Antonio Di Palma works in coloured wood; Chiara Dynys finds a new way of making paintings by moulding her canvasses outside and inside; Amedeo Martegani has placed the idea of the image inside the ready-made object; Nicola Ponzio has made the use of extremely diverse materials his particular speciality; Luca Quartana merges conceptual ideas and the relationships between poor materials; Oliviero Rainaldi is in the clear position of revitalising Arte Povera; Luigi Stoisa treats a Minimalist idea with 'poor' or simple subjects; Carmine Tornincasa renders the reading of space possible in a revival of Classical sculpture.

But if young Italian art is no longer to be found in the area of quotation and Post-Modernism, in which direction is it going? In my opinion the renewal of certain more rigorous styles is a general symptom of the need for a commitment to thought in art and, therefore, its practices, which while assimilating all the cynicism and eclecticism of Pop Art and the Transavanguardia considers it right to take up the diligence and analysis of Arte Povera and Conceptualism. Perhaps we find ourselves confronted by the first orphan generation of Joseph Beuys and Andy Warhol. Do we find before us an attempt to reconcile design and sensitivity? In my opinion, this is the general tendency of young Italian art. A tendency which deep down has forgotten nothing and which nevertheless will not be encumbered by memory.

Marco Mazzucconi, *Ads for an identity*, 1991, photograph on aluminium, 125x130cm

Richard Long, *A Clearing, A Six Day Walk in the Hoggar, The Sahara*, 1988

V

SCULPTURE AND EARTHWORKS

Georg Herold, *Globus*, 1986, mixed media (detail)

NEW GERMAN SCULPTURE

THE LEGACY OF BEUYS

Andreas Franzke

Rebecca Horn, *Pendulum with India Yellow Pigment*, 1986, installation, Theatre Steinhof Festival, Vienna

Within the enormously broad range of contemporary art, probably no artist has had as lasting an influence as Joseph Beuys. His work has had a formative impact on very different modes of artistic expression over the last three decades and it is primarily due to him that a broader public first became more aware of artistic questions. By sparking off such controversies over his work and his

person, he gave rise to the discussion on current trends. Moreover, the enormous influence he achieved as an artist has not diminished, it is still as alive and potent as ever. Beuys was both a driving force and catalyst for artistic perspectives and developments. He had a unique ability to attract generations of young sculptors, painters, performance and video artists as well as representatives of the literary and music scene and stimulate them in their own work. Innumerable artists had to face up to the questions Beuys raised, in order to find their own way in a scene that was characterised by a great range of information and a corresponding openness in its media. Beuys' attraction as an artist was not limited to German art; he had an international reputation.

Much as those who knew him personally were fascinated by Beuys, his personality and influence were not limited to his immediate circle and pupils, but affected the thinking of a whole generation. His influence extended beyond the art scene into social and political fields. This was largely due to the fact that Beuys naturally went beyond the narrow traditional limits of art, in both his impact and his work. He put into practice – preferably with direct participation by the public – his vision of a link between art and life, which was his central intellectual concern, manifesting an artistic approach which included the whole of human existence.

Beuys' public involvement was not only part of his effect, it was a way to widen the artistic means of expression which he so emphatically strove for. Simply the consistent use of actions as an instrument, for example, ensured that his work was not only seen by a small circle of initiates but achieved a considerable impact on the public at large. Interestingly, Beuys began his career as a sculptor, but he soon moved beyond the traditional limits of the medium to find new forms of sculptural activity and thought. Installations and performances quickly replaced traditional material. In the course of his development, Beuys was not only to give major impulses to forms, but in his dedication to the objective of a creative expansion of the possibilities of the medium, he was also to demonstrate what importance the contemporary artist should attach to experiment and a permanent questioning of the results.

As far as the materials he used were concerned, his practice was extremely creative and adventurous. He moved forward into areas and used materials that had never been used in the context of art before, and imbued them with qualities that had an entirely new significance based on an intellectual concept.

It is only to be expected that with his wider vision of the pictorial means and his belief that the artist is absolutely free to use every conceivable material, Beuys would prove a particularly creative force in object art. His influence here was indeed

223

great and it was also extremely varied. It is basically due to him that subsequent artists began to question the medium of sculpture, to declare its technical, material, creative and aesthetic framework, until then subject to a relatively narrow, obsolete interpretation. In this context Beuys offered convincing examples in his own works, which could provoke and stimulate at the same time. His intellectual approach set standards in its political and social dimension. In retrospect, it is hardly surprising that at the end of the 60s when the political structures began to change, Beuys was a dominant and leading figure.

Beuys was not only a successful pioneer before his conflict with the authorities and the ensuing suspension of his teaching at the Düsseldorf Academy, but even when he could no longer hold a public teaching appointment, his influence if anything, grew.

It would be idle to list all the artistic movements and artists who have been influenced by Beuys, in their own work and the ideas on which they are based, or in their approach and attitude as artists. Without him the development of German art after the Second World War, its emancipation after years of isolation and finally its participation in major manifestations of the international avant-garde would have been very much less

that they are completely open in their choice of materials and methods, but for all of them the main artistic concern is an extremely severe conceptional and formal clarity.

The influence of Joseph Beuys is not equally evident in all of these artists, although in some way they are all influenced by his ideas and by his insistence on a completely open avant-garde that should include references outside art.

Most interesting are the object artists who took up what Beuys started but have taken this further independently and consistently, and reached solutions that on the one hand were influenced by Beuys and on the other have become almost completely emancipated from him.

In that context Reiner Ruthenbeck is particularly interesting. He was a pupil of Beuys at the Düsseldorf Academy, but his work soon led him to an individual statement. That applies both to the pictorial and material means which Ruthenbeck uses and to their aesthetic and intellectual purpose. Altogether Ruthenbeck's work is distinguished by a hermetic severity. It has an astonishing economy of very lapidary means and materials.

With this restriction the artist achieves a dense expression with a highly evocative aura. In the 60s, Ruthenbeck drew on

L to R: Reinhard Mucha, *Wartesaal* (detail); Felix Droese, *Five Silent Witnesses*, 1981, five wooden planks, 255x230x6cm

rich or extensive.

That applies particularly to object art and three-dimensional installations, where the German art scene has produced a number of outstanding contemporary figures who have won international recognition. They include such artists as Reinhard Mucha, Meuser, Harald Klingelhöller, Rosemarie Trockel, Georg Herold, Thomas Schütte, Hubert Kiecol, Katharina Fritsch and Bogomir Ecker, all born around 1950. Each of them has developed independent, individual formulations which are also characteristic of the state of German art today and are setting international standards. Their work generally combines a conceptual direction and the opposition this necessarily entails, with the expressive-figurative tendencies represented by artists of the same generation. Some of these object artists – and one could name others with similar artistic concerns – were pupils of Beuys or began their artistic development in an intellectual climate that depended on his powers of attraction and influence.

Refreshingly different as the works by these artists, who cannot really be called sculptors in the narrower sense, are, most of them have an obvious factor in common: namely that they all more or less explicitly involve space. Another common factor is

models in the Italian *Arte Povera* movement as well as Beuys' works in his choice of material. It is mainly his subsequent installations that distantly recall concepts from his teacher.

Ruthenbeck's latest works, spatially related constellations and individual objects, are of particularly disarming severity. The objects suggest familiarity and alienation at once; they are clearly identifiable as pieces of furniture, but they seem poetically alienated and distant from the everyday scene. Accordingly they imbue their surroundings with tension, they are disruptive factors in an artistically effective way. This observation also applies to the more severe concepts with minimal geometric structures. Entirely in the tradition of Beuys, Ruthenbeck has extended his three-dimensional pictorial repertoire to include kinetic effects, light, and tone. In that context too he has always been concerned to achieve extreme discipline and clarity.

Rebecca Horn did not study under Beuys. Since the early 70s she has produced a series of interesting works that are characterised by a high degree of independence and conviction. Initially she incorporated her own person in videos, and in that respect transmuted certain ideas of Beuys into an independent, highly suggestive vision in a way that is sovereign and reflective. But in her later work she has increasingly liberated herself from this approach without losing any intensity of expression.

Rebecca Horn's objects and installations have become more perfect and refined in the course of time, and the materials have taken on their own value and significance. Operated by invisible integrated motors, the objects become action in the room, and their secret functionalism is evocative of ritual. As with Beuys and yet in quite a different way, the objects are imbued with a mystical, obsessive aura. The technical perfectionism and the costly materials represent a distanced world in which raw materials and vehement impulses create a tension-laden contrast that abruptly shatters the suggestion of stillness.

In Reiner Ruthenbeck and Rebecca Horn, we have artists literally of the first hour as far as the influence of Beuys on three-dimensional art is concerned. We could name other representatives of that generation, among them the painters Palermo and Polke, both of whom realised some objects at an early stage that are clearly products of the climate created by Beuys in Düsseldorf. However, let us concentrate on those members of the contemporary scene who are particularly characteristic of the German object and space-related art of today.

works of this artist is their seeming triviality, both in regard to their pictorial means and in their contents. Herold thematicises specimen ideas and modes of thought of the anonymous everyman of our much-prized media age and transposes these with comparatively disarming banality into objects. His favourite materials are from the building industry, such as wooden slats and tiles. They are not of high quality, and this deliberate downplaying gives them an unexpected effect.

That is particularly evident in works in which he imitates contemporary technology in rough constructions using simple roofing lathes. The models literally mock the standard of such mechanisms and they are further alienated by the legends they bear and the labels that are applied.

Herold's objects and their statements are as foreign to normal ideas as are their materials. They are concepts that are open to experiment and demand from the viewer an active perception and intellectual penetration. The trivial language is only a means to undermine the worn-out language of conformism.

The deliberate faults in what should be perfection and the seeming lack of pictorial skills, that impression of improvisation in the work of Georg Herold, are in complete contrast to the

L to R: Bogomir Ecker, *Spring, Bell, Red Base*, 1986; Reiner Ruthenbeck, *Intersecting Blue, Red on Two Mirrors*, 1989, foil on mirror

Felix Droese, born in 1950, was a student of Beuys and Peter Brüning at the Düsseldorf Academy. Unlike Rebecca Horn, his objects and installations are not ritualistic and obsessive, they are symbolic and intense. Accusations of contemporary politics play a role, as do protests of modern conditions in general. Whether he is formulating his ideas in drawings, developing them in the form of monumental shadow-silhouettes cut out in paper, or building them up from worn-out objects and remnants he has found, Droese is always concerned with themes related to the responsibility and freedom of the individual, the human condition itself.

Like Beuys, Droese poses existential questions, he is concerned to articulate his position in his artistic work and take sides; he reacts to situations. He sees his artistic work as a way of making the present transparent for himself and others, of countering the world of technology and machines with something on the sensuous level. In that context his multi-part objects, made of a wide range of materials, have a very direct impact on the viewer; they challenge him directly to think it out for himself.

The works of Georg Herold are quite different, both in their ironic distance and in their formal language. Characteristic of the

perfection and precision displayed by Katharina Fritsch. Her replicas of objects or animals, her people made in series from one mould all have a striking anonymity. With their evident and emphatic perfection they make a particularly lasting impression.

While Katharina Fritsch takes the sphere of our collective everyday perception as occasion for her objects and installations, and confronts us with this, we experience them on the one hand as familiar things and on the other as alien ciphers that are further distanced by their artificiality and strangeness. They make us think, if only because of their presence outside their normal ambience, and they awaken memories. The artist offers us prototypes from the realm of our experience, but by shaping these to technical perfection and without any personal handwriting she makes them function as disruptive factors and so sets off a deliberately steered perception or gives rise to dreams.

Of all the artists who followed Beuys in moving away from the traditional practices of sculpture and as far as possible from formal aesthetic conventions, in order to realise a new three-dimensional pictoral language saturated with complex meaning, Reinhard Mucha has the greatest potential and intensity. His concern with collective history as the basic precondition for

Rosemarie Trockel, *Untitled (Amuse)*, 1989, glass, wood, linen, linen pillow, 121.3x47.6x47.6cm

coping with existence itself has opened entirely new perspectives for contemporary object and installation art.

Mucha's constructions – whether made of objects he has found or ordinary practical things – have a striking precision and severity. This artist consistently renounces anything casual, the position and role of every detail is calculated; the relations of elements that incorporate a historical reference and those that cite the present are subject to control. So it is only too understandable that the artist directly relates each of his installations in a new and unique way to the situation he has found, and is forced to modify them when they are exhibited again in order to adapt them to the new room in which they are to stand.

That consistency in itself shows how radically Mucha sees his concepts, how serious is his concern to create models of memories that have coalesced into pictures. In these memories, which he communicates through observed phenomena, he reflects himself; his struggle for acknowledgement of his own existence can be traced and it is at the same time hermetically embedded in the collective – and naturally a component related to the social element is also involved.

Meuser likewise attempts to come to terms with space in his works, and in their severely constructivist vocabulary of forms, his objects also indicate concern with phenomena of day-to-day visual experience and observations. The artist intensifies this in the individual piece or in tension-laden combinations, making them pregnant ciphers, whose significance combines technical elements with those that reflect an elementary sense of form.

The work of Meuser is based on the interaction of these two components. He was a pupil of Beuys at the Düsseldorf Academy, although today his origin in Beuys' class is hardly evident in his works. The artist has moved away from the influence of his teacher in a very characteristic and autonomous way and worked out for himself his own language of forms. It is related to the space around him, and to the intensive dialogue which Meuser's works conduct with the room in which they stand.

That applies under different conditions to the constructions of Harald Klingelhöller. They are much more speculative and artificial as is evident in the material he uses. This artist prefers to use cardboard, which he handles with great skill, building formal constellations which, although related to the interior, certainly have the power of unexpected monumentality.

Klingelhöller's repertoire of forms clearly points to a sign, to pictorial ciphers that are either geometric in origin or stand in relation to letters. They are always abstracts, basic elements of forms, concentrated on themselves, and often their pronouncements are influenced by the way they are arranged and varied. They are like elements of building blocks. The artist arranges and orders them so that allegorical references result, the attraction of which is greatly enhanced by the choice of title. In Klingelhöller's works, linguistic metaphors are transcended in sculptural manifestations. These are usually displayed inside a room but they can certainly have their effect in the open air.

Hubert Kiecol and Thomas Schütte have created sculptures and objects that are very precise, both formally and thematically. Both these artists are concerned with architecture. Kiecol, for instance, has repeatedly intensified basic architectural elements into block-like concrete sculptures. Although the reference to house types is very evident, the vivid impact of these works is their dominant characteristic. This is due on the one hand to the expressiveness of concrete as a material and secondly to the Cubist compactness.

Thomas Schütte has also used forms from architecture and everyday things which he models into objects. Some of his ironic and sophisticated objects could be enlarged and placed outdoors as 'monuments' and so directly confront the ambience on which they are ultimately based. More than Kiecol's works, those of Schütte definitely have a model character, and this is apparent even when the works are exhibited outdoors on an appropriately large scale. It is this model character which is their particular quality.

The constructive formal transparency that is characteristic of the work of Meuser and Klingelhöller is not the main concern of an artist like Rosemarie Trockel. She stresses the free availability of pictorial means and the contents of her work can range from a private mythology through the manifestation of philosophical, political and social contexts. Found objects, photomontages, castings, and copies of everyday objects are used by her as individual pieces or in combination to achieve extremely evocative results. Not infrequently her objects reflect the stimulus of Beuys, in their combinative approach and even faintly in the materials used as well.

The works of Rosemarie Trockel are distinguished by their high degree of sensuality. This gives them their unmistakeable penetration and it also provides the basis for expression through artistic means of the questions that keep pressing to the fore with an evocative insistence. Rosemarie Trockel succeeds in realising an imaginative depiction of her private ideas, and views the object in a way that is at once very general but also laden with secret emotion, with its sensuous radiation. That she is very adventurous and unconventional in her choice of means definitely helps her suggestive artistic vision. In addition, the variety of media she uses – here too she is in the Beuys tradition – permits her to tackle politically-oriented contents directly and communicate these through emblems that are decipherable.

Not least in respect to its general reference to Beuys, the monumental three-dimensional work *The High Priestess,* which Anselm Kiefer completed in 1989, is of particular interest, although it is rooted in a fascinating way in the pictorial language of Kiefer's paintings. It is impressive to see how the artist has intensified his vocabulary of the monumental in presenting about 200 lead books in two mighty steel bookcases. Each of the huge folios is so heavy that several people are needed to lift and move it. On the leaden pages of the books the artist has stuck photos, clay and hairs, in some he has even pressed peas into the pages. He has also used torn-out scraps of newspaper and exposed the metal plates to the weather before he worked on them, laying them out of doors or in the studio to let them take imprints. Accidental markings, history, the atmosphere, allegorical elements, general and personal things, the original material and speculation are all combined, absorbed and sublimated in an artistic concept.

Characteristically the shelves bear the inscriptions 'Euphrates' and 'Tigris'. It is a reference to the legendary area with its two rivers, that existed before Classical Antiquity, in which the forces collected there would remain powerful through all time.

Lead played a part in Kiefer's pictures before *The High Priestess.* He used the same metal for his only other free-standing sculpture, made in 1985, a winged palette. Lead suggests a heavy finality and it also conveys the impression of sacred determinedness. This is what communicates itself to the viewer in the new work. He stands before the powerful manifestation of an intellectualised attempt to illuminate existence that has found expression in art. His reaction can at first only be intuitive, before it stimulates him to collect his perception and reflection, and with emotional and psychological determination, to face up to the challenge of this work.

Within the new and latest sculpture the object dominates, objects occur in an extreme variety of forms and, whether as individual pieces or installations, most of them are designed in close relation to their surrounding space. Moreover, among the three-dimensional works made in the last few years, a conceptual approach, oriented to powerful forms with a differentiated

Harald Klingelhöller, *Above L to R*: *Schlaf tief* (Sleep deeply); *Das Unheil soll menschliche Züge haben* (Disaster should have human features);
Below: *Ich bin hier, Du bist hier* (I am here you are here), 1989, cardboard, cast iron, steel, mirror

choice of material predominates. New media are certainly used and these artists are particularly free and inventive in their use of found objects and references to the process of civilisation.

That is particularly impressive in Reinhard Mucha's work. The precision of his formal economy and the intellectual penetration of the contents of his model-like objects convince with their concentrated visual force, in which collective experiences are surprisingly directly present. Their anonymity works like a glass in which personal elements collect and are reflected back onto the viewer. Mucha always feels unsure whether he should see the banal objects only as facts in space or identify their language with more complex recollections.

Mucha seeks a very exact relation to space, and the same can be said of the installations by Rebecca Horn, although she uses different means. Her materialised and mechanised obsessive rituals transform the space to a stage. It becomes a major partner and a factor that plays a decisive part in the effect. Rosemarie Trockel, on the other hand, does not seek a comparable spatial relation in most of her three-dimensional works. Her main concern is to convey the contents. Her statement can be experienced without being fixed to any specific spatial conditions. Anselm Kiefer's first great sculptural work should actually be seen in the same context. That is probably also due to the fact that it is closely related, in both its iconography and its material formulation, to the artist's painting. *The High Priestess* must be seen as the work of a painter, who has opened new perspectives of expression by moving into a medium that he does not normally use.

Since the late 19th century the most important painters of the modern movement have successfully taken the same step, and Kiefer has taken it with a kind of assemblage that, taken purely externally, does recall Beuys. This is evident in the use of shelves and rough material, although Kiefer has transmuted the ideas of his former teacher into his own imagination, which is full of history and myths, in a very complex way.

The influence of Joseph Beuys, which finds expression more in the intellectual climate than in a formal or aesthetic sense, has proved extraordinarily stimulating on a whole generation of three-dimensional artists. Many of them have already won international recognition, particularly the German object artists. Those born around 1950 clearly reveal their intellectual and artistic heritage in their concepts and installations. But that has certainly not prevented them from finding independent solutions. It is evident that exciting and highly relevant works, determining their position in regard to pictorial problems, are to be expected of them in the future.

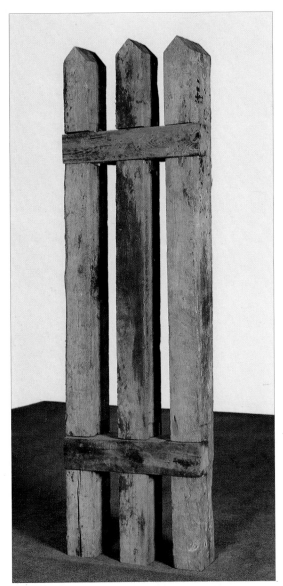 

L to R: Hubert Kiecol, *Untitled*, 1983, three joined wooden beams, 260x74.5x21cm; Meuser, *Monument for the 24 November 1983*, 1983, iron, 219x94x94cm

Anish Kapoor, *Black Earth*, 1983, polystyrene, cement, earth, acrylic medium and pigment, four parts, 259x571.5x236cm overall.
'I am Indian but to see everything in terms of nationality is limiting. I don't see myself as an Indian Artist; neither do I see myself as a British artist. I am an artist who works in Britain. The work has to be looked at from as wide a base as possible. If we accept that Western culture is in crisis, then there are some issues which throw this into relief. For example, decoration in Indian art is written into a philosophical view of the world. It is about abundance, fecundity, about the world as a generative unity. Taken out of context in the West it is merely decorative, there is no other way of dealing with it. This is bound to change though. By the year 2000 there will be around 50 million non-European people living in Europe. Let's hope they define a new art that will state itself forcefully in the mainstream.'
From an interview with Majorie Allthorpe-Guyton, 1990

MARY ROSE BEAUMONT
NEW DIRECTIONS IN INTERNATIONAL SCULPTURE

Christian Boltanski, *Bougies*, 1987-88, five figurines in painted leather with metal supports

The main problem when discussing new international sculpture is its sheer diversity. One may attempt to categorise it, which is fairly futile, since no artist can be confined within any one category. However, futile or not, I am going to map out some broad areas, if only to make it easier to read the contemporary scene. One can say with muted conviction that some sculptors incline to classicism,

others to the romantic and organic. More confidently, one can assert that architecture, not for the first time, has dictated sculptural forms; the best of architectonic furniture-sculpture is very elegant, the worst resembles children's building blocks. Installations fall into a nebulous area somewhere between architecture and performance.

The sculptor who seems, at the time of writing, to bestride the narrow world like a Colossus is Richard Serra, whose work defies easy categorisation. From Kassel and Munster, to Paris, London and New York, Serra's sculptures are ubiquitous. Massive and threatening, they sometimes seem like bully-boys, battering the viewer into submission. Yet, despite or perhaps because of the permanent nature of the steel in which they are constructed, they inspire feelings of insecurity and unease, partly because of the fearful angle at which the elements are poised, or, as in *House of Cards (One Ton Prop)*, 1968-69 (Saatchi Collection), where the sheets of steel are merely propped against each other, they make one feel that a mere sneeze might cause them to slide, slicing off one's feet.

Serra has made many site-specific works which have been variously received. His *Tilted Arc* in Foley Square, Manhattan, attracted vituperative comment from those who worked in the vicinity, which was countered with equal ferocity by the artist. His sculpture for Saint Louis, Missouri, also aroused contro-

versy, but the length of the gestation period allowed the citizenry to voice their objections and to accept what appeared to be the inevitable. The situation in Paris was different, *Clara Clara* should have been installed at the Pompidou Centre for the Serra exhibition there, but the foundations were found to be inadequate. The sculpture was moved, on a temporary basis, to the Tuileries Gardens where, situated on the axis which runs from the Louvre to the Arc de Triomphe, it proved to be extraordinarily appropriate. The piece has now been bought by the city of Paris and re-erected at another location.

For *Documenta* 8 in Kassel, Serra constructed in cor-ten steel the ultimate in road blocks. The end of a street was shut off by a 20ft-high wall of metal, with arms of equal height reaching out before and behind. This double-sided box-like enclosure which was supposed to remain inviolate, turned out to be irresistible to motorists who parked happily within its confines. The most sucessful of the site-specific pieces was at Munster, where Serra had to match the genuine rivalry of the Baroque palace courtyard in which his sculpture was to be installed. The highly ornate palace facade is slightly concave. Serra echoed this by setting two concave steel wings at right angles to the facade. The sculpture, perfectly framed in the gateway and complementing the curving forms behind it was a rare example of art and architecture, separated by 200 years.

Richard Serra, *Maillart Extended*, 1988, forged steel, two posts and lintel elements installed at opposite ends of the pedestrian passage of Grandfey Viaduct, Switzerland, 144x12x12cm. 'Weight is a value for me, not that it is any more compelling than lightness, but I simply know more about weight than lightness and therefore I have more to say about it, more to say about the balancing of weight, the diminishing of weight, the addition and subtraction of weight, the concentration of weight, the rigging of weight, the propping of weight, the placement of weight, the locking of weight, the psychological effects of weight, the disorientation of weight, the disequilibrium of weight, the rotation of weight, the movement of weight, the directionality of weight, the shape of weight. I have more to say about the perpetual and meticulous adjustments of weight, more to say about the pleasure derived from the exactitude of the laws of gravity. I have more to say about the processing of the weight of steel, more to say about the forge, the rolling mill and the open-hearth.'
Richard Serra, 1988

A concern with history and with the spiritual informs the work of a number of German sculptors. It is curious how many women artists suggest in their work the fragility of life, and the hovering presence of death. Rebecca Horn, in her performances, videos and installations, always conveys a sense of evanescence bordering on tragic loss. She sometimes counterbalances the premonition of loss with an attempt at protection. In 1975 she made *Paradise Widow*, a feather-covered, womb-like hollow space into which the artist herself retreated during the course of a performance. Her chosen site in Munster was redolent of death: a mediaeval tower which had been used as a torture chamber from the Middle Ages until the end of the Nazi era. Horn, in choosing to work on this site, was not exorcising death but reminding visitors of man's inhumanity to man. In the dark recesses of the tower, little steel hammers, illuminated only by night-lights, knocked unrhythmically against the brick walls. It was as if one had descended into the caves of the Nibelungen; a spirit of evil and revenge haunted one's passage. To emerge into the daylight brought a sense of relief and the hope of redemption, tempered by the sight of a snake (the cause of man's fall from grace) in a glass case and a dark pool into which a single drop of water fell with monotonous regularity from the transparent roof above; a relentless reminder of the passage of time.

Christian Boltanski's area of activity is close to that of Rebecca Horn. He too sets up implicit memorials to the dead. In Kassel, a small prison-like room was crammed with photographs of missing persons, many of them children, placed against barriers made of cage wire. He too uses night-lights as a metaphor for vigils over the dead; or shadows to suggest the insubstantiality of the living.

Ulrich Ruckriem's granite slabs are to be encountered everywhere in Germany, in museums and galleries as well as, more appropriately, in the open. In an interior space these forms seem almost to crouch, as if unable to fulfil their potential. Outdoors, the stones seem able to breathe, standing proud in the sunlight. The sheer size of the granite is impressive in itself, and the fact that the material is so little affected by the sculptor's chisel, gives it a primitive, Stonehenge quality. In Kassel, Ruckriem erected a *Stone Museum* on a derelict car park, which became quite simply a holy place, a place of worship, and a wry comment on the status of museums in the present day. He accepted the challenge of church architecture in 1977 when he placed blocks of Dolomite granite at a short distance from the Petruskirche in Munster; whether in opposition or in harmony it is up to the viewer to decide. Ruckriem's wedge shapes echo the bays and buttresses of the church, the sculptures leaning towards the building as if to acknowledge gracefully its architectural priority.

Sculpture as furniture or furniture-sculpture holds the stage both in Europe and America, and the artist with the highest profile, simply in numerical terms, is Scott Burton. Burton's wood or formica garden seats, granite or marble chairs, wooden or cast-iron tables, are everywhere, in and out of the gallery. As objects they are extraordinarily beautiful, since Burton uses his materials with a delicate sensibility which enhances their intrinsic qualities. Sometimes there is a quirky perversity in his conception of the sculpture, as if he wants both to confirm and deny its usefulness at one and the same time. His pair of park benches in Munster are expansive semi-circles but the seats are minuscule; a formula he repeats in the Equitable Life Building in New York. In these installations he enjoys combining the natural with the man-made, using his furniture to enclose growing trees and plants. The chairs and tables, and even the Madame Récamier-style chaise-longue, can actually be used, a rare distinction among the growing army of furniture-sculptors. They are the late 20th-century equivalent of Gerrit Rietveld's 1918 *Chair*, as elegant a piece of furniture-sculpture as can be imagined.

Classicism and the New

The term 'classical' is an all-embracing one, as dangerous and as non-specific as 'romantic'. In nearly all sculpture which is overtly classical there are romantic undertones, although the reverse is unlikely to be so. In the strictest sense a classicist is a follower of the restrained style of antiquity, whereas a romantic artist prefers irregular beauty to finish and proportion, subordinating form to matter. It is axiomatic that rules such as these are made only to be broken.

Classicism as we understand it today can be loosely divided into three parts: sculpture which is deliberately archaeological, delving into antiquity, real or imagined, for its inspiration; sculpture which quotes from classical imagery, which may be unadulterated or disguised, but in either case subverted; or sculpture which is regular in form and ordered in execution. There are of course artists who escape any such neat categorisation but whose work may yet be considered classical.

Anne and Patrick Poirier are among the foremost archaeologists of classical antiquity, constructing fragments of ruins and breathing new life into civilisations long dead. In 1980, they made a model based on a time-worn Egyptian temple doorway called, nostalgically, *Lost Archetypes*, and, at the Bath International Festival in 1986, they made an outdoor installation of broken columns and a miniature aqueduct which was entitled *Archaeological Model*. In 1979, they constructed a model of Hadrian's Villa in plaster, back-projecting onto it a photograph of a sculpted head (a genuine classical remain) of Hadrian's favourite, the boy Antinous. By associating the real, in this case a photograph of an existing object, with the reconstructed past, they are combining ancient and modern in a single image.

Charles Simonds builds tiny dwellings in terracotta, thereby inventing a wholly imaginary civilisation and the appearance of fragments of an ancient city on a platform, usually at table-top level. There are no figures, although by implication there are traces of a vanished human presence. To begin with, Simonds constructed his clustered architectural pieces outside, in rough areas of New York, Paris and Dublin. In 1978, he was invited to build a dwelling in a hollowed-out wall at the Venice Biennale, but in the nature of things, these constructions had a short life-span and he was forced indoors to build in more sheltered spaces. These buildings usually take the form of classic geometrical shapes, such as circles and pyramids, but also of convoluted labyrinths and spirals embodying sexual overtones. Religion and ritual are integral elements in his work. A classic example is *Ritual Tower*, 1980, which resembles a ruined Mayan temple set in a lunar landscape. Interestingly, Jackie Ferrara constructed a huge stepped edifice in red cedar in 1981, based on Mayan temple architecture, for the Laumeier Sculpture Park in St Louis, Missiouri. The difference lies in the fact that Charles Simonds is inventing a civilisation that never was, whereas Jackie Ferrara is building a new structure which stems from an ancient prototype. Recently there have been signs that Simonds' classicism is breaking up; organic and natural forms are increasingly evident, as is indicated by *Rock Flower*, 1986, which is formed from irregular, flame-like curves.

Also at the Laumeier Sculpture Park, are deliberately archaeologising sculptures by Walter Dusenbery. *Porta Barga* consists of two marble columns and a lintel which evokes the time-eroded character of the remains of an ancient arcade. The arch has an air of displacement, as if it had suddenly been reft from Pompeii or Herculaneum. Dusenbury also makes fragmented sculptures which dissemble an air of antiquity. *Mure*, 1975, in red travertine, has a hammered surface bordering a smooth arch form and an inner post. The arch and post forms have been inverted, thus removing them from a literal association with antiquity and positing a clear sexual allusion.

Ulrich Rückriem, *Untitled* (detail), 1989, dolomite stone, four parts, each 1800x1100x35cm

Stephen Cox uses forms borrowed from antiquity as naturally as breathing. He is very much affected by the place where he is working, using the local marble or stone for his sculpture. The Tate Gallery piece *Tondo: We Must Always Turn South*, 1981, was made in Verona from St Ambrosia marble. The tondo shape is classically derived but, as well as the smooth oval of the apricot-coloured marble, the surrounding area is hammered and gouged into a halo of flames, a device which transforms it into a symbol of the warmth of the Italian sun. When Cox went to India, he worked with local people in the local material, granite, producing a remarkable body of work which, whilst nodding in the direction of Indian temple sculpture, is yet unmistakeably Western. An example of this use of local tradition is *Rock Cut: Holy Family*, 1986, a piece which consists of many large fragments surrounding a central image of five separate pieces on which is carved the Holy Family. The forms are related to Indian rock carvings, especially that of St Joseph, who assumes the position of the blessing Buddha.

Edward Allington uses the language of classicism in a way similar to that in which it was appropriated by the architects and sculptors of the Renaissance from the disinterred remains of ancient Rome. But Allington subverts his imagery, so that it becomes an ornamental fantasy, making his classical or baroque shapes perform impossible feats. His use of materials, too, belies their function. Plaster is the vehicle for his 'ideal standard forms' (itself a tongue-in-cheek description) and he uses plastic bricks to make an *Architectural Fragment*, 1984, the teetering column of glued-together bricks terminating in a bastardised classical capital with acanthus leaves and volutes improperly applied. Allington ensures that his audience is aware that he considers that the language of classicism which he chooses to use is dead.

Cy Twombly is better known as a painter than as a sculptor. An American who has lived in Rome for nearly 30 years, he inscribes words, such as 'Orpheus' or 'Leda and the swan', on his gnomically scrawled paintings to reassure us that we are in mythic country. Less well-known perhaps are his sculptures, which also evoke resonances of a mythic or archaic past, such as a palm-leaf fan or a fibre-glass construction of a bound bundle of sticks which force comparison with the pipes of Pan.

Although the Italian artist Arnaldo Pomodoro's early interests lay more in the direction of technology, he now invokes his heritage in *Three Columns*, 1969, made individually in gold, silver and steel. The first two refer to a greater or lesser extent to antiquity, the silver one being a specific quotation from Trajan's column while the steel column is uncompromisingly high-tech.

Mario Rossi also uses classical references in both painting and sculpture, often borrowing a sculptural image from antiquity for his work on paper. In his sculpture he will use an Ionic column, such as *Phenomenon, 1870*, 1986, into which he inserts a fat candle, immediately transforming it into a piece of church furniture. He subverts this notion by setting the column on an overturned tree, so that it serves as the tree trunk as well.

There are also those sculptors who use well-known, almost hackneyed imagery, altered or added to only to a minute extent. What could be more banal than a plaster statue of Venus, such as is sold to countless hordes of tourists in a variety of sizes and media? Some 30 years ago, during the era of Arte Povera, Venus was used by Michelangelo Pistoletto in *Venus of Rags*, an installation in which the goddess of beauty turns her back to the viewer and faces a huge pile of dirty rags, symbolising the contrast between the pampered luxury of the 'beautiful people' and those on the margins of society. As a symbol she has lost none of her power and has been, and no doubt continues to be, used to suit many an artist's purpose in a variety of ways. In 1987, Ian Hamilton Finlay used a plaster cast of the Venus de' Medici, his 'minimal intervention' being a red silk thread around her neck, a reference to the revolutionary Terror in 1794 when French women wore threads of red silk around their necks in memory of their guillotined friends and relations. This tiny detail posits a whole new historical dimension whereby once again, the not-so-distant past and antiquity are brought into collision.

Perhaps the least complicated idea of classicism is that of ordered simplicity, the reductive path which was pursued by Minimalists, particularly in America. Sol LeWitt is the *nom pareil* of this group, both in the monumentality of his wall drawings and in the cool geometric configurations of his sculptures. His *Serial Projects* of the 1960s and the *Modular Structures* of the early 1970s are architectural in conception, whereas the *Incomplete Open Cubes* of the mid-1970s are, as their titles suggest, purely geometric, although they are sometimes baffling in their lack of logic. 'Irrational thoughts should be followed absolutely and logically', he has said, which leaves us no nearer to comprehension.

Donald Judd's name is often paired with that of LeWitt's but, despite his parallel interest in modular structures, his untitled pieces are less open to structural analysis, more enclosed in form and more teasing to the perceptions by means of light and colour. The open-ended cube in clear anodised aluminium and violet plexiglass of 1969 and the open-topped copper box coated inside with red lacquer of 1973 are, besides being mysterious, quite frankly beautiful, a word which Judd may not consider to be a term of praise.

Although his detractors may claim that he is a one-idea-only artist, in that all his sculptures are permutations of identical units, there is something absolutely classical in the calm certainty of Carl Andre's work. The series of *Equivalents* (I-VlII), each made of 120 firebricks differently laid out, are paralleled in serenity by the floor pieces in squares of various metals. The pieces which speak of a prehistoric era are the red cedar sculptures of 1981, *Furrow* and *Hell Gate*, whose hieratic forms and open architecture have something of the grandeur of the Lion Gate at Mycenae or the great walls at Tyrins.

Eduardo Chillida, now in his 60s, has achieved in his later years a style of calm classicism. Always a welder, never a carver or a modeller, in the 1950s and 1960s, Chillida fashioned entirely abstract configurations which embody a sense of suppressed anguish. In the 1980s, his sculptures have become more expansive and, although some of them are concerned with mortality, they have a breadth of vision which expresses acceptance of the changes and chances of this fleeting world. He makes direct reference to the pre-classical past in *Stele of Agamemnon*, 1982, in corten steel, which takes the form of a curved facade into which is cut a scalloped space, possibly a shield or a mask, which recalls those soul-stirring words of Heinrich Schliemann when he was excavating the ruins at Mycenae: 'Today I looked upon the face of Agamemnon'. His *Stele for a Friend*, 1987, is the simple shape of a Japanese neck pillow, vastly enlarged, signalling perhaps a paradigm for eternal rest.

Alice Aycock is a young American whose fantastic structures are based on scientific prototypes which she elaborates in a Protean way. Although they display a certain illogicality in the same way that Tinguely's machines refuse to conform to any kind of rationale, they do have a sound starting-point in architecture, which she wilfully proceeds to deconstruct. She uses such epic titles as *The Machine That Makes the World*, 1979: a huge wooden construction somewhat resembling a submarine, which can, with difficulty, be entered. The piece that comes closest to classicism, if only on account of its title, is *The Miraculating Machine in the Garden (Tower of the Winds)*, 1981, in mixed media, which includes bells, antennae and a cyclotron pipe system for sending vibrations. Her *Tower of the Winds* has more, I suspect, to do with modern technology than the 1st-century BC monu-

Edward Allington, *Above*: *An Apollo Admiring Two Vases*, 1988, black painted wood, resin and plastic; *Below L to R*: *Saturnus*, 1988; *Three, Four and Five*, 1988, both ink and emulsion on paper on canvas. The drawings and monochrome sculptures of Edward Allington translate the myths of classical antiquity into claustrophobic modern settings where collections of dislocated, often repetitive fragments of architecture, sculpture and other artefacts have become categorically confused, questioning the authenticity of language codes through the artificial, playful nature of their presentation; above all creating a sense of loss of continuity with the past. 'For me with classical reference there is no nostalgia, it is no more than a mode, a basis for thinking, a starting point.'

ment in Athens, although there is a degree of formal precision which permits the analogy.

A Romantic Vision

In his essay 'British Romantic Artists' included in *Aspects of British Art*, published by Collins in 1947, John Piper wrote: 'Romantic art . . . is the result of a vision that can see in things something significant beyond ordinary significance: something, that for a moment seems to contain the whole world; and, when the moment is past, carries over some comment on life or experience besides the comment on appearances.'

In the same year Geoffrey Grigson wrote: 'Romantic artists of all countries share a tendency to be emotional and unintellectual about their art, to mix their art intimately with their religion, which was often of a personal, unorthodox, mystical kind.' Piper's statement still holds true 40 years later, but Grigson's seems hopelessly dated – trapped in the era of neo-romanticism, of which he was a leading exponent. Artists are not, with the possible exception of the naïve or 'outsiders', unintellectual, and the word passionate would be an improvement on emotional. Religion seems to be now, as then, out of place, although the personal, unorthodox and mystical are still valid.

Francesco Clemente was born in Naples and, although he now divides his time between Rome, New York and Madras, he retains the spiritual link with the past which is inherent in Southern Italians. On the one hand there is the inescapable presence of Pompeii and Herculaneum, a constant reminder of a past civilisation, and on the other there are the churches with their dark interiors and paintings of saints and martyrs. Caravaggio spent some time in Naples when he was forced to flee from Rome after killing a man in a brawl, and it is there that he painted the great altarpiece in the Church of the Pio Monte della Misericordia, showing *The Seven Acts of Mercy*. Clemente stirs into his folk memory of pre-Christian art and Neapolitan Renaissance art a knowledge of Hindu iconography and an interest in metaphysical systems. It is the human body, usually his own, which forms the core of his work. In Madras in 1983, with the help of local artisans, he created a whole battalion of little figures, each 68cm high, in papier-maché and clay. Each figure is identical and – a surreal touch – they are the same from both sides. They have the appearance of having just been resurrected from an earthy grave and seem, in John Piper's words, 'to carry over some comment on life or experience besides the comment on appearances'.

Mimmo Paladino was also born in the south of Italy, near Benevento and his works carry within them a sense of an indefinable antiquity, of prehistoric rites and rituals whose meaning we can only speculate on. *A Surrounded Figure*, 1983, combines references to Chinese tomb sculpture with suggestions of Egyptian wall painting, particularly in the Anubis-like creature which leers fawningly up at the seated figure. Evil is disturbingly present. In 1984, Paladino made a huge bronze portal entitled *South*, which was exhibited outside the Italian Pavilion at the 1988 Venice Biennale. Covered with human and animal figures, rods, poles and a conflagration, it would seem to be Paladino's modernist version of Rodin's *Gates of Hell*.

German artists have always been drawn to Mediterranean culture, and therefore inevitably to Italy, but they have tended to take from it the romantic and the mythological, rather than the classical aspects of its earlier civilisations. Markus Lüpertz has lived and worked in Milan, from where he could look both eastwards to Greece, and to the riches of her cultural past, and westwards to France, where once again the figure of Rodin must be invoked as the begetter of new possibilities for 20th-century sculpture. Lupertz's *Shepherd*, 1986, draws on the classical prototype of the 6th-century BC Attic sculpture, *The Calf Bearer*, in the Acropolis Museum in Athens, but he has interpreted it in a

rough, deliberately anti-classical manner more in tune with Picasso's *Man with a Lamb*, 1943. The meaning of Lupertz's sculpture is ambiguous: is the lamb being brought to the slaughter, as the calf was in the Attic sculpture, or is it being protected from harm, as is Picasso's? The challenge of Rodin's *Burgers of Calais* inspired Lüpertz to make a series of *Burghers of Florence* in 1983, a work comprising painted bronze heads, at once coarse and humorous, ranging from the Prince to a gaping tourist. Lüpertz is a ruthless appropriator, but the images he represents are incontrovertibly his own.

Landscape and natural forms played a large part in the sculpture of the 1980s, perhaps because of the increased interest in the environment and the knowledge of the perilous state of the world's resources. Richard Long's activities take several forms, but they are all aimed at one goal, that of self-identification with the landscape, sometimes in the most ephemeral way, and of making a record of it. Long takes lengthy walks, sometimes as close to home as on Dartmoor or in Ireland, at other times as far afield as South America or Nepal. He always logs his journey carefully on a map. At various stopping places he gently rearranges the landscape, building a cairn of stones or treading a track through a field of daisies. He photographs these 'interferences', knowing that, after his departure, nature will reassert herself and wipe out all traces of man's presence. In the gallery, Long displays the maps and photographs, with a few framed gnomic phrases, whilst on the floor is a circle or line of stones, slate or slivers of wood. The physical presence of these natural objects is very powerful, representing where the artist's foot has trodden; the floor pieces are often complemented by imprints on the wall made by dipping his hand into the mud of the River Avon, near where he lives, and making a kind of mandorla or sacred circle.

David Nash is also entirely dependent on nature for both his materials and his inspiration. He lives in a remote part of North Wales, principally using wood for his sculptures. He too 'interferes' with nature in the mildest way, perhaps tying or grafting trees so that they will gradually form a sculptural design, or he will place a boulder in a mountain stream which the movement of the water will displace or erode. Nash never cuts down a living tree, using only wood from fallen trees to form his sculptures. The principle of growth is important to him, and many of his works continue to change long after they are made, cracking and expanding. In one series he created stoves in different materials, recording them in photographs. The ceramic and wood stoves survived as shells but, as might be expected, the ice stove melted.

Wolfgang Laib uses basic organic and fragile materials – milk, pollen, rice – which are for him full of symbols and possess an energy and power which he says he could not create himself. His rice houses, which are laid directly on the floor, are wooden structures covered with metal, pierced with a small, round hole and filled with rice to the point of overflowing. Laib says: 'They have the form of a house and also of a reliquary of the Middle Ages or of a Muslim tomb, which contains the bones of saints.' They also contain an implicit comment on the world's starving millions. In 1977, Laib made his first *Pollen Piece*. From mid-February, he collects pollen from the meadows and forests surrounding his studio and stores them in small jars, keeping the types of flowers separate. He says: 'Pollen has incredible colours which you could never paint.' They are extremely beautiful, which is his avowed aim, but one cannot help having a nagging doubt about the deprived bees.

Traditionally the Japanese have been obsessed with wood as a sacred material possessing magical properties, as shown by the fact that the many statues of the Buddha in their temples are more often carved in wood than cast in metal. Contemporary artists have continued this tradition of wood-carving. Shigeo Toya uses

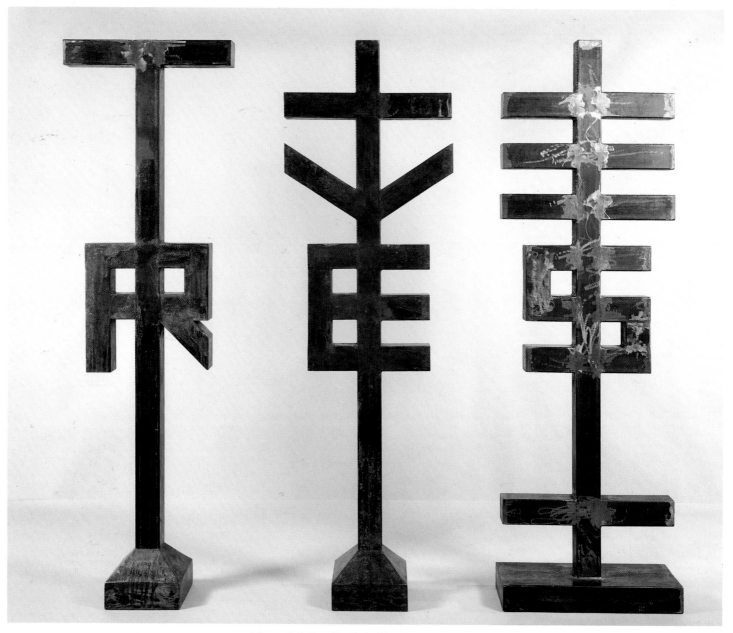

Mimmo Paladino, *Untitled*, 1987, iron in three parts

wood blocks which he works with a chainsaw or hatchet to produce deep intersecting notches. The split and indented surface is then rubbed with plaster of Paris or pigments. Toya's *Range of Mountains*, 1985, is a group of these notched and coloured wooden boulders set on a striated circular wood base which is itself a cross-section of a tree trunk. The material quality of the wood is more important than the associations which it provokes. In this context it is interesting to record that at Venice, a stone's throw from the Japanese Pavilion, there was a sculpture by Philip King entitled *Shogun*, 1988, which incorporated hefty chunks of wood within an open metal framework. It encapsulates in a powerful piece the Westerner's notion of a Japanese warrior.

An artist who combines living trees with figures alternately carved from bark or cast in bronze, all sprouting from terracotta pots, is Giuseppe Penone. The effect is of unrestrained vegetation and the twisted, distorted sprites are undoubtedly romantic.

Mystery and perhaps a certain ambiguity, whether of form or content, are dualities inherent in romanticism. Richard Deacon's shapes are open to several interpretations, some of which have literary sources hinted at in their titles. *Falling on Deaf Ears*, 1984,

in galvanised steel and canvas, suggests the story of Ulysses stuffing his companions' ears with wax and strapping himself to the mast in order not to be seduced by the song of the Sirens, whilst the upthrust member may be seen as the prow of a ship or as a phallus. *For Those who have Ears No 2*, 1983, as well as its manifest biblical reference, refers to Orpheus, inspired by Rilke's 'Sonnets to Orpheus'. The intricately curved laminated wood shapes can be read as an inner ear, as breasts or buttocks; or, taking the whole configuration together, as a nesting bird; or again, and most appropriately, a lyre, Orpheus' instrument and the romantic symbol of creativity.

Mystery is also an integral part of Alison Wilding's sculpture, which resists any attempt at literal interpretation. It is concerned with a femaleness, which is emphatically not to do with feminism, but rather with what it is like to be a woman. Much of her work is to do with enclosure or protection: a larger form enfolds or contains a smaller one, as in Henry Moore's *Two Forms*, 1934, in pynkado wood (Museum of Modern Art, New York), which he said could be regarded as a mother and child, the larger form sheltering the smaller. A similar intent is evident in Wilding's *Curvaturae*, 1985, while enclosure is more complete in *Hearth*,

Guiseppe Penone, *Ongle et pierres lithos*, 1988, lithographic stone and glass, 50x520x190cm

1986, a single hollow monolith, slit down one side and terminating in a thin arch. Yielding to the temptation to search for equivalents, it could be seen as having a formal affinity with Piero della Francesca's *Madonna del Pal* in a tiny chapel near Arezzo in which two angels part curtains to reveal the pregnant Madonna. It can also more obviously be seen as a vagina. Wilding reveals her interest in alchemy in *Hemlock III*, 1986, made from lime, hemlock, lead, beeswax and pigment. It is an enormously evocative piece, the dish shape of the upper element containing the poisonous ingredients. The sense of evil is palpable.

The sculptures by Shirazeh Houshiary in the early 1980s were biomorphic and archetypal. They were made of straw and earth, moulded over wooden armatures. *Listen to the Tale of the Reed*, 1982, exhibited at the Serpentine Gallery in 1984, is composed of five separate elements, zoomorphic in the variety of shapes they evoked, from man to dinosaur, inspired by a Persian legend. Since then, her work has become intentionally more abstract and architectural. *Echo*, 1985, is composed of flat planes and sharp corners, yet there is in the horizontal spread and upthrust members, a suggestion of a reclining figure whose head and knees rise upwards. The indentations have a kind of lilting poetry: she says 'the works are about fragmenting the whole – there are echoes, but nothing is whole.' The intention of the work is to express the immaterial in visible terms.

Luciano Fabro is a magician. He belongs to the Arte Povera group, and uses a great range of materials to effect his transformations. At ROSC, 1988, he installed a line of white eggs (they had to be pure white) which represented both perfect form and the birth of the world. In 1986, in the exhibition *Falls the Shadow*, at the Hayward Gallery, he was represented by an installation entitled *Iconography* which, although it dates from 1975, can justifiably be considered in the context of his continuing interests in the 1980s. The work consisted of a wooden table covered with an exquisite linen tablecloth, on which were laid clear glass dishes each containing water filled up to a certain level, and a glass object. The resonances were multiple, the clearest being an equation with the *Last Supper*, but after the participants had left the table.

There is another category which could be classified as romantic, although some may consider this distasteful. For I think those sculptures which are concerned with the imminent destruction of

David Nash, (going clockwise), *Mountain Bowl*, *Six Birch Spoons*, *Inside Outside*, *Descending Sheaves*, *Vessel and Volume*, 1990, installation view

the earth are romantic in the same way that John Martin's apocalyptic paintings of cosmic upheavals, such as *The Great Day of His Wrath* or *The Destruction of Sodom and Gomorrah*, are indisputably romantic.

Tony Cragg, Britain's representative at the 1988 Venice Biennale, has always been socially conscious, but his vision has darkened in recent years. Since the late 1970s, he has used urban detritus, such as discarded bits of plastic and wooden objects which have long since outlived their useful life, to create sculptures that express his anxiety for the future of the human race in an increasingly man-made environment. Cragg practised only briefly as a laboratory technician, but it has left him with an obsessive interest in chemistry. One of the most impressive pieces at Venice was a tripartite sculpture called *On the Savannah*, 1988. The three huge vessels, which are based on laboratory or engineering shapes, represent human and animal forms, threatening by their very size and their uncompromising anonymity. Cragg sees clearly and his honesty forces him to be a prophet of doom.

Enzo Cucchi, in common with Clemente and Paladino, is concerned with Italy's legendary and mythological past. In *A Painting which Grazes the Sea*, 1983, a stormy sky and turbulent sea are the setting for a dark ship creeping across the horizon. The sticks attached to the surface must be seen as driftwood, perhaps from a sunken boat. The ship may equally well be a battle cruiser or an evocation of Dante's barque crossing the Styx. Skulls, so often present in Cucchi's work, bob about forebodingly in the sea. The ultimate despairing sculpture is *Drawings Living in the Earth's Fear*, 1983. A blasted tree trunk stands solitary amid a devastated landscape. No living being has survived, and the scorched earth looks as if it will never bloom again. Cucchi's sculpture says it all: it is the end.

It is easier to pinpoint romanticism in literature, music or painting than in sculpture. But metaphor and allegory, with a mixture of appropriation from the past, are among the ingredients of contemporary romanticism which have abandoned rhetoric in favour of a poetic equivalent.

Pluralism and the International Scene

The Walker Art Center in Minneapolis organised an exhibition in 1988 entitled *Sculpture Inside Outside*, which explored four salient approaches to recent American sculpture: figuration

David Mach, *Adding Fuel to the Fire*, 1987, installation view in Barcelona

(references to the human body, as well as descriptions of recognisable objects); organic abstraction (references to natural forms and processes); transformed objects (processes and combining and/or modifying actual objects); and architectural abstraction (allusions to architecture and construction processes). This pluralism is not exclusive to America and we may widen the discussion to include British and European sculptors, with particular reference to the exhibition *Starlit Waters* at the Tate Gallery, Liverpool.

Figuration is perhaps the most difficult area in which to be convincing. Dealing with the human figure, although theoretically nearest to a known reality, poses the problem of banality and shallowness, one narrowly avoided by such artists as John de Andrea, Walter Segal and Duane Hanson, who quite literally reproduce the human figure, but with a twist which changes its context. In Britain, the sculptor who engages most directly with the human body is Antony Gormley. His engagement could not be closer, since the body he uses is his own and the person who models him from life is his wife. Ironically, it is only just over 100 years since Rodin was accused and berated (unjustly, as it happened) for having modelled *The Age of Bronze* from life, a

process which was then considered cheating. In *Ça change . . .* Gormley's body is modelled in plaster, which is then hacked off him, reassembled in the chosen position and covered with lead. This inert material makes the sculpture metaphorically, as well as literally, heavy. The featureless head and undefined hands and feet make the figures pregnant with mystery and, to compound the imagery of birth, he often assumes the foetal position. His most discussed, and abused, sculpture is the Janus figure on the walls of Derry. By facing both ways it is intended to bring hope in either direction.

Peter Shelton has points in common with Gormley, not least that he creates eccentric anatomical fragments in cast metal, often based on his own body. He describes these skins or shells as 'tight fitting architecture' and, like Gormley, by using himself as model he seeks to break down traditional distinctions between mind and body. More overtly figurative, but perhaps concomitantly more disconcerting, are Judith Shea's translations of Cycladic or classical Greek sculptures. Her bronze torsos are headless and armless, incapable of thought or action, victims of an unknown violation. Besides their classical resonance they also resemble shop-window mannequins which are a reflection

241

Luciano Fabro, *Paolo Uccello, 1450-1989*, 1989 steel, 1200x1200cm

of Shea's early career in fashion design. *Che Cosa Dice?* 1986, is a robed woman's contour placed in a corner supporting an oak stanchion. It has unmistakable associations with Christ carrying the cross, elided, because of its femaleness, with the figure perhaps of one of the Marys or perhaps of St Veronica. Quite different in spirit, but still emitting an atmosphere of despair, is *He and She*, 1984. The limbless woman's body is closely draped, as if in a winding sheet, enclosed by an uninhabited man's overcoat. Any idea of enfolding or protection is negated by the starkness of the image.

Organic abstraction covers an enormous field and takes many forms, often with suggestions of shapes readily recognisable in nature. Walter Lobe transcribes forms from nature quite literally. To make *Killer Hill C W*, 1985, he placed heavy sheets of aluminium over rocks and trees and hammered them until impressions of the underlying forms were revealed. Their very massiveness makes one feel that the hill is there to be climbed and the trees to be leaned on. They are a chunk of reality removed from its context and presented in an art gallery as an abstract form which yet contains within it the permanence of nature in the face of the impermanence of human life. Jene Highstein also uses forms directly culled from nature. *Palm 11*, 1986, whilst bearing a relationship to a stunted palm tree, more closely resembles a shaving brush or a giant phallus.

Martin Puryear also favours forms reminiscent of those in nature – trees and rocks as with Lobe – but he radically simplifies their shapes, rather than transforming them. He has also been influenced by objects from nomadic cultures, such as pottery, basketry, jewellery and portable architecture, perhaps as a result of his service in the Peace Corps in Africa. *Nobless 0*, 1987, is made of three sections of red cedar, coated with aluminium paint, terminating in a point like a witch's hat, which could be equally well interpreted as a Thai stupa. John Newman's forms are a synthesis of mechanical and organic themes. Like Puryear he enjoys enigmatic and jokey titles. *Tolled Belle*, 1987, in cast and fabricated aluminium (the fabrication involves twisting and bending planes of metal), partly refers to the shape of a bell, but is complicated by other elements with ambiguous orifices which have sexual connotations.

Anish Kapoor's mysterious shapes in glowing primary colours at once combine architecture with eroticism. Their bases are shapes constructed from wood and coated with pure pigment spilling over into the surrounding area. The reticulated red shapes in *As if to celebrate, I discovered a mountain blooming with red flowers*, 1981, are offset by a pair of elongated ovals, with holes in the top surface, closely conjoined like breasts with inverted nipples, or lips presented together in a kiss. *1000 Names* contains a direct reference to Kapoor's Indian origins in that the many protuberances can be read as the multi-breasted goddess Kali, so often carved on Indian temples.

Adopted plant forms are also found in Tom Butter's fibreglass and resin sculptures, but the allusion is to submarine rather than terrestrial life. In a sculpture such as *S C*, the translucent forms speak of undersea flora waving gently in a slowly moving current. *D D*, 1982, in the exhibition at the Metropolitan Museum of Art, New York, *The 1980s: A New Generation*, is altogether less beneficent; it is equipped with rows of teeth which put one in mind of a shark or a killer whale. More recently Butter has made semi-transparent architectural structures, such as *In Irons*, 1986, in fibreglass, resin and maple, where the central upright strut is wrapped or enclosed by a thin membrane of wood veneer.

A discussion of transformed objects can cover the widest possible spectrum. The process of art itself is a transformation, and the only question is to what extent the object has been transformed. If we take the most direct means of transformation, it accords with the Surrealist notion of removing an object from its context. A piano seems peculiarly susceptible to subversion. To take two examples: the first is Walter Martin's *Snail snail come out of your hole, or else I'll beat you black as a coal*, 1987, in styrofoam, wood, rubber and fibreglass, in which a grand piano lies up-ended, its legs in the air in a pathetically undignified position, like a beetle unable to right itself. A piece of sheet music lies on the ground, underlining the unplayability of the piano. A ball of twine sits in the viewer's space, a length from it snaking towards the piano like an umbilical cord, so that we are drawn willy-nilly into the incomprehensible drama. Secondly, a piano was used as a surrogate for the self in Helen Chadwick's personal life-history entitled *Ego Geometria Sum: The Piano – Aged 9 Years*, 1983. Chadwick used a series of objects, such as an incubator, a font and a perambulator, to portray herself at various stages in her life, as a way of defining the past. The piano itself, made of painted wood, was being silently played by disembodied hands and instead of pedals there were feet. By using objects as stand-ins for the artist's self, and negating their purpose, Chadwick was exploring the growth of her own sensibilities and perceptions, and asserting that we are culturally determined by the objects around us.

David Mach also transforms objects by a witty destruction of our preconceptions. He makes the conceptually impossible possible. How could a seal balance a car on its nose? In real life it could not, but in art it can. Similarly, he makes a gaggle of Cindy dolls and teddy bears carrying a tree trunk, giving it the slightly ominous title of *If you go down to the woods*. One of Mach's most recent manifestations has been *101 Dalmatians* at the Tate Gallery, a most elaborate installation which, with the help of assistants, took him three weeks to build. The Dalmatians were doing impossible things, balancing washing-machines on their noses and supporting cupboards in their teeth, feats achieved with the help of a good deal of sophisticated engineering. 'What is the point?' many will ask. Apart from the element of fun, a rare enough commodity, it is an exercise in sleight-of-hand, playing perception off against conception.

New Yorker Donald Lipski is quoted in *Art in America*, November 1985, as saying: 'I wasn't trained as a sculptor, so I glue my stuff together or tie it together. I can melt wax on the stove and pour it in. Fabrication takes much too long.' That sounds like a flip New York artist, and indeed Lipski does have something in common with Jeff Koons, the ex-commodity broker who increased his fortune by turning to sculpture, immortalising such commodity-orientated objects as a Jim Beam train and a travel bar by casting them in stainless steel – stainless steel, according to him, being more democratic and accessible than bronze. In 1983 Lipski fabricated – no, glued together – the base and cradle of an old-fashioned telephone, balancing on top a glowing glass sphere which reflects the viewer and his surroundings. The rotund belly and head of Koons' cast stainless-steel *Rabbit*, 1986, similarly reflects the viewer. Both objects have, whether one likes it or not, an undeniably iconic form.

In another mood, Lipski has this year piled up a triangular mountain of marine buoys, enigmatically entitled *Balzac*. Was he thinking of Rodin's majestic figure with its huge extruded belly? Marine buoys are again used in *The West*, 1987, made of painted steel, corroded pennies and silicone adhesive. The spheres are joined together at one point, as if locked in a passionate embrace. They too have anthropomorphic associations reminiscent of Brancusi's two conjoined figures in *Le Baiser*, 1907. Lipski's use of a wide range of discarded materials and his ingenious conjunction of disparate objects seem to pay a sardonic homage to the fruits of the industrial age.

The British artist who uses discarded materials most poignantly is Bill Woodrow. His *Twin-Tub with Guitar*, 1981, is just exactly that. From an elderly redundant washing-machine he cut

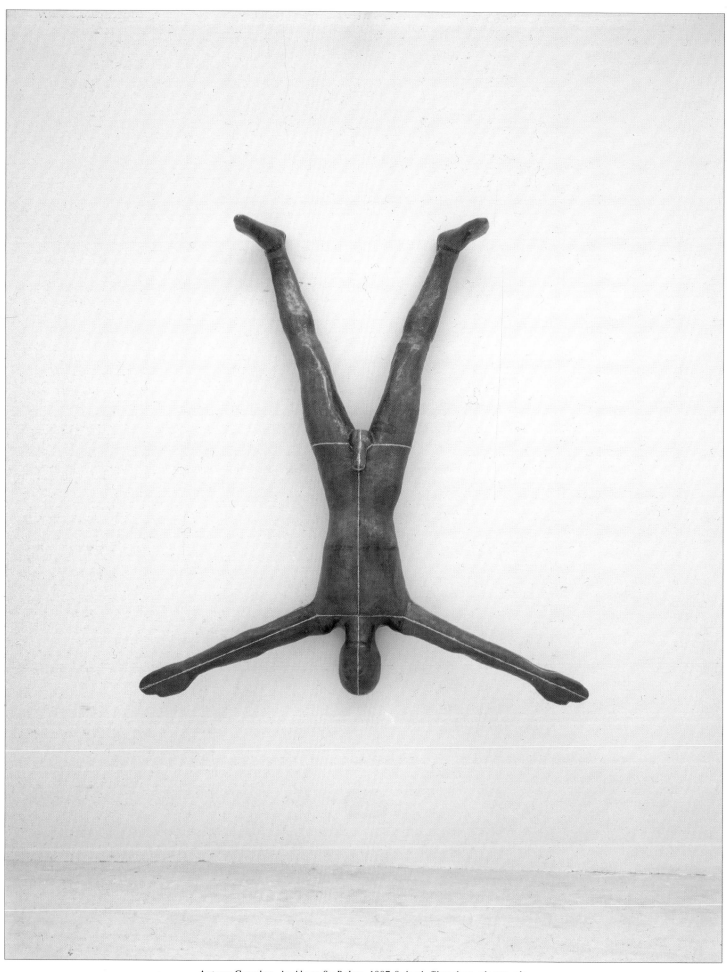

Antony Gormley, *As Above So Below*, 1987-8, lead, fibreglass, plaster, air

Tony Cragg

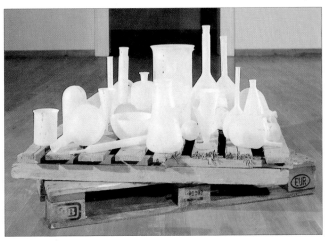

Silicate, 1988, glass and wood

– You do not come to things by chance . . . How is a sculpture constructed? What is the first basic step?

I have two or three usual ways of starting. I can literally be in my bed, or I can be sitting somewhere, or be in the middle of a meal and have a sort of vision . . .

– A vision of something elaborate, or an object?

I can't call it an idea, rather a sense of fascination about something that I don't immediately recognise, but whose presence grows in my mind until it connects itself with other parts of my experience which I've already dematerialised. So, I then go to my studio and think about these things while I begin to work . . . My second method is completely free and more pliable: it is a good way of getting right down to working with the material. Let's take as an example a traditional material like clay which has its limitations since, if I move, it moves! I look, I think, I move: it moves! And so, through a process of thousands of decisions, it takes on a form! It is the same with painting. A painter is always busy moving. There are thousands of decisions involved before a painting is finished.

– You'd define yourself as a sculptor, wouldn't you?

Yes. It's the most appropriate way to describe my activity, although I'm not keen on the idea of object-maker.

– But have you ever painted? Was there a moment when you broke away from painting?

I can tell you exactly what happened; it's a very simple story yet a very significant one in my life. I spent my first year studying at a very traditional college (we were taught landscape painting, life-drawing, still-life, perspective) . . . After that year, I was able to enrol at another college in London. But for five months in between, I worked in a foundry. I used to work from 7.30 in the evening to 7.30 in the morning, pouring hot metal into moulds that were lined up all the way

down the factory, where it would cool and turn from red to black. The moulds would then fall over on to the ground, spilling out black sand. At the end of the night, we would move this mountain of black sand! It was something incredibly dynamic and fantastic. I was 20 at the time, and working that hard made me feel very strong. By the time I began college again, it had become physically impossible for me to do painting. I was at the peak of my strength and energy. I needed to move, to build, to create things.

– So, it was a confrontation with reality which became the decisive factor. . . You use elements from everyday life, and yet current events do not really figure in your subject matter. Instead, you withdraw these objects, giving them a diachronic dimension. Even so, do you see elements of realism in your work?

These elements are sort of reference marks, things that one can name. In the end, they in fact establish their own reality without one being able to say that it is real. What would a realistic artist be? Someone who accepts everything as being real and so never does anything?!

– What do the materials that you use represent? It seems to me that the materials are a base, but not the be all and end all of your work.

The *Arte Povera* generation and the artists at the end of the 60s and 70s incorporated a great number of non-artistic materials into the sphere of art. They reaffirmed and reinforced Duchamp's idea that ordinary, banal objects could still be the media for important information, for emotion. And all the while, they were adding to the vocabulary of materials, they were also adding to the techniques of art, so that in the end we've come to a point where there's no interest for an artist in associating himself with one material alone: it's a little simplistic and uncreative. For my part, I have been associated with plastics (although I don't know if I am the first to use them). Apart from carrying the idea of detritus

(already exploited by many artists and of no interest to me) these plastics were a little like materials that I have invented and brought from non-art to art. All materials are free to be used in the building of a sculpture, in relative proportion to the things that surround us: there are not many natural things in my house, not my studio, nor my town; nor even the countryside – we could say that nature itself has changed radically. It is a totally relative notion (a forest may be considered to be an artificial object).

My aim is to go beyond an object or material: to decode it. I attempt to fill, with my own capacity for invention, the sphere which surrounds it. For example, plastic can be seen in various ways: as rubbish; as an interesting material in the context of art; as a material with surprising vividness; or as something allegorical. This material can make the long transition from being refuse to being something that could really have a meaning. That's why I insist on the fact that the material is only a medium. In terms of sculpture, it is ultimately not the material which is of prime importance. This becomes clear with a personality like Gandhi; in the end he almost ceased to be material; becoming nothing but spirit. What would have remained of Gandhi? Nothing, were it not for his spirit.

– Is this method of collecting and giving a meaning to poor and invented materials related to your interest in science and scientific subjects?

Yes. I'm fascinated by science. In fact, my education was geared more toward science than arts and the tendency to analyse has never left me. I'm becoming more and more deeply convinced that the division between the arts and science is false. It is a cultural misapprehension that has separated the two. The philosophy of nature, science and art have, in a strange way, moved apart.

Interview with Demosthenes Davvetas, 1988

Shirazeh Houshiary, *Fire*, 1987, copper

out the shape of a guitar – nothing removed, nothing added. He had simply transformed a piece of machinery no longer able to perform its rightful function into a work of art, at the same time commenting on the built-in obsolescence of present-day commodities. Cars, the ultimate commodity and status symbol, have often been used by Woodrow. In *Car Door, Armchair* and *Incident*, 1981, a gun is fashioned from the interior of the car door, and part of the upholstery is splattered against the wall; the incident in question is clearly a fatal accident. Woodrow's comments on the human condition have become darker. In 1986, one of his entries for the Turner Prize at the Tate was *Self-Portrait in the Nuclear Age*, which showed the artist's severed head suspended in mid-air, a map of the world torn off in strips and attached to an empty tailcoat. Woodrow's transformations are warnings against the cupidity and greed of humanity summed up in the title of several of his works – *Ship of Fools*.

The area of architectural abstraction is wide and ever-growing. There are sculptures resembling miniature buildings, real or fantastic, sculptures in the form of pieces of furniture, serviceable or simulated, and sculptures laboriously fashioned to represent domestic artifacts. Michael Singer makes airy constructions of ash-wood and stone, such as *Cloud Hands Ritual Series*, 1982-3, carefully interlacing the thin wooden struts like a game of spillikins; remove one length of wood and the whole edifice would collapse. The delicacy of the structure has something of the mystery and ritual architecture of Giacometti's *Palace at 4am* and also some affinity with Alice Aycock's illogical structures. Using closed rather than open forms Steven Woodward builds structures which seem to contain a kind of compressed energy. *Another Conundrum*, 1988, in wood, modified bitumen and steel paint, is shaped like the hull of a ship interrupted by triangles at back and sides, the interior voids filled with an evenly spaced lattice. Set on a flat rooftop against a backdrop of skyscrapers, it exudes an air of solid authority which contrasts with Singer's and Aycock's apparently evanescent constructions.

Closer to actual building construction principles are Brouwer Hatcher's follies. His conceptions are cosmic, embracing ancient civilisations equally with modern technology, his titles evocative of a past that never was. *Prophecy of the Ancients*, 1988, in cast stone, stainless steel, bronze and mixed media, is an elegant open edifice reminiscent of Buckminster Fuller's geodesic domes. Six tapering stone columns support a circular, transparent mesh-structure from which are improbably suspended a variety of shiny, brightly hued objects including turtles, fish, ladders and chairs, as well as purely geometric forms. The lightness of the structure, besides the obvious fascination of Brouwer's weird selection of objects, forces the viewer's attention upwards, looking at and through the mesh.

One of the most impressive of architectural sculptors is the Catalan Susana Solano, who represented Spain at the 1988 Venice Biennale. She makes enormously solid and threatening pieces out of such materials as galvanised steel, steel mesh and cement. They contain the 'Keep out' or 'Watch out' quality of Richard Serra's gigantic curved metal walls. *Entre Limites*, a particularly striking piece shown at the Antony Reynolds Gallery early in 1988, is a three-sided wire-mesh cage against a wall. Inside is a metal trunk, its lid propped open by a steel bar which is wedged upwards and forwards to a square plate fixed to the front of the cage. The four corners are supported by tower-like columns, the whole edifice redolent of watch-towers, concentration camps and coffins. It is a meditation on death; violent death caused by man's inhumanity to man.

The work of Robert Gober is a cross between the categories of architectural abstraction and transformed objects. His domestic sinks are laboriously recreated out of plaster, wood, steel, wire lath and semi-gloss enamel, with slightly unnerving modifications of scale. They can be seen as a homage to Duchamp, although Duchamp's modification of a real urinal was merely to alter its orientation so that it became useless. Gober's wooden *Play Pen*, 1986, is almost embarrassing in its faithfulness to the real thing. Only its placing in a gallery makes it into an art-object. It would otherwise be equally at home in a nursery. Gober lets his sense of humour go in *Partially Buried Sink*, 1986-7, in which the top of the eponymous sink peeps out from the surrounding sward like a tombstone in a grassy cemetery.

From the foregoing, although certain tendencies have been highlighted, it would seem that sculpture in America and Western Europe is more varied than it has been at any time in history. Figuration, whilst eschewing the academic, is dependent implicitly and explicitly on the human figure. Abstraction, whether organic or architectural, is alive and well, the latter of necessity closer to factual realisation, although the objects often subvert the concept. Transformed objects contain within themselves the contradiction between seeing and knowing. For the Surrealists the 'marvellous' was the supreme quality, but it is not a quality confined to Surrealism.

To me the very plurality of the sculpture under discussion is a marvellous phenomenon. It is not that anything goes, which implies laxity and a lack of moral fibre, but that everything goes, given that it has some bearing on the human condition. If artists are searching for personal symbols, and I believe that art is always, to a greater or lesser degree, such a search, it may be that the quest is also one for stability in an increasingly uncertain world.

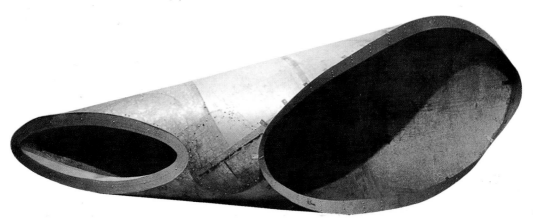

Richard Deacon, *Untitled*, 1980, galvanised steel, 125x345x125cm

Above: Drumlanrig Sweet Chestnut, Autumn 1988; *Below*: Castres and London Plane Leaves, Autumn 1988

ANDY GOLDSWORTHY
GEOMETRY & NATURE
An Art & Design *Interview*

Yorkshire Sculpture Park Sweet Chestnut, Summer 1988

I use the architectural qualities of the leaf. The sculptures rely on the architecture of the leaf for their
strength. They are about the way things grow, the way they are built. The progression is so important,
the growth-progression in the building of the leaf work. **Andy Goldsworthy, 1990**

– What is it that most appeals to you about a place where you decide to work?
The quality of the unexpected is something that interests me because that is what I find in the land. I go out to work and I don't really know what I am going to make and I discover things that have always been there, but are totally unexpected . . . Some time ago I had an exhibition in the old transport museum in Glasgow of 18 snowballs that were kept in a deep freeze. I wanted a kind of tough industrial empty space in an urban situation where these snowballs would melt. I think the unlikeliness of finding snowballs in the middle of summer in that place helped the exhibition.

– Would you say that an important aspect in your work is bringing the natural landscape into the urban context?
I think that the work I do in an urban context is exploring that relationship; perhaps the best work I ever made in a building is a hole I dug into the Serpentine Gallery floor. I dug the earth out and the earth lay around the hole and it looked very, very black. In that work I touched the nature of the building and brought the earth from underneath. That is what I would like to try and do in an urban situation, just to touch the nature of that place.

– So your work is actually responding to a specific context?
At my best.

– And in your exhibition of leaf sculptures at the Natural History
Museum do you feel that you succeeded in responding to the site?
Not with the same degree of success. I made two leaf works out of leaves in front of the Natural History Museum that went into the show. I pinned one work to the wall of the museum with thorns but I certainly didn't put my fingers through the wall and feel what was behind. So in a way it was a little bit superficial in that respect. I am very conscious of the space and what it means.

– Would you work with found materials in an urban environment as readily as you do in a natural landscape?
I have problems with manufactured materials in that I don't understand them, I can't feel their relationship to source; so that's why I work with the land directly. When I work with a leaf, it's not just a leaf, it's growth, it's life, it's water, it's space, it's air. All the materials I work with window into the experience of growth and I cannot feel that connection when working with plastic. But I do a lot of work with old roofing slate. At Fabian Carlsson, for instance, I made two installations with roofing slate. I came to London and we went collecting slate from where they were roofing. By reassembling slate in this tightly compacted form, I hoped it would have some of the energy it had in the quarry. That for me is a material which still retains a lot of its meaning.

– So you are always primarily aiming to return to the source of a material?

It is making visible the relationship between material and source that is the important thing.

– You were brought up on the boundaries between nature and a city; has the dialogue between the two played a significant role in defining your thinking?

I'm very aware of the relationship between the two. I'm conscious of not wanting to become some sort of romantic in the landscape, escaping from the city. I work in wild and remote places but I also work in urban situations. A lot of the work that is mistaken for being in wild and remote places is in fact made in cities and on patches of waste ground. I love those kinds of places.

– Can we discuss your work with leaves and the thinking behind these sculptures?

I feel very strongly about the place of common things, the neglected things which, because of their commonness, are not appreciated. A lot of the leaves I use are from the sycamore which is not the most loved tree of all. It is also a fantastic leaf to learn from . . . There are many small things that I make on the ground. I often rub earth into leaves to mix the leaves with things and doing this I began to notice the vein structure of the leaves, how there is this prominent geometry. Very gradually the leaves I was working with became more three-dimensional and I began to use the architecture of the leaf to make forms which eventually led to these. What is important about the work here is that the shapes come out of the leaf.

– Do you have a preconceived idea of the form you want to create before you begin working with the leaves?

I have a certain direction in which I want to take the leaf. Usually, when I have finished one work, I know the direction of the next because of what I have learnt while working with that one. For instance, there is one with London plane leaves where the cube comes out of the leaf's vein structure which has this right angle to it, which produces the square.

– It's interesting, because when you think of organic forms you don't tend to think in terms of geometry.

I used to think, when I first started working outside, that geometry was an arrogance imposed upon the land by people, but then I realised that it was an arrogance to think that people had invented geometry. It's within nature and all forms are to be found there. And for me, geometry doesn't necessarily represent the heavy-handed touch of man. It's just the way in which it is generally employed.

– So in a sense the leaf sculptures might be said to represent an architectural concept, in that you are working with the structure of the material to create a geometrical form.

Oh for sure, I use the architectural qualities of the leaf. The sculptures rely on the architecture of the leaf for their strength. They are about the way things grow, the way they are built. The progression, the growth-progression, is so important in the building of a leaf work.

– What about other forms like the cone and the horn? I believe that these forms evolved out of the sweet chestnut leaf?

The sweet chestnut leaf has a centre vein different to the plane leaf, which has the triangle, and it's also a very supple leaf so it can be bent. The first horn that I made began by bending the leaf. Then, wanting to make that a little bit bigger, I folded one leaf in the fold of another so that it became continuous and I just kept adding and adding. The first one I made grew into a spire and fell to bits very quickly. It had very little structural strength. I began to explore a way of giving it strength and this resulted in the spine. Because the leaves are very close together and pinned with thorns they are very strong.

– Do you feel that you are exploring new ground, in an artistic sense, without the weight of history that tends to dominate other art forms?

I have been working outside for about 15 years, and each day I go out I understand a little more about the materials and the place they come from, the weather, the seasons, etc; it's a growing, accumulating body of understanding that gives me the energy to carry on. It's not something that is static, I'm continually learning, and it's an intensely personal knowledge. I never feel that I am breaking new ground, but on the other hand I do not feel the weight of history. What I have noticed is that I am beginning to feed off things intuitively; because the land has been worked for thousands of years I see man's touch as part of that nature and I am working with that also. Dry-stone walls form a part of that and I've made sculpture that has used these walls.

– How did your ice sculptures come about?

Winter itself is an important part of the land and of all the seasons, and it has always held a particular fascination for me. Winter has always been the test of my commitment to the land. I wanted to work outside everyday, not just on the nice days. When I learnt to survive it I loved it! Winter comes from the North, which is one of the few places you can actually go to find its source. These sculptures were a response to the snow that could be cut into blocks. There were all different types of snow, but the wind-blown snow you can carve into lumps and can work with. The things that I made were very architectural: some used light and some used the architecture of the snow. It wasn't really until the very end of my stay that we made a snow house, an igloo, and then I realised how many things I had discovered and had been helped to discover by my assistant's understanding of snow through the building of igloos.

– Did you feel that the force of the sculptures was lost in the sense that the viewer was, inevitably, only able to experience the work visually, through the medium of photography?

Well a lot was lost, but when people see blue skies and snow they think it's warm, whereas with images taken on cloudy days people think that it is cold. In fact it's the reverse: when there is a blue sky it is really intensely cold. That was interesting for me and made me realise how I perceive the cold. After that we went to the North Pole itself and we were there for three or four days. The sun was going round at the same height all day; it never goes down. I made a piece of work that I think reflected the sun going round. When you stood in the middle of the enclosure, you were looking out through these rays and everywhere you looked was South, there was no West or East, and North was there. The only other place you can do that is the South Pole. It's such an important place that I made sure that the work would soon be destroyed; it was made next to a crack. It was the one place I felt that no person should leave any trace.

The photograph is an integral part of the whole process. The photograph is very important to me as a working record. I have a record of almost everything I have made; so I can look back on my past works and establish a dialogue with them which is very important.

– Are you conscious of a sense of spirituality in your work, in your concern with the elements and with returning to the source?

There is a deep sense of spirituality, but it doesn't manifest itself in any sort of religion. I can't explain that; the nearest I can say is that the places that I work in are a little bit like houses that you may have lived in. If you have lived in a house for a long time and you move, no matter whether you pass that house again, there's a feeling for it, there is an intimacy and a feeling of understanding; and that's how I feel for places I have worked in. Before I work with them they are strangers, I don't understand them and have no relationship with them.

RUPERT MARTIN
SPACES, PLACES AND LANDMARKS
Environmental Art

Kier Smith, *The Iron Road*, 1986, Jarrah Wood, Forest of Dean Sculpture Project

A distinction can be drawn with environmental art between places and spaces, between the changing character of a place with its layers of history, and the more neutral gallery space, which the artist can temporarily make his own. Some artists choose to work in both domains, recognising the different connotations which are imparted to their work. Whilst the work of Richard Long and Andy

Goldsworthy is predominantly made outdoors using natural materials, their work can be conveyed into the gallery space through the medium of photography and the written word. The photograph mediates between the uninhabited place and the public space, and it also mediates between the transience of the work and the more permanent imprint made by the light emanating from it. A further dimension is added by the artist bringing material from the land into the gallery space and composing a work within the parameters of that space. Richard Long's *Magpie Line*, shown recently at the Tate Gallery, Liverpool, requires an act of the imagination to complete it, with its suggestion of infinite extension. Wolfgang Laib's rectangles of pure pollen bring to mind the meditative process of gathering the pollen, which glows with an inner radiance coming from the accumulation of these myriad particles of life. A similar reverence for nature as a life-giving force is apparent in the works of Garry Miller, whose photograms reveal the transparency of each fragile leaf, illuminated from within as if by a divine light. The mystical dimension to Laib's and Miller's work is combined with a sensitivity to the fragility of nature and the delicate balance that is required in our relationship to God's creation.

To work in the environment, to evolve a sculpture within a certain place or with a place in mind, to collaborate with the processes of nature requires a certain humility and an understanding of the transience of things. Even the most durable materials such as stone and iron corrode or crack when exposed to the elements. The best works are therefore those which in their choice of materials, scale and position acknowledge that the place is more important than the object and that any intervention is at best semi-permanent. The ethos of the museum to preserve and conserve, cannot apply to works of art in the environment, although it is important that maintenance is carried out for both aesthetic and safety purposes.

The concept of the Sculpture Park lies somewhere in between the museum and the land, aspiring to the freedom of the open-air setting, but confined by the boundaries of the park and the civilising notion of the 'landscape'. They continue the 18th-century concept of art being a tasteful adjunct to nature, a humanising of the land that implies ownership and decorum. In his urge to possess the land, man has to leave his mark upon it, whether by planting a flag, constructing earthwork fortifications, placing an obelisk on the top of a hill or digging a mine-shaft into it. By contrast, the most enduring works of art are those which like the Aboriginal Songlines live in the imagination and belong to the whole culture. In their belief, the land itself is continually being sung into existence through the activity of the imagination, and landmarks have an interior significance, a hidden value. As Bruce Chatwyn wrote in *The Songlines*: 'In theory, at least, the whole of Australia could be read as a musical score. There was hardly a rock or creek in the country that could not or had not been sung.' The nearest we have come to this kind of freedom is in the work of Richard Long, a latter-day nomad whose subtle and often transitory marks on the land are kept alive in the photographic image or in words which evoke place and passage. Richard Long's vocabulary of forms – circle, line, spiral – are common to many cultures, and relate to earlier ways of making marks on the land. Environmental artists often make connections with the religious origins of stone circles and standing stones in their choice of forms and materials. In an increasingly secular age, this is both more difficult and more important as an alternative to the urban-based consumer culture which dominates our media. By putting us in touch with nature, works of art can help us to identify with places and alert us to the 'unseen landscapes' about which Paul Nash wrote, 'unseen because not seen'. The Romantic notion of the spirit of place is seen afresh in the light of a rigorous logic, a clarity of expression characteristic of the Classical idiom with its emphasis on proportion.

Perhaps the best known examples of sculpture in the open air, the form that most environmental art in this country takes, are the

giving them enough space in which to breathe, there has recently been a movement away from this idea of collecting works of art and putting them in the landscape. The new approach has involved artists getting to know a stretch of land and evolving ideas for sculpture out of their response to a specific place. This process has been developed most notably in Grizedale Forest where with the collaboration of the Forestry Commission, annual residencies have been taking place since 1978, when David Nash became the first artist to work there. This approach exemplified in the work of Nash is a new form of the truth to materials philosophy of the 1930s, and is also partly a reaction to the Pop artists' love of plastic, fibre-glass and other artificial materials. All except one of the sculptures in Grizedale are made using indigenous wood and stone. Nash's contributions included channelling the element of water through fallen branches in *Wooden Waterway*, and revealing the inner vitality of the tree in the sculpture *Running Table*. Nash's attitude to the elements and to nature underlies the ethos of the Grizedale Project which has had a significant influence on the development of outdoor sculpture in this country.

The same truth to materials and propriety of placing is

Forest of Dean, *L to R*: *Stuart Frost,* Bracken Ring, 1986; Yvette Martin, *The Four Seasons*, 1986; Cornelia Parker, *Hanging Fire*, 1988, cast iron

works of Henry Moore purchased in the 1950s by Sir William Keswick and sited with great sensitivity on the edge of a remote moor in Dumfriesshire. The photographs of these works have been often reproduced and have been influential in the development of the idea of placing works of art in the landscape. Moore's own comments show how much he was aware of the way in which a landscape can bring out one aspect of a sculpture. Writing of his *Standing Figure*, the first sculpture to be sited at Glenkiln he said: 'In the bleak and lonely setting of a grouse moor, the figure itself becomes an image of loneliness, and on its outcrop of rock, its lean, skeletonic form stands out sharp and clear against the sky, looking as if stripped to the bone by the winds of several centuries.' In a similar way, the *Upright Motif No 1* becomes a part of the landscape, appearing from the distance like an ancient Celtic cross. The siting of this sculpture took into account both the lie of the land and the local usage, since it occupies the place where the artist on his visit to Glenkiln saw a shepherd surveying his sheep. The identification of the sculpture with the place is complete in the name by which it is now known, the *Glenkiln Cross*.

However well the sculptures by Moore have been placed,

apparent in the *New Milestones Project* inaugurated by Common Ground with a pilot scheme in Dorset. Their method differs in that they aim to involve local people in the process of commissioning a work of art that in some way celebrates the land they inhabit. Two of these commissions were organised in collaboration with the Weld Estate which adjoins a stretch of unspoilt coastline at East Lulworth. The response of both artists was similar in that both sought, in the words of Peter Randall-Page, 'to make a work which would relate to the intimacy of human scale – something on which to refocus the senses before returning to the enormity of land, sea and sky.' Both he and Simon Thomas chose a theme and material that was appropriate to the place. For Peter Randall-Page, the abundance of fossils in the area and the rhythms of the hills, 'sweeping in broad rounded curves', provided the starting point for three shell-like forms. The material is a local limestone, blue Purbeck marble, consisting of tiny fossilised gastropod shells, and is commonly found in church architecture. The sense of preciousness, created by the material which is now no longer quarried, is further enhanced by the placing of each subject in a dry-stone wall niche to suggest a wayside shrine before which one can pause for contemplation and recollection. An indicator of how people have responded is evident in the way that the rounded surfaces have been polished by constant touching, in the same way that the knee of Moore's *Madonna and Child* in St Matthew's Church, Northampton has been made smooth by people touching the sculpture. The freedom which people have to explore the tactile dimension of sculpture, denied them in museums or exhibitions, is one of the strongest attractions of outdoor sculpture.

Simon Thomas' four carvings of enlarged seed forms relate to the usage of this particular stretch of land for the cultivation of wheat, one of the earliest such sites in the country. The sculptures thus draw attention to the history and unique character of the place, and are made out of weathered oak from the estate. Their placing in a field where sheep graze is also fortuitous. As Joanna Morland who set up the pilot scheme in Dorset writes in the book, *New Milestones: Sculpture, Community and the Land*, 'the oak wooden seeds appear to be much used and enjoyed by the sheep as scratching posts and wind breaks, and the oak has benefitted from the quantities of lanolin from the sheep's fleeces which burnishes and protects the wood. A happy co-existence!'

Both these works of art involve sequences or clusters of small

comments on the dividing line between fact and fantasy, reality and the imagination. The black shapes of the deer moving in a herd through the forest are caught in silhouette, with their secret 'thoughts' revealed in brightly coloured emblematic flower, tree, fish and bird forms on their head, back or tail. Whilst the subject of both these works is appropriate to the Forest of Dean, their materials are not; Keir Smith's railway sleepers were made for use in the London Underground from Jarrah Eucalyptus, an oily wood which delays rotting, and Zadok Ben David's deer are prosaically made by applying a black stained car-filler to a metal armature. Although such materials are not indigenous, they are right for the wet weather conditions common in the Dean.

By contrast, the wood used in the work of Magdalena Jetelovà and Bruce Allan are appropriate but their subjects, a giant chair-like structure entitled *Place*, and a staircase that leads nowhere entitled *Observatory*, seem to be out of place. And yet, displaced in location and in scale, their very incongruity and simplicity of form is effective. As with the stained glass *Cathedral* window it is the area they occupy and the space that they include which is of vital importance. Kevin Atherton's concept includes the tall pillared trees which you walk through to reach the east window

L to R: Kevin Atherton, *Cathedral*, 1986, stained glass, Forest of Dean; Simon Thomas, *Seed Forms*, 1988, oak, New Milestones Project, Dorset

objects which enlarge the scope of the sculpture, and actively involve people in walking alongside, round or through the interconnected elements. This aspect of participation through walking is a vital part of works of art in the open, since it enables them to be seen from near and far, from different viewpoints, with different horizons, and in varying weather conditions which affect the mood of the sculpture. In the *Forest of Dean Sculpture Project*, several artists have made similar clusters to explore, which relate also to the character of the Dean. Keir Smith's *The Iron Road*, consists of 20 railway sleepers embedded in a curve of the old railway line from Cinderford to Lydney. Out of each sleeper an image has been carved that relates to some aspect of the forest whether rural or industrial. Each sleeper can be looked at in isolation, or read as a sequence of images which compose a poem. The sculptures do not make up a narrative but through recurring images compose a kind of elegy to the intrinsic life of the forest which man has helped to shape. They add to the landmarks which have been left from centuries of mining, smelting and forestry, the aim being to reinterpret the forest through the eye of the imagination. Another sequence is the group of seven deer by Israeli artist, Zadok Ben David, which

of the Cathedral. The sculpture acts as a catalyst, drawing attention not just to itself but to the wood in which it is placed, and to the connection between the sanctuary of the forest and the gloom of the Cathedral with its forest of pillars. Placed on the brow of a hill overlooking the Cannop Valley, the animated figure of Magdalena Jetelovà's sculpture surveys the landscape. It is a place, a kind of woodhenge which we can enter, whose portals frame the landscape and direct our gaze outwards to include the length of the wooded Cannop Valley. The experience reminds one of Moore's eloquent description of the *Recumbent Figure*, 1936, made for Chermayeff's house overlooking the Sussex Downs, in which he speaks of becoming aware of 'giving outdoor sculpture a far-seeing gaze. My figure looked out across a great sweep of the Downs, and her gaze gathered in the horizon.'

As *Place* draws our gaze outwards to embrace the horizon, so Cornelia Parker's work, *Hanging Fire* draws the eye upward into the crown of a clump of five sycamore trees from which it is suspended 15 feet above the ground. The canopy of the trees creates a dark green space in which the bright orange of the rusting cast-iron glows like fire. Through the work Cornelia

Parker explores the symbolism of crowns and fire, and uses an indigenous metal, iron, cast in the nearby Cannop Foundry: 'Fire has many spiritual associations, in a biblical sense as the manifestation of the Holy Ghost, or in the metaphoric sense describing, for example, the vigour of thought, the warmth of affection or burning passion', while: 'A falling crown points to the subconscious, the roots beneath the tree and the source of regeneration.' The colour of the rusted crown of flames enables it both to blend with the leaves in autumn and to be distinct from them in the summer.

In recent years there has been an increase in environmental art projects, outdoor exhibitions, garden festivals and public art commissions. A new way of working has emerged which does not depend on the commercial galleries who are often unable to take on the younger artists. Making work in and for the environment offers young artists the opportunity to prove themselves, and to develop their skill and their vision in difficult terrain and in sometimes daunting weather conditions. At the same time the problems to be found in making work outdoors are not to be underestimated either by the artist or the commissioning agency.

Environmental art functions on a number of levels, generating a new and healthy interest in art on the part of people who may never visit an art gallery, exposing sculpture to the vagaries of the weather, helping to inculcate a respect for the environment and an increased awareness of an ecology that holds man, animal and plant in a fragile equilibrium, fostering a renewed concern for spiritual values which go against the grain of our rational, materialistic society, and generating new works of art by a younger generation of artists, inspired by the work of Henry Moore, Ian Hamilton Finlay, Richard Long, David Nash and Andy Goldsworthy to work in harmony with nature and expose their work in the light of day. If the 1980s is the decade which saw the revival of painting, and the 1990s promises to become the decade in which sculpture comes to the fore, then the greatest scope for the development of sculptural ideas could lie in its interaction with and integration into the environment which we are once more beginning to cherish.

Peter Randall-Page, *Wayside Carving*, 1988, stone, New Milestones Project, Dorset

Chris Drury, *Above L to R: Shelter for the 4 Days on Muckish, Co Donegal; Falling Water Stupa; Below: Stone Lavo – Mageroya Island, Finland*

Lo spazio è curvo o diritto (detail), 1990, twigs, glass, clamps, etc, installation Museo d'Arte Contemporanea Luigi Pecci, Prato. 'The smell of the bundles of sticks is the smell of sweat + the smell of the earth pulled toward the sun . . . the bundle of sticks is mute and dark in colour and so like blotting paper absorbs the noises of the cosmos and of life, and the blinding lights of the sun.' **Mario Merz**

MARIO MERZ

THE SPACE IS CURVED OR STRAIGHT

Untitled, 1979, metal tubes, clamps, stones, neon tubes, installation Castello Colonna, Genazzano, igloo 300x600cm, spiral 350cm

Organised by Amnon Barzel at the Museo d'Arte Contemporanea Luigi Pecci in Prato, Lo spazio è curvo o diritto *signifies the first realisation of Merz's concept of incorporating a museum space into a work of art. In this text, Barzel analyses the thinking behind Merz's spiral which, conceived as the geometrical representation of Fibonacci's numbers, forms a dialogue with the linear space at Prato.*

It begins and opens up to encircle all the square museum spaces in its curved energetic vector. From the terracotta inner piazza, it breaks in and then out, re-enters and breaks out again. The spiral of beech and chestnut twigs – *povera* natural elements – embraces the industrial architecture (iron I-beams, glowing white porcelain on steel); objects are not arrested in given spaces, but all the space is incorporated into one work of art. With this project in Prato, with its 300-metre long spiralling metal and twig structure, Merz has realised, for the first time, a concept he has carried with him since 1970, when he planned to encircle the Haus Lange Museum by Mies van der Rohe in Krefeld with a spiral, a project which was never brought to term. For 20 years, the concept has ripened, waiting for the right moment to be realised.

'This project is synthetic instead of analytic. The Museum in Prato permits the *formation* of a work instead of its *deformation.*'[1] The seed of the spiral was planted in the thick layers of a painting done in 1963 in Pisa, the town of Leonardo Fibonacci; the spiral being the geometrical visualisation of Fibonacci's series of numbers. This form crossed the spiral drawings with the snails in their centres to reach the mega-spiral in Prato, and to continue to grow as a dynamic expansion of the mind which starves to reach the endless distances of the universe.

In the consistency of his language, Merz is the big renovator: with the Prato curved spaces embracing the straight, he proposes a new concept in the philosophy of art and art creation. It is not environmental, since it relates to all scales, from the microscopic structure of the one-celled *foraminifera* that inhabit the seas, to the galaxies above. Spiral movement delineates a centre and a 'whole', combined with gravitational pull which creates the solar systems, their suns and planets. Fibonacci numbers bear the secret of growth, of order (in Ancient Greek, 'cosmos' means order), of planets, of the Nautilus, and of the twig spiral around and in the museum. The public space is within an art form; Merz makes a 180 degree turn away from the idea of artworks simply *in* a public space such as the museum. On two occasions, once in a letter to Harald Szeeman in 1972 and once in a 1985 talk with him, Merz concentrated on the idea of working within an igloo, in continuous contact with the public: 'The place where this micro-organic city (the igloo) is to be implanted must be public and must become public. The most interesting public place is the Mies van der Rohe Museum in Berlin.'[2] Now it's no longer the 'settlement' of the artist in the igloo in the museum, but it's the igloos, the paintings, the neon, and the twigs, the stones, and the stuffed birds, which all move along the stream of the total work of art, along the spiral which moves like a whirlpool, entering and exiting, as the East enters the West and the West enters the East. On a wrapped mass of newspapers, like a river of Kafka despairs, like corridors of bureaucratic files of horrors, Fibonacci

Above: *Untitled* (detail), 1982, igloo, glass, twigs, bread, installation Palacio de las Alhajas, Madrid; *Below*: *Spiral table*, 1982, metal tubes, stone, painted stone, bamboo, neon tubes, plaster, fruit, vegetables, branches, wax, bottle, installation Flow Ace Gallery, Venice, California. 'The fruit is with its weight. It bears with itself the decadent, decorative side of its own decomposition.' **Mario Merz**

numbers proliferate and run across as if looking for their sanity, for an outlet. The works together are like letters combined into phrases which accumulate to create a poem. 'Our knowledge builds a big system. And only within this system does each particle attain the value we attribute to it,'[3] wrote Wittgenstein. Within this spiral, which is the real and the imagined combined, we perceive the art of Mario Merz: a dynamic renovation of the language of images.

For Merz, 'the spiral is a humble drawing. It always represents the "incandescent" phenomenon of the spirit in the cosmic universe.'[4] Germano Celant, in an essay about Merz, writes that the 'act of drawing, of making art, is "existence in motion", a continuous moving and straying that involves the appropriation and deepening of the surrounding space.'[5]

The place itself, the house and the earth, are melted into non-conformist dynamism, into a spark of anarchic energy ignited by the friction of the crystalised idea with the movement of the spiral, like the snail; like the rectilinear space of the museum, which melts into the curved twig-course.

The igloo encloses a curved space for one who is concerned, a sign of the one who touches the earth. It is opaque and transparent. On its curved face the neon words are seen, like a brand or a tattoo. But movement dominates over the place, the earth. Geography is becoming past history, and the spiral – which enters and exits like the East to the West and West to the East – passes frontiers, and is a testimony to our time. To its rhythms. Merz is close to reality, to society, to the real. And this was the spirit of Arte Povera. C*he fare?* was the question. *Che fare* is the answer in itself. To ask about real time meant to perceive the reality of society, of the one within society who stands between the eye of the spiral storm and its remotest reaches imaginable in the universe.

The political concerns of Merz were exposed most radically in two crucial works: *Giap's Igloo,* 1986, his first igloo ('If the enemy concentrates, he loses ground; if he disperses, he loses strength'), and the igloo done in Jerusalem in 1983, whose surface Merz covered with flat bread loaves, alongside bread shapes made out of the earth from a refugee camp near Jericho, on the shores of the Dead Sea. Earth and bread with dramatic political intuition. The space of the igloo is the 'place', the body, the heat of the earth. 'For the early Kabbalists, as for Aristotle, "place" and "space" were identical. There was no such thing as abstract, metaphorical "place". Everything was place, even heaven,' wrote Thomas B Hess in 1972,[6] and we related it to the installation of Mario Merz at the inaugural exhibition of the Prato Museum, *Europe Now,* 1988. Now, the igloo, the place within the 'art place' – the museum – is all within the enlarging twig spiral which enters and exits, as West enters East and East enters West – to embrace the infinite.

Amnon Barzel, 'Museo Merz', Prato, 1990

Notes

1 From a conversation between M Merz and A Barzel, Prato, April 1990.
2 *Mario Merz,* Kunsthaus Zurich, 1985, p8.
3 *On Certainty,* paragraph 20.3. Basil Blackwell, Oxford 1968.
4 Prato, April, 1990.
5 Germano Celant, 'The Organic Flow of Art' in *Mario Merz,* Milano, 1989, catalogue for the exhibition at the Solomon R Guggenheim Museum N Y, p16.
6 Thomas B Hess, B*arnett Newman,* exhib cat, The Tate Gallery, London, 1972.

8,5,3, 1985, metal tubes, glass, clamps, twigs, neon tubes, installation Chapelle Saint Louis de la Salpêtrière, Paris, 1987

ACKNOWLEDGEMENTS

We should like to thank the artists and writers for allowing us to reproduce their work and also the numerous galleries, museums and collections who have provided us with illustrations, many of whom have waived their fees. For text and illustrations, credits are as follows:

Front Cover Gerhard Richter, *Abstract Picture*, (detail), 1984, oil, 190x500cm, Marian Goodman and Sperone-Westwater Galleries, New York; **Front Flap** Luciano Fabro, *Two nudes descending a staircase dancing the boogie-woogie*, 1989, marble, steel, dimensions variable, collection Ydessa Hendeles, Ydessa Hendeles Foundation, Toronto, photo SteinGladstone Gallery, New York; **Half-Title** Anish Kapoor, *Mother as a Mountain*, 1985, wood, gesso and pigment, 140x275x105cm, Lisson Gallery, London, collection Walker Art Center, Minneapolis; **Frontis** Daniel Buren, *Coïncidence ou: La Place des Colonnes*, 1984, Moderna Museet, Stockholm; **Title** Jeff Koons, *Jeff and Ilona (Made in Heaven)*, 1990, painted wood, 127x271.8x137.2cm, Sonnabend Gallery, New York, photo by AC Papadakis; **Introduction** *p6* Anselm Kiefer, *The High Priestess/Zweistromland*, (details), 1985-89, the artist and Anthony d'Offay Gallery, London.

I
BACKGROUND TO NEW ART

p8 Robert Rauschenberg, *BED*, 1955, combine painting, 191x80x16.5cm, © DACS 1991, photo Leo Castelli Gallery, New York.

Joseph Beuys – Man Is Sculpture,

pp10-21: This text was originally published in *Soleil immatériel: Chemins dans l'art contemporain*, Editions Galilée, Paris 1989, translation from the French by Vivian Constantinopoulos. All illustrations © DACS 1991; *p10* installation at Hessischen Landesmuseum Darmstadt; *p11* installation at Wilhelm-Lehmbruck Museum Duisburg; *p12* Kröller-Müller Museum Otterlo; *pp14, 18* and *21* photos Anthony d'Offay Gallery, London; *p16 above* photo by A Tüllmann; *below* photo by C Tisdall; *p18* extracts from interviews with William Furlong, Anthony d'Offay, Oct 1985, and Stuart Morgan,

Parkett No 7 1986, p66; *p19* extract from speech in *In Memoriam Joseph Beuys: Obituaries, Essays, Speeches,* Inter Nationes, pp35-55.

Warhol as Art History

pp22-27: This is an edited version of a text originally published in the exhibition catalogue, *Andy Warhol: A Retrospective*, ed Kynaston McShine, Museum of Modern Art, New York, 1989. Illustrations courtesy the following: *p24 LtoR* the Estate of Ad Reinhardt, collection Whitney Museum, New York; © 1991 Sol Lewitt/ARS, New York, photo John Weber Gallery, New York, collection Eva LeWitt, Chester, Connecticut; *p25 LtoR* © DACS 1991, collection Whitney Museum, New York; © DACS 1991; *p26* © DACS 1991, photo Anthony d'Offay Gallery, London.

Photography, Language
and the Mass Media

pp28-39: This article, edited by *Art & Design* was originally published in the exhibition catalogue *A Forest of Signs – Art in the Crisis of Representation*, 1989, The Museum of Contemporary Art, Los Angeles. Illustrations courtesy the following: *p28* the artist and Sonnabend Gallery, New York, collection Dakis Joannou; *p29* collection Daniel Buren; *p30* the artists, photo by Bill Jacobson studio; *p31* collection Städtische Kunsthalle, Düsseldorf; *p32 above* © 1991 Bruce Nauman/ARS, New York; *below* the artist; *p36* Lisson Gallery, London; *p39* John Weber Gallery, New York.

II
TOWARDS A
DEFINITION OF NEW ART

p40 Joseph Kosuth, *Zero & Not, (New York)*, 1986, offset printing on paper, Leo Castelli Gallery, New York, courtesy the artist.

Robert Rosenblum – Towards
a Definition of New Art

pp42-69: This piece was compiled from a series of interviews conducted by former House Editors, Hugh Cumming and Clare Farrow, and taken from past issues of *Art & Design* as well as from speeches given at Tate Gallery Symposia in London organised by Academy Editions. Illustrations

courtesy the following: *p42* Barbara Gladstone Gallery, New York *p43* Sonnabend Gallery, New York; *p44* Anthony d'Offay Gallery, London; *p45* Mary Boone Gallery, New York; *p46* the artist; **Romanticism and Retrospection** *p47* public freehold photograph, the artist; *p50* © DACS 1991; *p51* Sperone-Westwater Gallery, New York, private collection, Switzerland; **Post-Modernism** *p52* Galerie Bruno Bischofberger, Zurich; *p55* Saatchi Collection, London; **The Art of Quotation** *p56* Metro Pictures, New York; *p57* Saatchi Collection, London; *p58* Mary Boone Gallery, New York, collection Eli and Edythe L Broad, Los Angeles; *p59* Sonnabend Gallery, New York; *p61 above* Mary Boone Gallery, New York, collection Thomas Ammann, Zurich; *below* Raab Gallery, London; **In Search of the New** *p64* Sonnabend Gallery, New York; *p65* The Museum of Contemporary Art, Los Angeles, gift of the Frederick R Weisman Art Foundation, Los Angeles, photo by Gene Ogami; *p66 LtoR* © 1991 Doug & Mike Starn/ARS, New York, collection John and Mabel Ringling Museum, Sarasota, Florida; Galerie Ghislaine Hussenot Paris; *p67 LtoR* Sonnabend Gallery, New York; Jay Gorney and Sonnabend Galleries, New York, photo by David Lubarsky; *p68* Josh Baer Gallery, New York.

Unexpressionism

pp70-79: This text is comprised of extracts from *Unexpressionism – Art Beyond the Contemporary*, Rizzoli, New York, 1989. Illustrations courtesy the following: *p70* the artist, photo Salama-Caro Gallery, London; *p71* the artist, photo Metro Pictures, New York; *p72* Barbara Gladstone Gallery, New York; *p73* and *p75* Galerie Max Hetzler, Cologne; *p74* Metro Pictures; *p76* Mary Boone Gallery, New York; *p77* Barbara Gladstone Gallery, New York, photo by Larry Lame; *p78* Josh Baer Gallery, New York, collection Oklahoma City Art Museum.

Image World: Art and Media Culture

pp80-83: This essay, excerpted and edited by *Art & Design*, is reprinted from the exhibition catalogue *Image World: Art and Media Culture,* eds Marvin Heiferman and Lisa Phillips with John Hanhardt, 1989, Whitney Museum of American Art, New

York. Illustrations courtesy the following: *p80* the artist, collection FC Gundlach; *p81* the artist and John Gibson Gallery, New York, collection Edward R Downe; *p83* 303 Gallery, New York, collection Steve Salzman.

The Strange Attraction of Chaos
pp84-87: An earlier version of this essay by curator Laura Trippi, 'Fractured Fairytales, Chaotic Regimes', appeared in the exhibition catalogue *Strange Attractors: Signs of Chaos*, The New Museum of Contemporary Art, New York, 1989; *p84* (Art)^n Laboratory, Illinois Institute of Technology.

European Sensibility Today
pp88-93: This essay was originally published in the exhibition catalogue *Europa Oggi*, 1988, Museo d'Arte Contemporanea, Prato, published by Centro Di della Edifimi, Florence, and Electa, Milan. Illustrations courtesy the following: *p88* Galerie Daniel Templon, Paris; *p89* Lisson Gallery, London, collection Reina Sofia, photo by Gareth Winters; *p90* Museo d'Arte Contemporanea, Prato; *p91* Galerie Konrad Fischer, Düsseldorf, artist's collection; *p92 above* Galerie Farideh Cadot, Paris; *below* collection Museo d'Arte Contemporanea, Prato, donation Palmucci family; *p93* Galleria Giorgio Persano, Turin.

The Art of Alchemy
pp94-101: Illustrations courtesy the following: *pp94* and *96* Galerie des Beaux-Arts, Brussels; *p95* the artist, Henry Moore Sculpture Trust, Dean Clough, Halifax; *p98* the artist and Anthony d'Offay Gallery, London; *p99* Gagosian Gallery, New York; *p100* Marlborough Fine Art, London.

**III
RETROSPECTION
AND THE POST-MODERN DISCOURSE**
pp104 Mimmo Paladino, *Lonely Sun*, 1986, mixed media on wood, courtesy Sperone-Westwater Gallery, New York, collection Museum of Modern Art, New York.

The Post-Avant-Garde
pp106-111: Illustrations courtesy the following: *p106* Metro Pictures, New York; *p107* the artist.

Two Paintings: Prefaces and Postscripts
pp112-115: We are grateful to the author for allowing us to reproduce extracts from RB Kitaj, *Hints for Young Painters (Prefaces and Postscripts)*, Thames & Hudson. The illustrations are courtesy Marlborough Fine Art, London.

Painting Words – Kiefer and Celan
pp116-121: All illustrations courtesy the artist *p116* collection Sanders, Amsterdam;

p118 Saatchi collection, London; *p119* private collection, New York; *p120* collection Mr & Mrs David Pincus, Pennsylvania; *p121* Anthony d'Offay Gallery, London, quote from Armin Zweite, '*The High Priestess*, Observations on a Sculpture by Anselm Kiefer', in Anselm Kiefer, *The High Priestess*, Thames & Hudson, in association with Anthony d'Offay Gallery, London, 1989.

Repeating Themes
pp122-125: Illustrations courtesy the following: *p122* © DACS 1991; *p123* the artist, collection Mr & Mrs Andrew Saul, New York; *p124* John Weber Gallery, New York, photo by Hans Haacke; *p125 above* the artist, private collection; *below* © DACS 1991.

New German Painting
pp126-133: Illustrations courtesy the following: *p126* Saatchi Collection, London; *p127* Galerie Gmyrek, Düsseldorf; *pp128, 133*, Galerie Michael Werner, Cologne; *p129 LtoR* Raab Gallery, London, collection of the artist, photo Solomon R Guggenheim; Raab Gallery; *p130* Galerie Gmyrek, collection Zentrum für Kunst und Medientechnologie, Karlsruhe; *p131* Michael Werner, collection Fröhelich, Stuttgart; *p132* Galerie Volker Fisher, Berlin.

David Salle – An Interview
pp134-137: Interview conducted by Clare Farrow. Illustrations courtesy the artist and Waddingtons Galleries, London.

The Italian Transavanguardia
pp138-141: Text Nicola Hodges. Illustrations courtesy the following: *p138* Galerie Bruno Bischofberger; *p139 LtoR* Anthony d'Offay Gallery, London; Hunts Manufacturing Company Arts Collection Programme, Philadelphia Museum of Art, photo Joan Broderick; *pp140, 141* Sperone-Westwater Gallery, New York; *p141* collection Emily and Jerry Spiegel, New York.

**IV
NEW CONCEPTUALISM
AND THE POLITICS OF ART**
pp142 Barbara Kruger, *Untitled (You are not yourself)*, 1983, Mary Boone Gallery, New York, collection Edward R Downe Jr.

Pop Art II – Jeff Koons & Co
pp144-151: *p144* Saatchi Collection, London; *p145* Jay Gorney Modern Art and Sonnabend Gallery, New York, photo by David Lubarsky; *p146* Donald Young Gallery, Chicago; *pp148-49* John Weber Gallery New York, artist's statements: DA Robbins, 'An interview with Allan McCollum', *Arts Magazine*, Oct 1985, Selma Klein Essink, interview 1989 and artist's

statement 1981, 'Allan McCollum; The function, Meaning and Value of an Artwork', *Allan McCollum*, 1989, Stedelijk Van Abbemuseum, Eindhoven, Serpentine Gallery, London, IVAM, Instituto Valenciano de Arte Moderno, Valencia; *p151* Sonnabend Gallery, New York.

Jeff Koons – The Power of Seduction
pp152-157: Interview by Clare Farrow. Illustrations courtesy the artist and Sonnabend Gallery, New York; *p153* photo by AC Papadakis.

Thoughts on *A Forest of Signs*
pp158-163: We would like to thank Sherrie Schottlaender of The Museum of Contemporary Art, Los Angeles for her help. Illustrations courtesy the following: *p158* Barbara Gladstone Gallery, New York; *p159* the artist and Mary Boone Gallery, New York; *p160-161* The Museum of Contemporary Art, Los Angeles, installation views from *A Forest of Signs: Art in the Crisis of Representation*, photos by Gene Ogami; *p162 above* The Museum of Contemporary Art, Los Angeles, gift of the Frederick R Weisman Art Foundation; *below* the Renaissance Society at the University of Chicago; *p163* 303 Gallery, New York.

Going Public
pp164-169: The author is an artist and critic currently teaching at the California Institute for the Arts. Illustrations courtesy the following: *p164* Fisher Park and Elephant House productions, photo by Chris Rodley, ICA, London; *p166* the artist; *p167* the artists; *p168* Mary Boone Gallery, New York; *p169* the artist, collection DIA Art Foundation.

Jenny Holzer – Space, Language, Time
pp170-175: We would like to thank Jenny Holzer for her assistance, and Alexis Summer at the Barbara Gladstone Gallery, New York for arranging the interview with Clare Farrow and for supplying material; *p170* photo by AC Papadakis; *p171* the Guggenheim Museum New York; *p173 below* Artspace, San Francisco, California; other illustrations courtesy Barbara Gladstone Gallery.

A Note on *Minnesota Abstract*
pp176-179: The author is Professor of Art History and History of Consciousness at the University of California, Santa Cruz; his books include *Between* and *The End of Art Theory: Criticism and Postmodernity*. Illustrations courtesy the following: *p176* and *179* Liliane & Michel Durand-Dessert, Paris; *p177* courtesy the artist.

Cindy Sherman – Behind the Image
pp180-187: Interview conducted by Vivian Constantinopoulos. Illustrations courtesy

Metro Pictures, New York and the Saatchi Collection, London.

Alternative Spaces in New York

pp188-189: 'Artist's Space', taken from Linda Cathcart's introduction to *A Decade of New Art*, 1984, 'The Alternative Museum', adapted from statements made in an interview between Gino Rodriguez and Roger Denson, 'Exit Art' was compiled from the organisers' statement; illustration *p188* courtesy Saatchi Collection.

Gerhard Richter's Facture

pp190-195: Text originally published in catalogue for Marian Goodman Gallery, New York, reproduced by permission of the author. All Illustrations courtesy the artist *p190* collection Barbara Nüsse Hamburg; *p191* collection Susan and Lewis Manilow, Chicago; *pp192* and *193* Anthony d'Offay, London; statements on *pp190, 1 92* and *193* compiled from interview by Wolfgang Pehnt, 1989, *A&D* 9/10 89 *German Art Now*.

Double Vision

pp196-205: Illustrations courtesy the following: *p196* the artist, Neue Galerie, Ludwig Collection, Aachen; *p197* and *204* Galerie Michael Werner, Cologne; *p200* John Weber Gallery, New York.

Daniel Buren – Sign and Context

pp206-213: We would like to thank Michel Baudson at Galerie Isy Brachot, Paris and Daniel Buren for their assistance. Interview conducted by Clare Farrow and translated by Vivian Constantinopoulos. The illustrations are by permission of the artist and are from his book, *Photo-Souvenirs 1965-1988*, 1988, Art Edition, Villeurbanne, France.

Conceptual Analysis

pp214-219: The author is an art critic and curator currently teaching History of Contemporary Art at the Accademia Statale di Belle Arti di Milano. Illustrations courtesy the following: *p214* the artist; *pp215, 216* and *219* Franz Paludetto, Turin; *p217* Studio La Citta, Verona; *p218* the artist.

V

SCULPTURE AND EARTHWORKS: AN EXPANDED FIELD

p220 Richard Long, *A Clearing, A Six Day Walk in the Hoggar, The Sahara*, 1988, courtesy the artist from the exhibition at the Tate Gallery, London, 1990.

New German Sculpture

pp222-229: Translated by Eileen Martin. Illustrations courtesy the following: *pp222* and *229* Galerie Max Hetzler, Cologne; *p223* Galerie Konrad Fisher, Düsseldorf; *p224 LtoR* Galerie Max Hetzler, photo by Ulrich Loock; Galerie Rudolf Zwirner, Cologne, collection HJ Müller, Kunstsammlung, Darmstadt; *p225 LtoR* Kölnischer Kunstverein, Cologne; the artist; *p226* Barbara Gladstone Gallery, New York, photo by Larry Lame; *p228* Whitechapel Art Gallery, London and Stedelijk Van Abbemuseum, Eindhoven.

New International Sculpture

pp230-247: This piece was adapted from a series of essays published in *Art & Design* magazine between 1987 and 1989. Illustrations courtesy the following: *p230* Lisson Gallery, London, private collection; *p231* Galerie Ghislaine Hussenot, Paris; *p232* the artist, photo by Werner Hannappel, Essen; *p234* Tate Gallery, London; *p236* Lisson Gallery, photos by Edward Woodman; *p238* Sperone-Westwater Gallery, New York; *p239* Galerie Liliane and Michel Durand-Dessert, Paris, photo by Adam Rzepka; *p240* Louver Gallery, New York, photo by D James Dee; *p241* the artist, installation at Metrónom Gallery, Barcelona; *p242* SteinGladstone Gallery, New York; *p244* the artist; *p245* Lisson Gallery, interview from *A&D* 9/10 88 *British Art Now*, translation from the French by Vivian Constantinopoulos; *p246* Lisson Gallery; *p247* artist's collection.

Andy Goldsworthy
– Geometry and Nature

pp248-250: Interview conducted by Clare Farrow. Illustrations courtesy the artist and Fabian Carlsson Gallery, London.

Spaces, Places and Landmarks

pp251-255: Illustrations courtesy the following: Works from the Forest of Dean provided by the author, who is organiser of the Forest of Dean Sculpture Project, in collaboration with Martin Orrom of the Forestry Commission, photos by Jamie Woodley and Sarah Quick, Junction Studio, Bristol; *p253 right* the artist and Albermarle Gallery, London; *p255* the artist.

Mario Merz
– The Space is Curved or Straight

pp256-259: We would like to thank Amnon Barzel at the Centro per L'Arte Contemporanea Luigi Pecci, Museo D'Arte Contemporanea, Prato for his permission to publish his introductory text together with installation photos from the catalogue *Lo spazio é curvo o diritto*, 1990, Hopeful Monster Editore, Florence.

INDEX